Peter Harding
+
Tony Moulam

Sarah Waugh Davis (Mac!)

Carmello 'o' Higgins (P. James)

Bob Pettigrew

C James

Stan Moore

J. Fish

Judith Appleby.

Eileen Gregson.

Pete Scott

Harry Pretty

Betty Bird (Gardian)
Roy + April Sawyer.
Gordon & Margaret Gadsby

C000139904

OREAD MOUNTAINEERING CLUB

50th Anniversary Journal
1949-1999

Edited by
Harry Pretty

Published by the Oread Mountaineering Club.
© Individual authors or the Oread Mountaineering Club.

ISBN 0-9535736-0-5

A CIP catalogue record for this book is available from the British Library.

Dust jacket from a watercolour of An Teallach and other sketches by Harry Pretty.

Prepared for printing by Journal Co-ordinator, Colin Hobday.
Printed by Bemrose Security Printing, Derby.

CONTENTS

IN THE BEGINNING 1949-1953

GOLDEN OLDIES – CONSOLIDATION 1953-1958

A TOUCH OF CLASS 1958-1970

THE MODERNS 1970-1990

TOWARDS THE POST MODERN 1990-1999

RITES OF PASSAGE

BEFORE THEIR TIME

END GAME

APPENDIX

EDITORIAL

When I took on the production of a Journal to celebrate fifty years of Oread history I was under no delusion as to the nature of the task. On reflection, perhaps I had been subconsciously preparing for some considerable time. But, in this context, nothing is certain. I only knew that the Oread Mountaineering Club had been at the centre of my life for many years and, with some certainty at last, I knew that there was a story to tell.

I was not universally encouraged and have been made aware that the mere telling of mountain exploits, however distinguished, is not a compelling reason for such effort and, at worst, takes on the mediocrity of recounting what we have been doing on our hols, for fifty years. I had, and still have, some sympathy with this point of view but have remained convinced that the telling of the Oread tale could be elevated beyond the level of sad nostalgia.

The period 1949-99 occupies a particular niche in the development of British mountaineering. As others have recounted the enormous influx of would be climbers in the aftermath of the second world war presented the older establishment with a problem. How were they to accommodate this mass of half rebellious youth, who, radicalised by recent experience, viewed the pre-war insularity of the senior clubs with something of a jaundiced eye? But the young men solved it themselves. They founded their own provincial and regional clubs throughout the U.K. They taught themselves to climb and set the post-war climbing scene firmly in the direction of egalitarianism. They did not need to wait upon selection for expeditions by the great and the good. They simply went and did it themselves.

Jack Longland said in his Foreword to 'Climb if you Will' in 1974: "Born of a mixture of ex-servicemen and their girls and some Technical College students; with tents, anoraks, and probably ropes, all ex W.D., the Oread came into existence pat on cue. The men (and the women) matched the need, and they were inspired by a fanaticism about mountains . . . but always mitigated by a humour which would not let them take themselves too seriously, by a Rabelaisian anarchism which inspired their doings in huts and pubs, by the civilising influence of girlfriends and wives who sometimes climbed as well as they did".

As usual J.L.L. got it about right. The historical differential is that of the many mountaineering clubs founded in the late '40's. The Oread is one of the few to survive as we approach the Millennium.

After some early theorising I found it impossible to visualise a definitive format. 'Climb if you Will' was inspired by the life and early demise of Geoff Hayes, with a smaller narrative section on Oread history, 1949-1974, by J. Ashcroft, P. Gardiner and the late Jean Russell. I have found it a useful reference. But the format of Oread 50 occupies a different spectrum and, in truth, is not the result of any detailed plan. It has simply grown organically from constant reference to what already exists. It has been mined from the rich veins of Oread writing, from fifty years of Newsletters and Journals, and supplemented by contemporary essays, some of which look back, while others contemplate the present, or even the future.

Seeking further inspiration I have admired the gravitas, and the style, of the recent C.C. Centenary Journal, but have not emulated Terry Gifford's method of selection by recommendation from a "panel of readers". The written word that tells the Oread story has been chosen entirely by myself and therefore, in my Editorial capacity, I have to take sole responsibility for its quality and suitability for its purpose. In doing this I have to be grateful for the unique nature of Oread records since the early '50's. Most mountaineering clubs who have maintained any literary record have only produced, at best, an annual Journal, whereas the Oread, for more than forty years, published monthly newsletters (with occasional gaps) that provide substantial written evidence of all that has transpired during this period. News, gossip, meet reports, politics, letters, verse, opinionated essays, and character assassinations have all been grist to the mill.

There is a general chronological sequence but, more significantly, the separation of various eras has occurred almost naturally and follows an order that is in step with the influence of Newsletters and their respective editors. Thus the initial high dictates of Charlie Cullum are essentially apposite to the Golden Oldies, and the intense energy of Geoff Hayes gives way to ambition and the special achievements of Chris Radcliffe and Peter Scott. The Oread, from the earliest years, has always been susceptible to real and imagined fault lines. Navel gazing, the angst of self criticism, and barely concealed defamation, are all represented in these pages. But so is the humour and barbed wit which in general are the chosen weapons.

So eighteen months later, it is finished. From our domestic moors and gritstone edges to high adventure in the great ranges, from Arctic to Antarctic, from winter epics on the Croz Spur to summer adventures on the Eigerwand (three separate Oread ascents), all part of this story; for Oreads have planted boots world wide – and, in the 1990's they are still at it. From the Andes and the remote Tien Shan of Central Asia, from Greenland, the States, Canada and the Ruwenzori, from Karakorum to eastern Nepal, there are still post cards from the edge.

But in many ways the essence, the "gay audacity" that others have identified, shines brightest in less exalted places. Somewhere between Penmaenmawr and Cwm Pennant, perhaps in the great empty quarter of Central Wales, amid the spatial distances of Bleaklow, or walking south from Marsden, or north from Edale, on a winter's night through snow filled groughs. There are ghosts and shadows in Lower Small Clough, Poltergeist Barn, and Bullstones, and in the verse of Jim Kershaw, and the prose of Brian West and others, you will surely find them.

Harry Pretty
Holbrook, January 1999.

George Sutton, Founder Member, on gully approach to Sugartop, South Georgia, 1955. *Photo: I. M. Brooker.*

ACKNOWLEDGEMENTS

The Committee (President, Clive Russell), after a hesitant start, have provided funds, without which this book would not have been possible and furthermore, exerting minimum influence, have left me to get on with it. Committee members Shirley Wainwright (Honorary Secretary) and Colin Hobday have been particularly encouraging throughout. In the final stages Colin Hobday, applying his professional skills, has organised and co-ordinated the entire technical process from earliest text to final print.

By solving one of my earliest problems I have to thank Andy Oakden's friend John Lee, and his assistants Jane and Lynda, for providing extended free access to photocopying facilities. They transformed a boring chore into a pleasant task.

For the arduous transcription of original text into hard copy I am specially indebted to Pam Weston, Uschi Hobday, Barbara Smedley and Mike Hayes – Oreads all.

Although selection of written work has remained an Editorial function throughout I deemed it wise to co-opt Colin Hobday, Gordon Gadsby, Jack Ashcroft and Chris Radcliffe to form a Picture Selection Committee "Good historical action shots . . . celebrate in visual terms your club's main achievements" advised Ken Wilson, and we have agreed. But persuading members to dig into their files, and the ultimate whittling down, has been hard work and occupied many months. In the same context I am grateful to Terry Gifford for sharing some of his problems as Editor of the Climber's Club Centenary Journal.

For the loan of photographs: J. Ashcroft, P. Bingham, R. A. Brown, Dr. I. M. Brooker, D. Burgess, K. Bryan, R. Colledge, D. C. Cullum, J. Fisher, G. Gadsby, the late G. Gibson, D. Gray, D. Guyler, C. Hobday, P. Holden, C. Hooley, J. Hudson, G. Male, M. Moore, A. J. J. Moulam (K. Broadbent), M. Padley, D. Penlington, R. G. Pettigrew, C. Radcliffe, G. Reynolds, P. Scott, R. Sedgwick, T. Smith, Tom Weir, D. Williams, J. Winfield, Derby Evening Telegraph, the Indian Express.

I am particularly appreciative of the Foreword by His Grace the Duke of Devonshire who generously acknowledges a long association with the Oread, its activities, and its Derbyshire home on the Chatsworth Estate. Further distinction is provided by introductory words from that long respected guru Peter Harding, and my old friend Tom Weir whom I first saw with some surprise as a mysterious dot on an arctic glacier in 1951.

Molly Pretty has continued from where she started in 1949, to provide general secretarial assistance throughout. John (Rock) Hudson has delved into the voluminous archives to provide facts and figures, and a sharp commentary on routine activities in his Rites of Passage.

At the risk of over extending my privilege I thank young Michael Gregson for allowing me to end in a vein of youthful optimism but, of course, my final dedication must go to George Sutton for inserting an advertisement in the Burton Daily Mail in March, 1949.

Harry Pretty

𝕮𝖍𝖆𝖙𝖘𝖜𝖔𝖗𝖙𝖍,
𝕭𝖆𝖐𝖊𝖜𝖊𝖑𝖑,
𝕯𝖊𝖗𝖇𝖞𝖘𝖍𝖎𝖗𝖊,
DE4 1PP

𝕭𝖆𝖘𝖑𝖔𝖜 582204

Nearly forty years ago the Oread M.C. invited me to become Patron of the Derbyshire Himalayan Expedition 1961 and, after meeting the team at Chatsworth in late 1960, I was pleased to accept.

They were very typical of the young ex-servicemen who had founded the club in 1949 and I was interested to learn that as early as 1951 and 1954 previous OREAD M.C. parties had climbed and explored in places as far apart as Arctic Norway and South Georgia (Antarctica). Some years later, in 1967 I believe, there was a further connection between the Chatsworth Estate and this very active mountaineering club. Chatsworth is at the heart of gritstone country that has played a significant role in the history of British rock climbing. Members of the Oread M.C. were very welcome when, thirty years ago, they established a Derbyshire home on the Chatsworth Estate. The association still prospers.

It is, therefore, a pleasure to recommend this volume, put together by Harry Pretty, a Founder Member, in which reminiscent tales from distant mountain ranges mingle happily with contemporary adventures closer to home. It is a book brimming with universal enthusiasms; middle-aged men climbing the north face of the Eiger, septuagenarians exploring remote parts of the Tien Shan in Central Asia, but always, and inevitably, returning with equal enthusiasm to the crags and moors of their native Peak District.

The Duke of Devonshire

FOREWORD . . .

It pleases me greatly to contribute a foreword to this special edition of the Oread Journal marking attainment of the club's first half century. Not only is the book a fine record of development for a climbing club which like many others was founded shortly after the second world war, it also reveals much about the club's character. From its 300 or so pages one can see why the Oread has outlived many of its contemporaries to come of age as one might say, a localised junior club whose activities and achievements have brought it to wider seniority. Maybe those early expeditions, to Lyngen and South Georgia, laid the foundations and created tradition. Certainly these events, more than anything else, distinguished the Oread from other small clubs formed around the same time. In reading about those early pioneering efforts, then tracing the club's subsequent history, one may well reach such a conclusion; but I will leave that to the reader. Finally I must say that this bound collection of stories, anecdotes and illustrations, mostly from earlier Oread journals, is a production of which the club and its editor can be justly proud. In its pages lies that magic recipe for longevity in a climbing club – an unquenchable quest for adventure among its youth, the endless supply of youthfulness in its elders and a touch of good humour to go with all this, and of course, the club's own hut in the hills.

Peter Harding

. . . AND SOME FURTHER WORDS OF INTRODUCTION

On Jekkevarre, as we ate our last sandwich we were looking at three sets of footprints on the north-east summit,[1] and decided we would follow them, hoping they would lead us to an easy way down. They didn't. But we did find a route through the massed pinnacles of a huge ice-fall overhanging the crags of the southern flank and it was a relief at last to reach level glacier ice, then rock slabs, giving way to moraine screes. At that moment we heard whistles, and bearing down on us were a couple of bearded climbers, their curiosity about us, as thoroughly aroused as our own. Then a mutual cry of recognition, as Adam Watson and Dick Brown recognised each other, having met in the Lofotens the previous year, and soon, we were shaking hands with him and Nobby Clarke. They must have sensed our weariness when they produced a bag of raisins and invited us to partake . . . It demanded will-power to take only a few for we were starving.

Back in the Oread camp we didn't need any pressing to have cups of sweet coffee since it was 11 p.m. and we had been on the go for 23 hours of first class rock and ice climbing. As for the cheerful Oread expeditioners, as well as climbing, they had been mapping the ridge lines and the movements of its glaciers past and present, and they had left Harry Pretty, and his plane table, at the head of the Lyngsdal Glacier when they had spotted us as three small dots descending the ice fall.

That was in 1951, and three years later Douglas Scott and I, were to have the pleasure of meeting up with some of the Oread in Glasgow, at Princes Dock, where the *Southern Opal* whaling ship was tied up, and about to take Sutton, Pretty, Ian Brooker, Webb and Dick Brown to South Georgia.

I have a recollection we managed an evening, rock scrambling on the Whangie, 12 miles north of Glasgow, which overlooks Loch Lomond and takes in a great sweep of peaks from west to east. I'm truly sorry North Wales is not nearer, or I would be at the 50th Anniversary din-din.

Tom Weir
Ross Loan, Gartocharn

---

[1] The footprints on the north east summit of Jekkevarre, partly followed by Tom Weir's party, were left by Dick Brown, Phillip Falkner, Nobby Clarke and Harry Pretty during first recorded complete traverse (West to East) in 20 hours, 23.07.51 — *Editor.*

In the Beginning
1949-1953

"Begin at the beginning" the king said gravely, "and go on till you come to the end, then stop".

Lewis Carroll, *Alice in Wonderland*.

Now a whole is that which has a beginning, a middle and an end.

Aristotle, 384-322BC, *Poesy*.

OREADS REGARDLESS 1949/50

GEORGE SUTTON

Soon after the war a minor social phenomenon took place with the emergence of many small climbing clubs, of which the Oread Mountaineering Club was one. Not that its Founder Members, when they first met to climb at Black Rocks in early Spring 1949, had any percipient thoughts of starting a club that would last for fifty years, or of forming friendships that would hold true for a lifetime. The more likely scenario was of early death and disaster, so brash was our daring, so vast our inexperience.

I was not new to the mountains, having rambled solo in Scotland and the Lake District. I belonged to several clubs, and had joined some of their outings. One in particular left me sceptical as to whether or not to continue climbing. It was a training weekend at Glan Dena. Two young men, full of enthusiasm, took me on my first granite climbs on Tryfan and Craig-yr-Ysfa. Easy climbs for them, but exciting and exhausting for me. The third man on a rope, climbing just ahead of us, suddenly peeled off and swung out over my head, and over a lot of space. "He's not encouraging me", I said to my leaders, which made them laugh. But at night my sleep was haunted by dreams as I climbed the day's routes all over again. Would I ever be as safe and nonchalant as my leaders? A few weeks later, these same two men, full of joy and promise, were killed on the Munich Climb, on Tryfan.

Wisdom advised me not to continue climbing, but the pull of the hills was like a drug. Mountains held my spirit in thrall, but I knew that I must improve my skill and stamina if I was to become a sound climber. Such dedication would mean climbing often, and learning techniques. The only way it was possible for me would be to climb on the Peak District gritstone, which was near and with experienced climbers. There were three fine climbers in my hometown. Peter Harding I already knew. He was at the height of his prowess in 1949, had pushed up the then standard of climbing and helped to produce the current Guide Book to Black Rocks. But although he gave me encouragement, he could not spare the time to train the group I had in mind.

Dr. Norman Cochran, with whom I had climbed on Ben Nevis, was Medical Officer of the town and his time already over-booked, and Wilf White who was described to me as one of the 'tigers' of the new Valkyrie Club, I had no contact with. Help came in the end from an unlikely source. A young man, Barry Tipper, in his late teens, was trying to teach me how to ride a motorcycle. My mother thought that all my leisure activities favoured congenial ways of committing suicide.

Barry said that he had two friends, also teen-agers named Paul Gardiner and David Penlington, who were very keen on climbing. We met, all four of us, at Paul's house and between cups of tea arranged a day visit to Black Rocks for Sunday March 20th 1949. Barry said there were two other men who might come also, "one is an ex-Paratrooper – and he knows Wilf White!" So, I had a new hemp rope, clinker boots, three teenagers, and possibly an ex-paratrooper for companions, – what more did I need? Some might have said courage, luck and a psychiatrist.

The day dawned cool and bright. Armed with sandwiches provided by my anxious mother I met Paul and Barry at the Bus Station. In Derby we were joined by Dave and a bonny, flaxen-haired young woman named Nan Smith. We were silent on the bus to Wirksworth, and not more talkative on the walk up to the crags. We hardly knew each other and had no shared experience. As we stepped off the bus and through the gate, another world embraced us; a jungle of shrubs and trees out of which, at the top of the hill, jutted the aggressive buttresses of the rocks, even in the brittle March sunlight looking dark and sinister.

We came across a mess of green canvas, much like another rock but purporting to be a tent even if sagging and unloved. Out of it fell or rolled two men. The unshaven one in monstrous camouflage anorak was introduced by Barry as Keith Axon, "The ex-Paratrooper". I felt the explanation was hardly necessary. The shock of tousled hair that followed him out was yet another teenager, Eddie Say. We shook hands all round. Keith rolled himself a cigarette, scowled at Nan, and nodded up the hill, "Wilf's up there, he's got Nat Allen with him".

The Black Rocks, or Stonnis, as they were called in 1822 when Rhodes visited them, were amongst the earliest gritstone outcrops to attract climbers. J. W. Puttrell climbed on them around 1890, as also did the great O. G. Jones. There followed several waves of climbers over the next half century, each adding new, More difficult climbs, and raising the standard of gritstone climbing in the process. In the 1920's came Fred Pigott, Morley Wood and George Bower, adding Lean Man's Climb and Lone Tree Gully. In the years of which I write, the British mountain world was still an intimate circle, and paths often crossed. So I frequently met George Bower, finding him a tough, friendly old man. Later came Jack Longland, Alf Bridge and Maurice Linnell, opening up Birch Tree Wall and Lone Tree Groove.

In 1933 came Eric Byne and Frank Elliott, adding yet more new routes. Some fifteen years later I was rather forlornly watching members of the Midland Association of Mountaineers climb on Black Rocks, when I was pounced upon by a man in a jacket, spectacles above a smile in a lean face, shock of greying hair topped by a flat cap. "Want to climb?" he said, producing a huge ancient hemp rope that probably started life with Edward Whymper. I climbed for several hours with him, being led up various old favourites, including Blind Man's Buttress. Other climbers sought his advice on standards. Afterwards I asked Harold Restall who he was. "Eric Byne", said Harold. Eric wrote of Harold as "the kindest and most generous personality I've ever met". Well, it had rubbed off on Eric. He would have made a brilliant youth worker. Both Harold and Eric were to be my sponsors for joining the Midland Association of Mountaineers – two finer men I never knew.

That meeting with Eric had been a year earlier, but today we did not have his strong personality with us to give confidence. It did not matter. Wilf and Nat took control of the situation giving up a day of their time to helping a group of beginners. This may not sound a big sacrifice, but the keen young men of the Valkyrie M. C. were in their turn the standard setters, and they wanted to get on with solving some of the unclimbed problems remaining on Peakland grit. We were divided up, roped up, and then coaxed, bullied and dragged up climbs varying from easy to very difficult. There was Sand Gully, Queens Parlour Gully, Fat Man's Chimney, and the amusing inside route of Queens Parlour Chimney. Dave showed a natural flair for rock-climbing, and soloed up the Stonnis Arete, and there was something in the way Keith was frowning at the rock that suggested a determination to lead as soon as possible. Eddie, Paul and I struggled manfully and were pleased with our day, even if we had lost skin in the process. "Gritstone rash", said Wilf, looking at the grazes.

There was a moment of mixed farce and drama which did much to bind us all together as a group and install Nan as our heroine. Wilf had decided to take Nan up Central Buttress, a pleasant route of about 70' with several short pitches. Nan had taken a rest in the Sentry Box, and had moved out on to the slab, finding it beyond her competence at the time. "My legs aren't long enough," she said, dolefully. We assured her, perhaps with a lack of delicacy, that there was nothing wrong with her legs. She did a desperate manoeuvre and arrived in an impossible position for tackling the slab, with her back to the rock, her toes stuck out in space. Nan's plight drew all to the scene, to advise, laugh, cheer. Wilf gave a quick squint from the top, rolled his eyes in astonishment and tightened his grip on the rope, "Can you turn, Nan?" said Dave. "No", decisive. "Can you put your left foot on that hold?" said Paul. "No" sharp edge to voice, implying what a fool idea. "Can you step down?" said Eddie. No reply, just a severe look at the speaker. "Jump off – Wilf will hold you"! Neither Wilf nor Nan thought much of that idea. Eventually, Keith moved up below Nan and with Wilf tugging and Keith pushing, Nan was able to turn and finish the climb.

The day was wearing on. Wilf and Nat moved off to climb together. "Care for a brew?" asked Keith. So, joyfully bearing our heroine with us, we achieved a further impossible task squeezing seven of us plus primus stove into Keith's tent.

We finished the day by taking it in turns to fall off the severe route on The Railway Slab. There was more loss of skin, and bruises, but gain in laughter and companionship. Somewhere along the way a club had been born, with a few lifelong friendships. Stangely, Barry never came out with us again, although he had been the catalyst that set all in motion. Wilf did not join the club, but we met often. Nat joined the club in later years, becoming its very popular president for a time. We went home in different mood; gone was the reserve; had we not suffered and triumphed together?

Two weeks later we converged on Black Rocks. We were joined this time by Harry and Molly Pretty. From this time on we mostly taught ourselves, learning from every climb we led, or did on a top rope. Dave and Keith led some of the climbs we had done on the previous meet. Harry soon showed that he intended to be a fully paid-up member of the outfit, by doing some climbs solo and following on others. Towards the end of the day he announced from the top of the crag that he was going to do an abseil. We were impressed. "Have you done one before?" I shouted. "Yes, dozens", cried Harry jauntily. "Last night", whispered Molly to me, "off the back of a chair". "Would you like a lifeline?" normal practice for a first abseil. "No, I'll manage," a bit edgy as he fussed about, fixing the rope. He re-appeared with coil of rope like knitting round his body. "Doesn't look right to me," I warned. "Well, it's got to do," said Harry crossly, and dropped off into space. I saw him hurtling down and hastily got out of the firing line. There was a jerk, as Harry braked, but he kept falling. No one had allowed for the elasticity of his new nylon rope. Feet short of the ground the rope held him and he came to rest, gently bobbing beside me, giving a breathless grin. "Bloody hell," said Keith, casually rolling a cigarette; it was the nearest Keith came to showing he had been startled, that and a wry smile at Harry. Everyone laughed; Harry had well and truly joined us. And for Harry and me it was the start of a climbing partnership which lasted for many years, on many a long trail, and in many a wild camp.

All through that summer, golden not just with sunshine, but with youth, we went weekly to the crags. Many were our adventures. We explored other outcrops, such as Stanage Edge and Roaches. We learned about chimneys, and laybacks, and lightweight camping and bivouacs. We did join meets with the M.A.M. to Cratcliffe and Kinder Scout. We tried ourselves on the tiny dolomite crag at Brassington, and retired, found wanting, to an old lady's house where we drank tea in the company of asthmatic cats. We camped in winter on Brown Knoll and nearly froze to death. New members were not dismayed by our reputation and so Roy Edwards, Frank Ewer and John Adderley and others joined us. We climbed in rain, sun and snow and sometimes by torchlight and moonlight. Harry went to Skye and returned with tales of the Cuillins and worn fingertips and told of how people hid away after dinner lest Cyril Machin should spirit them up another climb. I met Harry most days in a corner cafe, to plan the weekends, holidays, even to speculate on higher hills. There was no other year in my life quite like 1949. At first the club was known as the Burton-on-Trent (Anorak) M.C. But it did not please us. One day I was striving for intellectual challenge, with the 'Daily Mirror' crossword – and came across a clue, "mountain nymphs. I looked it up and found 'Oreads' and put the idea to the others. We liked it and so the Oread M.C. came into being, a club that startled even some members with its stated aim, 'Mountaineering regardless'.

The early Oread years owe much to the contribution made by three very different men – Cyril Machin, Eric Byne and Oliver Jones. Cyril came late to mountaineering, but was soon a legend to his many friends for his enthusiasm, energy, courtesy and exploits. If people said that a climber had come back from a Ben Nevis gully in the middle of the night, or taken a frightened plumber up a rock climb, or survived an avalanche and climbed back up again, we knew it had to be Cyril. He joined many of the first gritstone meets, sharing our climbs, barns, coffee and lives, holding back when our wilder enthusiasms cut across his own gentler views. He first met us as a group on Stanage. Keith and Eddie had chosen to bivouac in Robin Hood's cave, which was several feet up the crag. In the morning, Eddie emerged blearily, having enjoyed a convivial evening in the pub the night before, missed his footing and fell out of the cave. Contact with the stony ground had the effect of almost waking him. An elegant, elderly gentleman bore down on him, hand extended in the famous Machin greeting, "Hello, I'm Cyril, are you Oread?" Eddie, bemused, confessed that he was, "Good, let's do a climb then" said Cyril, which is the only time ever that Eddie did Black Hawk Traverse Right, or any other climb, before breakfast. There was only one thing we could do with Cyril, so we made him our first President, an office to which he brought dignity and style during 1949 and 1950.

As the year advanced, Eric Byne came more into our lives, urging us on to ever more desperate deeds. There was at the time no greater authority on Derbyshire gritstone than Eric, and he was a prominent member of the Gritstone Guide Committee, which was parcelling out the Guide Book work still to be done. Joe Brown, Wilf, Nat and other stalwarts of the Valkyrie M.C. were grappling with routes on the Great Buttress and the rest of Froggatt Edge. Eric thought that Oreads ought to tackle the Baslow area, which included Baslow, Birchen, Gardoms edges and Chatsworth Rocks, a task for which we were not ready as climbers, but we did it. On a hot summer day all of us attacked the bare crags of Birchen and rattled off all the known climbs. Baslow edge took us into the autumn. We were now well known in the Robin Hood Inn, where we congregated in the back room with old Charlie and sang songs not acceptable in other establishments. It seems incredible now to remember that Gladys, a good lady of substantial build, would take our orders and stagger down huge steps into the cellar to get big jugs of ale filled, then carry them back up.

Gardoms Edge was quite a different matter. A long outcrop of mainly isolated buttresses and, with winter upon us, if anything toughened us up, it was Gardoms. Just wading through the dense vegetation to reach the buttresses was energy taking. Eric had named his three Unconquerables – The Unconquerable Cracks on Stanage, The Rivelin needle on Rivelin edge and Moyers Buttress on Gardoms. The unconquerable Cracks were fortunately not our problem, in any case Albert Shutt led the L.H. in 1945 and Joe Brown and Wilf White led the R.H. in 1949. The Rivelin Needle was also out of our area, but then Dick Brown and members of The Sheffield University M.C. managed to lead the Spiral Route without artificial aids. That left us with Moyer's Buttress until Eric discovered yet another unsolved route. He was standing on a massive buttress on Gardoms in the long dark raincoat he favoured. He said it kept the rain away; we said he looked like an undertaker and that's how it got its name, The Undertaker's Buttress. They were quite outside our capability but otherwise we tackled the Edge, week after week; crag after crag.

There were adventures. I shall tell of only one. Dave set out on a top rope to try out a steep wall. There seemed to be some big steps in it, but an enticing looking crack for a handhold high up. Dave, in the fullness of time reached for this crack, and pulled away on it. Next second a huge boulder swivelled out of the wall like a door opening on a hinge, leaving Dave dangling with a half-ton of rock of uncertain temper for company. The rock was finally kicked away but Dave felt that he had done his bit. So Cyril set out on the next attempt. He tried in boots, he tried in rubbers, he tried in socks and finally in bare feet, regardless that it was a bleak November day. Finally he was lowered off the crag, blue with cold and was sick. Then he went back and finished the climb. Hence its accolade as President's Wall.

We had climbed a few times with a giant of a man, Oliver Jones, who in his youth had worked his way round the Canadian Northlands, coming home again with the grand-dad of all rucksacks, a guitar and a stock of ballads, both sad and salty. He fitted easily into our company. I invited him to join a meet at Roaches and Hen Cloud. We climbed all of a hot summer day on those spectacular crags, and, as usual, went to The Three Horseshoes after. We did not know that the most memorable feature of the weekend was still to come. At nearing midnight, the evening was so still and hot that someone suggested a bivouac on Hen Cloud. We gathered candles, water, stoves and food and found a grassy hollow near the summit of the Cloud. No-one who was there will ever forget Molly making pancakes as fast as we could eat them, by the light of the candles set on the rocks, or of lying down to sleep under the stars, and waking in the morning to distant farm noises. Oliver certainly did not.

When Oliver was invited to speak at our first Dinner in November 1949, he asked "Do I need a dinner jacket, shall I bring my guitar, and will I be sleeping on a hilltop?" That first Dinner was at Fox House Inn. Jack Longland and Alf Bridge were the Principal Guests. The price of the three-course meal was five shillings and sixpence, or about twenty-seven decimal pence. Eighteen people sat down to dinner. The radicals of the club had not wanted to toast the Queen, but Cyril felt that it was traditional, so because of that and for love of Cyril, the Queen was toasted. Oliver spoke so well that he was invited every year after, usually speaking earthy words of wisdom from the Bible, to those who were married during the year and presenting them with a pewter tankard. As we thought, Keith and Nan were the first recipients; June and I still have our tankard dated 1962.

There is, of course, so much left unsaid. How Keith's stove had a habit of erupting in the tent, being flung out in flaming orbit, followed by some pithy adjectives. How we tried to climb Crib Goch at night, on snow, that first Christmas. How Roy Edwards thumbed a lift off a motor-cyclist, as the speed climbed up to 100 mph, Roy asked, "Are you Wilf White?" "Yes." "Well, can I get off then?" And Harry, up to his knees in mud trying to climb the Moated Boulder on Kinder Scout. And so many other stories.

MEET ONE – BLACK ROCKS

DAVID PENLINGTON

Following a letter written by George Sutton and published in the Burton Daily Mail a number of local "mountaineers" were drawn together on a meet at Black Rocks, Cromford.

The Sunday dawned fine and a group made up of George Sutton, Roy Edwards, Harry and Molly Pretty, Paul Gardiner and Dave Penlington boarded the 9.00 am bus from Derby to Wirksworth. We were to meet Eddie Say and Keith Axon at the crag where they had been camping overnight.

Walking up the hill from Wirksworth to Black Rocks it was obvious that each was assessing each other as to ability and experience. Smith, Gardiner and Penlington were known to each other having fallen off various Derbyshire outcrops.

Sutton, recently demobbed from the R.A.F. was the eldest. He was a member of the M.A.M., so must have 'done a bit'. He was dressed in ex army anorak, ARP warden's trousers, tucked into ex naval sea boot stockings and clinkered boots. Edwards, a young chap in cut down raincoat admitted that it was his first time out. Pretty was the big question mark. We quickly learnt that he was going to Skye with the M.A.M. in a few weeks time. He was wearing new boots (Robert Lawrie), a white roll neck sweater (not obviously ex R.N.) and an alpine style felt trilby. He certainly looked the part fitting exactly the description of "the Gen Man", as described by Pete Perkins, a local 'hard lad'; in one of his many tales. He also carried a brand new ¾ wt (8mm dia) nylon rope. This was the first nylon rope most of the group had seen and possibly the first one ever to be used at Black Rocks. Less than half the diameter of our hemp ropes and said to be several times stronger.

Axon, not long out of a certain notorious and mutinous airborne division and Say were found on Stonnis Buttress. They were friends of Wilf White another hardman and secretary of the Valkyrie M.C. We climbed and fell off various routes; no one ventured onto any really difficult climbs.

Towards the end of the day our "Gen Man" announced that he must abseil on the nylon rope. We all quickly gathered round. Pretty placed the rope around a pine tree, stood astride it, passed it across his body and over a shoulder, the classic method. Slings and karabiners were quite uncommon in those days. Walking backwards to the cliff edge the rope tensioned, in doing so it reduced to half it's original diameter. None of us had seen the elongation of nylon before. Pretty was now some four to five feet below the top of the crag looking like a yoyo on a string. "He'll cut his leg off," someone said. He then dropped out of sight; the rope was in full tension over the rock edge. He must have swung across below the overhang; the rope moved several feet sideways, in so doing the outer strands of the rope frayed and sprang apart under the tension. "Bloody hell, he's a gonner," cried Axon. Sutton went pale, believing the Club was finished before it had started. Gardiner and Edwards sprinted to the foot of the rocks to pick up the remains. The rope slackened, "Next one" came a shout from below. We looked at each other but someone said it was time to go for the bus. A few minutes later the party was descending the hill back to Wirksworth.

D.P.'s memoir of Meet One is actually a compilation of Meet One (Sunday 20.03.49) and Meet Two (a fortnight later) as described in George Sutton's Oreads Regardless 1949/50. I apologise for duplicating the story of the "famous abseil" which has proved too difficult to eliminate without mangling both articles — *Editor*.

48 YEARS WITH THE OREAD

TONY MOULAM

From about 1944, pre-dating the Sound of Music by 15 years, the Derbyshire hills were full of the sounds of climbing clubs being formed. This phenomenon was due in part to the vast post-war increase in the number of active climbers and the difficulty they had in gaining membership of one of the senior clubs. The twin centres of this ferment were Derby and Burton upon Trent and the innovations included The Stonnis (Peter Harding, Tony Moulam, Ernie Phillips, Ronnie Lee, Dick Meyer and Nobby Millward), The Valkyrie (Wilf White, Nat Allen, Chuck Cook and Don Chapman) and The Innominate (Norman Kershaw is the only one I remember, but there must have been more). These three clubs all transmuted into something else, or became defunct, within a matter of a few years but many of their former members eventually joined the Oread which was built to last! George Sutton was the founding father and its nuclear group included Harry Pretty, Dave Penlington and Keith Axon.

I think that I first met Harry Pretty and David Penlington at Pen y Gwrd at the end of September 1949, only about six months after the Oread had been formed in March. I was probably pontificating at the bar, having been in North Wales since August 25th getting the leg I had injured in a hitch-hiking accident fit, so that I could climb when I went up to Manchester University. Harry tells me that I gave him and Dave Penlington the benefit of my wisdom, whether about climbing, as we had just returned from our first attempt on Ogof Direct, or which beer to drink. I do not remember!

Being one of the few members of the CC in the north in those days I first represented the club at the Oread dinner at the Scotsman's Pack in Hathersage on 1st December 1951, the year that George, Harry and several other members had been to Lyngen. Although the food, the drink and the speeches were good, and I think we were treated to one of Oliver Jones' bagpipe accompanied monologues; the talk in the bar of that initial exploit remains with me as the highlight of the evening.

The club grew stronger and more entertaining year by year and made visits to Spitzbergen in 1952 and South Georgia in 1954. The latter trip was enlivened by Dick Brown, a recruit from the SUMC, who, early in the night, allegedly turned over in his sleeping bag on the beach and woke all the penguins, so creating such pandemonium that no-one got any more sleep.

After some tribulation a ground breaking Himalayan expedition was organised with the help of the Mount Everest Foundation and sponsors who donated large quantities of Christmas pudding. By then Dennis Gray had become an Oread, and he recounts that an overweight party left from Liverpool in May 1961 for Kulu. The leader was Bob Pettigrew, because he had been there before and Dennis, Ray Handley, Derrick Burgess, Trevor Panther, Jack Ashcroft and Steve Read made up the rest of what became a very successful and enjoyable exploit.

I must now move forward to 25th November 1972. The occasion was the 23rd annual dinner of the OMC, by now at the Green Man in Ashbourne. David Cox and I were the two main guests and we were well entertained by the now traditional pantomime, with its bearded ladies, other accomplished artists, and Harry Pretty's impersonation of Edward VII. However the evening was made for me by the presentation of a commemorative plate. This is one of my most treasured possessions, and as it is unique, it must be beyond price. It marks the 21st Anniversary of my Oread Dining as although I had not attended every dinner since 1951, it must have seemed to the committee as if I had.

My latest appearance to date was at the 28th Dinner in 1977. This time Harding was an official guest, whereas I had been invited by Jo and Bryan Royle. Johnny Welbourn, another relic of the Stonnis, was there which gave me an excuse (as if I ever needed one) to carouse into the night. The next day saw the Mynnyd Fell race but after the Club's usual generous and open handed hospitality, I sacrificed myself and tried to be a useful marshall counting people in!

I now look forward to the 50th year Jubilee Dinner for a reunion with many friends, and a new generation of Oread, and hope to survive for many more years of association with your vibrant and long lived club, whose motto might, or should, be "Climb Every Mountain".

GEORGE SUTTON   *Newsletter, November 1957*

I enclose a bill for the Oreads' first Annual Dinner. It will be seen that 17 people attended; that £5.15.6. was spent on Dinners; and £1.13.9. on beer.

IN AT THE DEEP END
CONTRIBUTION TO *CLIMBS ON GRITSTONE*
VOLUME 2, THE SHEFFIELD AREA
EDITED: ERIC BYNE 1949-1950

Extract from Eric Byne's introduction to The Baslow Edges, *Climbs on Gritstone*, Volume 2, published in 1951

> "...So began an all out effort on the part of the Oread members, prominent amongst whom were Dave Penlington, George Sutton, Keith Axon, Harry Pretty, Edwin Say, Miss N. Smith (later Axon), Mrs M. Pretty, Frank Ewers, Paul Gardiner, Joe Moor, John Adderley, Cyril Machin, Eric Byne, Roy Edwards and Lorna Peake, the latter proved to be an inspiring influence purely by her presence."

> "With tremendous enthusiasm the guide work progressed and climbing took place in heat waves, gales, pouring rain and by moonlight. On one notable day on Birchen Edge, eight hours climbing in blistering heat mopped up these rocks and left but little of the climbers to be mopped. This day saw Keith Axon's two new routes: Nelson's Nemesis and Horatio's Horror".

> "The greatest efforts have been reserved for Gardoms Edge. Adverse weather conditions have tended to prevent rubber climbing and this has meant a slowing up of climbing pace and an excess of harder work. Despite this the enthusiasm of Dave Penlington, Keith Axon, Harry Pretty and Edwin Say, whipped on by George Sutton and Eric Byne (hard taskmasters) has led to many new routes. Axon's pioneering of Gardom's Gate and Oread Climb have been a stimulus. President's wall, after attempts in boots, rubbers, socks and bare feet was finally ascended by the President – Cyril Machin. Finally in spring 1950 Dave Penlington capped all his previous efforts by the lead of Blenheim Buttress."

As Sutton has inferred in Oreads Regardless our climbing experience was barely adequate for the harder routes on Gardoms. But it was an intensive work out and at the end of six months, climbing every weekend, we began to feel more like veterans.

Immediately to the north the Valkyrie were operating: Nat Allen, Slim Sorrell, Whillans, Wilf and Mary White, Joe Brown, Janes, Handley and others engaged in the early Froggatt and Curbar classics. Further to the north the Sheffield University M.C. and the Peak C.C. were similarly engaged on Stanage. By the spring of 1950 we all knew each other. We caught the same bus from Bakewell to Derby every Sunday night causing chaos down the centre aisle with our ropes, rucksacks and tents. We sang the same songs and occasionally we climbed together. Nat Allen led me up many routes on Froggatt and Stanage that were beyond my capability as a leader. Not infrequently we encountered the Birmingham Cave and Crag (Stan Moore, Trevor Jones, Peter Knapp, Nobby Clarke), and of course if you were very lucky you came across the Stonnis stars: Peter Harding, Tony Moulam, Ernie Phillips, Ronnie Lee (later Phillips), Nobby Millward, Graham Robinson, Dick Meyer, Dave Sampson etc.

Editor

TREADING WATER
WHITEHALL OPEN PURSUITS CENTRE

When Jack Longland, supported by Alf Bridge, outlined his objectives for Whitehall in 1950 before an invited audience, mainly comprising Peak District climbers, his proposal that local mountaineering clubs would provide a core of voluntary instructors was enthusiastically received. In this age when you need a Mountain Leadership Certificate to take a party under instruction over Thorpe Cloud, Longland's faith in his assembled troops was remarkable.

Many Oreads and climbing friends from other clubs were regular week-end instructors and some, notably George Sutton, Cyril Machin, Trevor Panther, Joe Brown and Harold Drasdo, were on the permanent staff for short periods.

Longland's faith in his voluntary instructors was not misplaced. A student was kind enough to acknowledge the quality of instruction received in a letter to the club:

> Dear Sir,
>
> I am writing as a student of White Hall, and would like to send an appreciation of the instructors who, I believe are Oreads.
>
> I arrived in Buxton on Feb. 26th with another student and two instructors. One was an Oread but the other would not identify himself. We were soon installed in a Spanish bar, and hours later we arrived at White Hall to the jingle of bottles.
>
> Saturday found three inches of snow outside, and parties were quickly dispersed to Shale Gully and to skiing. I was in the Gully Party. One member wore a boater which stopped falling stones from hitting the last man. In the afternoon we went skiing. The least said the better. In the evening a slide show by Messrs. Brown and Falkner was followed by a social evening. Stan Moore and Dick Brown did a complete traverse on the wall of the lounge.
>
> Sunday proved amusing to the Gully Party. An instructor went crampons (sic) over balaclava down the Gully but was not hurt. He said it was a controlled glissade. Over lunch certain Oreads gave imitations of penguins which were very good – at least everyone had indigestion that afternoon.
>
> I should like to thank the members of the Oread concerned for some very useful instructions throughout the weekend.
>
> *D.R. Hammond*

Editor

MAKING WAVES
Oread Lyngen (Arctic Norway) Expedition 1951

It was George Sutton's initiative and eclectic research that led to the formation of the Lyngen party in late 1950 and early 1951.

There was little published on climbing in this northern alpine region since A.C. Journals in 1897 and '98 when Haskett Smith, Hastings, W.C.Slingsby, Norman Collie and the Norwegian Hogrenning had explored extensively. Mrs Elizabeth Main, with her guides the Imbodens (father and son), had published a book at the turn of the century on her climbing exploration of the peninsula. Other than that all was silence. Peaks climbed mostly had one ascent only and clearly there were many unclimbed peaks and multitudinous new routes waiting. (We knew nothing of Guy Barlow's solo visits at the time).

The available maps were extremely vague and, in practice, were found to be profoundly inaccurate in many areas. So the proper identification of peaks, glaciers etc. inevitably became a prime object.

The coming together of climbers on the Edges, and at Whitehall, was a significant element in party selection: George Sutton (leader), Harry Pretty, Stan Moore, Ken (Nobby) Clarke, Dick Brown, Phillip Falkner, Bob Pettigrew, together with Patrick Parks and Alick Bartholomew (both C.U.M.C.).

Pettigrew, in the course of National Service, was serving with R.A.F. Mountain Rescue at Harpur Hill, Buxton at that time and was temporarily released on full pay for the three-month period. He was thus the only paid member of the party and thereby deemed a professional. In consequence he was considered to have the status of an alpine porter and was subsequently rewarded as such by presentation at the 1952 Annual Dinner, of a very dubious watch.

The overall activities between June and late August 1951 were described in some detail in 'Climb if you Will', published in 1974, and suffice it to say that approximately 45 peaks were climbed, a number of which were completely first ascents and a great majority of the remainder were new routes. Some serious glacier mapping was carried out and Pretty subsequently produced a ridge line map which clarified previous uncertainties and copies of which were used by many following parties, including Dutch, French and German. The original, and copies of same have unfortunately been lost but a record of peaks identified and climbed was passed to the Norway Travel Association (Per Prag) and was published both in U.K. and Norway.

Further Lyngen ventures by Oread members, R. A. Brown, P. R. Falkner, R. G. Pettigrew, and T. Panther ensued in 1952, '53 and '54 all of which resulted in first ascents and new routes on previously climbed peaks.

Whilst still undergraduates at Leeds, and still unknown to the Oread, Chris Radcliffe and Peter Scott forced some typically hard routes in the Lyngsdal and other areas (Leeds University, Lyddon Hall Mountaineering Expedition to Lyngen 1965).

The glacier survey carried out by Brown and Pretty in 1951 proved to be a useful preamble to the more serious endeavours of South Georgia (1954/55). The Lyngen maps, filed away for forty-seven years, were sent to the Norwegian Glacier Research Institute (Norsk Bremuseum) in 1998, and acknowledged with thanks.

Editor

British South Georgia Expedition 1954/55: Dr. I. M. Brooker, Richard A. Brown, Harry Pretty, Clive Webb, George Sutton, Shackleton's Cross behind. *Photo: B.S.G.E. 1954/55 Collection.*

Oread MC Lyngen (Arctic Norway) Expedition 1951: Alick Bartholomew, Patrick Parks, Harry Pretty, Bob Pettigrew, George Sutton, Dick Brown, Phil Falkner (in front), Stan Moore, Ken Clarke (missing). *Photo: Oread Lyngen Collection.*

Scottish Mountaineers and Oreads meet. Lyngen (Arctic Norway) 1951: Stan Moore, Adam Watson, Douglas Scott, Pat Parks, Phil Falkner, Bob Pettigrew (see Foreword by Tom Weir). *Photo: Tom Weir.*

THE ENIGMA – A SMALL PIECE OF NORTHERN HISTORY

HARRY PRETTY

On Saturday 7th July 1951, in a bivvy tent, well exposed to a bitter north wind, and several hundred feet above the eastern shoreline of Lyngen Fjord, Nobby Clarke woke up at 7 o'clock declaring that since we'd only been in our bags for two hours it must still be a.m. It took some astute observation of the sun to convince him that it was p.m., and we had slept for fourteen hours.

Others of the 1951 Oread party (Sutton, Moore and Pettigrew) were simultaneously engaged in more serious business on the west side of the peninsula among the Jagervasstinder. "You both have damaged ankles" they said, "You might as well get some gentle exercise and do a reccy up the east side". So we'd left with 60lb sacks, a week's food.

We had spotted the peak during the previous night's trek north towards the coastal settlement of Kopang, well illuminated by the glories of the midnight sun. A magnificent spire, far to the west, above rolling snowfields, and a glacier narrowly constrained by coastal peaks, its snout in a deep ravine some 800' above sea level.

Our maps (courtesy R.G.S.), dated 1912-1913, a vague arrangement of contours, were merely indicative. Individual peaks and glaciers, or any separation between permanent ice and exposed rock, was not shown. But months of research among the writings of Hastings, Haskett – Smith and W.C. Slingsby in the A.C. Journals for 1897, '98 (the last known serious exploration of Lyngen) had implanted some knowledge of the main ranges and the most celebrated individual peaks. These early explorer climbers had written of Lenangentind as perhaps the finest of the northern peaks, and I was convinced that the soaring mix of steep ridge and great couloirs, now framed by our tent door, could be none other.

Reconnaissance of the approaches from a 3,800' heap of tot, known locally as Golborre, proved fruitless since cloud enveloped us from the start and our descent of its northern face to glacier margins owed something to divine provenance as the compass needle merely gyrated when required to provide vital information in descent from its tottering ridge. But an ancient card in an old oxo tin provided first evidence that Dr. Guy Barlow had been in the area, and had reached the summit on 13th August 1927. This was, we could only assume, the Barlow who with E.W. Steeple, H.B. Buckle and A.H. Doughty had made first ascents of such Tryfan classics as Gashed Crag (1902), Grooved Arete (1911) and 1st Pinnacle Rib (1914). We were not even sure whether he was still alive.

At 08.00, Monday, 9th July, from a camp in birch scrub behind Kopang we set off for the big one. Previous research provided no evidence that Lenangentind had ever been attempted from the east. The distant magic of the great S.E. ridge, rising from unknown snowfields, would be a first.

It is not my intention to provide a detailed narrative of this splendid day. Within the context of this article a mere outline will suffice.

At 11.40 at 2,200' we were negotiating crevasses in mist, and it was 15.15 before we attained the left hand rib of the S.E. ridge, from where we viewed the major peaks of south Lyngen, and clouds boiling up over Finland and Sweden to the south east. My diary notes " — reached summit at 20.15 after difficult climb, towers, notches, rotten snow aretes on the L.H., hard crusted, with masses of unstable snow on R.H. Cold N.E. wind throughout. Totally clear sky above continuous cloud layer at 3,000'. Main couloir avalanched when we tried to turn steep face. Summit cairn with small tin, indecipherable Norwegian names dated 1937 ('ascent from W. Col'). Also card left by Dr. Guy Barlow, Birmingham University, 03.08.27 ('ascent from W. Col')."

Mount Paget (2,934m), South Georgia from camp on Upper Nordenskjold Glacier.   *Photo: R. A. Brown.*

Trollhul, South West coast, South Georgia, Cape Disappointment behind.   *Photo: H. Pretty.*

I noted that 03.08.27 was my second birthday. Diary continues " — Left summit at 21.40 to descend West ridge to Col of previous ascents. Reached Col after tricky descent over ice glazed rocks and treacherous double cornices, verglas very troublesome, very tired. Reached knife edged snow of West Col at 02.10, finishing with a blind abseil of 70', rope barely adequate, but fortuitous small ledge below overhang".

A steep descent on avalanche debris, some wandering about in mist on the upper snowfields eventually found our old steps of 15 hours ago, and a fast unrelenting descent took us to the glacier snout and its frozen tarn by 04.40. The murderously loose ravine of the Kopang gorge slowed us down and it was 07.45 when we found our tent, with some difficulty, in thick birch scrub, 24 hours after setting out.

One hours brief rest and we were trekking to Kopang, to be ferried by row boat to the little fjord steamer at 19.00. By 20.00 we had landed at Lyngseidet, and were back in base at 21.00, exactly 37 hours after we had departed camp for the ascent.

In retrospect it has to be one of the most memorable mountain days of my life. Not by reason of extreme difficulty but more from the exciting uncertainties of a new route on a superb peak amid the unforgettable atmosphere and colours of those northern latitudes.

That we had climbed Lenangentind harboured no doubts and the others, returning from hard days among the Jegervasstinder, seemed a little put out that, in a few days of assumed recuperation, we had knocked off the plum.

Weeks later, Saturday, 18th August, the team (Sutton, Moore, Clarke, Pettigrew, Falkner and R.A. Brown) on the little Kvaloy, en route for Tromsö and the big ship that would take us south to Bergen. Rounding the northern tip of the peninsula we had a fine view of the major northern peaks, most of which we'd climbed during the past three months. But there was a problem. What was the major peak between Lenangentind (that K.G.C. and I had climbed in July) and the northern Jegervasstinder, where the others had been simultaneously engaged? Among the voluminous clarification and identification of Lyngen peaks, which was a major objective of the party, it was an enigma and remained so for many months. Eventually further research identified two peaks north of Jegervasstind, Lenangentind and Strupentind. Nobby and I had climbed the latter so, among the confusion, no-one of the Oread party had set foot on the much prized Lenangentind. These uncertainties remained throughout the period that I was producing a mountaineer's ridge line map of the peninsula in 1952/53, and were only resolved when, entirely by accident, I met the still extant and very clear minded Dr. Guy Barlow at the North Wales CC Dinner in '53. He identified Strupentind and could not understand that in my diary I had misquoted his 1927 card as referring to Lenangentind – and I have never understood it either.

In November 1953 he wrote to me from Port Dinorwic and it is this letter of total recall that is my main interest in re-telling this small piece of mountaineering history. It has never been reproduced before.

He wrote:

> "My climbing in the Lyngen region was in 1926, '27 and '28, with a camp at Kopang in '27 and '28. Strupentind was my first climb from Kopang. In Kopang they told me the name was Kopangtind. Route over glacier up to West Skar (Col – *Editor*) and then by 1,500' ridge to summit. I made the height 5,200'. There was no cairn so I built one, 3-4', at the highest point and put my card in the tin which had been used for a spare film. It would be interesting to know how much of my cairn you found. Also did you have difficulty in making out my note? For actually I wrote 'ascent from Skar on N.W. in eight hours from Kopang', No mention of Lenangentind as your account states. I was in no confusion about names as, at the time, the name for me was Kopangtind. Also I was not expecting to find it the highest peak for, from Kjostind in 1926, I had seen three peaks higher than Kjostind

itself (these included Lenangentind and Strupentind of course). Unfortunately a change in the weather compelled me to start my descent after only 20 mins on the summit. Kopang was reached in 6 hours.

It was almost a year later that I heard from Hastings that he and Hogrenning had made an ascent in 1901. They left a small cairn but concluded that in 26 years it had been blown away. It is surprising that my cairn stood so well.

Hastings said they called it Strupentind, and he made it clear to me that the highest peak to the W. had the name Lenganentind. In 1928 I traversed most of the ridges and peaks S. of Lenangentind but did not get up more than 300' of that peak from its S. Skar. Afterwards I was sorry I did not persist, but it was the end of a very long day. I do not remember seeing any printed account of the ascent made by Hastings but probably there is some note in the A.C.J. It would be interesting to know if you found such.[1] Hastings was the pioneer of Lyngen. Slingsby, I believe, only joined Hastings for one or more seasons. If you publish anything please give Hastings first place.

You certainly would not find any account of my climbs in that region for nothing has been published. In fact since these climbs were done *alone* it did not seem desirable to say much about them – at that time anyway. In later years my interests were deflected to other places.

I hope the above notes may serve to clear up a few points. It only remains to thank you most sincerely for your very kind invitation to your Annual Dinner, but I regret being unable to attend.

Yours truly,
G. Barlow.

P.S. It is not correct to associate Steeple's name with Gashed Crag.

[1] I subsequently found a reference by Hastings in the A.C.J., but I have forgotten the year, but probably 1901.

The book I was working on at this time, an account of the history of climbing in North Norway, was never published, and work on same was subsumed by preparations for the South Georgia Expedition 1954/55. The M.S. still remains, although a section has been lost.

R. A. Brown and P. R. Falkner subsequently made a new route on Lenangentind in 1953 — *Editor.*

THE FIRST MEET IN GLENCOE

JOHN FISHER

This must have been Easter 1952 and the arrangement was that a good number of Oreads would join some Barnsley M. C. people on a coach to Glencoe. The writer, after another 8–4 shift, all packed up and ready for public transport to Derby Station, was much dismayed by the failure of the bus to appear. Full of aggressive enterprise I dragooned a local motorcyclist who had just entered a barber's shop and for two and six (12.5p) got him to take me the two miles to the Station. Thence to Glencoe in sixteen hours, where Gibson, Webb and others camped at the meeting of the Three Waters and the Barnsley crowd, being mainly skiers, walked up with tents and gear to the Meall a Bhuiridh plateau. Our party of Harby (real M.A.M.), Burgess (a.k.a. Handley M.A.M.) and Fisher (a.k.a. Cholmondeley Smith M.A.M.) took up quarters in the S.M.C. hut at Laggangarbh. Neither Ch. Smith nor Handley knew of this misrepresentation. Bill Murray arrived later at the otherwise empty hut and thought it only curious that these English occupants addressed each other with names which did not fit the hut entry. He was a gentleman and did not explore this discrepancy.

That same day of arrival we did two climbs including Red Slab on the Rannoch Wall where we got lost. I became alarmed and leader Burgess placed a peg. In the following days a traverse of Aonach Eagach and all the Bidean summits were done in sunny Alpine conditions. No transport, of course. After Bidean we were potentially too late for a drink at the Kingshouse so Bill Murray and one of his friends (quoted in his books) volunteered to wash our pots! After taking drinks orders from D.B. and M.H., Fisher ran to the Kingshouse to get them before closing time (at 9pm in those days) but forgot the orders. Burgess was rather ungracious when, on arrival, he was offered milk stout, instead of bitter beer. Altogether a memorable and joyful Scottish meet.

LYNGEN – OREAD VENTURE II

Newsletter, September 1953

The earlier party (Phil Falkner, Dick Brown and Barry Cook) has succeeded in climbing the south Face of Jekkevarre. The climb took 11 hours, was 4,000' long, and had some severe pitches. Part of it had been done earlier by an Edinburgh party.

P.R.F. says of the route, "Imagine the Tower Ridge (of Ben Nevis), with the Douglas Boulder enlarged to about 2,200', so that it forms more than half the ridge – that is the Great Ridge or Storeggen of Jekkevarre."

The other pair (Bob Pettigrew and Trevor Panther) have made the first ascent of Skartind and accompanied by Dick Brown have also climbed the infamous "Slangetind".

With two weeks in hand the expedition has ascended ten major peaks, three of them first ascents, and six new routes.

D.C.C.

Storeggen was subsequently climbed by C. Radcliffe and P. Scott in 1965, possibly the second ascent. They were benighted in a blizzard on the summit of Jekkevarre – the highest summit in Arctic Norway. – *Editor.*

Golden Oldies

Consolidation 1953-1958

Although meets and general information circulars were produced during the years 1949-53 the first monthly newsletter did not appear until June 1953 under the editorship of Douglas Charles Cullum.

It quickly established a reputation for excellence which has never been surpassed and was particularly admired for the variety of its Editorials and editorial features, such as Oreads in Shorts, and the often scathing Profiles of sundry members. It was simultaneously serious, informative, comic, and often surreal – *Editor*.

EDITORIALS
(EXTRACTS)

Newsletter Vol. 1, No. 1, June 1953

In presenting this, our first newsletter (which, it is hoped, will subsequently appear monthly), a few comments seem necessary concerning its functions, its raison d'etre, and the nature of its contents.

In a small club, where there is plenty of contact between all the members, the personal touch needs no refreshing. It generates a spirit of intimacy embracing its whole membership, thus closely uniting the club. It is this, in fact, that makes a club a club, and not just a crowd of individuals, and it is what we call the club spirit. To my mind this is the most delightful and the most valuable benefit we derive from membership, whatever the nature of the club.

Recently the Oread has been growing rapidly, and shows every sign of continuing to do so (in fact, it may be said that we have left infancy behind and are commencing adultery!) With this rapid growth, we have inevitably lost something of the closeness, for one cannot possibly follow unaided the many and varied activities of our present seventy or so members. The broad functions of this newsletter is to help to restore and maintain the close personal relationships which make membership of the Oread worth while.

D. C. Cullum

Newsletter, January 1954

Whether you prefer to join the ladies on the Marsden – Rowsley walk or Gibson on his pub-crawl, to climb severes in Llanberis or browse in idyllic Cwm Silyn, to follow the trade routes up Stanage or to explore Agden, there is something for you. Let Oread boots tramp every hill, scale every crag! Let Oread tents be seen on every moor, by every lake and cliff! Let the click of Oread shutters reverberate through the land, in preparation for the second Photo Meet! Let our ice axes never rust, our ropes never be coiled, our Primuses never grow cold, and our tankards never run dry, and 1954 will indeed be a Happy New Year!

D. C. Cullum

PROFILES
(EXTRACTS)

GEORGE SUTTON   *Newsletter, June 1953*

The man who, in 1949 gave birth to the Oread and, in doing so, discovered that although he had been delivered of persistently tiny baby it was, persistently, a noisy, argumentative, and troublesome one and, above all, remarkably virile for its size. It is apt that he should be President in a year when a fine growth of membership has lent some authority to the original and still extant virility.

A man whose life has been a constant search for the solution to a series of unusual and highly original problems. Of the earlier of these, little is known, beyond the fact that they appear to be connected with the more dubious parts of Rangoon, Singapore, and other points east of Bombay. (1942-45)

More latterly there was an attempt to penetrate the mountainous part of New Guinea, followed by the founding of this club, and the concept of an Oread expedition. It is no small thing that George Sutton inspired, planned and led a mountaineering and scientific expedition to Arctic Norway in 1951 which has been described as, "one of the most efficient of small British expeditions of more recent times". In 1952 he led the British Spitzbergen Expedition with a party of five Cambridge Scientists. If in Lyngen he produced a lyric, in Spitzbergen he achieved an epic.

Somewhat gaunt in appearance and ascetic by nature, he is, on any kind of rock as a second, the answer to a leader's prayer. On snow or ice is apt to be a different person, and only thoroughly happy when leading. Once led a horrible ice-pitch on N.E. Ridge of Nevis, and had to give a top rope to several following parties – wrote delirious letters to his friends on the subject.

Is alleged to have saved Bob Pettigrew's life in Lyngen, rescuing him from an arctic swamp, but has almost succeeded in living it down.

Our President has, in the field of mountaineering, his biggest problem yet to solve (South Georgia). But whatever the outcome he might be remembered as the man, who amid the misfortunes of 1950, wrote ... "The north and be damned," and I'm damned if we weren't.

Anon

Some Profiles appeared under the by-line of the author. Others were, as above, submitted anonymously – *Editor.*

RICHARD A. BROWN   *Newsletter, July 1953*

His bearded, dignified, almost noble appearance contrasts strikingly with his youthful sense of fun. A true disciple of Rabelais, he has long been the hero of countless legendary exploits and orgies; exploits of astonishing variety, but all characterised by some outlandish episode exhibiting the true Brownian genius. Whether climbing Arctic mountains, or supping Cointreau in a Sheffield den of vice, Richard "A". Brown makes a delightful if bewildering companion. He undoubtedly possesses a great future – but what sort of future is anybody's guess.

P. R. Falkner

ALBERT SHUTT   *Newsletter, August 1953*

In 1942-3 Albert, then a lad of 14 years, became a protégé of Macleod of the Sheffield Climbing Club, and could be seen leading in shorts such severe routes on Stanage as Black Slab original route and the Trinity Wall climbs. At that time rubber gym shoes were a rarity possessed by few and tricouni nails impossible to buy locally, so Albert learned to climb and lead V. S. routes in hob-nailed boots.

Always keen on exploration and new routes, to both bars and rocks, "Our Albert", spent considerable time forcing new ways up virgin rock, only to find later that the deflowering had already taken place. Nevertheless he was probably the first to combine the girdle traverses of Robin Hood and Black Hawk, thus giving over 1,000' of climbing on Stanage. With Tom Probert he made the first ascent of the Left Unconquerable Crack, but the Right one eluded him. The following weekend he celebrated by falling off Nether Tor and breaking his ankle.

In later years he worked out numerous routes on White Hall rocks and, with R. A. Brown and P. Carr explored Rake's Rocks near Laddow. Surely no more fitting explorers could have been found, as witness the names of the routes they discovered – Orgy, Dissipation, Degradation, etc.

E. Byne

OUTDOOR MEETS (U.K.)
CWM SILYN

Newsletter, June 1953 (Extract)

A coach will run at the usual times on the Friday evening – Nottingham Midland Station 6.30 p.m., Derby Market 7.10 p.m., Burton (Queen's Hotel) 7.40 p.m. Friends and guests are of course welcome. Deposits of 10/- should be sent to P. R. Falkner, 14 Queens Drive, Beeston, by June 6th at the latest.

P. R. Falkner

COACH MEETS

Newsletter, July 1953 (Extract)

Since the Llanberis meet last February, the failing support for long-distance coaches has given cause for some anxiety. The Easter meet only just survived; the Ogwen and Wasdale projects were so feebly supported that not even a 14-seater could be operated without financial loss.

Reasons can be found for these failures. Perhaps we are attempting too many long distance meets; perhaps we have visited Ogwen too often recently; perhaps the Coronation holiday arrangements "killed" the Whitsun meet. Perhaps this, perhaps that, perhaps the other; an apologist can find plausible excuses for anything.

D. C. Cullum

KINDER DOWNFALL

Newsletter, October 1953 (Extract)

A most successful meet from the point of view of weather and attendance. The sun shone and Oreads rolled up in thousands – well, twenty came and brought ten friends. Among these were Jack Longland and his son John, who joined our Naiad section by getting wet through climbing the waterfall.

D. C. Cullum

HARSTON ROCKS (JOINT MEET WITH M.A.M.)

Newsletter, December 1953 (Extract)

The day that it was and the location of the rocks deserved a better turnout for a joint meet. Only eleven put in an appearance. However, enthusiasm grew the more they explored, for Harston is a place to improve technique. Everyone expressed a desire to come again.

The party, being small, kept together and worked from the Froghall end of the valley, searching and climbing wherever possible, to the Harston Rock where the highlight of the day was Ernie Marshall's ascent of the Helix Route – a magnificent climb.

D. C. Cullum

John Fisher has averred that, on this occasion, Dave Penlington led Helix – *Editor.*

FIRST OREAD PHOTO MEET, BASLOW, OCTOBER 1953

This meet was a glorious success. The response exceeded all expectations, in both quality and quantity. On Saturday afternoon over two hundred photographs, almost all of a high standard adorned the walls of the room at the Prince of Wales, Baslow. The exhibition showed in a striking way the wide range of the Club's activities. There were photographs not only of all standard British climbing areas, but also of nearly all the principal Alpine districts, and places as far afield as Spitzbergen and Lyngen. The first prize in the Pictorial Section went to Geoff Gibson for a superb study of the Pigne d'Arolla. Bob Pettigrew won the first prize for the photograph of greatest interest to the Club, with his extraordinary "Moulin Rouge", starring a grotesque simian Brown. In both categories the President and Mike Moore were the runners-up. In the evening, Phil Falkner, Gerry Britton and Dick Brown gave a display of colour slides.

Revelry continued to a late hour on Saturday. Malcolm Padley gave a display of aquatic sports in the horse trough at the Robin Hood. Then at midnight there was climbing on Birchen Edge by the light of electric torches and occasional fireworks. Somehow a jumping cracker found its way into a tent containing Mike Moore and his lady friend, who had camped far away from the common herd.

On Sunday morning there was the astonishing sight of a Viking and a "toff" in tails and a cricket cap climbing the Prom. Conditions were superb throughout Sunday – mellow autumn sunshine, blue skies, golden bracken and warm rock provided an idyllic setting for the day's climbing activities. Details of climbs and parties are not important. Some enjoyed themselves strenuously, others quietly; the overall impression was of a wonderfully happy weekend for everyone.

D. C. Cullum

OREADS IN SHORTS 1953

Sayings of an expeditionary: "Old Bob would have his budgie if Anne knew that he snored". – *S. G. Moore.*

"How can you be christened Nobby Clarke?" – *Nobby Clarke.*

Quote of the month: "Of course, I feel that bread is essentially a platform for butter" – *Geoff Gibson.*

Bright idea for campers: Geoff Gibson had a nylon pan-scrubber at the Idwal camp. It made washing up a pleasure (almost), and both weight and cost are negligible. Recommended. (Real progress in the era of nylon ropes and bowlines — *Editor*).

Dick Brown celebrated the Coronation by pegging part way up High Tor. This procedure stopped the traffic on the A6 and aroused the interest, but not the fury, of the law.

Oread venture 2 (P. R. Falkner, R. A. Brown) reports the ascent of two virgin peaks, the Lyngstraltind (4,750') and the Store Gjemmentind (4,810'). The party has also climbed three new routes, the North Face of the Rodbjergtind, the East Ridge of the Festningen, and the Hemmeligtind by the West Face and South Ridge. (Lyngen – North Norway).

Bob Pettigrew and Trevor Panther will shortly join the expedition.

Oreads and "Coves and Crogs" had a grand drinking and singing session in Zermatt, and outsang all opposition until midnight.

Stan Moore made this season's first guideless ascent of the Taschorn. It took him 27 hours. He was also heard by several witnesses to decline to drink beer. There is no previous known instance of this. (And no further instance either – *Editor*).

Nobby Clarke and Stan Moore also did the Mer de Glace face of the Grepon this season. Good show both.

Conversation between two (male) Oreads:

A: "You know, a fine thing about the Club is that there's not a man among them with whom I wouldn't gladly spend a weekend".

B: "And there's not a woman among them either, with whom ...."

ASPIRATIONS

In succession to Cyril Machin and Eric Byne, George Sutton was elected President in 1953. After returning from Spitzbergen (1952) he was now in the throes of organising an expedition to South Georgia for 1954/55.

GEORGE SUTTON   *Newsletter (Extract), August 1953*

The Oread now more numerous, have chosen one of the first few to be their President in this fifth year of activity. One who is aware of the honour, and will strive by word and example to influence for good the character of the club, and thus project the same ideals and philosophy into the mountaineering world.

One who has struggled in those four years to preserve the original ideals – the gay audacity: the friendly welcome to novices: the high standard of all round ability: the philosophy of loving to climb hills, to see hills, to be among hills, and not to regard hills merely as a display case for prowess – in fact, those many things which bind together to become the fibre of the club's character, and the common spirit of its members.

Quote of the century: "Unhappy men! If you are thus weary of your lives, is it so difficult for you to find ropes and precipices?" – Antonius, proconsul of Asia during the reign of Trajan. (Gibbon, "Decline and Fall of the Roman Empire", Ch.XVl.)

PROFILES
(*EXTRACTS*)

R. G. PETTIGREW   *Newsletter, October 1953*

Robert Gavin Pettigrew started his career as a climber at the age of twelve, by the surreptitious reading of books on mountaineering (but only those by the "correct" authors) in the school library. There was no practical outcome until 1947, when he set out to climb Snowdon from Caernarvon. He gave up at Llanberis and spent a fortnight at the Rectory there. At Christmas the same year he traversed Crib Goch under snow and ice, armed only with a fireman's axe. He survived.

The salient events of his subsequent career may be outlined as follows:–

1948:   Brief dalliance with Innominate. Made first acquaintance with gritstone with Messrs. Kershaw, Perkins and Wagstaff. Revisited Rectory.

1949:   Joined R.A.F. Posted to Mountain Rescue at Buxton.

1950:   Met Graham Brown at Chamonix during an R.A.F.M.A. meet. Climbed Mont Blanc and Savoy Alps with him. Started getting his pictures in the papers.

1951:   Met Harry Pretty at White Hall and was invited to join Lyngen expedition. Got three months' paid leave (largely due to Harry's intervention) and discovery of this caused him to be dubbed "professional", "not quite a gentleman" and finally "porter".

1952:   Climbed in Stubai and Zillertal.

1953:   Joined Oread Venture 11 (Loughborough College section).

Handsome, athletic, bearded Bob Pettigrew, known and loved by millions for his enthralling broadcasts, has endeared himself to the Oread by (among other things) his boundless youthful enthusiasm for everything he undertakes. This occasionally leads him to make more engagements than he can possibly keep, and to utter "pettigrewisms".

D. C. Cullum

MOLLY PRETTY
Newsletter, November 1953

Molly shares with Nan Axon the distinction of being one of the Club's two feminine founder members. She is a woman whose charm has endeared her to many Oreads, and whose intelligence is built into the very foundations of he Club.

One remembers the happy adventures – how she and Harry helped pitch a tent in the Allt a Mhuillin at Easter and then went to the pictures; how she led us blithely across the high pass to Torridon in deep snow, of a glorious sunny walk from Malham Cove to Ingleton, and Drambuie that night in the "Wheatsheaf" – and a score of other days and nights.

Her 21st, for instance, celebrated in a haze of rum at our spiritual home, Baslow, inspired a moonlight ascent by a band of Oreads, not strictly sober, who clawed, hauled, pushed, cursed and sang their way gloriously to the top, Uncle Eric in the lead.

Those alone who shared the Lyngen/51 adventure will know just how much it owed to her help as a typist and even greater service as hostess to the ever-hungry horde of conspirators.

G. A. Sutton

REMINISCENCE
DO YOU KNOW?

ERIC BYNE
Newsletter November 1953

(1)   That Chuck Cook of the old Valkyrie band once, for a small wager, leapt from the top of Froggatt Pinnacle across the steep gully. No doubt "Cook's Leap" would make excellent bergschrund practice.

(2)   That Four Jack's Cabin on Grindsbrook, Kinderscout, derives its name from four Edale gamekeepers, all named Jack, who rebuilt it in 1932. One of these four, Jack Tym, once nearly shot the balaclava from the Vice-President's head. He said he thought it was a hare.

(3)   That Goliath's Groove was so named by Peter Harding, who led the first ascent, to commemorate the effort of David Sampson, who as third man laybacked the crack all the way.

(4)   That the climbing term "to layback" originated about 1921 at Stanage as an American Wisecrack by Rice K. Evans, and so began to be used by the Rucksack Club tigers of that period.

(5)   "The best position for the rope is over both hips, held with the hands near together in front. In this position the climber is less likely to be pulled forward and lose his balance than when the shoulder belay is used. My theory was once severely tested and proved its worth".

   – *from "Falling off Rock" by Maurice Linnell, in the M.U.M.C. Journal, 1933.* (How now, Tarbuck?)

(6)   "........as soon as the blizzard commenced, Norah conked and refused to budge. They dragged her as far as they could, and in doing so lost their bearings, and because she was a big girl, and they but small men, they decided to shelter in a peat trench. All night, Fred and Albert sang and acted the goat just to keep those two girls awake. They tried everything, but the trouble was that Norah had no will. She gave up and just wouldn't try, and so she died ......"

   – *from a letter relating to a tragedy in 1936 on Howden Chest, near Abbey Brook.*

OREADS IN SHORTS 1953-54

Molly and Harry Pretty spent a holiday in the Northwest Highlands of Scotland early in October, during which they visited Dr. Longstaff, one of the greatest figures of Himalayan exploration. It seems that Harry has joined the clergy – at any rate, whilst at Torridon on the journey north, he received a letter from Dr. Longstaff addressed to the rev. H. Pretty. The church is ever with us.....

As a result of this pilgrimage to Achiltibuie, Dr. Tom Longstaff became a Patron of the British South Georgia Expedition 1954/55 in its application to the Mount Everest Foundation – *Editor.*

Overheard in the Berwyns:

"What size is your camera Phil?" "Thirty five millimetres, if it hasn't shrunk."

Department of Rude remarks (Managers Falkner and Brown):

"You're not so much a seasoned Mountaineer as a pickled one, Cullum."

"Pretty, you look more like a worn-out male ballerina every day."

The perennial question of a Club badge has been revived once more. R.A.B. (Brown, not Butler) has produced an original design featuring Nelson's Monument on Birchen. As the voting was close on this question at the A.G.M., perhaps you would care to communicate your views to the Editor.

A fine display of pegging technique was given at Froggatt on April 4th, by Nat Allen, aided and abetted by (among others) Ray Handley and Derrick Burgess. The show, which was watched by a large and appreciative audience; provoked Pete Janes to utter the Quote of the Month: "Just like climbing a lavatory chain, isn't it?

Coming out of a pub (it was closing time) in Coniston, Jim Winfield was greeted by two young ladies who asked, "Are you in the Orrid Mountaineering Club?" The girl's names turned out to be Cyn and Virginia – an ill-assorted pair, by the sound of things.

Many Oreads spent Easter in Scotland. Messrs Gibson, Cole, Webb, Dearden and Parslow camped in Glencoe. Harby, Fisher and Burgess stayed at Lagangarbh; and the South Georgia party camped on the summit of Nevis.

Remark by small boy lying at the top of Froggatt, watching Ron Dearden following Marion Cooke up a climb: "Ooh, look – there's another missus coming up."

LETTERS TO THE EDITOR
DECEMBER 1953 – MARCH 1954

The following anonymous communication has been received:

This Oread Newsletter? Nothing but the journal of an association of back-patters and as far as that goes, written entirely by that horrible shower who seem to run the Club – that Nottingham crowd, I mean; Falkner and his gang of imbeciles. Nearly every article bears either his or D.C.C.'s initial. All very nice, of course, but a bit thick really, especially if you don't happen to live there.

Reading the thing, one would seriously think that the Oread only had about a dozen folk in it. Damn great long-winded chunks about past and future meets, a few senseless remarks by individuals we've never heard of and an enormous Editorial, usually insulting the average member and suggesting he's barely literate. And they have the cheek to ask "Dear member, contribute something please." No sir, I won't!

Come, sir, a few facts: First, Phil Falkner is the only Committee Member (presumably your horrible shower) who lives in Nottingham. Second, apart from the offensive D.C.C. and the loathsome P.R.F. there have been twenty-three contributions to date. Third, only a dozen folks indeed: forty-three of our membership of sixty-nine have received mention at some time. Fourth, if reports of meets and the doings of unfamiliar members are not the concern of a Newsletter, what the hell is? Fifth, no member has yet complained of insults to his literacy: perhaps self-consciousness is your trouble. Sixth, if you write sense as well as you write abuse, I request – nay COMMAND you, sir, to write a serious article — *Newsletter Editor).*

Sir,

I am distressed to see that you have published in the Oread Newsletter a scurrilous and anonymous attack upon the Club, and certain of its members who are my friends. Whilst admitting that we should allow all sides free opinion-expression, I feel that there is a considerable body of opinion in the club who have been disturbed by this unfounded and ill-informed attack, and I urge that in future, all who would write such material should have the courage of their convictions and append their name. I am sir

Yours sincerely
Richard A. Brown

25

Sir:

I see in your February issue that you publish a letter by one Richard A. Brown attacking writers of anonymous letters. Shame on him that he should wish us all to be exhibitionists and flaunt our names at the end of our epistles.

In the case of the particular anonymous writer, however, who so upset Mr. Brown by writing in the December Newsletter, perhaps I can expose him. Those who wish to meet him should look for an eccentric gentleman with fiery beard and Sellotaped spectacles, who may be seen wandering around Gritstone edges dressed in Edwardian evening dress. In other words Mr. Brown, I think you are suffering from schizophrenia.

"Ezra".

PEAK PERSONALITIES

ERIC BYNE   *Newsletter, February 1954*

HARRY SCARLET set of in 1939 to walk around the world, selling picture postcards of himself. He reached Naples and climbed Vesuvius, then Hitler intervened.

PETER HARDING did his first climb in January 1944 – Sand Gully at Black Rocks, accompanied by Ronnie Lee, now Ronnie Phillips of the Oread. Believe it or not, Harding states that it took him well over an hour to do this climb. Ronnie, incidentally, is the only girl to have climbed Suicide Wall at Cratcliffe.

I remember also the shocked look on Cyril Machin's face, as Pretty, under the influence of several pints of best (deliberately supplied by others), stood up in that extra room at the Robin Hood and gave that superb rendering concerning forty ladies of doubtful virtue who were lined up in the Strand. Those nights of song and wine have gone down in the history of the Oread. They were nights of gladness and madness, nights of moonshine and rum-inspired ascents on Birchen – of Oliver Jones and his guitar – and Dick Brown's presence, in top hat, swallow tail coat and red football jersey.

Memory flashes to Stanage, with clear cut pictures of the dinner meet which saw Wilf White climbing superbly in nails up Goliath's Groove, followed by Herr Toni Demetz in vibrams. The wonder of a Dolomite guide on gritstone and his plaintive statement – "Nein, Nein, Nein, Vibram no good!"

E. H. Pryor was responsible for the foundation of the Mountain Rescue Committee in 1927. He was accidentally knocked off the top pitch of the Long Climb at Laddow and broke his thigh. The rough carry and handling down to Crowden with the primitive apparatus then available irreparably damaged the great sciatic nerve. Dr. Wilson Hey, after desperate efforts, was forced to amputate. The Rucksack Club presented Pryor with a car.

D. C. CULLUM   *Newsletter (Extract), February 1956*

We announce with sorrow the death of Dr. Wilson Hey, at the age of 73. Wilson Hey was a keen mountaineer almost to the end of his life, but his greatest contribution to mountaineering was in the field of mountain rescue. In 1927 he amputated the leg of a climber following an accident on Laddow, and it was largely as a result of that accident that the Mountain Rescue Committee came into being. Wilson Hey figured prominently in the history of that body, and for fifteen years he supplied morphine at his own expense for the relief of injured climbers, in face of a Home Office ruling that supplies of the drug were not to be made generally available for that purpose. It is largely due to his sustained efforts to bring about a reversal of that ruling that morphine is now included in all mountain rescue medical kits. Oreads will remember him as the proposer of the toast, "The Oread" at the Annual Dinner of 1952. Many other mountaineers have cause to remember him with gratitude, and indeed his memory will be respected as long as there are mountaineering accidents.

EARLY ALPINE

Oread parties were in the Swiss Alps as early as 1951, '52 and '53, notably Geoff Gibson, Peter Cole, Malcolm Padley, Ron Dearden, Clive Webb, Bob Parslow and John Adderley but little information appeared in Newsletters — *Editor.*

ERNIE PHILLIPS   *Newsletters (Extracts) 1954*

Ernie Phillips, Pete Janes and the Handleys went to Chamonix and Zermatt for their holidays. Ernie writes:

"At Chamonix we met Ray Colledge, and both Rays went off via Courmayeur to do the Peuterey Ridge on Mont Blanc. In the meantime the rest of us went to the Couvercle hut and snatched the S.W. Ridge on the Moine. When we returned to Chamonix we found that the Mont Blanc party had been unable to get on the Peuterey at all, due to high wind and snow. We then adjourned to Zermatt by road, and then up to the Taschutte. I tried the Alphubel with Pete Janes, and the two Rays tried the Teufelsgrat on the Taschorn, both parties being turned back by bad weather. Back to Zermatt, and then up to the Hornlihutte for the Hornli Ridge of the Matterhorn. This just went, and took 14 hours from hut to hut in vicious conditions. This effort expended the party, and we returned via Grindelwald, Interlaken, Lucerne and places north. Judy still asserts that the first words which greeted her when she set foot on foreign soil were, "Have you any food parcels for Yugoslavia?""

PHIL FALKNER

We went up to a hut immediately on arrival in Zermatt, and knocked off three "viertausenders" in four days; Allalinhorn, Strahlhorn and Rimpfishorn. The first two were snow plods. The Rimpfishorn was rather more interesting. We did it on the way to another hut and this involved carrying sacks up to 13,000 feet. We descended to Zermatt on the Friday and after that got rather out of step with the weather. After $1\frac{1}{2}$ hours Clive[1] felt unwell and decided to return. Gerald[2] went with him and I continued with Mike[3]. We reached the Solvay hut at noon. This was very late. We were in cloud and a few snowflakes were falling, so we retreated to Zermatt.

Monday was an off day; the weather was perfect. Tuesday Mike and I plodded back up to the hut and the weather deteriorated again. But on Wednesday we did climb the Matterhorn despite a heavy snowstorm and several Swiss guides who used my rope as a handrail while I was on difficult rock. Friday Colin Morris and I went to the Betemps hut. Saturday was wet but on Sunday we did the 6,000' ascent of Monte Rosa between 2.45 and 8.00 a.m.

The next Tuesday I went to the Taschutte and on Wednesday did the Alphubel by the Rotgrat, a good climb but plastered with new snow. Chunky[4] arrived on Saturday. The weather broke up and was bad for a week. We managed two climbs – the Trifthorn and the Zinal Rothorn. The next day we found 2" of snow and more falling, so we retreated to the valley.

It really seemed like the end of the season. Chunky went to the Italian Riviera. I did one more climb – Monte Rosa again, this time with Dick Burgess. The weather had remained foul until nearly the end.

[1]Clive Webb. [2]Gerald Parsons. [3]Mike Turner. [4]Chunky Cartwright.

Question Mark, Stanage, Brian and Marion Cooke.
Photo: M. Padley.

Rusty Wall, Stanage, Nobby Millward climbing, 1947.
Photo: A.J.J. Moulam Collection.

Robin Hood's Stride, Stanage, Keith Axon climbing.
1949. Nan Smith (Axon) and Dave Penlington
observing.   *Photo: G. Sutton.*

Marsden to Rowsley Walk 1953. Arrival Rowsley,
Geoff Gibson, Mike Moore, Roger Turner, Clive Webb
(Sports Jacket and Tricounis).   *Photo: Jim Winfield.*

Pioneers of the 40's. The Stonnis M.C., 1947: Norman Horsefield, Ernie Phillips, Dave Sampson, Graham Robinson, Dick Meyer, *unknown*, Brian Mayfield, Alf Bridge, Norman Millward, *unknown*, Kay Hardy, John Sargent. In front: Ronnie Lee (Phillips), Peter Harding. *Photo: Ken Broadbent – The A.J.J. Moulam Collection.*

Dave Penlington on Grooved Arête, Tryfan, with Ken Griffiths, 1949. *Photo: H. Pretty.*

Oreads at Rainster Rocks, 1958: Burns, Fisher, Gardiners, Ashcrofts, Hooleys, Axons, Allens, Janes', Pettigrew, Cookes, Telfer, Blackrock (sundry children appertaining to Axons, Cookes, Prettys, Allens). *Photo: H. Pretty.*

Glencoe, 1950's. Bob Parslow, Peter Cole, Clive Webb, Ron Dearden. *Photo: Geoff Gibson.*

First Oread Photo Meet, The Prince of Wales, Baslow, 1952. John Welbourn, Betty Wright, Ken Wright, Charlie Cullum, Mary Cullum, Ron Dearden, Brian Cooke. *Photo: Geoff Gibson.*

Snowdon Horseshoe 1950's: Mixed group including R. Parslow, M. Moore, C. Webb, J. Fisher, T. Statham, Larry Lambe, Mary Cullum, J. Welbourn (others unknown).   *Photo: Charlie Cullum.*

Snowdon Summit 1954: Dennis Badcott, Jack Ashcroft, Jim Kershaw, Clive Webb, John Fisher, Jim Winfield, Ron Dearden (sitting), Roger Turner.   *Photo: G. Gibson.*

31

Oliver Jones.
Photo: J. Hudson.

Phillip R. Falkner, 1969.
Photo: H. Pretty.

Brian Cooke.
Photo: H. Pretty.

Ray Colledge and David Appleby.
Photo: H. Pretty.

THE LONG WALKS

Long walks have been part of the Oread tradition from the earliest days. The Bullstones Meet in December, commencing with a night crossing of Kinder, to the Snake, was probably the earliest and continued as a regular epic for at least 21 years, although Lower Small Clough became the objective after the vandalisation of the Bullstones cabins. "Bullstones" still appears on Meets lists, but the name more in memory, since these modern bog-fests can take place anywhere across trackless upland country and are only defined by the inevitable bivvy in atrocious weather.

Marsden to Rowsley, Colne to Rowsley, (a Falkner special), the Welsh 3,000's, Aber to Cwm Pennant (Bryn y Wern), and, ultimately, Penmaenmawr to Cwm Pennant, have also left their mark and created their own legends.

Apart from Snowdonia the "Welsh Walks", of desperate memory, regularly negotiated that empty quarter of central Wales from Abergwesyn to the Berwyns, from Cynwyd to the Arenigs, from Cwmystwyth over Pumlumon Fawr to Machynlleth, from Dolgellau to Rhyd ddu over the Rhinogs. The mysteries of Mignent and the Claerwen moors on a bad day live forever in the sub conscious − *Editor.*

COLNE-MARSDEN-ROWSLEY, MAY 1954 (EXTRACT)   *R. G. Pettigrew*

On Saturday, the first party left the bivouac at 6.00 a.m. and traversed all the summits to arrive at the Yorkshire Bridge Inn by 5.40 p.m. Ken Wright's party came next; Charlie Cullum administered to the needs of the ladies in the third party, in which fine work he was eventually assisted by fabulous Falkner, (with the party in transit from Colne). Various people were posted as "missing", noticeably the Hon. Sec., Clive Webb. But all had visited the Yorkshire Bridge Inn by midnight on Saturday. Meanwhile the leader had departed alone at 6.25 p.m. Saturday and reached Rowsley at 11.15 p.m.

The majority concluded the walk in leisurely fashion on Sunday. A special word of congratulation is due to the two ladies, Mary Cullum and Jean Challands, also Glenn Gundry, a non-member who accompanied the Colne party.

A word about the Colne party. They got within nine miles of Marsden on Friday night, losing Clive on the way. On Saturday Glenn Gundry left the others behind by running a good deal of the way. However, they re-united at Yorkshire Bridge, and all four finished the seventy-mile course. A fine achievement, and a fine weekend all round.

MARSDEN-ROWSLEY, MAY 1955 (EXTRACTS)   *R. G. Pettigrew*

It is with regret that I have to report a lamentable lack of support for this traditional stroll down the Pennines. To my knowledge only seven members of the Club attempted any stage of it and they were strung out over a considerable section of the Pennine Way. These isolated blobs of Oreads failed to coalesce during the entire weekend and comprised, from North to South: Phil. Falkner, Charlie Cullum and Gerald Parsons, who started from Colne on Friday evening; Dave Penlington, who did a solo from Littleborough − at last my curiosity is satisfied as to the owner of the Vibram prints whose footsteps we dogged from Wildboar Clough to Win Hill − and finally John Welbourn, Laurie Burns, Bob England (Loughborough College M.C.) and Bob Pettigrew, who made the usual nocturnal entry into Marsden by train − one day I shall visit Marsden in daylight, just to satisfy my curiosity!

Being such a small party, a trade union was formed quickly to determine pace. It was decided that the weekend would be enjoyable and so an excellent start was made by obtaining accommodation in the hospitable "Isle of Skye". Joan Littlewood had a mournful tale to tell. The dear old I. of S. is probably to be destroyed in a month's time because its effluent drains into the catchment area of the new Huddersfield reservoir. Consequently, we made the most of our stay there, eventually departing about 10.45 on Saturday.

P. R. Falkner

"On Saturday, May 7th, at 10.15 p.m., having walked the 53 miles from Colne, I staggered into the Yorkshire Bridge Inn and looked round for the welcoming faces of fellow Oreads. Alas, not an Oread to be seen!"

Dear Sir,

As you are well aware, at the beginning of May the Club Meet took the form of a walk, from either Colne or Marsden to Rowsley. A lengthy circular appeared from the Meet Leader, telling us all where to assemble, where we were to meet en route and even giving times of buses.

After the walk, which eight people claimed to have done, we heard stories saying how they had repeatedly missed each other the whole way down. Three people claimed to have started from Colne, one from Littleborough and four from Marsden. I suggest, Mr. Editor, that there has been collusion with them; in fact I suggest that none of these people actually did the walk at all.

Let us first of all examine the stories. Party A claim that they started from Colne and walked southward, following the route, called at the Isle of Skye and that on Saturday night they also called in at the Yorkshire Bridge Inn, as per the Meet Leader's instructions. Party B, our soloist (he actually claims to have done the whole thing by himself) started at Littleborough and he also says he was in the Y.B. on Saturday night, that he did not see Party A in there and that he left at 9.30 p.m. Now I feel that here's the pertinent question – who has ever heard of an Oread who left a pub before closing time? Party C, which included the Meet Leader (none other than the King of the Arctic, R.G.P.) slept at the Isle of Skye, walked down towards Rowsley, finding a handkerchief which Party B claimed to have dropped (this I suggest, was sent through the post) and camped on the summit of Win Hill.

Now in my youth I once ascended Win Hill and found that the summit was small, fairly pointed and rocky. But Party C, having two expeditionaries on its strength, found no difficulty in erecting a large tent and sleeping there on Saturday night. Party A, according to their claims, followed Party C down the walk, went over Win Hill and into the Y.B. I should like to ask Party C if the tent was secure during the night and why on earth they didn't stop another party walking through their portable bedroom. I should like to ask Party A how they managed to walk through a tent supposedly containing four Oreads without even seeing it.

Lastly, I must say that as I walked from Skipton to Matlock and didn't see anybody, I suggest that I was the only Oread out on the walk during the weekend.

Yours faithfully
IN VINO VERITAS

MORE PROFILES
(EXTRACTS)

DOUGLAS CHARLES CULLUM
Newsletter, February 1954

When, in 1945, Charlie Cullum was inveigled into accompanying me on a short holiday in North Wales, he could hardly have known what he was starting. With great trepidation we ascended the North Ridge of Tryfan, and a couple of days later, with even greater trepidation, we traversed Crib Goch. Before we realised it we were incurably afflicted with dementia montis.

The following year, having borrowed a rope, we began our rock-climbing career with the Ordinary on the Milestone, Charlie in the lead. In the years that followed, Charlie became an accomplished all-round mountaineer, with a strong predilection for camping in remote places in any weather.

But Charlie is not just a good climber. He is a man of many parts (and in quite large parts too!). Apart from chemistry, his job, his interests include music, art, literature, photography and drinking – serious drinking, I mean, as opposed to mere celebratory drinking.

Early in 1952 Charlie joined the Oread, and soon became one of its staunchest supporters – a pillar of truly Doric proportions. On June 14th of the same year he married Mary. June 1953 saw the production of the first Oread Newsletter, a venture for which Charlie has earned the congratulations of the whole Club.

Perhaps the best description of Charlie is a man who for nine years has been one of my stoutest friends, and who, as the years go by, becomes even stouter.

P. R. Falkner

JOHN FISHER
Newsletter, September 1954

John "Drws, Meall a' Bhuiridh", Fisher, for the benefit of Oreads who do not know him, is a tall thin person, who might be called good-looking by his friends. He has a long reach and fantastically thin legs, thin face, and a very engaging smile; in fact a physique and a personality all his own.

He began climbing well over three years ago and at once achieved fame by getting a severe telling off from the late George Bower, for climbing in tricounis at Brassington. Shortly after that he attended a course at white Hall, where he met Penlington. Through "Penno" he joined the ranks of the Oread and has been on the downgrade ever since.

Apart from climbing, John is a student at Birmingham University, where he is studying dental surgery. It has been suggested that he chose Birmingham because he could than become a member of the M.A.M. for five shillings per annum. University life has changed him. Whether for better or worse is hard to judge, but at least he has introduced a new song to the Club, which was culled from that seat of learning – a famous ditty entitled, "Good Morning, Mr. Fisherman".

Anon

THE OREAD
Newsletter, June 1954

"But who are ye in rags and rotten shoes,
You dirty-bearded, blocking up the way?"

"We are the pilgrims, master; we will go
Always a little further; it may be
Beyond that last blue mountain barred with snow."

In 1949 that answer might well have been forthcoming and, in the event, would surely have been proclaimed with the arrogance of youth. Likely enough it would have been made in blatantly overconfident fashion, aggressively, in a way calculated to hide any inward misgivings as to the ultimate truth. But it is important that at least it would have been made; that within the small nucleus of founder members an essential element was to be found, for otherwise this would never have been written.

By many standards a curiously composed group, brought together by fortuitous circumstance and a newspaper advertisement, it nevertheless fought its own battles, mainly internecine, and within a year had established a character which, although self-avowedly unorthodox, delivered itself into strictest conformity by this very assertion. To be sympathetic to the ideas and customs of the long established, large and prosperous clubs was as good a way as any of achieving social ostracism from the 1949 committee of the Oread – and in that year, eighty per cent of the Oread constituted the committee. It was an inevitable reaction against certain pre-war attitudes, which had endowed many of the larger clubs with some of the aspects of the "closed shop". But there were mellowing influences.

In some way or other Cyril Machin was acquired, and he, by his singular example, unwittingly did more to indicate a general direction than was apparent at the time – but then of course, Cyril was the most unorthodox of them all. His name and strange accomplishments were legendary, and no man in the short history of the Oread has been regarded with quite the same affection as that accorded to C.B.M. in the early days.

The sudden flowering that produced the Gibson-Moore combination will be remembered for the acrimony that resulted from its impact upon an otherwise quiet and orderly A.G.M. But when the heat of that debate has passed beyond recall it will still be remembered for the promise it gave of new strength and integrity of vision. And in these ideas that came from this new source, from Gibson and Moore, from Penlington and Wright, was there not a refreshing hint of return to basics.

Into new and almost untried hands the influence passed, and the result was a bracing up, an increase of efficiency, of authoritative administration. There were new members, and a quickening of life, for there had been a draught of air, perhaps a little uncomfortable at first, which in practice proved to have many of the virtues of its original promise.

Up to the present day, four men can be said to have influenced fundamentally the growth and contemporary character of the Oread. Of these, Sutton, Machin and Byne have been previously mentioned. Without any shadow of doubt Gibson is the fourth. With quiet genius he has woven those threads which in the last eighteen months have lent a new and richer texture to Oread activities.

This was the era of the Baslow Area Guide, when the Club did not miss a weekend's climbing on the Edges over a period of four months. There can be little doubt that in giving the Oread a job to do, by issuing his demands, and imposing his personality at such a critical point, Eric Byne, together with George Sutton, ensured that this Oread would be no transitory "seven days wonder" for now there was a spirit, already they were "a little further".

From 1950 to the present day three periods of differing thought and influence can be discerned, all of which have moulded the Club's present character. There is what might be termed the Woodbine Cottage era, from '50 to the early months of '52, followed by the Gibson-Moore coup d'etat, with its subsequent "Administrative Reform and Consolidation policies – and lastly, from early '52 to the present, there has appeared a new culture which will almost undoubtedly be known as the Beeston Period.

Lyngen '51 will always be associated with the first of these, and although much has been said of this venture by now, it is a simple and sober fact that Lyngen is still the greatest, bravest, and most inspiring achievement of the Oread.

The Beeston Period is contemporary history, too close for analysis and too blatantly alive and vigorous to require critical review. Prolific with efficiency and new enterprise, birth place of a second northern venture, it is the proper residuary legatee of the Woodbine Cottage ghosts. As the home of one, Falkner, patron of all the singular and ancient arts, it already has the air of being guaranteed a place in future legend.

And what of the remainder? What of the ordinary member – this creature who calls himself an Oread? What are they like, these people who, by their degree of collective loyalty and spirit, can carry the Oread yet "a little further", or destroy all that which has been achieved?

University lecturer, metal worker, student and clerk, surveyor and typist, geologist and housewife, engineer and "out of work" – all of them, and a score of other denominations, are Oreads – and many of them, still young to the ways of the mountains, are like G. K. Chesterton's "Secret People" and have not spoken yet.

Anon

OREADS IN SHORTS 1955

Just before the great event, Phil Falkner made the Quote of the Month: "They're serving teas in the room where Professor Graham Brown met Pettigrew!"

Annual Dinner, Baslow

Bob Pettigrew has been spending his summer holidays at Butlin's Holiday Camp at Filey – as a barman. He landed an Honours Diploma in Physical Education at Loughborough this summer – congratulations, Bob.

The following was found written on a menu card after the Dinner:

> Out in Tibet
> There's no publicity yet.
> Hence the Yeti who
> Had never heard of Pettigrew.

Kilchoan proved to be somewhat larger than we had expected, with about twenty houses, a small general store, and an excellent pub, and, of all things, a petrol pump. However, when we bought three gallons of petrol a few days later, and the young lady said, "Fifteen an' threepence, please", we were somewhat taken aback! – *Ernie Phillips.*

The same weekend, Eric Byne was principal guest at the S.U.M.C. dinner at the Marquis of Granby. On the Sunday, Eric, with Frank Fitzgerald, (President S.U.M.C.), and Maurice Twentyman, climbed the North Face of Back Tor under very icy conditions, taking four hours. Eric believes this may be a first winter ascent.

It was signing on time at the Labour Exchange. The aristocrats of the Nottingham Branch, distinguished by their collars and ties, were queuing at Box No. 3. The clerk broke the news to me gently: "Now take it easy Jim", he said, "I don't want to alarm you, but there's some danger of us finding you a job in the near future. If I were you I'd get out of the district for a few days – just wait until things get back to normal". The thought of the Cairngorms in February sprang to mind, and thus it was that I found myself on a northbound train a day later (available for immediate recall for interview – Poste Restante, Aviemore). – *Jim Kershaw.*

BRITISH SOUTH GEORGIA EXPEDITION 1954-1955

A COMMENT

Serious planning started in 1953. George Sutton (in Burton-on-Trent) gave up his job to devote himself full time, and Dick Brown alternated between Sheffield University and various building sites. The Rectory at Stanton-by Bridge (Harry and Molly Pretty) became the administrative H.Q. and ultimately became temporary repository of nearly 8 tons of food and equipment, most of which had been acquired gratis or at greatly reduced cost. After many set backs we gathered sufficient backers (John Hunt, Jack Longland, Dr. Tom Longstaff, Tom Weir, Bill Murray, Bill Tilman) to persuade the newly formed Mount Everest Foundation to provide a grant; small in amount but influential in other negotiations. The Daily Telegraph (Sir Colin Coote), and several other foundations, also gave donations. A book deal was concluded with Chatto and Windus, and Sir Martin Lindsay D.S.O. C.B.E., M.P. (pre-war polar explorer with Gino Watkins) opened innumerable doors and became principal patron.

All this commitment had been made but, in April 1954, we still had no way of getting to S.G. In a letter Bill Tilman suggested that we forget S.G. and re-assemble as his crew for his first voyage on Mischief 1 to Cape Horn and Chilean Fjordland. But we gritted our teeth and gambled on something turning up.

H.K. Salvesen, who still ran the shore based whaling station at Leith Harbour (S.G.), had declined our pleas for passage on one of his supply ships, and it took a personal visit by Sutton and Brown to his home in Edinburgh to change his mind, mere weeks before the Southern Opal was due to sail south in August 1954. He also requested that our medical man, Dr. Ian Brooker, should act as ship's surgeon on the voyage south. At this time Squadron Leader Brooker was a senior medical officer in the R.A.F., serving in Germany. He obtained temporary release on full pay (a parallel with Pettigrew in 1951). Clive Webb, just back from the Alps, resigned as Oread Sec. to join the party.

We sailed from Glasgow on 20-8-54 and after a circuitous voyage, not without incident, arrived in S.G. on 30-9-54. The expedition returned to U.K. (Liverpool) on 30-4-55. The full story was told in George Sutton's book Glacier Island, Chatto and Windus 1957, and the first successful ascent of a major S.G. peak, by Brooker and Webb, was described in the Oread book *Climb if you Will* (1974) (Mount Gregor subsequently re-named Mount Brooker)

I hope the following offerings may shed some light on this truly unique island when it was still a little known base for whalers and sealers, and before it achieved significance in the Falklands Conflict and, more latterly, as a regular stop off for Antarctic cruise ships — *Editor.*

From a letter to Charlie Cullum:

> Had a go at Paget from Nordenskjold Glacier, and could not force ice-fall (3,000') to col. Spent ten days on the glacier, and two in the ice-fall. Ascended one peak of near 5,000'[1] and several minor summits. It would be a long and difficult job to climb Paget this side – Harry reports that the other side looks even worse. The same problems attach to all the main range peaks, except that Paget is 1,500' higher than most. On the North side of the second summit of Paget a vertical wall of around 7,000' drops into a Great Cwm, a tremendous thing. I think we'll get up Paget eventually but it may wreck all other plans.

[1]Now named Sutton Crag – *Editor.*

THE BEACH

HARRY PRETTY

With consummate ease the sealers landed us in a small bay, forcing the pram through a heaving sea only moderately restrained by skeins of loose brash ice – broken remnants from glacier ice-falls that plunged into the sea on all sides. The surf was always heavy on this south-west coast of the island for, in these latitudes, the constant westerlies drive the Southern Ocean relentlessly, and only the precipitous coastline of South Georgia intervenes.

On the previous night, a little to the north-west, we had run for shelter into a small cove close by the entrance to the great open fjord of King Haakon Bay. It was here in 1916 that Shackleton ended his epic 17-day open-boat voyage from Elephant Island, where the remainder of his crew, unknown to the rest of a world immersed in World War I, still awaited rescue following the crushing of their vessel, the *Endurance*, in the Weddell Sea.

It is the most powerful tale of survival in the entire history of Antarctic exploration, and close proximity to the scene of this historic landfall pervaded the mind as the little Albatros, with its mixed Norwegian and South American crew, pushed through loose ice, searching for some nook or cranny where the drapery of icefall relented to provide a feasible landing place.

The sealers had no name for this baylet. They had been here before but infrequently – too often choked by ice, they said. It was a pessimistic thought since the season was nearly at an end, and we, a party of five, were relying on a pick-up in two weeks' time.

There were perhaps 300 elephant seals hauled out. Near the end of the breeding season, and space being limited, the harems under the dictate of some 20 mature bulls, were packed tight between sea and cliff. Some of the frenzy of the early mating season had abated, but our arrival was sufficient disturbance to cause several large males to rear in mutual confrontation – still protective of their polygamous rights.

Drenched from standing waist-deep to unload gear amid pulverising waves and floating ice, we made haste to shift boxes, tents, skis and sledges to a safe recess, in anticipation of turmoil as the sealers commenced their dispatch of the resident males – one bullet each at close quarters.

But sudden death had no effect on slumbering females or dependent pups. Blood spurted inconsequentially over the living and the dead and there was no message in its flow among rocks and shingle, or where it soaked down into the black volcanic sand.

But then at the sea's edge, each wave broke to run foaming red up the steep black shelf, a stained torrent swirling through a litter of stranded, pale green ice. There was something more momentous in this red tide, in the stain that encroached further and further out across the bay, but it remained beyond definition.

Within an hour the sealers' work was done. The dead bulls had been flensed and the circular rafts of blubber, rope-toggled together, towed back to the Albatros, hove to beyond the inshore ice. The men, encased in black suits and wielding their long flensing knives against the backdrop of a boisterous and blemished sea, made a macabre tableau – Dantesque came to mind. But they were our friends. They were men to be trusted and they had proved it more than once. They waved as the landing pram was poled through the brash ice towards a waiting motorboat – "Two weeks, ja!" It was time to establish a foothold on this bleak coast.

Even as we started to shift gear off the beach, new bulls were coming ashore to take over the territory. From our first camp, high above the beach, the noise of combat between marauding males could be heard above the general cacophony of seals and roaring surf. It went on far into the night.

Two days of climbing reconnaissance quickly established our position on this western and unmapped side of the main range. Access through the complexities of the coastal ice-falls to the vast inland ice-sheets that might lead to our objective, Mount Paget, would not be easy. The unravelling of the route and the ultimate two-man push to the south-east is a story that has been told elsewhere. It is a brief but familiar tale of arduous travel across a sterile interior. It is about blizzards and white-outs, fear and failure, and ultimate survival.

But I saw little of this. Injured in a recent crevasse fall, I was relegated to more scientific tasks and I spent long solitary days with theodolite and camera on the summits of nearby coastal peaks. Slow, grinding ascents that were often frustrated by the sudden onset of westerly squalls that made observations impossible, and retreat a prerequisite of my own survival.

But there were days of magic brilliance when the great ice peaks of the main range seared the imagination, and icebergs from the deep south floated like fairy-tale castles on a glittering sea. It was in the early evening of such a day that I missed my way across a steepening gully and found myself forced to descend to our landing beach. It was a different place.

The massive corpses of those seals killed and flensed 10 days before had already been picked down to skeletal remains by scavenging petrels. Several skuas still raked around inside the long rib-cavities, pulling at a few remaining strings of flesh. At one end of a shallow pool, a young seal splashed and playfully gnawed an old cow. Down by the foam line, two seals lay flat on black shelving sand, pointing downwards into each oncoming wave. The water broke around their pointed snouts and washed smoothly over their streamlined bulk. As the water ran, they reflected pale blue-green light from a part of the sky far out beyond the inshore ice.

An untidy group of mature cows included several of the new bulls, inert hulks now that the violent fires of spring and early summer were dead. Soon they would return to the sea. The beach would be washed clean by winter storms, cleansed of the bones, the desiccated remnants of flesh and the torn scraps of fur that lay like abandoned trivia.

I remembered the noise and clamour of the beach when we had come pushing through the surf – the squeal of new-born pups and the roar and snarl of the old bulls. I remembered the sudden death of day-old pups pulped by the massive bulk of the lusting, never seeing bulls. Now there was a strange hush. A few gentoo penguins ejected from the arched face of a wave, moved with lightning speed up the sand, to stand preening and squawking like old gossips.

Pure white sheathbills moved unconcerned over rock, dozing penguin, or dead seal, picking their way deliberately, yet delicately, from one morsel of excreta to another. And I suddenly saw this beach for what it was: a world oblivious and uncaring of death that stank on every few yards of sand and shingle, as heedless of death as the mountains at my back.

It was a strange moment when, for a time, the rhythm of life and death seemed clear and strong. The often tritely expressed impermanence of human affairs was, in that moment, sharply three-dimensional.

This beach, it seemed, was the other place. At my back the world of ice – sterile, without life, giving birth only to the ice that choked the sea's edge. In front, this place where life and death lay inextricably mixed, but a place without fear. There was no malevolence in this world; the natural order prevailed, and not even the strong could always escape.

This article originally published in *B.B.C. Wildlife* magazine, August 1990.

CHRISTMAS IN RETROSPECT

HARRY PRETTY   *Newsletter, January 1959*

For most people Christmas has a particular flavour. Quite unlike any other time of the year it provides its own atmosphere and among those fortunate enough to spend it in the company of family and friends it is frequently memorable. My own Christmases have been spent variously: – quietly at home, uproariously at "Tyn-yShanty" and Bryn-y-Wern, and once on a railway station in Montreal. The story I propose to relate concerns a Christmas quite different from any of these – unique in some ways, but with the familiar spirit that seems essential to all good Christmas stories. That it is nostalgic, and not without sentiment, I freely admit. For this I make no excuse since this was the way of it.

On December 23rd 1954 Dick Brown and myself left a camp between the Lyell and Geikie Glaciers to return to base for a five-day break. The others had left two days before. We had been in the field for four heart-breaking weeks of awful weather that had resulted in frustration and considerable mental strain.

In addition to continuing physical disability I was personally feeling spiritually exhausted – an ulcerated mouth and inexplicable sores on my face seemed merely incidental.

Ironically the 23rd was a calm golden day. The crunchy glare ice of the Lyell Glacier reflected a fierce hard light. Sugartop, Paulsen, and Fluted Peak rode above us – uncompromising, majestic shapes. Magnificent in scale, beautiful in every detail of fluted ice face and pinnacled ridge they seemed a little unreal after so many weeks during which they had only been seen at infrequent intervals.

Late that night we crossed the barren scree of Echo Pass and glissaded the short snow margin of a small residual glacier. Above us snow petrels, insubstantial and slightly ethereal, floated about a spiny crag. Around us, in bat like flight, we saw the dark shape and white rump of Wilson's petrel. Visible only in flickering snatches close about our heads it was a friendly and familiar presence with none of the remote mysteriousness that seemed to surround those pure white birds nesting high above on a snowy crag.

Below us was Grytviken, King Edward Point, and our hut barely discernible against the steep scree of Mt. Duse. Beyond the Hobarts a single catcher with a red and blue funnel circled gracefully across still dark water that here and there reflected a coppery sun-glow. Two grounded bergs gleamed, as though lit from inside, against the monochrome uniformity of the Sandebugten mountains.

The physical misery of that last descent is now only a blur, but I recall with sharpness and precision the calm and peaceful beauty of that pre-Christmas night. Through Pesca whaling station, silent and seemingly deserted, across the flensing plan still slimy and blood red from the day's whales, and by way of the familiar shore track we returned to base. As though to remind us of other things snow began to fall before we reached the hut so that, in our tatty snow decorated windproofs, our entrance upon a party already hilariously in full swing seemed strange and incongruous.

Father Christmas came on the morning of the 24th. He came in the way that all things come to S. Georgia – from the sea, and we waited for him with almost the same expectancy as did the three young Falkland Island children to whom ships were as buses in other children's lives. He came in the shape of old Hans Kristofferson aboard the little Sabra. Old Hans, a character even in a community of characters, wearing his ancient red dressing gown, and red woolly hat and an enormous white cotton wool beard made a curious though charming spectacle as he brought his ship alongside.

First came Hans with a little Norwegian Christmas tree decorated with tinsel, candles and flags – then came all the boxes and parcels, presents for everybody on the Point. This, it seemed, was yet another S. Georgia – when Christmas came in as an old whaler dressed in shabby makeshift but so delightfully carrying out his mission that it was no matter. Easy to forget that he was familiar Hans with his bent leg and cherubic features. Easy to see him as a symbol of his race and kind as he handed presents to the three children who stood half bemused, beyond expression in their excitement. A shaking of limp hands, a quaint inclination of the head and he was off again – back to the minute open bridge of Sabra where his red bobbined head suddenly appeared above the side screen. Hands wrestled with the sticking plaster and cotton wool, which threatened to cut off speech, and we heard his "Laggo – aft!".

The last we saw of Father Christmas was a blob of white and a waving arm as Sabra, ever mindful of her whaling days, heeled over deck awash, into the channel inside the Hobart rocks; and then he was gone, behind the headland that carries Shackleton's plain wooden cross – and I was left with an impression of simplicity and kindness that would be difficult to forget.

RETURN

HARRY PRETTY   *Newsletter (Extract), January 1956*

We left south Georgia in the latter half of a miserably raw afternoon – sliding out past small stranded growler bergs at the entrance to Leith Harbour – past Mutton Island and the Black Rocks until, clearing Cape Saunders for the last time, we stood out to sea with only a score of bergs to keep us company.

Drab coastal peaks above the Fortuna Glacier, where it tumbles into the sea, were almost the last we saw of the island and we thought it an unfriendly scene. Years of travel brood fatalism towards departures and this it seemed was just another – uninspired and without particular merit.

There was therefore, a certain thrill on being called over to starboard some time later to see what was our genuine last view of the island wherein we had found such combination of men, mountains, birds and beasts, in an environment so creative of strange atmospheres that one can only acknowledge the impossibility of conveying the singular impressiveness of the place.

For a short while there was a glow of light over the southern peaks. The familiar double pyramid of Cape Charlotte projected a blackened finger toward off-shore bergs – seen only as pale tabular shapes against sea and sky, both of which remained indistinguishable one from the other.

Precisely four weeks later we entered the Mersey.

POLITICS
A.G.M. 1954

(Extract)

The Treasurer Ken Griffiths was brief. Our bank balance stood at £12.9.6d and cash in hand amounted to £6.17.10d. 26 members had so far paid this year's subscription. There had been a slight loss on coaches, but recent coach meets had shown a profit. The Hut Fund had reached £37.19.6d.

Newsletter (Extract), August 1954

MEETING EXTRAORDINARY: At the Burbage Meet a group of people presented to the Hon. Secretary a request for an Extraordinary General Meeting. The subject to be discussed is that "the present Committee is unrepresentative.....owing to the large number of changes in the Committee since the last A.G.M." The facts are that there have been three resignations and two of the vacancies have been filled by the top two "runners-up" at the A.G.M. The third is still vacant owing to the difficulty of co-opting a suitable member. Everything has been perfectly constitutional, and far from being unrepresentative the present Committee is as representative as it possibly could be. So how the signatories of the request will uphold their claim, or what they expect to gain by calling an E.G.M., is difficult to see. It really is most Extraordinary.

D. C. Cullum

Extraordinary General Meeting   *Newsletter (Extract), December 1954*

The extraordinary General Meeting, called by five members to discuss whether not the present Committee was representative of the Club, was held on the afternoon of November 13th (a sinister date!). Eric Byne was in the chair, and he took a strong line from the beginning. Feelings were soon aroused, the temperature of the meeting ran high, and there were some sharp exchanges. Perhaps the wisest words were those of Bob Pettigrew, to the effect that the true spirit of the Oread seemed to be absent. At length the chairman forced the Five to admit that the Committee was in fact constitutionally representative, and when put to the vote, thirteen hands were raised in support of the Committee and six against, about a third of the small number present abstaining.

D. C. Cullum

A.G.M. 1955 (Extract)

Ken Griffiths, the retiring Hon. Treasurer, next presented his report. His announcement that we were still solvent (£4.9.3d!) was warmly received. All but four members had paid up for 1954, and subs. amounted to £29.1.6d, and total income was almost £50. The Secretary's expenses had been less, the Meets Secretary's more (£9.18.0d) and the Newsletter had paid for itself. The Dinner had shown a loss of £2.

Solvency may have been on a knife edge, but democratic rights were fiercely defended — *Editor.*

"DISASTROUS CHANCES......"

Newsletter, May 1954

We have just learnt with regret that the fatal accident on Tower Ridge of Nevis at Easter involved a party of our friends, the Polaris M.C. The body of Mrs. Betty Emery was recovered by six Oreads (Sutton, Pretty, Cartwright, Falkner, Pettigrew and Jones), with members of the Rock and Ice Club and Polaris M.C. We offer our sympathy to relatives and friends of the dead woman.

During the night following the accident members of the S.M.C. (Dr. Norman Cochrane) and Rock and Ice (Brown and Whillans etc.) struggled to raise the body onto the eastern traverse. The Oread party (arriving overnight) completed the task as far as the summit plateau where the R.A.F. Mountain rescue took over. Betty Emery's companions (Eileen Gregory, Ernie Snow) were uninjured, but suffered a car accident on their journey south, and were hospitalised at Dumfries. They were subsequently visited by the Oread party during their return south – *Editor.*

Newsletter, June 1954

We regret to announce that on May 9th, Cyril Machin fell from Castle Naze whilst abseiling. It is believed that the rope slipped over the belay. He sustained injuries to his back and is at present in Manchester Royal Infirmary. He is remarkably cheerful and his condition is improving. Any member wishing to visit him will be welcome to stay at the Cullum's flat.

C.B.M. was seriously injured and after along spell in hospital, he recovered, but was encumbered by metal braces for the remainder of his life — *Editor.*

Newsletter, June 1958

During the early part of May there was an accident on "Cloggy" in which members of the Oread were concerned. A hold, which at the time was vital, broke away and Don Chapman fell from approximately thirty feet above his second – Derrick Burgess. Burgess held him from a difficult position and the belay remained intact. Chapman, who sustained injury to an ankle and temporary concussion, was able to assist in his own evacuation to the bottom of the crag. Ray Handley, Nat Allen and Ray Colledge were of the party and on the same climb. The ultimate evacuation down to car in Llanberis, and thence to hospital, was carried out entirely by the party concerned and Nat is reported as having carried the victim bodily for half a mile over ground where combined tactics were difficult. Don was in hospital only a short time and can be seen most Tuesday evenings in the "Bell", albeit with plaster cast, and walking stick.

In these days when not only accidents, but stupidity and sheer ignorance seem to be on the increase rather than the reverse, it is pleasant (if one can use the word in this context) to hear of an accident properly restricted to the role of minor incident owing to the skill, efficiency, and coolness of the persons concerned.

D. C. Cullum

"Wherein I spake of most disastrous chances of moving accidents by flood and field,
Of hair-breadth 'scapes I' the imminent deadly breach".

Othello (1, iii, 134)

THE MATTERHORN

Records indicate that Ray Handley, Peter Janes and Ernie Phillips were the first Oreads to reach the summit, by the Hornli, in 1954. Since then successful ascents from all sides, including the North Face, have been made by various Oread parties although curiously few accounts have been submitted to Newsletters or Journals. Enough to say, in the context of what follows, they have all been accomplished without injury although I seem to remember that P.R.Falkner dropped a brand new camera down the North Face in 1954.

This brief aside is merely a foreword to my inclusion of the Rev. Joseph M'Cormick's letter to The Times recording the disastrous end to Mr. Whymper's first ascent which started on Thursday, 13th July 1865.

The original cutting from The Times was given to me nearly fifty years ago by Gerry Britton who was an enthusiastic early Oread member, a man of substance, sometime Trustee of the Club, who was at the heart of club affairs in the 1950's, only to disappear south in pursuit of a sailing career, whereupon all contact was lost.

It is quite outside the context of this Journal, but I value the original, and have thought it worthy of a wider audience and, in particular, those of an historical bent. — *Editor.*

MATTERHORN
TO THE EDITOR OF THE TIMES

Sir, – As the news of the fatal accident on the Matterhorn must by this time have reached England, I think it right for the sake of the friends of those who have been killed, and to prevent mistakes, to give a correct account of it, and of what has taken place with reference to it.

Some months ago the Rev. Charles Hudson determined to ascend the Matterhorn this season. Before leaving England he invented and had made a kind of ladder for scaling precipices.

Mr. Birkbeck and I agreed to accompany him on his expedition. On arriving in Zermatt on Wednesday, the 12th inst., he met with Mr. Whymper, who for some years past has been anxious to conquer the Matterhorn, and has made several attempts to do so. They agreed to work together. Mr. Birkbeck and I were both prevented from joining them. Lord Francis Douglas, who had made several successful ascents this season, and had been with Mr. Whymper for a few days previously, and Mr. Hadow, who had been up some high mountains with Mr. Hudson, were allowed to go with them. Having secured the services of Michel Croz, one of the best of the Chamonix guides, and of Peter Taugevald and his son, they started on their expedition on Thursday morning. That night they slept on the Hornli arrête, and at 3.40 a.m. on Friday they began the ascent by the rocks on the left of it. They met with no great difficulty, and reached the top about 2 o'clock. There they were in the greatest delight at the accomplishment of their purpose. We saw them distinctly from Zermatt. About 3 o'clock they began the descent. Soon after they were all roped together. Croz was first, Hadow next; then came Hudson, Lord Francis Douglas, Peter Taugevald, Whymper, and Peter Taugevald's son. Not far from the summit they had to pass over a difficult and rather dangerous place. It was a decline of snow and rock, with very indifferent holding for the feet. They were descending with great caution, when Whymper was startled by an exclamation from Croz, and the next moment he saw Hadow and Croz flying downwards. The weight of the two falling men jerked Hudson and Lord Francis Douglas from their feet. The two Taugevalds and Whymper, having a warning of a second or two from the time that Croz called out, planted themselves as firmly as possible, to hold the others up. The pressure upon the rope was too much. It broke, and Croz, Hadow, Hudson, and Lord Francis Douglas fell headlong down the slope and shot out of sight over a fearful precipice.

Mr. Whymper's feelings at this time may be imagined. The two remaining guides were so completely unnerved by the calamity which had befallen their companions that he found it difficult to descend with them. He and they spent a miserable night on the mountain at a great height. As they came down they looked in all directions for some traces of their companions, but from the shape of the mountain they could not catch even a glimpse of them. At 10.30 a.m. On Saturday they reached Zermatt.

Though he had no hope that any of his companions were alive, Mr. Whymper immediately sent guides to search for them. In the evening they returned to tell us that they had been able with the aid of their telescopes to see where they lay, but had been prevented by the width of the crevasses from reaching them. Being a friend of Mr. Hudson, Mr. Whymper sent for me. I had gone to the Corner Grat. On my return it was too late to do anything that day. After consulting together Mr. Whymper and I agreed to start in search of our friends on the following morning at 1 o'clock. The Rev. J. Robertson and Mr.

Phillpotts most kindly volunteered to accompany us. The Zermatt guides refused to go with us, as it would be Sunday, and urged us, as there was no hope of saving lives, to defer our expedition until they had made preparations for overcoming the difficulties of the way. Mr. Whymper, though exhausted by upwards of 60 hours work, gallantly refused to accede to their request. Franz Andermatten of Sass; the brothers Lochmatter, of Macugnaga; and Fredric Payot and Jean Tairraz, of Chamonix, generously offered their services for the expedition. We hope their names will not be forgotten.

After an arduous walk, in which we were exposed to much danger, we reached the snow field on to which our friends had fallen. When we looked up at the 4,000 feet above us, and observed how they must have bumped from rock to rock before they reached the bottom, we knew they could not be alive, and we feared that they would be so awfully mangled that we should not be able to recognize them. Our worst fears were realized. We found no traces of Lord Francis Douglas, with the exception of some trifling articles of dress. His body must either have remained on some of the rocks above or been buried deeply in the snow. Croz lay near to Hadow. Hudson was 50 yards from them.

From the state of their remains, the danger of the place (for it is exposed to showers of stones), and the very great difficulty of the way to it, we came to the conclusion that the best thing we could do would be to bury them in the snow. We drew them all to one spot, covered them with snow, read over them the 90th Psalm from a Prayer-book taken from poor Hudson's pocket, repeated some prayers and a few words from the Burial service, and left them.

They are mourned here with heartfelt grief, and the greatest sympathy is expressed for the bereaved. Mr. Seiler, the landlord of this hotel, and his wife have assisted us in every way in their power. They are deeply distressed at what has happened.

Your obedient servant,
JOSEPH M'CORMICK, Chaplain at Zermatt.
Hotel du Mont Rose
July 17/1865

LETTERS . . . TO THE EDITOR
SEPTEMBER 1954

Dear Sir,

Accuse an Oread of bad rope management and he or she will be highly indignant, but the fact remains that a dangerous practice has arisen, mainly due to the current fashion of wearing a spliced abseil sling and karabiner. These slings which are intended to serve as aid in roping down (and to promote a neat waist line) are being used far too often as a form of belay and in almost all cases are unsatisfactory for the latter purpose. The limits of adjustment of a standard spliced loop are far too narrow to cope with all belay situations and I have seen on many occasions such a loop used where it appeared to be convenient, where in fact a far superior belay existed out of range of the loop. At least one fatal accident (where the second was killed and not the leader) has been attributed to the use of a sling as a means of belaying, and on our Stanage meet of May 1st/2nd I saw a situation which would almost certainly have resulted in injury to the second had the leader or the third man come off. And, in this particular case, had the person referred to used the climbing rope instead of a sling, a belay could have been devised that would have held a coach and four.

It is my opinion that where an abseil sling can be used, the climbing rope would in almost all cases be more effective. This is not intended to preclude the use of a knotted loop suitably adjusted or the use of nylon cord in certain circumstances.

So harking back to the reference to the Stanage meet – if the cap fits wear it!

Yours sincerely,
G. R. Gibson.

Dear Sir,

So Gibson, having at last mastered the intricacies of the bowline, now sees fit to dictate rope technique. He has never been the same since he went to Ken Tarbuck's lecture at Derby. After hearing this he immediately rushed out and bought 20 ft. of nylon shoelace which he wraps round his waist like a corset. This, like the bunch of pitons which he takes to the Alps each year, is never used but is fully approved by Stephen Potter.

To get down to actual cases, I personally have never climbed with a coach and four. This I assume is just another example of Gibson's D.Ts. As the person foully libelled by him I must insist that I was climbing with two ordinary people. As leader I was sitting at the top of the climb – belayed with the climbing rope to a rock the size of the one at Gibraltar. My second was a few feet from the top on a ledge, back-stopped by me and belayed by a spliced sling. I could have further safeguarded him by riveting him to the rocks with pitons but unfortunately I did not realise that Gibson was passing at the time.

However, I bear no ill feeling towards Gibson, and I wish him luck with his 20 ft. of shoelace. Should he desire a change from his Tarbuck knot, might I suggest that he use the one advocated by Albert Pierrepoint? *

Yours etc.,
R. V. Dearden

* For those short on historical facts, Mr Pierrepoint was the Official Executioner in more barbaric times — *Editor.*

Letter from a Dog   *Newsletter, September 1955*

Dear Editor,

Excuse my bad writing, my paws are still sore – those inhuman brutes Burns and Moore – that's what I want to tell you: the truth about the Pennine Way. It was nothing but a publicity stunt to get a year's supply of "Lassie" free. I don't like "Lassie" anyway. Three men and a dog on the Pennine Way – what a headline. Lawrie said, "Walkies". I didn't know it was two-hundred-and-fifty-mile-walkies. I walked four times as far as they did anyway, and the thousands of trees we passed, let alone the rain-gauges, no dog could have done himself justice. A good job they didn't know I was bluffing most of the time. That Moore was laughing at me, powdering my tail with "Apple Blossom". I don't know what I'd have done without Jim Kershaw, letting me use his sleeping bag and eat off his plate. It was a real pleasure to lick his face every morning. As for Burns, I had to take him home from Alston, he's led me a human's life ever since. I'm going to run away to a circus or something, just see if I don't. Keep my name secret.

Yours,
An embittered Corgi.

Moyers Buttress Climbed *Newsletter, September 1955*

The following is an extract from a letter written by Peter Biven of Leicester and addressed to Eric Byne:

"Please forgive my not answering your letter promptly, but you know you were, in a very small way, responsible for that. You see, in your letter you said that Moyer's Buttress on Gardom's Edge had not yet been led. This started off a chain of events which culminated in a week's leave in Derbyshire, and I am happy to say that we succeeded, and Moyer's Buttress is no longer the "last great problem". I finally led it on Wednesday Sept. 7th (but I had been up it twice on a top rope the previous day). I put a chockstone on the square block under the overhang, to protect the corner move which is the crux. My second man, Trevor Peck, was belayed down to prevent "yo-yoing" if you know what I mean."

"As regards the standard, it is Exceptionally Severe on almost every move, the final one being almost as hard as the crux. A friend took a series of pictures which I am hoping will turn out."

Eric Byne adds the following note: Peter Biven, by his lead of this, and of Congo Corner on Mississippi Buttress on Stanage, proves his right to stand alongside Joe Brown as one of the great rock climbers of today. It is worth noting that he has also led the overhang crack on the right hand wall of Moyer's Buttress, the Sloth on the Roaches, and moreover has led in nails on a wet and windy day, that superb climb on Harecliffe Rocher, the Whittler.

JOHN ADDERLEY GOES NORTH *Newsletter (Extract), September 1955*

The next morning I continued up the Glen, (Carnach – Knoydart, *Editor*) which got steadily wilder. I had a lot of difficulty negotiating cliffs, trees and burns but finally passed by Lochan nam Breac when, to my surprise, I turned a corner in the Glen and came upon a dam stretching across the valley. It was the same old story of Hydro-Electric Power.

Visiting the work camp I was given a meal of scones and tea and offered a lift to Tomdoun by the engineer. I accepted and in a few minutes I was back on to a highway and civilisation; passing on the way miles of new roads, gashes in the hillside for pipelines and other atrocities that go with a Hydro-Electric scheme – "so essential to the economy of the country".

This brought me back to reality and getting my thumb out I set it to work, and made my way to the Isle of Skye. I arrived in Glen Brittle without many incidents, having done a couple of small hills on the way.

I met Bill Brooker of Aberdeen at Macrae's and together we did a few climbs – Cioch West, Cioch Direct, Walwark's Route on the Upper Buttress, Crack of Doom and Direct Finish, Fluted Buttress on Sgurr Mhic Coinnich and Waterpipe Gully (not direct). The highlight of the climbing came for me when it was my turn to lead through on the second pitch of Mallory's on Sron na Ciche. Bill said the hard move was ten feet up. At ten feet I found the hard move, but Bill had omitted to say it lasted for the next twenty feet. For those who don't know it, it is a slab. It's quite safe really – you can't fall off – there aren't any holds to fall from. We continued up the arete above Mallory's and finished up the top part of Amphitheatre Wall, a delightful finish – short run-outs, vertical and rock like sandpaper.

We had a couple of off-days, after a Scottish dance, during which we ate, slept, swam in the sea and stooked corn. We left for Applecross in pouring rain, the first for a fortnight. Bill had mentioned a shelter in the form of a road-menders' hut, complete with stove. It turned out to be a minute box, belayed to the mountainside with wire at the point where the road makes four 180 degree turns in half a mile. The stove had fallen to pieces; dirt of ages was piled high on the floor and it was infested with huge sluggish flies. I was lured out one day to do No. 1 Buttress on Sgurr a'Chaorachain. The formation of the rock was like a series of gritstone edges piled one on top of the other, giving rise to many airy situations.

The next day we started home. At Aberdeen I left Bill and started hitching the following morning. I arrived home 36 hours later swearing I would never hitchhike again. Funny, though – I remember saying that last year – and the year before that!

The first written evidence of an Oread in Knoydart. Bill Brooker; a very distinguished Scottish climber, companion of Tom Patey and subsequently President of the S.M.C. His older brother, Dr. Ian Brooker. Was a member of the Oread South Georgia Expedition 1954/55 and made the first ascent of Mount Brooker with ex-Oread Secretary Clive Webb — *Editor.*

ACQUISITIONS

"He would be setting up as a man of property next, with a place in the country" John Galsworthy, *The Man of Property.*

BRYN-Y-WERN

D. PENLINGTON

The third weekend of April '55 was perfect for rock climbing, warm but not too hot, the rock dry and cool. Climbing had started early so shortly after midday a large group had descended to the Bowling Green below Froggatt for refreshment.

A few weeks before at the A.G.M. the problem of finding a club hut had been discussed at length. A look in Derbyshire or outside the main Welsh valleys was suggested.

"We've looked everywhere, either the rent is prohibitive or you need to rebuild the place" said Ernie. Burns uttered uncomplimentary words about landlords in general. Someone mentioned that John Neill's guide to Cwm Silyn and Tremadoc was about to be published. John Adderley said he had done a few new routes on Tremadoc with Stan Moore and Trevor Jones. He was convinced it would rank with the `Three Cliffs` when cleaned up. Others were more doubtful; Ernie quoted descriptions from records in the C.C. journal, "Trees and vegetation with a little scrambling. Some vegetation, hardly a climb, A route to be avoided until a forest fire can be arranged". Some said Ted Dance had recorded a number of routes on Moel Hebog. Was this a new area just opening up? Mick Moore and I decided we would take a look the following weekend.

An early start was made, we decided a direct line to Portmadoc via Shrewsbury, the Tannat Valley and Ffestiniog was the best way. Most of this route was new to us but proved to be quite quick and we arrived in Portmadoc by mid morning. Seeking out the local Estate agent was no problem, only one existed. This was no other than Tom Parry himself, "Auctioneer and Land agent, Portmadoc and Caernarvon". His office was by the harbour; we explained our mission to his secretary. A few minutes later we were explaining it to T.P. himself. Standing at the side of his desk in Welsh Tweed plus four suit, brown boots and gold watch chain, his piercing eyes looked us up and down, a few searching questions and replies must have impressed him. "Well" he said, "I think I have just the place for you. It's part of an estate bought by a mine owner from the Midlands. The house was last lived in by the vicar of Pennant and Dolbenmaen. The rent is £1 per week". He produced a map," here it is, Bryn-y-Wern, stands above the river. Take the key and have a look. We close at 1 p.m.".

49

We thanked him and took the key. Outside we looked at our map, yes there it was, clearly marked Bryn-y-Wern. "Must be quite a place to be marked," said Mick. We noted the way to go. What would we find, what condition could such a place be in for £1 per week? Many questions went through our minds.

We passed the church round the two right angle bends and stopped on the bridge over the Dwyfor. There in the trees was this fine looking house. "That must be it," said Mick, opening the gate of the drive.

From the outside all looked good, roof and windows intact. We opened the front door and walked in; a good sized hall, large rooms on either side, bit of a mess from a few dead rooks that must have come down the chimney, rear kitchen damp rear wall, second kitchen clear and dry. Upstairs five bedrooms, bath and W.C., all too good to be true. Outside we forced a way through the undergrowth. The wooded hillside at the rear was full of fallen timber, plenty to last a number of years.

We now had a problem, if we did not agree to rent, would someone else step in? Could we agree to take the place without reporting back to the Committee? Was the area right? Few Oreads had their own transport. Many other problems entered our minds. We decided it was too good to miss.

On our return to Portmadoc T.P.'s secretary typed out an agreement, we retained the key, T.P. locked his office, we shook T.P. by the hand and departed.

Mick purchased a brush and shovel to clean the mess on the floors. We walked up the valley, looked at crags and ridges and decided we had done the right thing. We slept on the lounge floor and it was a peaceful night. We did not know the history of the house then.

BRYN-Y-WERN

Newsletter (Extract), May 1955

The acquisition of a hut is one of the greatest events in the history of the club. The Oread has now arrived and Mike Moore and his hut sub-committee have earned all the praise and thanks we can offer them. Not content with the tremendous effort exerted in finding this palatial residence, which is now ours, Mike is among the most enthusiastic workers in equipping and decorating. Not that there is any lack of enthusiasm elsewhere.

D. C. Cullum

OFFICIAL OPENING

Newsletter (Extract), July 1955

The official opening is to take place on the Cwm Silin Meet on September 17th and by that time we should be capable of accommodating at least thirty members.

It has been said that the acquisition of a hut is one of the great events in the history of the Club. All of us who have been to Bryn-y-Wern realise its immense potential and the effect it can have on the Club's future. But those who will most fully appreciate its value will be those who, by putting something of themselves into it, will help to write this page of Club history which members of the future can only read.

Its real worth will be realised only if we rediscover there, that unique spirit of companionship without which the Oread cannot flourish.

Mike Moore – Chairman Huts Sub Committee

Progress Report IV (Extract)

Expenses will be heavy in 1956. It is hoped that members will make the most of B.-y-W. and encourage others to do so. Only in this way shall we be able to cover our running costs and save money for future improvements. Remember even Welbourn considers it worth while at 2/6 per night!

Dave Penlington

HOLES IN THE GROUND

Editorial   *Newsletter (Extract), February 1956*

Underground warfare appears to have broken out between the pro- and anti- caving groups within the Club. This issue contains more letters on this subject. These letters and "Claustrophobia's" original complaint have one common feature which reveals the sinister nature of the whole controversy. They are all anonymous. Anti-cavers as well as cavers are afraid to do battle in the full light of day, and hurl their missiles from the obscurity of noms-de-plumes. One cannot help feeling that so much secrecy must veil other, more deadly, skirmishes – brief but bloody encounters involving stabs in the back with sharpened pitons, cleaving of skulls with ice-axes, throttlings with nylon line and other "such bitter business as the day would quake to look on".

D. C. Cullum

Correspondence   *Newsletter (Extract), February 1956*

Dear Sir,

It was with some dismay that we read the second communication from your correspondent Claustrophobia in the December Newsletter, having thought that his initial letter would have been sufficient to set the wheels in motion. These grotesques must be removed from our midst. We ourselves rushed financial assistance, and bitterly regret that we were forced by our Bank Manager to limit our support to the two lire note to which he refers.

We have however initiated a research programme to determine the psycho of the caving proselytes by means of a Gallop Pole (sic. — *Editor*). A statistical analysis of the results has revealed piffling arguments.

Other minor points revealed were opinions ranging from "All Nature's wonders are worth a little effort to see" to "You can get a crafty snog in the dark if you organise the party properly".

However we ourselves will have none of these arguments, and prefer to stand, like Cortez, silent upon a peak in Darien. The bar sinister must be removed from the escutcheon of the Oread, or at least converted into a four-ale bar.

Your obedient servant,

"Pithecanthropus Erectus".

P.S. We investigated five rifts and two adits in the Via Gellia the weekend after Christmas, but were unable to find any trace of the "underground lake three-quarters of a mile long" described in glowing terms by Penlington.

Crypt Chambers, Lower Creep, Jugholes, Matlock.

51

EDITORIALS
(*EXTRACTS*)

Newsletter, May 1956

Recently I was in Llanberis. This fact is not in itself remarkable. What is remarkable is the change that has come over the place since I was first there, eleven years ago. Not only physically – though heaps of rusting cans and broken glass bear witness to the diligent efforts of the litter-lout in recent times – but in the type of climber one meets there, the type of climb he does, and above all the extraordinary atmosphere which pervades the valley. The latter is so powerful that when a stranger asked me what I had done the previous day, I felt an acute sense of shame when I replied, "The horseshoe", so much that I was obliged to add, by way of excuse, "Just showing a lady round, you know". For it is old-fashioned to go to Llanberis to climb mountains; one goes there to climb the Three Cliffs; and the Three Cliffs are, to a layman's eye (and I am a layman in these matters), little outcrops of crag which land their conquerors within comfortable spitting distance of their cars. (Assuming they want to spit on their cars, of course.) Eleven years ago most of the rock of these cliffs was considered unclimbable, and not long enough or high enough to be interesting anyway. Today they are the valley's principal attraction. Their hardest routes are, it turns out, surprisingly long, and though not impossible, are at any rate highly improbable. This change is symptomatic of the revolution which has swept over rock-climbing during the last decade. Strange to think that many Oreads who are not yet thirty belong to a bygone generation of rock-climbers, a generation that has, in a sense, had its day.

D. C. Cullum

Newsletter, August 1956

Although the Mustagh Tower is not among the highest of the Himalayas, its ascent on July 6th and 7th by Hartog's expedition and the re-ascent by the French party a few days later, is one of the most astonishing double events in the history of climbing. Notwithstanding Brown's (Dick's not Joe's) assertion that there was an easy ridge at the back, it was widely held that the Tower would never be climbed. And now it's been done twice in a week! Panther must be feeling a bit sore about it, for he was planning an expedition to the peak with Penlington and Pettigrew in 1958. (The three of them sound like a music-hall trio). Disappointed though they must be from a personal point of view, it is to be hoped that they will not abandon their plans, for in two years' time the Mustagh Tower will, for all practical purposes, be a virgin summit. The difficulties involved in its ascent will by then be quite different and perhaps greater than they were last month. Never let it be said that a bunch of Oreads were interested only in the glory attaching to a "first".

During my recent fortnight at Bryn-y-Wern, I wandered up to look at this Craig Isallt where parties keep gardening. I couldn't help being a little disturbed about two things – firstly that people should choose to spend days of good mountaineering weather on a crag little bigger than a gritstone outcrop when there are far worthier crags within easy distance, and secondly the ravages wrought (with the best intentions) by the "gardeners". The second of these seems to me the more important. Kicking down bits of turf, patches of moss or the odd clump of heather is one thing, but chopping down trees and stripping vegetation wholesale is another. Non-climbers are likely to see no distinction between this sort of climbing and sheer vandalism. And is it really worth it when some of the buttresses unearthed are no more than thirty feet high? Enthusiasm for opening up new crags is a fine thing, but it would be a pity if misguided enthusiasm earned us a reputation for bad behaviour and lack of regard for the countryside.

D. C. Cullum

Newsletter, December 1956

The Dinner was as usual a great success and it is unfortunate that this issue contains no account of it. The move to the Rutland was a good one, for the meal itself was first-class and of ample quantity, and the dining-room was much more sumptuous than we have previously enjoyed "in another place".

All this was in keeping with the increasing respectability of the Club, upon which at least one speaker commented. The speeches too were of a high order. Two other events made the evening particularly enjoyable. One of these was the re-appearance of Cyril Machin after his accident at Castle Naze in May 1954. Cyril is one of the Club's most remarkable members, in more ways than one, and it was obvious that everyone was very pleased to see him again. The other event was the President's announcement of the election of Alf Bridge and Jack Longland to honorary membership. Both of these men are not only outstanding mountaineers in their own right but have also made very great contributions to the progress of the sport. They have both been associated with the Oread since the earliest days and the Club has benefited much by the association. It is hoped that each will take his membership of the Oread seriously, that is, as a very practical business, and take as full a part as possible in Club activities. Both are busy men, Alf in organising expeditions and Jack in training mountaineers to send on them. But we look forward to seeing them on meets – and to reading their articles in the Newsletter.

D. C. Cullum

SELECTIONS FROM OREAD VERSE
IN A MINING CAMP

Away from the bar, gin and blare
I gaze at the tropical night.
Do those same stars, weeping there,
yet give that shrouded light
which, in another world, witnesses the setting out
of youth's bravery, still furled
in sleep-bemused, devout
step, on to the glacier ?

Enclosing all, the jungle, voracious
with black movement, would dispel
this stored treasure, gracious
in that ability to quell
a despair of damp, heat-sodden ways,
and make of these a boulder
to surmount with memory's days
of rock and ice, rose-tinted – a white shoulder
of rest, pleasures won.

No – in some small act
some form, some thought,
does each day refract
the encompassing greenery, and abort
the russet ways which ever sleep
in the mind's most precious keep.

Peter Cole
Burma, November 1955

Unquiet Night

No water trickles down the ice,
And silence shouts
Across the dimming light,
The corniced ridge
No longer bares a razor edge of fire;
And I,
Upon the plunging edge of night,
Sing songs of praise to solitude,
Until the flickering bat-like bird
Has fled before the sudden wind,
Shorewards, – beyond the rising drift of snow.

No silence now,
The night is hideous and loud,
With blizzard winds rough-tongued,
And fresh from brawling in the southern ice;
But I,
Within my down bag lying,
Storm-drowned amid the seething wrack of snow,
No longer sing;
The eye-like mind, once strong,
Is blind to all the discipline of years,
And knows at last the shapeless underworld
Of unfamiliar fear

Harry Pretty
South Georgia 1955

Ascent of S.C. Gully

Beneath the riven precipice we wait,
Feeling the need to put on anoraks
And sweaters, nylon- link ourselves in fate,
Ascending, kicking footsteps in the snow
Until the underlay of ice requires
The keener penetration of an axe,
Changing the leader when he tires.
We circumvent a patch of doubtful ice
By traversing up to the left on rock,
Each poised in turn upon an airy slab,
A flimsy knot belay to take the shock
Of a sudden fall,
The leader taut in readiness
To stem the rush of burning rope
That follows the frantic hands
Bereft of fingerholds of hope.
Ahead, a slope of sixty foot of ice
Is sculptured step by step, until a face
Of rotten rock looms high above our stance,
Stripped of its winter carapace.

And now
The coire shadows lengthen far below,
The menace of approaching darkness
Spurs us on;
There is no choice, the pitch must go.
Hand by hand seeking,
Probing, testing the shattered rock,
Foot by foot trusting,
Avoiding the loosened block
Until the glassy lip is reached,
The friction of a vibram sole on ice
Between oneself and paradise,
The gully's last defence is breached.
Treasure the moment passing fleet
As toiling up that frozen labyrinthine street,
The cornice, promise,
Gold in the dying sun
Heralds the rising star on Bidean.

Jim Kershaw
Stob Coire Nan Lochan, Easter 1956

COMIC RELIEF
AWAKE, AWAKE O OREAD

Awake, awake O Oread,
Arise famed heroes of the past,
O fabled names of founder days,
The Club is sinking fast.

Put on your mouldered anoraks,
Search out your rusted iron,
Arise, the tigers of the past,
Restore V.S. to Zion.

Jim Kershaw

(A chorus of resurrected Oreads despairingly chants the following to the clanking of chains of karabiners, pitons, hammers and associated ironmongery which they drag behind them.)

Where are the hard men,
Where are the serious men,
The men with the bloodied hands?

(Stop reading the poem, you degenerate shower, and either do 100 press-ups, or hand traverse round the picture rail.)

Carry on reading now with a better conscience.

Present day Oreads lounge in bars,
Go to the hills in sleek black cars,
Pseudo-mountaineers in Teddy-boy suits,
Frolic about on moderate routes.

(Have you read any good V.S. routes lately?)

> Where are the hard men,
> Where are the serious men,
> The men with bloodied hands?
>
> So rise, you men of long ago,
> That criticise the present,
> Attend some meets to demonstrate
> That V.S. routes are pleasant

Newsletter, July 1955

"A CRITIC REARS HIS VENOMED HEAD ...."

POME

> William McGonegall
> Wrote poetry that was absolutely abominable.
> Cole's blank verse
> Is worse.
>
> (As for Jim,
> H'm.)
> Even the Editorial prose
> Has a touch of rose.
>
> This may not be sublime
> But it does rime.

Les Langworthy
Newsletter, January 1956

To the "onlie begetter of this ensuing sonnet", Mr. L.L.

> And now a critic rears his venomed head,
> Assails the work of gifted poets three,
> McGonegall in Ulster long since dead,
> Myself, and Cole beyond the Bengal Sea.
> I perused the address list for his name,
> And found that Langworthy or Leese, but two,
> Could cruelly have vilified our fame,
> Befouled the old, and seared the budding new.
> I scanned the books of Oread in vain,
> To see a word or line he wrote before.
> Why did he vie with verse and wit inane
> To emulate his betters on that score?
> Before he sneers at fruits of others' wealth,
> Well may he try to write the like himself.

(What price Marlowe now?)

I append brief extracts from the post I received following the issue of the January Newsletter.

"This is an insult to Clan Mcgonegall; an apology or the names of his seconds. The Mcgonegall, Killabeg House, Co. Donegal."....... "Carry on writing, Jim. – Five Boilermakers, Scunthorpe." ...."The workers are behind you. – Trades Council, Runcorn." ....."Disregard recent criticism. I regard your work as promising. – T.S.E – t" ......and finally a touching tribute from "Your old friends at No. 3 Box, Unemployment Exchange, Nottingham."

Yours,
Jim Kershaw.

Newsletter, February 1956

PEAK PERSONALITIES
BLOODY BILL THE BOGTROTTER

ERIC BYNE   *Newsletter, February 1955*

Bill was a product of the Manchester Rambling Club before the 1914-18 war. He and his companion, the famous Harry Gilliat, explored the fastnesses of Bleaklow and Kinder, and then around 1922 joined the Rucksack Club – a move that was to open a vista of new friends and great deeds, and to earn him the sobriquet of "Bloody Bill the Bogtrotter". No walking feat was too long, no open air bivouac too wet or too cold for this tough moorland wanderer, and it was to his own inventive genius that we owe many famous high level bog trots of today. "The Three Inns Walk", the "Double Marsden Edale", and many all night bogtrotting crossings of Bleaklow, Kinder, and Black Hill were all planned and executed by him, often under vile conditions of rain, blizzards, and pitch black nights, during which the use of torches was considered taboo and progress was always a matter of skilled compass work.

Other areas also received his attention – the Berwyns – the Welsh three thousands – and the Scottish four thousands which he and Gilliat accomplished in the fantastic time of 11 hours and 8 minutes walking plus four hours travel by car which transported them from the Ben Nevis area to the Cairngorms. However, perhaps his most famous expedition was the planning, inauguration and execution of that great "milestone misery", the 70 mile "Colne to Rowsley", in 1926 – a master route which today is considered the greatest classic in the peak, and a feat of considerable endurance if accomplished under winter conditions. A little later it was Gilliat who extended the course from Colne to Matlock in an incredible time of under 24 hours, a record which probably still stands today.

By now you will be wondering who is this "Bloody Bill", this man who for a wager of a pint of shandy once walked barefooted over the hills from Derwent Village to Edale, and who once was noted for his hospitality at Tunstead, that calling house between Hayfield and Kinder Low.

In later life he became the inspirer of youth, took over the licences of the Church Hotel and the Nag's Head at Edale, became a Rural District Councillor – and indefatigable worker for the Peak District Branch of the Council for Preservation of Rural England – fought strenuously and successfully against the steel magnates who attempted to industrialise the Edale Valley with great steel works, and indirectly planned many great walks and inspired many great walkers with his slogans of reward for success, such as "A pint on the House", or, (as in the case of the 120 mile Tan Hill to Cat and Fiddle) "Breakfast on the House".

He is still there at Edale – jovial, friendly, ever ready to greet the climber, mountaineer, and bogtrotter – always willing to listen to the deeds of the day, to pass comment, to give advice, to help plan a Route, and to pull you a pint of the best. That is "Bloody Bill the Bogtrotter", mine host of the Nag's Head inn at Edale – none other than our old friend – Fred Heardman.

Uncle Alf

Eric Byne   *Newsletter, June 1956 (Extract)*

You may have met him in the peak. His reputation is now legendary, and his kindness to the young enthusiastic mountaineers is proverbial. Usually one can be sure of seeing him at one of the annual dinners of the Oread Mountaineering Club, for Uncle Alf is often an honoured and privileged guest, either of some individual member, or of the club itself.

To go back to the start of Alf Bridge's career is to retrace one's footsteps back to the period that was principally noteworthy for the enterprise of Fergus Graham in forcing a direct route to Moss Ledge on Scafell Pinnacle. It was an era noted for the climbing tigers who were reared or trained on the gritstone outcrops of the Peak District. Rice K. Evans, the American Vice Consul in Sheffield, and the one time leading light on Stanage, had departed back to his native land. J.W.Puttrell was 56 years old, still climbing, and an established authority on the geology and the cavern systems of Derbyshire. And such ferocious tigers as A.S.Piggot, Morley Wood and George Bower were now truly exploiting the techniques learnt on gritstone, adding new routes over a widely distributed area in the Lake District, Scotland, and North Wales. Harry Kelly, using his gritstone knowledge, was also busy vomiting forth new routes on Scafell with the precision of a machine – and, of these, perhaps his best effort was the discovery of a new route up the Central Buttress, by way of Moss Ghyll Groove.

This then was the period which saw the introduction to climbing of Alf Bridge, a young Manchester lad with unusually prehensile fingers, and a great strength of arms, shoulders and legs. His initiation took place at the Staffordshire Roaches, under the tuition of Robert Burns of the Rucksack Club, and it is said that on this, his first day, he revealed the promise of the skill to come, by leading the climb known as "Via Dolorosa".

So the fire was lit, the ambition to do great things was born – not only in the climbing world but also on the high moorland plateaux. As a walker he proved superb, being possessed of lungs of leather, and leg muscles of spring steel which nothing could completely tire. He became a member of that brilliant band of Peakland fell walkers, "The Bogtrotter's Club", whose feats soon became legendary with such routes as the Double Marsden Edale, Colne to Rowsley, Penistone to Macclesfield, and Greenfield to Macclesfield, all being traversed in exceedingly fast times. By 1927 his toughness and popularity received full recognition, for he was elected the President of this group of "grough greyhounds".

One of his famous excursions during this period was a walk from Greenfield to Chinley, travelling light, with only food, primus and pans in his rucksack, rubber gym shoes on his feet, and going via Laddow, Wildboar Clough, Slippery Stones, Stanage, Cratcliffe Tor, Castle Naze and Combs. It started as a light-hearted affair, and the intention of doing various climbs at each of the famous outcrops and edges which he reached. All went well as far as Cratcliffe, where a rapid ascent of the Hermitage Crack and the Giant's Staircase, followed by the twin towers of Robin Hood's Stride, saw the passing of a precious hour and the appearance of several fine specimens of blisters on each heel. This, of course, was not to be wondered at, for approximately 24 hours had passed since his departure from Greenfield at noon on Saturday, and for the majority of this time he had been either walking or climbing.

The continuation of the walk from Cratcliffe to Castle Naze, via the Limestone Dales, is a long and tedious one, and Bridge, traversing this section during the hot afternoon of this sunny day, found it to be "sheer purgatory". It was 6.30 p.m. before, tired and thirsty, he could gaze down from the crags of Castle Naze at the promised land of the valley of Combs. Worn out, he struggled up A.P. Chimney, trod gingerly on blistered heels across the "Scoop", and flogged himself wearily up the safe but clinging cleft of Deep Chimney.

These were the halcyon days, with such great personalities in the walking world of the Peak District as Eustace Thomas, Fred Heardman, Harry Gilliat, and many others, to look up to. With such people as an inspiration, to be used as a "mighty yardstick", is it any wonder that the "Bogtrotter's Club" became fell walkers of the highest grade? With Ben Bennet, reputed to be one of the most brilliant members, Alf Bridge succeeded in walking the full length (North to South) of the one inch Ordnance Survey Peak District tourist map – from Penistone to Ashbourne in the remarkably fast time of 10 hours 20 minutes – a fantastic speed for this 51 mile journey, made possible no doubt by the fact that the southern portion of this route included many miles of roadwork, thus giving rubber shod feet the opportunity of accomplishing faster times than would normally have been possible had it been purely cross country travel.

More people will perhaps know of him as the Oxygen adviser of the successful 1953 expedition to Everest; others perhaps will think of him as the secretary of the successful 1955 expedition to Kanchenjunga; but I, who have known him over 20 years, remember him as a great lover of the Peak, a great bogtrotter, a superb cragsman of Herculean strength and considerable courage. The companion of Maurice Linnell and the great Colin Kirkus, and the man who introduced, taught, and practised the "Technique of Falling"

Tough weekenders, bivouackers and walkers gradually turned more and more to the high wild moorlands and the gritstone crags – being influenced by such people as Fred Heardman, Harry Gilliat, Robert Burns and Alfred Bridge, whose reputations were now well known amongst the elite.

As for Alf Bridge, he, unknown to himself, was at the crossroads, needing only a touch from some other domineering personality to take him to further heights. Then it happened; for at the close of a summer's day on Cratcliffe Tor he met Maurice Linnell, and thus a friendship and climbing partnership was born which was to lead to many great days and fine expeditions on the crags of Wales and the Lake District. Both he and Linnell were strong individualists with strong views about many things and therefore found much in common, both as climbers and as men.

Linnell at this period, a product and founder of the Manchester University Mountaineering Club, was now progressing to that zenith when he would crown his climbing career by the pioneering of the East Face of Scafell, and the Narrow Slab on the West Buttress of Clogwyn Dur Arddu. Tall, slim, with a long face, lantern jaw, shock of black hair, and keen eyes, one sensed instantly the drive and determination that lay behind the gentle smile which could light up his whole countenance. His life was spent in keeping himself fit for climbing and, in the training of himself to withstand cold, hunger, fatigue, and great effort, he would have found no-one more suitable than Alf Bridge. Both he and Alf had a reputation for imperturbability in the presence of impending danger or averted danger, and neither would turn a hair but simply carry on climbing calmly upwards.

In Manchester these two tigers had a regular meeting place, where they would sit over coffee and talk about climbing and the routes they planned to do. It was here that the Girdle Traverse of Pillar Rock was first mooted, seized upon enthusiastically, and then planned in meticulous detail, until that day, in 1931, when the expedition was finally transformed into fact. However, before this took place there were many exciting weekends on gritstone, on one of which they bivouacked under the Black Rocks of Cromford, and Bridge, in great form, led the first ascent of the direct start to Longland's Birch Tree Wall, using the thin slanting crack which had repelled the layback efforts of Longland's experimental advance the previous year.

There were also meetings with Ivan Waller, the tough Cambridge University mountaineer who reigned as undisputed monarch and "grand inquisitor" at Black Rocks – Ivan who would bundle Alf into his Alvis and tear away at terrific speed to some other climbing ground, anxious to make as complete a day or weekend as would satisfy his restless spirit. These were great days, with Alf in 1930 leading Waller and Longland on the first ascent of that ferocious super-direct finish to Lean Man's Climb on Black Rocks – truly an incredible effort, considering that no previous inspection of this overhang was made. No wonder that it remained unrecorded for almost 15 years, when its pioneers considered it to be totally unjustifiable.

By 1931 the partnership of Linnell and Bridge was firmly cemented. There were grand times in the Lakes with A. B. Hargreaves, and it was these three who added the Girdle Traverse of The Pillar Rock, Linnell in the lead and Alf as last man. Gimmer Crag also proved attractive and George Bower's route of Hiatus was varied by a terrific new finish. On gritstone Alf was also busy – new routes on Fairbrook Edge of Kinderscout, and an important visit to Stanage where he pioneered a route up the thin delicate crack now known as Robin Hood's Innominate. There was some snow about and a little ice yet, despite these disadvantages, he managed to force a continuation up the overleaning Cave Gully Wall – a most exposed climb above the level of the well known Cave Traverse.

The greatest year for Alf was perhaps 1932, for that was the time of the start of his friendship with the great Colin Kirkus. It was the period of intensive exploration on Clogwyn Dur Arddu and Kirkus's great pioneering routes. Here Alf teamed up to help in the production of such famous routes as Curving Crack and the Direct finish to East Buttress. He also, on a visit to the Lakes, led the first ascent of the safer and exposed Route 2 of Esk Buttress.

Then came 1934 and tragedy as Linnell was swept to his death and Kirkus severely injured by an avalanche on the Castles of Ben Nevis. This marked the end of a phase in British rock climbing. Kirkus was never the same, and he too was to die during the war on one of the great Hamburg Bomber Raids. Only Alf Bridge remained, trained Commandos, kept alive the memories of his two friends by his reminiscences, encouraged those who came to follow, and became "Good old Uncle Alf!"

EVEN MORE PROFILES
(EXTRACTS)

P. R. FALKNER
Newsletter, October 1954

An interesting species of bogtrotter. Lives in Nottingham, lecturing in chemistry at the Technical College. Also frequently found in public houses, concert halls, public houses, jazz clubs, and public houses. Shows almost pathological enthusiasm for fireworks.

Took D. C. Cullum climbing for the first time in 1945. Has frequently regretted it since. Though no tiger, has led a good number of severes. Lengthy holidays enable him to climb for several months a year. Does so. Usually spends Easter in Scotland, doing snow and ice climbs and marathon walks. Migrates to Alps for the summer. Has also been twice to Lyngen (1951, 1953).

Very energetic. Cannot bear weekends at home. Retires to Derbyshire moors and crags instead. Camps all over the place, does long walks (eg. Colne – Rowsley this year) and delights in attempting record numbers of climbs in one day. Steady leader, reliable second – once held a leader who fell over 100'. Smokes continually, rendering atmosphere in tent impossible for those with lungs. Not true that he made first ascent of Tryfan.

Anon

PETER JANES (WHYMPER, SOMETIMES TODHUNTER)
Newsletter, January 1956

When Janes came of age, his doting parents provided the wherewithal for a holiday in Zermatt. On this occasion only the Zermatterhof was good enough for him. The last time he visited the resort, being more or less self-supporting, he shared the top attic at the Bahnhof with three other people at one franc a night. Janes is the second tightest chap in the Club with money (no prizes for guessing the first!). As an example of his parsimony, it should be noted that he budgets for one roll of film a year. One of the shots, of course, guarantees first prize at the Club Photographic Meet.

If you see a photograph of Pete himself, you will always find him standing, back to the camera, on a pinnacle of rock in the middle foreground, a lone rampant figure looking out over a panorama of peaks ranging to infinity. Hence the sobriquet "Whymper".

Although we have never been fortunate enough to be entertained by his histrionic ability, his friends tell us that he treads a pretty board. He's no mean performer on boards that turn up at the front, either. (Prior to Janes' electrifying appearances in the legendary Ilam Hall pantomimes – *Editor*.)

In the art, or craft, of professional diner-out he is second only to Tony Moulam. He dines out regularly with everyone we know, and a lot of people we don't know. In recompense, on odd occasions, he disburses small samples of his mother's cooking as a rare elixir. If he ever makes a mistake and invites you home for a meal, acceptance with alacrity is recommended.

There is no doubt, however, that Pete's wit is his outstanding talent. No other member has the ability of raconteur, punster or fool to compare with him. His prowess in the extempore is as outstanding as his belching is voluminous. Everyone agrees that he is an asset at a Meet or any gathering.

Anon

MEMORY HOLD THE DOOR

"Here with foul shirts and fouler breath, were the climbing heroes. Summits had fallen, and men had perished, aspirations had withered, and marriages ruined, for this and this alone: that hard men in stinking pubs might have great wealth of memory."

Adapted from Magnus Merriman, E. Linklater – *Editor*.

"Fond memory brings the light of other days around me, the smiles, the tears, of boyhood years." *Thomas Moore.*

MEMORIES OF THE FIFTIES

PHILLIP FALKNER (SEPTUAGENARIAN)

Nowadays, when the pundits of the media comment on the years just after the second world war, they portray a dull, dreary, depressing time. Britain was exhausted and almost bankrupt after six years of war; everything was run-down and shabby; many items were still in short supply and food rationing dragged on into the 1950s, but for those of us who were young at the time, life did not seem at all depressing. We were glad to have survived the war and for anyone interested in hill walking or mountaineering, there was everything to go for. Wartime restrictions on travel had been lifted and the Alps were again accessible. Camping and climbing equipment was available cheaply from army surplus shops and travel was relatively cheap.

It was an exciting time. In Britain a new generation of rock climbers were pioneering new hard routes on gritstone and in Wales and the Lakes, and many of us were finding our way around the Alps after years of deprivation. One thing, however, still seemed pretty remote. This was the opportunity to explore and to make first ascents of hitherto unclimbed mountains. Few of us then had the resources to visit the great mountain ranges such as the Himalaya or the Andes where such opportunities were to be found.

Then, in 1949/50 a few chance meetings opened up a new and intriguing opportunity. On 4th November 1950, on Edale station, I met Harry Pretty, accompanied by Dick Brown, whom I had first met at the C.I.C. hut on Ben Nevis at Easter 1949, and Eric Byne. With a few others we spent a not too uncomfortable night at the Poltergeist barn and had an enjoyable traverse of Kinderscout the next day.

The other significant meeting came only five weeks later when on Sunday 11th December 1950 I met George Sutton in a café in Bakewell where we were both waiting for buses to get us home. George and I quickly discovered that we had a number of friends in common. I learned from George that in the previous year he, Eric, and Harry, with some friends from the Derby/Burton area had launched a new mountaineering club, The Oread, and that for 1951 they were planning a surveying and climbing expedition to a place called Lyngen in Arctic Norway, where there were still unmapped and unclimbed alpine mountains of around 5,000/6,000' rising steeply from sea-level. I was overjoyed when, shortly afterwards, Dick Brown, who'd already had experience of climbing in the Lofoten Isles, and I were invited to join the Lyngen expedition in the summer of 1951.

Much has been written about Lyngen '51 and I will not attempt to give a detailed account here. To sum up, it was an extraordinary party made up of eight people who came from widely different backgrounds but who all got on splendidly together. We had a lot of first rate climbing with several new routes, and a notable achievement of the expedition, under Harry's guidance, was the production of the first reasonably accurate sketch map of the interior of the Lyngen peninsula, previously existing maps being hopelessly inaccurate and misleading. For myself the memory I cherish most was the first ascent by Stan Moore and myself of a previously unrecorded, impressive rock peak which we called Klokketörn (Clock-tower).

Throughout the 1950s regular Oread meets were the most enjoyable feature of one's life. A notable feature of those days was the gloriously carefree irreverent attitude to established conventions and procedures. A club that started off with its purpose summed up in two words "Mountaineering regardless" was clearly something new and different. We were always ready to take part in new ventures, and if sometime adventurousness just over-stepped the boundary into what the more cautious might regard as rashness, then good fortune always seemed to be with us when we needed it.

Many of these early ventures originated either in Harry and Molly's picturesquely named Woodbine Cottage, or in my suburban semi in Beeston which I shared with Charlie and Mary Cullum. Charlie was my most regular climbing companion in those days and our series of Easters spent in the Scottish Highlands could fill many pages. A unique memory is of a bus journey from Achnasheen to Torridon, when one of the locals on the bus kept passing us a bottle of whisky and insisting that we drank, so that when we reached Torridon we were almost too sloshed to pitch our tent. That holiday was also memorable for successive traverses of the ridges of Ben Alligin, Liathach and Bheinn Eighe in splendid alpine conditions. The last of the three had a darker moment. On the summit ridge, in thick mist and a howling gale we came across a fragment of a Lancaster bomber, and nearby, the frozen body of a young airman. They had been there for about a week and until we reported it, The RAF Mountain Rescue had been unable to locate the wreckage.

Another regular feature of those days was the annual Marsden to Rowsley (or Baslow) walk. For the first one, in late October 1952, six of us arrived in Marsden on a cold dark showery evening, with no accommodation arranged and only minimal bivouac equipment. Having fortified ourselves with beer and fish and chips, we were huddling disconsolately in a bus shelter pondering the next move, when a passing policeman took pity on us and suggested that we try the gas-works. There the friendly night shift made us welcome and found us comfortable bunks in a warm cabin where we slept very well and were woken with cups of hot tea when the day shift arrived to take over. During Saturday we crossed Black Hill, Bleaklow, Kinder and Win Hill, arriving at the Nag's Head, Edale in the dark. Another stroke of luck, – the genial landlord, Fred Heardman, himself a great hill walker, let us spend the night sleeping in his living room. The next day the four of us, Geoff Gibson, Mike Moore, Dave Penlington and I forced our weary selves down the succession of gritstone edges to Baslow. Two years later, Ron Dearden, Clive Webb and I completed the much longer and arduous route from Colne to Rowsley. Early on during the walk Ron and I ate nearly all of Clive's supply of Kendal mint cake, intending to share ours with him later. Unfortunately we then left him behind on his own for most of the rest of the 70 miles. Clive has never forgotten this and reminded me of it quite recently.

In 1953 there was another Lyngen expedition with Dick Brown, Barry Cooke and myself, joined for a while by Bob Pettigrew and Trevor Panther from Loughborough College. Like its predecessor this expedition went very well; we made several first ascents and produced an amended and extended version of the map, which remained the best one of the area until a few years later the Norwegian authorities did a proper aerial survey. (for anyone interested, my own account of the '52 and '53 expeditions can be found in the Climbers Club Journals for the years 1952 and 1954).

One final episode from those years: At Easter 1954, Sutton, Pretty, Chunky Cartwright, and I took two new tents, prototypes for the forthcoming South Georgia expedition, to test on the summit of Ben Nevis, which we thought would give as near approach to Antarctic conditions as we were likely to find in Britain. Ironically we had the most perfect weather, cold but dry, calm and sunny all the time. It was no test at all for the tents. Chunky and I, camping on the summit plateau, had no problems, whilst the other tent, down in Glen Nevis, was damaged by cows – not an anticipated Antarctic hazard! (Edgintons were not amused since the tents had not been paid for — *Editor.*)

From our summit camp, one glorious fine morning, Chunky and I descended to the Allt a Mhuillin, climbed Tower Ridge in quick time and had lunch in our tent. We then descended to the foot of the crags again and climbed Northeast Buttress in the afternoon, finishing at dusk. I still don't know whether both of these climbs have been done in one day in snow conditions, before or since, but we felt mighty chuffed at the time!

FIRST IMPRESSIONS

CHRIS MARTIN

I was introduced to MIKE GADD by a close friend in 1956. I recall having a discussion with Mike in the Shire Hall in Nottingham, the outcome of which was an invitation to attend the joint MAM/OREAD meet at Bryn-y-Wern on Nov.3rd and 4th 1956 with Mike Harby as meet leader.

I departed from Beeston with MIKE and ANN GADD, MIKE TURNER and his wife, RON DEARDEN plus a.n.other in Mike (T)s Standard Vanguard car en route B.y.W. The journey was uneventful until we came to the Welsh Mountains with the twisting roads and Mike driving as though he was in the Monte Carlo Rally, when all of a sudden, the front near side front door flew open and I was almost ejected from the front bench seat. Fortunately for me I was grabbed by a very welcome hand and saved from being dumped on a Welsh hillside. What had I let myself in for?

Eventually, arriving at the hut in the early hours of Sat. morning, I was allocated a top bunk in the hut. What seemed like hours later a character crept into the room wearing a long black heavy overcoat and proceeded to remove the coat, roll it out on the floor. Curl up in it and promptly fall asleep. This was my first encounter with LAURIE BURNS.

The following day was a tramp over the local hills, collecting wood for the bonfire to be held on Black Rock Sands that evening. No outstanding recollections until the evening when the clubs congregated on the beach for the bonfire and fireworks display. This was when I, an innocent young towny from Nottingham was introduced to certain members of the Oread (names with held for good reason) who proceeded to romp around the sands, despite the weather, in the nude (some still sporting a pipe in the mouth). What an eye opener! My eyes must have been on stalks. I had heard of the Druids and their rituals, but no one had mentioned the initiation ceremony of the Oreads. I held my breath.... But luckily participation was optional and this shy bashful lad opted out. Was I joining a mountaineering club or a nudist club?

The Sunday morning was a stroll across the hills adjacent to the hut with what I thought was the local landowner. Dressed in tweed plus fours (looking very much the part) and in deep discussion with senior members of the club was a very distinguished gentleman. This later turned out to be DAVE PENLINGTON (at that time hut warden).

The friendliness of the club members this initial weekend, followed by attending the Annual Dinner on the 24th Nov. 56 confirmed my decision to apply for membership. It is this friendliness that has made the club so successful in the 40 years of my being a member, even when one lives so far away. Lets hope it continues.

REMEMBERING

KEN GRIFFITHS

Whilst perusing old diaries, I came upon the following entry for 26th June 1977: "Off at 06.30, arrived at Tan-yr-Wyddfa 10.30". What is so special about that you may conjecture.

Memories came flooding back: My wife Gwenda and I were running a Residential Establishment for Physically Handicapped and Delicate Children on the edge of Ilkley Moor. Most of these youngsters had led very sheltered lives, including much hospitalisation and had missed out on much of the fun and games ordinary youngsters enjoyed.

So following intensive rehabilitation training our thoughts concentrated on ways to enhance their improvement in physical health and outlook. Whitehall, (Jack Longland's Derbyshire Centre) might be a wee bit too exacting at this stage.

But what about the Oread hut in North Wales at Rhyd Ddu? With the whole hearted and generous co-operation of the club we ran, for several years, an annual summer training programme at Tan-yr-Wyddfa, and what a difference it made. Several were able to gain "I have climbed Snowdon" badges and thereby inspiring others to join the next expedition. All of them the better able to meet life's challenges.

It is all a long time ago but, as an octogenarian I am fortunate in having retired to the Lake District and I can still enjoy a good trek on the fells. My last outing was a delightful amble over Red Pike, High Stile, High Crag and Haystacks to the Honister youth hostel.

Some of my most treasured memories!:

Dave Penlington (to whom I am indebted for early rock and ice experiences) and our trip to Chamonix in 1952/53: two nights snowed in at a refuge on Mont Blanc. Some years later Dave introduced me to easy routes on Cloggy, starting with the 30' layback on Curving Crack.

A visit to Poltergeist Barn with Harry and Molly Pretty with baby Laura strapped to an ex W.D. carrying frame, quite happy despite the bleakness of winter.

Knowing Eric Byne, such a quiet and unassuming man, and through him getting to know Alf Bridge.

Geoff Gibson, dear gentle Geoff, our club secretary in 1952/53 and with whose party we reconnoitred the Dent D'Herens and Dent Blanche route from Arolla to Zermatt.

Accompanying Bob Pettigrew to Lyngen (Arctic Norway) in 1954 to climb Jekkevarrenebbe.

With George Sutton in the Julian Alps following his return from South Georgia.

As I write, within view, a most precious memento: a pewter tankard inscribed: "To Ken and Gwenda from the Oread M.C., November 1957," to mark our marriage in August 1957.

Gwenda Griffiths died, 1st July 1976 — *Editor.*

OUR TIME WITH THE OREAD

CHUCK AND MARGARET HOOLEY

I am a little uncertain as to when and where Margaret's and my own association with the Oread began. Inevitably combinations of dates and times are always difficult to remember possibly obscured by my service with Bomber Command in the Royal Air Force from 1945 to 1948. It is perhaps easier to remember events. As I recall many earlier Oreads migrated from Clubs like the Derby Mercury and the Valkyrie. John Welbourn and I emerged from these two clubs in the late forties. I spent some time climbing with Wilf White in Cornwall and later joined with Colin Morris and his friends. Margaret was on the scene by this time and Colin had taken unto himself a wife and we climbed extensively on Black Rocks at Cromford and the Derwent Edges. It was whilst traversing at mid-height along the Curbar Edges, a recognised and difficult activity in those days, that we came upon a group at the base of the crag. An unkempt bunch to behold. Most were attired in ex army gear which is not surprising considering the year. One could hear names like Pretty, Sutton and Moore being bandied about. Had we stumbled, albeit at altitude across the embryo Oread. They had I learned later just returned from an expedition to South Georgia thereby laying down one of the earlier chapters in the history of Oread achievements. Some weeks later Margaret and I were, for reasons unclear, at the Bell Hotel in Sadler Gate, Derby. The Bell we had heard was where the Oread met on Tuesday evenings. Faces from the past were there, from the Valkyrie and the Mercury: Pete Janes, Fred and Brenda Allen, Ray Handley, Ernie and Ronni Phillips, Norman and Judy Millward etc. Our acceptance into the Oread started at the Bell followed by membership and our first Christmas meet at Bryn-y-Wern, the club hut in Cwm Pennant, North Wales. This hut, the club's first, was renowned for its ghostly atmosphere. Who's going in first to light the tilley lamps? This question was always asked by first arrivals on Friday evening. I personally witnessed an apple move out of a fruit bowl and roll across in my direction. Not many members would spend the night alone at Bryn-y-Wern. Ronni Langworthy did, but then it would be a brave ghost who tackled Ronni!

Memorable times with the Oread included activities abroad: two weeks mountaineering in Norway in 1961 with Ronni and Les Langworthy, journeying on foot across the Hardangervidder Glacier where Captain Scott trained for his polar expedition; travelling north to Jotunheimen to ascend Norway's highest summit Galdhopiggen; taking part in Jack Ashcroft's expedition to the Bernina Alps from the Italian side and, following this, visits to the Ortler Mountains with Laurie Burns and Clive Webb. These were all milestones.

In our Oread years several notable events occurred. In the mid-1960's at the behest of many members I created a Mountain Rescue Team (call sign Alpha). It was purely voluntary and attracted about 30 members. Its role was to give support to the Peak District Mountain Rescue Organisation which was very active then. The team no longer exists. The call outs became minimal – perhaps it was the mild winters, or the invention of climbing walls.

Another event was the eviction from Bryn-y-Wern, not due to Oread behaviour, but to the owner shuffling off his mortal coil and the selling of the property. A search for another property in North Wales ensued and, on May 28th 1958, a Conveyance and a Deed of trust were signed making the Oreads the owners of another hut, an authentic Welsh four bedroomed house, a freehold property documented as 'Snowdon View' and now re-named in Welsh as Tan-yr-Wyddfa. Money was loaned to the club by the members and it was purchased for the princely sum of five hundred and fifty pounds.

The earliest record in the deeds is of an indenture of lease dated 30th October 1895 between Lady Ann Watkin, wife of Sir Edward Watkin Baronet, and one David Jones of the Temperance Hotel, Rhydd-Ddu, now known as the Cwellyn Arms. This places the hut at approximately one hundred and three years old.

The Oread left Bryn-y-Wern on October 26th 1958 and moved into Tan-yr-Wyddfa. A photograph in the book 'Climb if you Will' records the event. So commenced another chapter in the annals of the Oread. There were opinions that it was in the wrong location. However it was near to Cwm Silyn, which offered good climbing, and Cloggy was just over the ridge. Also one could walk out the front door and up Snowdon. It is so popular now that it always has bookings into the next year, and weekends have to be reserved for use by its own club members. The first Hut Custodians were Dave Penlington and Fred Allen. I took over from Fred in 1962 until 1966 followed by John Corden, Dave Appleby and John Welbourn. I took over again from John Welbourn around 1977/78 and am still in place in 1998. In the last forty years there have been many improvements to the hut. There are those who remember those first few years of a single cold water tap and the outside toilet to which brave mountaineers had to escort their womenfolk on a dark stormy night. The toilet from which an attempt was made to put Ray Handley into orbit with the help of army cadet corps explosives! The hut now has L.P.G. Gas on tap, hot and cold showers, and yes, three indoor toilets.

The Oread also has a hut in Derbyshire. The club took out a lease in 1968 with the Chatsworth Estates on an old Sawmill site with a cottage called Heathy Lea, located near the Derwent Edges. It is a Grade 2 listed building and is serving the club well as a base in Derbyshire where the club grew up and developed. Heathy Lea was acquired as a result of Harry Pretty's erstwhile negotiations with the Chatsworth Estate. Both huts are served by a single management committee with myself as incumbent 'Custodian'. The burning of Heathy Lea, if not recorded, would soon be forgotten. On Thursday 25th October 1990 it was found that burglars had broken in, stolen a cash box and axe, made a pile of books, papers and furniture in the lounge, and set fire to it. The culprits presumably, must have been well brought up for they closed doors as they left which snuffed out the fire and only £1,958.82 worth of damage was done.

You are permitted to think that this article is mostly about our time with Oread huts. If I were ever to possess Harry Pretty's superb turn of phrase (Playboy of the Alpine World, page 176, in 'Climb if you Will') I could write a book about our forty plus years with the Oread. However, as the Journal is to be a record of the Oreads' fifty years and, as I also firmly believe, without a club hut few mountaineering clubs would have survived that number of years, the history of our huts should be recorded.

In 1976 Margaret suffered a Sub-Arachnoid Haemorrhage. Eight hours of brain surgery left her with limited speech and mobility, but she survived. The effect on our life with the Oread was dramatically changed. Overnight I became a life long carer and our normal mountaineering activities were severely curtailed. We now realise that "Our Time With The Oread" was, and we hope will continue to be, a major part of our lives. We maintain contact with members and mountains through our work with the huts. We always look forward to meeting members on their Derbyshire walks at the lunch time rendezvous and quaff a pint or two (non alcoholic of course) before driving home, often giving lifts to hip replacements, knackered knees and other coffin dodgers.

The term "coffin dodgers" was, I understand, initiated by young Weston, son of "Weston the Old" — *Editor.*

EARLY DAYS IN THE OREAD

COLIN HOBDAY

In the 50's few people had their own transport. My love of the outdoors, cycling, and joining the C.T.C., led to meeting Dave Weston and a lasting friendship.

During winter, walking became the interest, and I joined the Derby Nomads with bus trips to Wales and the Lake District at the weekend.

The natural progression was to climbing so buying a full weight nylon rope for £6 from the Y.H.A. shop in Leopold Street I headed for Kinderscout (why Kinder I have no idea). A few months later, this time with a guide book, we walked from Wirksworth to Brassington and camped at Rainster Rocks. Whilst trying some of the climbs on Sunday morning who should come along but John and Ruth Welbourn. So my first introduction to the Oread, with an invite to the Bell on a Tuesday evening. In those days the Bell was an important focal point for the Oread with discussions for the weekend and arrangements of lifts. A35 vans were the main form of transport with four people going to Wales for 10 shillings (or 50p in new money).

Memories of many meets spring to mind. Camping at Birchen, Ben Froggatt's farm, with his usual greeting, "Is Welbourn with you?"

Big walks also proved popular in the 60's/70's. Marsden to Rowsley in particular brings back memories. Catching the train on a Friday evening to Manchester where we were met by Phil Falkner whose job it was to guide us quickly between railway stations so that we could catch our connection to Marsden. A dozen or so Oreads laden with heavy rucksacks trudged in single file through a back entrance of M & S to emerge out of the main entrance.

Once in Marsden a few beers, followed by a visit to the chippy, before walking up to a bivvy at the remains of the Isle of Skye pub, only to be visited by the Police who soon climbed over the wall and joined us for a brew. Saturday consisted of traversing Black Hill and Bleaklow to bivvy at "Penlingtons Plantation" (Stanage), finishing the walk on Sunday down the edges to Rowsley.

There were Alpine Meets (family meets) to the Bernina, Cogne, Zillertal, Clampère, and my own meet at Trafoie in July 1980, a super campsite, matched by an excellent turnout of Oreads with families, total 40 people. Many routes were done including the Ortler 3,905m.

It is possible to go on for hours recalling one's memories of my early days with the Oread and the many happy years it has given me.

More recently, many years on the Huts sub-committee, and as Hut Booking Secretary, have provided a different perspective. A few facts:

Some nights the phone never stops ringing while other times not so much as a murmur, that's how it goes when dealing with hut bookings.

The Oread is very fortunate in having two properties, one in Snowdonia at Rhyd-Ddu, Wales, and the other in the heart of the Peak District on the Chatsworth Estate.

Tan-yr-Wyddfa appears in the B.M.C. hut list and therefore attracts many enquiries and bookings. The hut is booked to guest clubs on 3 weeks a month with 1 room of 6 beds always available for members. Many clubs request bookings year after year, coming from as far a field as Glasgow and Brighton.

Over the years we have been successful in negotiating reciprocal rights with other clubs who also own property:-

Swiss Alpine Club T.C.C.
Climbers Club
Yorkshire Ramblers
Lancashire Cave & Crag
K. Fellfarers

Over a twelve-month period Tan-yr-Wyddfa is visited by around 36 clubs and Heathy Lea, 12 clubs. This involves a considerable amount of administration, confirming bookings, taking deposits, sending keys and information and, finally, the collection of fees and the return of keys.

Finally no visit to the hut would be complete without someone leaving items behind, ranging from maps, compasses, boots and watches. Very little is actually claimed and returned to its owner.

FIRST ENCOUNTERS

ERIC BYNE
Jim Winfield

Eric Byne was without doubt my main inspiration for the love of mountains and mountaineering. It was as a young man that I first met him and I was not at that time climbing to a very high standard.

Without having seen me before, the Great Man enquired as to what I had done that day and it was with some trepidation that I informed him of my modest achievements. He proceeded to recall his past enjoyment of the very climbs I had done and my attitude to mountains was cemented for life; to enjoy the sport at whatever level of expertise one can achieve. I find that the ageing process and diminishing ability do not lessen my enjoyment of the hills.

Shortly after our meeting, I was fortunate enough to enjoy a holiday in Skye together with Eric and his climbing partner, Charlie Ashbury.

I am sure that my experience of Eric Byne's enthusiasm are echoed by a great many people who had the pleasure of his encouragement and his company.

JACK ASHCROFT

My meeting with Jack, Hebog Ashcroft was on a Derbyshire walking meet. Jack had written to the club indicating his interest in joining a mountaineering club and was invited to join this particular meet, and my duties were to meet him, introduce him, and generally to put him at ease during the weekend. Hebog duly turned up with his friend Dennis and this was the commencement of a great relationship with the Oread. Jack has been, and still is, a pillar of the club. The same year we were both at the meet at Dow Crag and enjoyed some superb rock climbing in the hottest Easter weather I can remember – though Jack seemed to be strangely distracted by outside interests. We have enjoyed some magnificent holidays with Dave Penlington and Roy Darnell. We had an assured arrangement for several years, always taking off the week at Whitsun. These weeks included the Pennine Way (a hard week), Coast to Coast, Scottish Four Thousanders, and Knoydart, and my enjoyment was greatly enhanced by the companionship of Jack, Dave and Roy.

JIM KERSHAW

My first meeting with Jim Kershaw was a most bizarre circumstance during a "Bullstones" meet.

I could not be free for the whole weekend and I arranged with Ron Dearden to take the bus during the Saturday and walk to Bullstones from the Flouch Inn, which would mean walking a considerable way in darkness. In the gathering gloom, Ron led the way by torchlight on a wet, cold and murky night.

A fall by Ron in dreadful conditions resulted in his smashing the torch, and my inability to carry a spare did nothing to calm his fury. I received a considerable tongue lashing about my inadequate equipment. The fact that I proceeded to produce two inflatable mattresses did nothing to diminish his ire. Our night afloat on the moor was spent in reasonable comfort, but not such comfort that we wished to lie in after daybreak.

It was whilst assembling our gear for a continuation to Bullstones that the bizarre meeting occurred. In the half light and murk an apparition, gradually approached our bivouac. This spectre actually spoke and asked, "Are you members of the Oread Mountaineering Club?"

Jim Kershaw had written to the club indicating his interest and had been invited to join the Bullstones meet. He also had come out on the Saturday and been benighted, quite close to Ron and myself. JK's equipment had been minimal and he appeared completely soaked and bedraggled. An appearance not improved by his wearing of an ex-army gas cape.

A later incident I remember vividly was during a Welsh meet at the Ynys Ettws Hut. Jim, entering the lounge area of the hut from the sleeping accommodation, forgot that his considerable height needed adjustment to negotiate the low stone doorway. The result was JK entering the lounge with severe bleeding and in a state of semi consciousness. He was advised by all to go and recover in the dormitory and he readily agreed. Misfortune struck again. Jim forgot the low stone doorway resulting in more bloodshed and complete unconsciousness.

LAURIE BURNS

The late "Lol" Burns was a long-standing member of the Oread who gave unstinting service as Treasurer for many years and it was in this capacity that I got to know him well.

I remember Lol Burns attending his first meet which was in Borrowdale when camping was allowed in the area, and the many Oread members, plus Lol as a prospective member, arrived by coach. I believe the year to be 1953.

Laurie established his camp and, attired in his normal outdoor gear, i.e. Surplus War Department clothing and a pair of "TUF" boots, proceeded to build the largest camp fire ever seen in Borrowdale. This enormous conflagration was fulfilled with the aid of an axe which would not have been out of place in the hands of a Canadian Lumberjack.

I seem to recall Dave Penlington turning up on this meet, arriving by motorcycle and attired in full military uniform, there being compulsory national service at that time.

Another memory of this meet concerns two members of the coach party, Mark Hayhurst and Joe Johnson who intended camping at Sty Head rather than Borrowdale. Nothing so extraordinary about this you would think. But in fact they accomplished the ascent to Sty Head accompanied by an Ex Army "bell tent", its size and bulk filling the whole of the aisle in the coach. This task was to be performed in the dead of night.

Returning to Laurie Burns; it was some years later that I had more frequent contact with Lol who by then was a well established member and holding the post of Treasurer. The then auditor of the Oread was one Reg Squires but I believe that he had to work overseas and therefore relinquished the duties of checking Laurie's book keeping and accounts. I was persuaded to take on the duties of Hon. Auditor by Burgess during a walking meet, and I have always suspected that DB knew of the horrors of this post, (perhaps from the previous incumbent, Reg Squires). But I was naive enough to believe the Burgess job description as "a piece of cake". DB's economy with he truth could have been an act of revenge for my leaving his climbing rope in the old Snowdon Hotel after a winter ascent. The truth was soon revealed and I quickly learned that standard and accepted practices meant nothing to Lol who had devised the most bizarre methodology for his book keeping and accounts. It was during the next few years, during Reg Squires' absence, that I got to know LB well, spending numerous evenings and weekends together trying to understand his unique methods. My appendage to the accounts of the words "Audited and Found Correct", were always made with tongue in cheek, due to my inability to fathom the system. It is due to Lol's honesty, rather than my auditing, that things were always correct. It was with some relief that I learned of Reg Squire's return to the UK and of his willingness to take on the role of auditor.

Although I regarded Lol as a non climber, his love of mountains and the outdoors was immense, as was his knowledge of mountaineering in general.

Laurie's walking activities were severely curtailed in his later years due to serious physical problems with feet and lower limbs, but he still got into the hills, and he told me with great enthusiasm of his bird watching in the islands off Scotland, accompanied by Doug Cook.

Laurie is much missed by his many friends and also by his Outdoor Gear suppliers; Wakefield's Army Stores.

Poltergeist Barn, Edale 1959 (Bullstones Meet). Ron Dearden, Bob Pettigrew, Jack Ashcroft, Clive Webb, Frank Goldsmith (rear).   *Photo: H. Pretty.*

Oyster Clough Cabin, December 1979: Dave Weston, Digger Williams, Harry Pretty, Ron Chambers, Dave Appleby, Peter Janes.   *Photo: Unknown.*

REFLECTIONS

JOHN FISHER

On an old photograph (page 72 overleaf)

Site: Outside the Roadmender's hut on the Llanberis Pass circa 1954. The hut is the corrugated iron structure, to the right of the massive roadside boulder, directly below Dinas Cromlech. Although the property of the local Council, it was regularly used as a base by the climbing cognoscenti of the time.

While these sketches verge on character assassination there is a clear club precedent for happy acceptance of this style. At club dinners in the past it was usual for the main club speaker to present the dug up dirt on the half dozen or so representatives of kindred clubs, much to the amusement of diners. There was never an action for slander.

David Penlington

Uncharacteristically churlish in demeanour here, presumably his V.Diff standard friends would not accompany him on V.S. climbs with dodgy stances and dubious belays. Recent information is that he has climbed all the Alpine four thousanders. An important O.M.C. member but something of an eminence grise who likes his own way but never tells you what it is.

Martin Ridges (I think)

An able and determined Manchester University climber. Friendly with D.P. and led some of the first ascents of hard climbs with O.M.C. members on Harston Rock. No real material for facetious comment or character assassination available.

John Fisher

Without seeming unduly unkind, the most apt description of his climbing competence is that Fisher occupied the front rank of the second rank. Noted as a rather timid operator who, as Burgess relates, was quite capable of leading the crux on a demanding route twice and then retreating with the comment that the climb was too difficult for him. A sort of human yo-yo. He has never been seen in a T-shirt or a pair of jeans and has read the Guardian only once. Sometimes called the Prince of Parsimony but that title is disputed by Pete Scott.

Geoff Gibson

One of the few gentlemen in the club and, on occasion, climbed with guides. Officer material with lots of social grace, style and one of those rare people about whom one never heard a bad word. To be envied. However, with a chap called Bob Pettigrew, also O.M.C. he forged a powerfully slow party unsurpassed by any in the club or, possibly, in the country. Even the most amiable and competent leader, on an easy but cold climb with them, could be rendered transiently insane by these men of insatiable patience.

Ernie Marshall

This picture represents his pre-Alistair Sim appearance of later years. Determined and ambitious, he was a Penlington acolyte who became important later on as a climber and guide book writer in the Peak. I don't think he had any sort of impediment but he always struck me as sporting a public school drawl with its classic underemphasis, delivered with overtones of the working class. He never used anyone's Christian name but then perhaps he was not of that persuasion in spite of Vaya con Dios!

71

Llanberis Pass 1954: M. Gadd, W. Richardson, E. Marshall, Geoff Gibson, *unknown, unknown,* J. Fisher, M. Ridges, D. Penlington (see Reflections by J. Fisher). *Photo: Mike Moore.*

Walter Richardson

Known as Wally. Small in stature but a great enthusiast and also pally with Penlington since both came from Rolleston on Dove, Sir Oswald Moseley's country seat. He is memorable for an arcane style of description, especially of young women who, in appropriate cases, he relates as having good form. Nothing to do with a visit to the Bwci (Welsh). Wally's trusting nature would have made him an excellent candidate for the depredations of financial advisers. It is worth noting that a lot of Oread people live in or have connections with Rolleston but I have not noticed any armbands or funny moustaches.

The last on the left

This man I shall take as Raymond Handley because the confusion gives me a platform from which to assail him in prose. It is not, of course, since Raymond enjoyed more exalted company and, anyway, always wore trousers of superior cut and style. He had the first pair of P.A.'s in this country, climbed with the best in the land and never let you forget it. Thoroughly tamed by his most recent wife, he enjoys golf and verbal fights with Fisher, always claiming that he has won. If you want to see a picture of him in 1950 look up p.140 of *Cumbrian Rock* by Jones and Milburn. I was hoping to see the caption to the picture would cite him as "unknown" but I fear it failed to give me that pleasure.

As a P.S. I gather from an informed source that the man is almost certainly Mike Gadd. I have nothing on him of consequence. Sorry old chap, but then you did become a colonial, having lived in New Zealand for thirty odd years.

H.P. SAUCE

JOHN FISHER

An attempt on the fourteen peaks was the major enterprise of the two-week industrial holiday available in August 1953 to Mike Moore and myself. Hitching to North Wales from Lichfield we spent the first week in the idyllic but unfrequented Cwm Cowarch, and the second in Ogwen. It had been agreed that, if I joined him on this major walk, he would climb rocks with me. I remember that Grooved Arete and the Direct Route, including Gibson's Chimney, were climbed in outsize Vibram soled, second hand boots. A.C.C. chap, name unknown, but even then a computer expert and ex-Cambridge, staying at Helyg, climbed with us on the Chasm and then joined up for a shot at the fourteen peaks. His boots were nailed and one of them had the sole secured to the upper by a loop of copper wire.

Starting from Foel Fras on the hottest day of that year, we completed the trip in just under sixteen hours but our new companion abandoned his effort after the Glyders. I think the wire broke.

Our camp was in Ogwen. The finish for us was Pen-Y-Pass, then without telephone, making it impossible at that late hour to arrange transport. Happily, as we rounded the twists on the flat towards P-Y-P, we were greeted by a crowd of young men led by our broken booted companion. They plied us with hot soup and tinned fruit and drove us back to Ogwen. It turned out that they were Sandhurst under-officers who had been drinking in the Royal (now Plas-Y-Brenin) and had made several trips to find us. No facetious comment here, just heartfelt thanks for their generosity.

Naturally, Mike and myself were elated at our success, slow though it was. Nevertheless we thought that we were the first Oreads to do so and that belief continued for 45 years. However, I recently mentioned the matter to Harry Pretty who, to put it bluntly, said that we were wrong because he and a bearded Brummie called Stan Moore had done it earlier. I did not hear, nor did Mike, any trumpets before 1953 but when a most senior, eminent, and respected ex-President, and to boot the assessor of this epistle, says so, you radiate the castor oil smile, tug the forelock, and retire.

I think, for the sake of an artful climax, J.F. has slightly misrepresented my words. I merely stated that in 1951 (when no one had the use of a car) S.G.M. and myself started our attempt on the 3,000's from Ogwen (Glan Dena) and thereby had to traverse the appropriate Carnedd summits twice before continuing over Tryfan, and the Glyders, in our quest for Snowdon — *Editor.*

"The memories of men are too frail a thread to hang history from" — *John Still.*

Newsletter, August 1956

REFLECTIONS

A time there was
When I believed the crystal spire
The unknown clouded pinnacle
The only summit of desire.
The years there were,
The precious years of youth,
Lost in the desert sands of learning
That surround the citadel of truth.
At length I scaled its adamantine face
And stood alone where no man stood before
Until my strength deserted hands and failing feet
Perforce began the bitter desolate retreat
Down to a black tarn shore.
But on the shore
I came to see
The summit that I strove to reach
Beneath my feet concealed,
For darkly mirrored in the lake
The beauty of the mountain was revealed.

Jim Kershaw

A PROLOGUE

JACK ASHCROFT

In my own case it all goes back to the early fifties when our guide -(students all) took us into a quarry in the Shropshire countryside and said, "Here, you put the rope up the front, behind the right leg, over the left shoulder and rope down like this —". Over the edge he went. "This can't be right" I thought, "climbing is about going up hill", and so I got a book out of the library, which put me right on the simple theory of what goes up must come down, safely. And that is what climbing is all about.

A few years later after a little more sophistication had been introduced in the use of karabiners, slings, belays, nailing patterns etc., a visit to Skye was called for. I had only found the enthusiasm of the Oread a few months previously and, before the Committee had barely accepted my application for membership, I was up and over the front face of Sgurr Dearg Bheag en route for the Inaccessible Pinnacle. There was a howling gale with negligible visibility. "I'll go ahead, looks alright", said the optimistic Jack and promptly disappeared into the mist. A short distance along the ridge I came back to Dearg Bheag to shout the others on. They were nowhere to be seen or heard, above the roar of the wind. "Came up here didn't I?" — 50 metres down — water running. "This isn't it". I came back up, scrambled onto the Bheag and stood there on that little pap, in the swirling mist with the words ringing in my ears, "due to the magnetic nature of the rocks, the compass is unreliable in the Cuillin". To have tied on a rope to start with wouldn't have been a bad idea!

Eventually the party was reunited: Janet McHarg (later Ashcroft), Mike Turner, Margaret Dearden and Ron Dearden.

Later that year a report appeared in the Newsletter contributed by Ron. "Jack got lost on a knife edge ridge". Not true. The party got parted due to the exuberance of youth, one more exuberant than the rest. Inpin was never seen that day.

I had come to live in Derby in 1953 soon after a weeks holiday in the Lakes.

Whilst staying overnight at Wall End Barn, Langdale, Albert Shutt of the Peak Climbing Club and Stanage Left Unconquerable fame said, "If you're going to live in Derby, the Oread is a good club". In the ODG next morning the headlines in the paper announced the death of a climber in the Alps, Arthur Dolphin. The Leeds climber had slipped on the descent of the South Face of the Geant. Albert was stunned by the news, as indeed all North Country climbers were as recalled in the Chapter An End by Harold Drasdo in his book The Ordinary Route.

I was in the Lakes with Trevor Wheat a Wolverhampton youth club friend at the time and my introduction to walking and climbing mountains had come about by joining the Birmingham College of advanced Technology Exploration Society. The Society mounted an expedition during my few years of membership, to the uninhabited Shiant Isles off the East Coast of Lewis. A study was made of the botany, marine biology, ornithology and geology of the islands. Whilst at Birmingham I did my first rock climbing and read Barford's Climbing in Britain, largely instructional and effectively the first handbook of the B.M.C. Then there was Colin Kirkus' Let's go Climbing – inspirational reading for the most unlikely novice to the climbing scene.

As Albert, Trevor and myself left the ODG and walked up Mickleden over Esk Hause to Portinscale on Derwent Water we talked a lot of climbing and Albert made known his early experiences of climbing with the Peak C.C. of Sheffield.

In the autumn of 1953 I was in Derby and met the Oread in their heartland; – The Bell Tuesday nights. Though my earliest experience of climbing had been through the Birmingham College everything came together in 1954 and my recreational interest was firmly established on mountain and moorland with the Oread. The spirit of the Club in the fifties was 'mountaineering regardless' – written into the Constitution. I soon discovered that diretissimo on the crag, as on mountain and moorland, was the watchword. Orpheus Wall, Top Sail, Trafalgar Wall at Birchen, Apple Arete, Finale Wall and Och Aye Wall at Gardoms were regular test pieces. The majority of the Club however preferred routes like NMC Crack, Whisky Wall and Moyers Climb. But the meet I enjoyed most during my first year with the Oread was the Marsden Rowsley walk. As Richard Gilbert wrote some years ago, "For many of us mountain walking provides the most elevating experience of all both literally and figuratively". Just as Arthur Dolphin's death in the Alps, described as 'An End' in Harold Drasdo's book, so Black Hill, Bleaklow, Kinder and the Gritstone Edges were a beginning for many Nottingham/Derby climbers in the 1950's. The Oread membership went from 35 in 1952 to 83 in 1955.

Having walked and climbed with the Club ever since the early 1950's, from the mountains of Snowdonia, the Lakes, to Scotland, the Alps and Himalaya, I always come back to the Peak District.

Big Country

"It's big country out there".

P. Janes (Early morning mantra)

Follies of 1956: Penmaenmawr to Bryn-y-Wern
P. R. Falkner

Prologue

Many years ago, when I was a young lad, I used to spend my summer holiday with my people at Penmaenmawr. From there I used to make excursions into the mountains, and, venturing a little further each year, in 1943 I succeeded in walking from Penmaenmawr to the top of Snowdon. In later years I looked back on this feat not without certain pride, but nevertheless regarded it as a piece of juvenile folly which I would not care to repeat. This year, however, with the Colne – Rowsley walk deleted from the Meet List, someone (Penlington, I believe) decided that a new marathon must be invented. So it came about that at 10.30 p.m. on Friday, the 1st of June, I found myself bivouacking in a wood above Penmaenmawr in the company of four other maniacs (and more arrived later), bent not only on repeating my youthful exploit, but extending it to include Moel Hebog and thus to end at Bryn-y-Wern.

The Event

We all rose at first light on Saturday, and before we set off arrangements were made with our gallant lady drivers – Betty in the Bedford, and Janet in the Pilot, – to take our gear and meet us at strategic points en route, to supply us with food and pick up casualties. (I was going to say simply "to attend to our needs", but then realised that the average Oread would certainly misunderstand my meaning.) The cars thus functioned as mobile canteens and ambulances.

A start was made at 5.30 a.m. In the lead were four enthusiasts, Penlington, Pettigrew, Hayes and Russell, who had a wild notion of including all 14 "dreitausenders" en route. The other group, Dearden, Parslow, Kershaw and Moore, (Mike), confined their ambitions to reaching B-y-W by any reasonably direct route. Somehow I became separated from both groups and did most of the walk on my own.

The weather rapidly deteriorated and we crossed the Carnedd summits in heavy rain and a furious gale – conditions which threatened to exhaust us all very quickly. Fortunately, the weather began to improve about 10.00 a.m. and for the rest of the day, though generally cool and dull, it was not actively unpleasant.

Descending direct from Carnedd Llewelyn, I reached Glan Dena at 10.40 a.m.; actually before the cars. The "enthusiasts" arrived about 11.00 a.m., having already stained their escutcheons by omitting Yr. Elen. They set off again at 11.30 a.m. for Tryfan and the Glyders, whilst at the same time I set off for the Devil's Kitchen col. The other party arrived at Glan Dena just before we left. Ron Dearden retired at this point.

From now on, apart from contacting the car drivers at Nant Peris at 2.00 p.m., I was on my own until nearly the end of the day. Ascending Snowdon via Cyrn Las, I reached the summit at 4.30 p.m., whilst the enthusiasts went via Crib Goch and were naturally later. At the summit was a B.B.C. mobile T.V. unit, which I presumed to be awaiting Pettigrew's arrival. I contrived to make a brief appearance before the cameras, then set off down to Beddgelert. The final pull up Moel Hebog was distinctly tiring; rather reminiscent of the pull up Win Hill at the end of the Marsden – Yorkshire Bridge Walk, only much more so as Moel Hebog is much bigger. Just below the summit I was delighted to meet the two surviving enthusiasts, Bob Pettigrew and Geoff Hayes. We reached the summit at 9.00 p.m., and feeling very weary but mightily pleased with ourselves, plodded into B-y-W at 10.00 p.m. The others had all crossed into Cwm Pennant by Bwlch Cwm Trwsgl (N. of Moel Lefn) and arrived half an hour earlier.

Support party: Betty Gardiner, Janet Penlington — *Editor.*

THE BRAZILIAN CONNECTION

NEWSLETTER EDITORIALS (EXTRACTS)

Newsletter, September 1955

Joe Brown will lead the world's hardest rock-climb and a new grade will have to be invented for it. The C.C. will refuse to follow Continental practice and just call it Grade VIII. An attempt on the world's seventeenth highest peak by a party of Brazilian schoolmistresses will be unsuccessful.

D. C. Cullum

Newsletter, November 1955

For me the most remarkable feature of the Dinner was the letter signed by three Brazilian ladies and read to the assembled multitude by our President. (How gratifying to learn that the fame of the Oread has spread so far, and that our "big sporting journal" finds readers in such distant lands.) These ladies apparently blame me for the failure of a party of Brazilian schoolmistresses to climb the world's seventeenth highest peak (by the way, can you name it?). I hasten to assure the ladies that in bringing this failure to the notice of the O.M.C. I intended no slur on Brazilian womanhood. However, as their letter seems to call for a reply, here goes.

Firstly, the picture of me alleged to have been sold to the ladies by a man with "much hair and glasses". I cannot imagine what was the object on my chin, said to resemble a dirty rabbit's tail, unless it was a fault in the negative. However, the fact that the ladies were "very disappointed Senoritas" leads me to believe that the pictures were not pictures of me at all. For how could any lady be disappointed?

Secondly, I must flatly deny the accusation that I said Brazilian mistresses were inactive in their sport. I said "schoolmistresses" (a totally different thing, in England if not in Brazil) and I said "our sport" (which may or may not be the same thing). I have never doubted that Brazilian mistresses are indeed "very serious in their sports" and "have much action". But rather than give the ladies proof, as they demand, that they are not active women, I demand proof that they are.

Thirdly, regarding the claim that I am known in Europe as a fast sportsman and have much influence – this I admit.

Fourthly, a simple matter of a scholarship. "Monstrum nulla virtute redemptum a vitiis" does not mean "a monster who's vices are not counterbalanced by a single virtue", but rather "a giant who's virtues are unsullied by a single vice". Modesty forbids further clarification of this point, but really, ladies, if you only knew.

But just a moment ..... one hesitates to impugn the integrity of our President ..... but why is the envelope containing the famous letter addressed in correct Portuguese to "Senor H. Pretty" while the missive itself commences in Italian, "Signor Presidente"? And why is one of the stamps on the envelope Brazilian and the other Mexican? Could we – all who were present at the Dinner – have been the victims of a hoax? Could it possibly be that the President's three Brazilian mistresses are not real people at all?

D. C. Cullum

These Newsletter Editorials had unexpected consequences since they upset Brazilian lady mountaineers and resulted in correspondence from their leader S. Carmello O'Higgins and ultimately, to her attendance as a guest at the 1960 Annual Dinner — *Editor.*

"SOME MEETS ARE LIKE THAT"

J. Kershaw

JOINT MEET WITH M.A.M., BRYN-Y-WERN
BONFIRE NIGHT, BLACK ROCK SANDS

November 1956

Extract

Only one President was present at the meet. We must have scared the one belonging to the M.A.M. However, ours, just to show that he is superior to normal mortals, went swimming. The first thing we knew about it was when a naked figure hurtled down the beach wearing what appeared to be a beard and sporran, and disappeared into the sea. Members were too staggered to take any action and allowed him to have his swim and get dressed again. Later on, however, when he went for another swim, he was joined by Mike Moore, and this time the alarm was given in time. Two naked figures were hotly pursued seawards by the "mob". One member, who had a surfeit of enthusiasm, ran in after them until the member concerned realised that paddling in climbing boots was uncomfortable. Rockets were lit and fired at the swimmers. Roman candles were lit to illuminate the scene and to fire at the naked human targets. No direct hits were scored but some very near misses were registered. Chestnuts and potatoes were roasted and eaten, songs sung in the firelight, and then everybody returned to Bryn-y-Wern and bed.

BULLSTONES CABIN

Autumn 1956

Extract

It was Lord Jim who offered us the pearl (cultured of course) when he spoke of Dylan Thomas. If you should see Moore equipped with a green plastic mackintosh, you will know that the wheel has come full circle. In any case it is probably sheer exhibitionism.

That night I dreamed. I was occupying a castle (of which R.A.Hodgkin spake) and as I remember it, Jim Bury was drawing the rent. There were men about me, dark and cadaverous, when suddenly a door was flung open and upon the threshold stood one, more lean, dark and cadaverous than any man I have ever seen. He wore a wolfskin cap and hung about his neck was a board on which was written in bold Trajan letters "JOHN WELBOURN, BAILIFF." There rose a great cry and amid the noise of thunderclaps I awoke to hear another voice from the outer darkness shouting "— Is Mike Moore there?" It all seemed a bit inconsequential for I knew that Moore had been living in castles like this for years. On coming to I recognised the voice of Geoff Hayes – my watch gave the time as 1 a.m.

Moore, who thought the intruder was a gamekeeper, kept on confusing the issue, but the facts were gradually established.

Geoff, with three companions, had come the hard way via Derwent Edge and Margery hill. It had taken them six and a half hours from Yorkshire Bridge. Having found us in the course of a solo reccy, Geoff returned to fetch his party who were waiting in the shelter of rocks some distance away.

Outside, the wind was getting up and it was raining. Inside, peace and quiet returned. Only the ghost of Gibson roamed abroad.

H. Pretty

RETURN FROM BULLSTONES

Autumn 1956

Extract

Two complete strangers were witness of the final scene. They observed with open incredulity the efforts of Len to heat soup on the rocking floor of a third class compartment. One can only assume that Len put on a special show for their benefit for his stove had behaved with perfect propriety among the draughts of Bullstones Cabin – and in defiance of his efforts to drown us all in a nauseous mess of tea and brussels. Within the space of ten minutes he produced every kind and size of flame but the right one, and managed to engulf us in dense blue smoke. The strangers left at the next stop. They spoke as though it was their destination, but we thought they were seeking air to breathe and the company of persons less addicted to pyromania. It is perhaps fortunate that Jim was not wearing his plastic mac; that Len never so much as mentioned Buenos Aires; and Mike spilled sardine oil only on himself and the President. Otherwise they might have thought us very odd. (others: Len Hatchett, Jim Kershaw, Mike Moore, Laurie Burns).

H. Pretty

A LITTLE LOVE GOES A LONG WAY

RETURN FROM BRYN-Y-WERN

Boxing Day 1956

Extract

Boxing Day dawned bright and clear, little did we know that most of the roads in North Wales were blocked by snow, and therefore it came as quite a shock when we heard the news over the radio. Bird and I set off on the homeward journey about 2.30 p.m. with Janet perched in the back for the short run to Tremadoc. However, we had only progressed about fifty yards when we became bogged down in the snow, wheels spinning madly. Ice-axes and six man-power soon dislodged us from this first drift, but this state of affairs was repeated several times before we eventually fought our way to the main road near Dolbenmaen.

The Tremadoc – Caernarvon road was found to be very "dicey" and we slithered from rut to rut into Portmadoc with hard packed snow grating on the sump and beating against the underside of the wings in a terrifying manner.

Janet (Hughes – later Penlington) was deposited at Portmadoc station and Bird and I, little realising how soon we should be seeing that outpost of British Railways again, pushed for Maentwrog. The causeway was crossed, we paid our 6d at the toll and from then on things began to go wrong. The snow became deeper and more compact so that we soon found that a number plate is an inefficient snow plough. At one point we found ourselves out of control and heading for the wall at far too great a velocity and it was then that we decided it was time to pack in .... . We turned round and ploughed back into Portmadoc. The rest of the journey home is a tale of looking for a garage on Boxing Day in Wales, of cold railway compartments, and even colder waiting rooms, of six hours in a sleeping bag on No. 4 platform, Crewe station, of continually swigging to keep out the cold, and other little odds and ends, like *getting engaged*, arriving at work late and then falling asleep over the desk. Anyone got a set of tyre chains to flog? .....

Paul Gardiner

GLENCOE

Easter 1956

Extract

Gerry Britton provided the car; Dave Penlington contributed a most handsome gadget – a most comprehensive piece of equipment, which cooked, washed up, aired sleeping bags, carried the rope, stimulated, inspired and simultaneously insured against all those rigours which beset us in the wilderness – he called it "Miss Hughes"[1].

From Stanton-by-Bridge to Glencoe in eight hours – overnight – to find Parslow, Turner, Kershaw & Co. encamped in Glen Etive.

"A rock climb on the Buachaille", said Penlington.

"An easy one", said the drivers – recollecting that Penlington had snored the hours away beneath a great heap of sleeping bags. "Crowberry Ridge", said Penlington, "— a moderate route".

The Buachaille is of an almost constant shape when seen from any point within the Eastern quadrant – a most confusing fact – so we consulted the book again, stretched our respective imaginations and thought it a pity that Murray couldn't have found someone who could draw the mountain in a recognisable fashion!

The second pitch was surprisingly hard – no belay in 110 feet, and D.P. ferreting about on toe holds. Gerry and myself traversed crab-like on to easier ground. The weather was perfect – we climbed in shirt sleeves.

A series of short entertaining walls followed. We professed to recognise the V.S. alternative fork in Crowberry Gully to our left. (All good front men can recognise at sight, preferably from a distance, the famous V.S. alternatives). Shortly afterwards Penlington was balancing about on the flank of an overhanging nose. It was a hard moderate, and it wouldn't go; so down into a snow-filled gully bed to find an exit by the right-hand wall where it grew upward to the roof of a shallow cave. We spied Crowberry Tower at the head of its ridge a long way to our right.

Apparently we had wandered without particular merit on to D Gully Buttress and, as someone once remarked to Smythe when he confessed to having merely connected different pitches of half a dozen routes on Lliwedd, – "You haven't done a real climb at all then".

Harry Pretty

[1]Janet Penlington (née Hughes) — *Editor.*

A LITTLE HISTORY

ERIC BYNE COMES CLEAN (*EXTRACT*)

Newsletter, May 1956

Now I have reached the age of no shame. If I don't wish to follow on a rope up a hard climb, I no longer feel guilty of cowardice, but answer complacently, "Ah, but you should have seen me a quarter of a century ago", when Clifford Moyer and I began rock climbing in 1927.

So let's begin then, and in my own modest manner I will tell you how good I was, so that you can compare the past glories with the shell you know now – you're getting this for nothing remember.

I was on the "Dole" and trying to satisfy my mother's ambition, which was to see me an expert banjoist like my Burton-on-Trent grandfather and uncles.

Face climbs at first appalled me. I had a highly developed sense of fear which, coupled with strength to weight ratio, usually meant that I could quite safely lead and climb the V.S.'s of our day, simply because fear and strength gave a clutch on handholds which would not be denied. Yet the fact remained that a hard lead on a face usually meant a nightmare afterwards. Believe it or not, I did make one or two hard new face routes, and yet doubt whether I should receive any credit for these. After all they were accidental, and only "went" because fear took hold and strong clutching hands took control and hauled the body up instead of allowing the brain to balance the body down. A typical example was the Count's Buttress on Stanage Wall End, a climb not repeated until Arthur Dolphin proved it still possible in 1950. Another route was the Tower Face Direct on Wall End, and the second ascent of this has been deferred until Easter of this year, when Peter Biven clawed his way up this unrelenting wall. I warned you I was going to tell you how good I was.

And so the years rolled on. I founded the Sheffield Climbing Club in 1933, and discovered that all my friends were better climbers than I. I went to the Lakes for the first time and, during a week of incessant heat wave, exhausted my companions (amongst whom was my future wife) by dragging them along to the ascent of nineteen climbs in Langdale, on Scafell, and around Great Gable, and all this on a diet of boiled potatoes, scalloped potatoes, fried potatoes, baked potatoes, raw potatoes, and bread. That's what a holiday on the "Dole" meant – and so you can imagine how like a millionaire I felt when a week later, I wrote an article on Moss Ghyll, sent it to the *Out of Doors* magazine, and received two guineas for it.

I was reaching my Peak form in 1934 when I came to Birmingham on the back of a lorry, with 10s.0d. in my pocket, and two heavy suitcases (mostly containing climbing gear). You've got to admit I was tough to come to a town like Brum! Could any place be more God-forsaken to one who had climbed every weekend on gritstone for six years? No Crags! No money! What would you do chum? I had a job with poor wages, but could manage to get to the Peak about once every six weekends. The remaining five I used to travel about on foot exploring the town. Sunday nights were spent in the Reference Library wading gradually through the complete set of the Fell and Rock Journals, and on one occasion I was "nabbed" at 10.30 p.m. by a copper who found me climbing on the town Hall. However, he too was a climber, a Cumberland native, and knew my landlady who came from Welsh Wales.

Then I had a break. J. W. Puttrell (God bless his name and memory) introduced me to E. W. Steeple, and the latter sponsored my membership to the M.A.M. I was the "baby" of the club, and they thought me mad. I gave them a lecture on grit which was so long-winded and detailed that it had to be continued at a further date. However, it brought me friends – R. E. W. Pritchards, the companion of H. M. Kelly, and Harold Restall, the kindest and most generous personality I've ever met. He took me to Wales, to the Cotswolds, to the Peak, and we climbed regularly together – and I repaid him by handing him over to the Sheffield Climbing Club's fiercest tiger on a joint Stanage meet. Harold climbed more V.S.s that day than all the rest of his climbing life and it's still a mystery how he managed to navigate his Morris Isis back to Brum. Perhaps the car should take the credit, for it's the same one he still uses, despite the passing of 20 years, and if it's possible for a car to possess a soul, then the Isis must certainly come within that category.

This period saw my wife and I putting up new routes on the Wall Buttress of Gardom's. Of these the best being perhaps the very severe Right Hand Crack. It was a hard lead. It still is a hard lead, and if you don't believe it, ask Ernie Marshall. He could tell you a tale about this crack.

After this, deterioration began. Lack of climbing opportunities during the War led to this, and when hostilities ceased I began to meet the new school: Harding, Dolphin and others. Then I knew that as a rock climber I had never been in the top class. My own trivial efforts could not be compared with those who produced such daring ascents on the cliffs of Llanberis, the precipice of Cloggy, or the steep crag of Gimmer.

Fortunately, at this time I met the "Burton Oread", liked Harry Pretty's flowing handlebar moustache, and remembered taking George Sutton up Blind Man's Buttress on Cromford Black Rocks, early in his career. The Guide Book work was beginning, and George and Harry's part in this is now history.

However, my rapidly declining standard on rock could no longer be denied. But my ego received a boost at this critical period. First I took over the Organisation of Meets for the M.A.M. Then White Hall was opened and I was able to exhibit my remaining talents to complete novices and, finally, the Sheffield Area Guide Book was published and proved a best seller. Life was rich, my friends many and sincere. The Oread made me President, then exalted me to Honorary membership. The Mountain Club saw fit to offer me Presidency. And so here I am, in all my glory, rich in friends numbering amongst the hundreds. I feel there can be no doubt that I must be good, despite the fact that George Sutton has been known to call me "stubborn", and Harry Pretty has said I've a "single track mind" (however, they are privileged). In view of all I have written, my ego needs but one more thing. I think I would be satisfied if Jim Kershaw were to pen a poem or ballad in my favour.

Yet perhaps even this would not satisfy my desires, for there is something else I would wish if it were possible – and that is, I'd like to go back – to see again Colin Kirkus on Stanage; or Maurice Linnell in Robin Hood's Cave; to follow Cliff Moyer up one of his face routes; to sun-bathe with Derrick Ritson, even to repeat the Robin Hood Girdle with Toni Nicholson; a Toni who started up Inverted V fully clothed and, several hours later, descended Flying Buttress completely nude except for socks.

ERIC BYNE   *Newsletter (Extract), November 1957*

The last time I was in Abbey Brook Cabins to sleep was about 1931, with Clifford Moyer and "Och Aye" (Jack) MacLeod. A howling wintry blizzard raged outside and idly with a pencil, I wrote on the wooden wall:

> "First it friz and then it blew,
> Then it friz and then it snew,
> And shortly after then
> It friz, and snew and blew again."

Perhaps this is not quite correct but anyway it was something like. It's a small world. I was walking down Millers Dale and Water Cum Jolly in the company of Harold Drasdo of White Hall and a number of tough-looking youths from Saltley College, when suddenly the bearded lad beside me burst out laughing, and as I gazed at him with amusement, he apologised and said, "Ever been in Abbey Brook Cabins?". "Sure", I said, "Before you were born though – why?". "Well", he replied, "I've always wanted to meet a guy called Eric Byne who wrote a verse on the wall, which often makes me laugh". Can you beat it?

LETTERS . . . TO THE EDITOR

MAKING THE RIGHT CONNECTIONS

Summer 1956

Dear Editor,

I would draw your attention to the article on Kuhtai in the March/April issue of the newsletter. I quote from the first paragraph " ......solved the problem of continental travel once and for all – have a sleeper ......" From my experience, this idea turned out to be a complete shambles!

On the outward bound journey to Austria, we were to connect up with the sleeping car at Aachen. So far so good! We had reasonable bunks and a not too broken night's rest. We requested a call for 7 a.m. the next morning, as we had to change again for the rest of the journey. At 9 a.m. we awoke with a start and looked out of the window. We were in railway sidings and quite, quite alone – no more coaches, no engine, and, to our horror, no conductor or official in sight. The fifteen or so travellers gathered together for consultation and after a while demanded from a passing linesman, in our best German, to know where we were. He informed us we were in Munich sidings but couldn't say where we were supposed to be going, then wandered off whistling. Nobody dare leave the train to trot back along the tracks to the station as sundry engines kept puffing along the lines and shunting us on to different sets of lines. Eventually, $4\frac{1}{2}$ hours later, we were rescued by an efficient looking engine and hooked on to a passing express. Through all this, we reached our destination 10 hours late.

We were naturally very wary on the return journey and so were delighted to discover that our sleeper had H. & C. running water, fitted carpets, wardrobes, and all mod. con. We spread ourselves out in this luxury, practically unpacking all our ski-ing gear, and settled down to a last bottle of wine and a good night's rest. However, such luck was not to be ours. At 2 a.m. there was a horrible grinding noise and we came to an abrupt halt. An agitated official came rushing down the corridor, yelling at us to get out, "Schnell, schnell", and we very hastily dressed and packed and jumped down on to the rails, thinking the train was on fire at least. It turned out that the back axle had broken. So we were pushed headlong into another train, which had pulled up alongside, and spent the remainder of the journey to Ostend on hard wooden seats, trying to catch up on our broken sleep.

And then I am recommended to "have a sleeper" – it's worth the extra quid": Not b— likely! From now on I take to the air.

"PEGASUS"

Dear Sir,

I was delighted to read in the May Newsletter the amusing, but no doubt apocryphal, account of the experiences of your correspondent "Pegasus" on the Continental Railways; it might almost have been culled from the pages of Jerome Klapka Jerome's Three Men on the Bummel, or should it be the Alps in 1864?

However, I can assure you, Sir, that we are unlikely to emulate his misfortunes, and, if I may, I will quote from the Travel Agent's plug:- ".....these coaches are the very last word in modern transport. By day the compartments have the appearance of superior 2nd class accommodation ...... deep soft seats and large wide windows. By night the attendant (it should read attendantesses – curves like linked Christies) transforms the interior into a sleeper .... Three wide foam rubber berths ....pillow and blankets .... reading lamps .... air conditioning" .... Etc. etc.

The fact lives up to the description, and one travels in this style, in one compartment, from Calais to Innsbruck. As far as I can see, there can be no snags – one can drink unlimited quantities of "vin ordinaire ouvert", and sleep until 9.00 a.m. with an easy mind.

I can only assume that "Pegasus" is a bloated plutocratic spendthrift and not a penniless proletarian like myself. Let us hope that his wings prove to be better than those of Icarus when he reaches the alpine sunshine!

Yours faithfully,
Ernie Phillips.

"Pappenhacker says that every time you are polite to a proletarian (sic) you are helping bolster up the capitalist system". Scoop, Evelyn Waugh.

No mention of "penniless proletarians"— *Editor.*

NEW BLOOD AND FUTURE VITALITY

Newsletter (Extract), February 1957

Dear Sir,

It is unreasonable to expect the same people to remain quite as keen year after year. The little band of youthful enthusiasts who built up the Oread in its early years are no longer quite so youthful and most of them have acquired ties and responsibilities of some kind. Also some of the novelty is bound to wear off. I still enjoy climbing on Tryfan and Stanage, and I hope that I shall go on doing so for a long time yet, but I will freely admit that I cannot get as excited over the prospect of a visit to these now familiar crags as I did twelve years ago when they were a new and enchanting prospect.

The third point follows from this. The future vitality of the club does depend very much on attracting keen young members who are coming to the hills for the first time; and I sometimes wonder if we are going the right way about this. These cosy family parties at Bryn-y-Wern are all very nice (I enjoy them immensely myself) but are they really what the younger people want? Trevor Panther's particular brand of fanaticism does not greatly appeal to me at the moment, but ten years ago I think it probably would have done, and I have a definite feeling that the injection of a bit of neo-Pantherism into the policy of the Oread might be all to the good.

Yours,
P. R. Falkner.

Editorial comment   *Newsletter, December 1957*

NEW BLOOD

Unpleasant stories have been circulating recently whose general burden is that more than one newcomer has been turned away from the Oread by the lack of welcome he has received; by the fact that members were so engrossed in their own little cliques that he could find no-one to climb with. If these stories are true (which I hope is not the case) they reveal a very shameful state of affairs indeed, and one which would have been inconceivable two or three years ago. The Oread has always in the past opened its heart to strangers; it was in fact its remarkable feeling of camaraderie that attracted me to it, and I am certain that that goes for a lot of other members too.

D. C. Cullum

Plus ça change, plus c'est la même chose — *Editor.*

CRAG SNIPPETS

DAWSON'S ROCKS

Newsletter, April 1957

Reference to an earlier article by Brian Richards describing climbs with Wilf White at Anchor Church (Ingleby) and Dawson's Rocks (sometimes referred to as Carver's Rocks).

Sir,

I have just received the Oread Newsletter for February and thought Brian Richards might like to know that Peter Harding and I did five or six routes, mainly S and VS standard, at Dawson's Rocks between 1945 and 1949. One I remember vividly, we called the Swashbuckle. It went over a rotten overhang near the middle of the cliff. Other climbs we named Oak Tree Crack, Stonnis Slab, Ash Tree Groove, Gorse Groove and Beech Corner. I doubt if I could identify these – at least without a visit!

Yours,
Tony Moulam.

The 1949 Oread also climbed at Dawson's Rocks — *Editor.*

WHITE HALL ROCKS

Newsletter, August 1957

All this waffle about which Sutton did the White Hall rocks guide – let me reveal the horrid truth. That indefatigable writer of guide books, Uncle Eric, despatched the inevitable wad of notes to Geoff Sutton, who asked me what I thought about them. When I had exhausted my full range of blasphemous comment, having but recently rescued the then President of the Oread (one H.P.) from a dilemma on these same cliffs, we decided on a fateful evening just to have a look at the crag again. Of course, the first climb Eric told us about in Mosedale's day was up a detached buttress (this, of course, is not unusual on White Hall rocks, since nothing is attached very firmly to anything else). By sitting on the main crag, six of us put our feet against the detached buttress and pushed – thus erasing one climb in entirety from any future guide book. It was some hours before Eric deigned to speak to us again – but as you perceive this setback did not deter him from writing his guide notes. On this fateful evening, I just missed Geoff Sutton's head by knocking a rock out of a V.S. which I was imprudent enough to climb (on a top rope). Several other near misses occurred. Eventually we gave up. If Geoff has since been on these cliffs, he is madder than I thought – they should be blown up! (New members, please note – there will be no blood feud or libel case between Eric Byne and myself – he knows me too well, and I've said the same thing for years anyway!).

George Sutton

CASTLE NAZE

Newsletter, November 1957

Vandals have levered off the top of Castle Naze Pinnacle, and the crag therefore is without a pinnacle.

TREMADOC — SCRATCH

Some few years ago a new group of cliffs was discovered near Tremadoc, climbing commenced, and some very fine new routes were worked out by members of various climbing clubs.

I heard about these cliffs some five years ago when the main climbing centres were the Llanberis Pass and the Ogwen Valley. It was said that these cliffs, being near the coast, provided excellent climbing when the higher crags were shrouded in mist and rain; this is quite true, but to get on to them and really enjoy the climbs fine weather is recommended as the difficulties can be as great as many in the Llanberis area.

I did one or two of the easier routes, and then two years ago I started doing some of the more difficult ones in the company of Harry Smith and Trevor Jones. One day Trevor and I went to do one of the harder routes called Scratch on a day that was damp but not raining. Trevor, who had done the route before, elected to lead and climbed without much difficulty to the first stance. This was a grass ledge apparently stuck to the face of the very steep slab by grass and mud alone; the belay was a very small spike. After I had joined him he led across the face of the slab to the foot of a very steep groove which constituted the crux of the climb. I joined him at the foot of it and he began to layback up it. I could see that the finger crack was greasy and the wall for the feet green, and as his rubbers kept slipping it looked to me that a descent would be necessary. After much grunting and groaning Trevor decided (as I had already) that it would not go that day. After changing positions I began to descend to the grass ledge and found that though the ascent of the slab had been fairly easy the reverse was not the case.

After a little time I managed to perform a descending mantleshelf and alighted on the grass ledge, feeling it shudder as I did so. I considered that the belay was not good enough to hold us if a slip occurred, and as the ledge seemed liable to collapse I decided to insert a piton. Trevor negotiated the wall with difficulty and as he let himself gingerly on to the ledge I felt it descending like a lift under me, slowly at first, and then with increasing speed. Trevor shouted: "Hold me!" which I tried to do whilst still descending, until with a slight jerk we were arrested by the rope through the peg. It quivered, but with a great feeling of relief I realised it was well and truly in, and Trevor by this time suspended from me facing outwards on the steep slab. I slowly lowered away until he was able to obtain footholds. Our descent continued without further mishap.

We vowed afterwards to handle gently in future any sea cliff grass which obviously had not the tenacity of the "Cloggy" variety.

Ray Handley

Originally printed in the M.A.M. Journal 1958.

TIMES CHANGE

"TEMPORA MUTANTUR, ET NOS MUTAMUR IN ILLIS". (HARRISON 1577)

1957 and 1958 were significant years. The Golden Oldies period was drawing to a close. An unforeseen crisis, concerning Bryn-y-Wern, enforced some hard decisions.

Charlie Cullum had lost some of his enthusiasm as Newsletter editor. He complained at lack of articles etc., and noted that, since his move to Manchester, he was no longer at the centre of club affairs. But in 1957 he continued to publish forceful Editorials fully up to the high standards that he had maintained since 1953. Extracts are reproduced below — *Editor.*

Editorial (Extract) *Newsletter, January 1957*

Two mountaineering tragedies occurred almost simultaneously during the last few days of 1956, one on the highest peak in Britain and the other on the highest peak in Europe. In neither case was anyone hurt in a fall; in both cases uninjured parties attempting to descend were killed by exposure. And there the parallel ends.

The Nevis victims were inexperienced in Scottish winter mountaineering, although they were all good rock climbers and one had led an ascent of the Matterhorn – but the weather on Nevis at Christmas is likely to be more violent than that on the Mattterhorn in midsummer, and the snow and ice conditions much worse. And although one newspaper said they intended to spend the night on the summit, they were not equipped for sleeping out. They also made a number of errors of judgement. First, it was rash to continue with their ascent of South Castle Gully in a blizzard when they could at least have got to the C.I.C. hut or the distillery, if not Fort William. Benighted in vile weather and unable to descend they chose a poor place for a bivouac and failed to construct any kind of a shelter. And perhaps the lone survivor erred in leaving his friends while he went for help, instead of flogging them into some kind of physical activity. But no one who was not there can pass judgement on that. However that may be, as soon as the alert was given parties set out from Fort William and spent three days searching the mountain in bad weather for four youths. Even when three bodies were found and it was certain that the fourth was also dead, the search for his body went on, at no small risk to the searchers, who knew that their efforts must be in vain.

This reflects great credit on all concerned, but who would have backed out? It is both a natural reaction and a moral obligation for a man to do all he can to help persons in desperate circumstances. No swimmer would refuse to go to the help of a drowning man; nor would any mountaineer fail to do all in his power to save fellow-mountaineers when they were threatened by death. Or so one would have said a month ago.

Vincedon and Henri slowly froze to death on Mont Blanc because a whole town full of expert mountaineers refused to lift a hand to help them. It was known by the evening of December 26th that the two students must be in serious difficulty, but although December 27th and 28th were gloriously fine, not a solitary guide set off to look for them. The French Air Force made several attempts to rescue them by helicopter, which continued during the bad weather of the last days of December, and which might have succeeded but for the crash in which a pilot was injured. Terray arrived in Chamonix on the 29th and went up the mountain the next day in foul weather with four others – all the support he could find. This gallant but pathetically small party turned back without reaching the doomed men, after misunderstanding a message from a helicopter. Their leader declared that if the guides had gone up in the good weather of December 27th, when the alarm was first raised, they could have effected a rescue without great danger or difficulty, for the snow conditions were not bad. But the guides of Chamonix had failed in their trust.

The Nevis victims were comparatively inexperienced and ill equipped. They got into difficulties because of the inexperience and consequent misjudgement. They died in spite of the endeavours of their would-be rescuers.

D.C.C.

Editorial (Extract) *Newsletter, May 1957*

In this issue is a letter from Ernie Phillips on the subject of litter. He speaks of "abominations in Langdale", and he speaks truly. Broken beer bottles on the summit of Bowfell were taken there by climbers, not Teddy boys. And the Achille Ratti Hut, next door to Raw Head Cottage, suffered damage at the hands of campers who broke in, and who must have been the owners of nice respectable cars which were parked outside on Easter Monday. Also at Easter, property in Borrowdale was maliciously damaged. The heap of cans and bottles in the Llanberis Pass reached an intolerable level a long time ago. Now the pertinent questions are, who is responsible, why do they do it and what can be done to prevent them?

There is no doubt that Teddy boys and other youngsters of a like outlook are in some measure to blame. The police are doing their best to deal with them, but the most effective measures are probably those adopted by the locals, notably in Langdale. These measures are of a homely nature, like pitching the culprits into rivers. But I hope and believe that the cult of vandalism for its own sake is a passing phenomenon, and that rough and ready self defence will probably tide us over.

D.C.C.

Editorial (Extract)   *Newsletter, September 1957*

In an Editorial I had been going on in pontifical tones about the uses and misuses of climbing ropes, and just as I reached the final peroration the typist put these words into my mouth: "False SECUTIRY is worse than none at all". Oh yes. I quite agree. If I couldn't have the real thing I'd rather do without altogether. Nothing worse than this shoddy imitation stuff hanging in festoons all over the crag. It's as bad as an Irishman demanding shamrock when over in Ireland there's whole mountains full of the genuine article. Real secutiry for me every time.

And then someone, writing up a new route, said, "Step out on to the fact of Marble Wall." Well, when you've been climbing on friction for the last fifty feet there's nothing more comforting than a good solid fact to step out on. This proves, if proof were needed, that a lot of modern routes aren't really there at all. They exist only in the imaginations of the people who climb them. I'm not suggesting that they don't actually climb them, only that they aren't there at all for ordinary people. A mod. Diff. is a fact. An XS isn't.

D.C.C.

BRYN-Y-WERN

The following items appeared in Newsletters for February, March, August and December 1957

Mrs. Hall, the owner of Bryn-y-Wern, is in the process of selling the estate. Her price (£5,000) is hopelessly beyond our means, and at present our only hope appears to be to negotiate a new lease with the purchaser, if any.

The minutes of the previous A.G.M. having been disposed of, Harry Pretty spoke about Bryn-y-Wern. Mrs. Hall had wanted to sell the estate but had changed her mind. She was unwilling to sign a ten-year lease in case her son wanted to live there. The Club has been given first option on the purchase, but the Committee had decided there was no chance of raising the £5,000 demanded. The present position was that we had paid rent up to the end of 1956 and Mrs. Hall had now promised to sign a three-year lease.

Bryn-y-Wern was recently offered for sale in the Manchester Guardian, though we are still negotiating for a three-year lease. The Club has not been officially notified.

The news about Bryn-y-Wern (see Oread in Shorts) is most disturbing. Of course, if the estate were sold it would not necessarily mean that we should lose the hut. In all probability the new owner would be willing to sign a new lease. The disturbing feature is that when Mrs. Hall nearly sold the estate last year, we asked her to give us the first chance of purchasing it if she decided after all to sell. We are at present negotiating for a longer lease.

Yet we have not been told officially that the estate is up for sale. The whole thing is being done almost surreptitiously, behind our backs. Of course, Mrs. Hall is not under any legal obligation to offer the property to us, but she is under a moral obligation. This by-passing of the Club does not suggest very good faith, and makes one wonder what sort of relations will exist between our landlady and ourselves if after all she should fail to find a purchaser.

Sir,

A point has now been reached where further discussion, negotiation, or search, is pointless unless there is an immediate response for a loan (in connection with a new hut). The North Wales district has been scoured several times. Many houses and buildings have been investigated and owners interviewed. Our need for a Club hut has been made known in any quarter where it was felt to be profitable. All with little success. The result is that it is now considered that the immediate purchase of a house or suitable building is the only solution, and that the renting or leasing is impracticable. One house is under consideration; that is by the church in Cwm Pennant, the probable price being in the region of £500.

However, obviously no approach can be made to the owner without something in the kitty, and it is imperative that this is done in the immediate future, for two reasons. First, the owner is undecided whether to sell or retain the house for renting to visitors on a weekly basis, and second, when the nuclear power station project (at Trawsfynnydd) gets under way all the available accommodation will be absorbed and a demand created which will place prices beyond our reach.

The Club membership exceeds 90, and even allowing for disinterested members, and those abroad and in H.M. Forces, the average loan required is only £7 – £10. Consider, for a loan of £7–£10 you can secure permanently a place in the hills. It would cost this amount to rent a house or even a caravan for one week in high summer, and you most certainly wouldn't get it back. A very few visits would repay you for the inconvenience of the loan. The actual terms of the repayment will be made clear by the Committee if any actual progress is made.

In my opinion if the appeal is unsuccessful any further effort with regard to the hut would be fruitless.

If anyone knows or can find a suitable place where the owner will come to terms, please come forward at once. The furniture from B-y-W can be transported there.

L. H. Burns, Hon. Treasurer.

BUT SOME THINGS GO ON FOREVER

In March 1957 Phillip Falkner took over the Presidency as the crisis over Bryn-y-Wern was about to unfold. But outdoor Meets, and other rites of passage, continued unabated. Jim Kershaw, at the height of his powers, also entertained. Pettigrew was about to go east ..... for the first time.

THERE WAS TROUBLE ON KINDER THE OTHER WEEK

The aristocracy had gone,
The landed gentry sunk to low estate,
The shooting rights on Kinder's barren lands
Were leased through agent delegate
To a financial brotherhood,
Seeking to wash with feathered blood
The taint of commerce from their hands.
Rag and bone kings and magnates in cotton
Assumed the sport of long-forgotten dukes.
A guard of keepers stood with gun in hand
To turn away with shot and foul rebukes
The gentle trespasser upon the land.

National Parks and rights of way
Were granted for the public use,
The People's Park Police were formed,
The Nag's Head made a calaboose
And some spare bureaucrat or other
Appointed the climbers' Big Brother.
Where formerly we roamed at will
Avoiding far-flung keepers,
Now voluntary Polizei
Sleuthhound our steps in creepers.

J. Kershaw

OREADS IN SHORTS 1957, 1958

Bob Pettigrew is now at the Outward Bound Sea School at Aberdovey, and flies out to Malaya in July ("to help Pete Cole found the S.E. Asia Section of the Oread"). Bob has recently been elected to the Alpine Club and consequently is entitled to drink with Falkner once more.

May 1957

During the day Peter Janes and Ray Handley had been arguing about the quickest way to get to Cwm Sylin from Bryn-y-Wern. The argument ended in Peter betting Ray he could run back to the hut quicker than Ray could motor back. Peter did the run in the fantastic time of 35 mins, but Ray beat him by 1 min. They agreed it was a close race and called off the bet, much to Janes' relief.

June 1957

The new C.C. journal contains accounts of several new routes by Oread parties. Pity they didn't think of putting them in their own Club's publication first.

June 1957

Ronni Phillips and Margaret Hooley, occupied in taking up the bathroom lino at B-y-W., found behind the lavatory waste pipe a perfume bottle labelled "Sweet Pea".

June 1957

The weekend of 28th/29th June provided us with a remarkable and perhaps unique occasion. It was the 30th Anniversary of Eric Byne's advent to climbing. To mark the event The Oread, The Peak, and the Mountain Club held a Joint Meet on Birchen Edge. Never have so many tents been pitched at Moorside Farm – approx. 60 I believe. On any other occasion it would have been nothing less than appalling – unless you like having some other person's guy lines running over, through, and across your tent. Ernie Phillips, hemmed in on all sides by tents of a lesser vintage than his own, resembled a light opera "Gypsy King" struggling to maintain the dignity of his Boer War W.D. surplus equippage. Mike Moore, close by, might have been one of his profligate sons.

Eric was there of course and appeared to be suffering from the royal malaise of overmuch hand shaking. There were people who hadn't been seen in years - Albert Shutt, Don Morrison, Eric Morrison - and a score of others. Dick Burger was to be seen, looking more Burgerish than ever. Nan and Keith Axon were there, and all in all it was a splendid gathering. For once, there was none of the usual ennui when "for he's a jolly good fellow" caught on towards the end of the party at the Prince of Wales. There were close on 200 climbers, active and retired, at the party and I doubt if there was a single one who did not have some reason to be grateful for the circumstances that led Eric Byne to find his spiritual home on the watershed moors of his native city thirty years ago.

Don Morrison (of Sheffield) has recently returned from Canada where he has been climbing and working. At Eric Byne's instigation he discovered the grave of Cliff Moyer in the R.A.F. Cemetery at Neepawa, not far from Winnipeg. Moyer was killed in a flying accident during the last war and apparently is well remembered by the people round about.

June 1957

Pettigrew arrives in the Far East ...

I arrived in Ipoh by air after a flight of four days via Germany, Italy, the Middle East, India, Burma and Siam. Jack Tucker, who has a fund of stories about Kanchenjunga and Huagaruncho (South America), the acting warden, met me off the plane and we travelled by car to the West coast at the mouth of the Dindings river where the school is situated. Across the Dindings channel opposite the school the heavily forested island of Pankor provided cover for men of force 136, including Freddy Spencer Chapman engaged in espionage and guerrilla warfare in Japanese occupied Malaya during the last war .....to be continued — *Editor.*

November 1957

But before he left ...read on:

14 PEAKS AND ALL THAT

R. G. PETTIGREW   *Newsletter (Extract), August 1957*

The weekend June 28/29th is listed innocently enough in the Club calendar as "Welsh training Walk" to be led by its instigator Dave Penlington.

As a club institution it is youthful since this was the first anniversary of the mountain crossing from Penmaenmawr to Bryn-y-Wern in the Pennant valley. There is little doubt that the original plan arose as a direct result of the abandonment by the Club of long training walks over homeland moors such as the Marsden-Rowsley and later the Colne-Rowsley. These were subjected to a good deal of adverse criticism because the limits were expanding and the pace increasing until Rowsley was once reached in under twenty-four hours from Marsden. That was not a good time, but it illustrated that the Oread had the potential to approach the great feats performed by the Bog-Trotters, one of whom Alf Bridge, is now an honorary member of the Oread. Destructive criticism such as the taunts of "Cross-Country runner" and the like should not deter those who wish for good general fitness in preparation for the Alps, or else-where, from attempting ambitious mountain walks. By this means, stamina and speed, qualities for which average British parties in the Alps are not noted, can be improved, the resulting efficiency makes for more enjoyable ascents and a greater margin of safety.

I have long been an avid protagonist of long mountain walks and, together with Falkner and Penlington, have taken part in all those organised by the Club.

Now Geoff Hayes, Jack Ashcroft, Mike Smith and others are carrying on the tradition whilst some of us must absent ourselves from the Oread scene.

On Friday evening, June 28th, two Oread transports rolled out of Derby on the first leg of Penlington's celebrated Welsh Training Walk. Their arrival at the dubious campsite was staggered by some three hours - Falkner getting his head down first, owing to the lure of fish and chips in St. Asaph, and an unusual quarry approach to the campsite advocated by R.G.P. from the navigator's seat in the Trojan.

The mean time spent in sleep by the two parties was under three hours and by 4 a.m., the participants were roused by Hayes, obviously under the erroneous impression that he had to meet the newspaper special. The ladies having received sealed orders for the day, Messrs. Falkner, Penlington, Ashcroft, Hayes, Smith and Pettigrew departed Craig Lwyd and headed South at a good pace.

Stopping only to write "Penlington" on a grinning horse's skull, the party moved over Drosgl into dubious navigational conditions.

I summarise the remainder of this Pettigrew opus — *Editor*.

06.00	Drum
07.00	Foel Fras
07.45	Carnedd Llewelyn
08.15	Yr Elen
09.40	Carnedd Dafydd
10.00	Pen yr Oleuwen: Cyril Machin provided tea at Glan Dena
12.00	Tryfan: Penlington had foot trouble and withdrew from 14 Peaks
13.15	Glyder Fach: divided into two parties
13.45	Glyder Fawr: (Pettigrew and Hayes only)
14.40	Y Garn (Ditto)
15.30	Elidir Fawr (Ditto)
16.00	Nant Peris
17.00	Snowdon summit (Ashcroft, Falkner, Penlington)
18.15	Crib Goch (Pettigrew, Hayes)
19.00	Snowdon summit (Ditto)
21.00	Yr Aran (Pettigrew alone)
–	Forestry camp site: Pettigrew rejoins Hayes
22.30	Moel Hebog (Pettigrew, Hayes. The other party passed over Hebog at 21.20)
00.30	Reached Bryn y Wern (Pettigrew and Hayes. The other party arrived B-y-W at 22.35

Total distance! 44 miles, 14,000' of ascent.

The 1998 brand of young Oread is not noted for this kind of punishment training prior to the Summer Alpine Meet — *Editor*.

BUT THERE ARE ALTERNATIVES

MOUNTAINS IN SPACE

HARRY PRETTY   *Newsletter (Extract), August 1957*

By Loch an Leaothaid we fished and shortly five 8 oz. trout were lying in the heather. On the southern shore of Leaothaid, which is three quarters of a mile long and 500 feet above sea-level, there is a camp site that mountaineer's dream of among the industrial grime of a winter's day in the Midlands. There, you find a strip of pink sand by the water's edge; much of it chewed up by the countless feet of thirsty deer. Behind, rises a steep amphitheatre dense with ancient twisty oaks, birch, and rowan; and lush with fern and moss. A mile to the east is the long west cliff of Quinag. Three miles away is Drumbeg on what must be one of the worst roads in Scotland - and long may it remain so. Twelve miles away by track and road is Lochinver. Nine miles by similar means is the Inchnadamph Hotel. The remainder is wilderness.

For myself I shall remember Loch an Leaothaid as it was on the evening of June 29th – the solitary figure of Brooker, thigh deep in the shallows, – a black shape moving slowly across a broad avenue of light that glittered down the water. A lone Northern Diver fishing in his own polished fashion on the edge of the light blaze. The only noise the intermittent humming of the reel and the light splash of minnow touching water. "Are you tired of watching"? said Brooker after several hours. "No", I replied, for this was the kind of night that had to last a long, long time.

ROCHES TO BUXTON

JIM KERSHAW   *Newsletter (Extract), November 1957*

Tents were packed at 2 p.m. and we followed the ridge of the Roches for some way, descending to the Dane via Blackbrook. Three Shire Heads was reached across country with an interesting diversion in the river, and the site of the S.C.C. roadman's shelter (Five Inns, '54 – see Gibsonian folklore). A lane running along a somewhat rusty stream was followed to Orchard Farm and a track past some old mine-shafts led on to Axe Edge.

The sky was cloudless. We watched the sun sink behind Orchard Farm, ridge on ridge of low veldt-like hills silhouetted by the warm smoky glow of the last daylight. In the East the moon had risen, faintly illuminating our path to the Buxton road.

It was one of the finest December days I can remember. For the rest, we met the Nottingham University M.C. returning from castle Naze and were kindly offered seats to Nottingham, a pleasant hour being spent in a pub between Ashbourne and Derby.

Example of frequent meetings with other clubs, all known to each other and assistance with travel so generously given. — *Editor.*

CHRISTMAS AT BRYN-Y-WERN 1957

RONNI PHILLIPS

Extract

Christmas day dawned, breakfast was eaten, some of the men cut fire wood, and some were dispatched to fetch the milk, which turned out to be a long errand as they were unable to pass the Cross Foxes without entering and sampling its wares. Some went climbing and walking and the rest of us, mainly the women, started to prepare our Christmas dinner. 90 potatoes were peeled, 180 brussel sprouts and 15 spanish onions were prepared. 60 bacon rolls were stuck on skewers, 10 pints of soup were made, 6 chickens were carved and their stuffing removed, 16 tins containing peas, beans and carrots and 10, containing fruit for fruit salad, were opened by John Fisher (I gave him this job to strengthen his arm in readiness for when he begins snatching teeth in earnest). 6 Christmas puddings were boiled, copious quantities of bread and rum sauce and gravy were made. Cheeses, biscuits, butter rolls and coffee were laid out. By 6.45 p.m. David arrived with the ice cream and by 7.00 o'clock everything was ready and we all sat down as one big family to eat. I don't think anyone complained about leaving the table still feeling hungry. The washing up and deck clearing operations were organised by John Fisher as usual, and everyone finally collapsed in the lounge where desultory drinking continued until the early hours of the morning.

The rest of the holiday period was marked in many and various activities. Parties climbed on Silyn and Tremadoc and the Snowdon Horseshoe was circuited under excellent conditions, although Pretty only managed to stay the course after ministrations of hot soup on the summit by a boy scout!

June Telfer was "initiated" on the summit of Snowdon by the Vice-president and Secretary, but details of the ceremony are known only to those present.

KERSHAW ENTERTAINS

DERBYSHIRE WEEKEND

Newsletter, January 1958

Ashbourne is a friendly sort of place. Moore, Geoff Hayes and myself arrived there on Saturday hot on the trail of Welbourn who had left for Dovedale on foot. It began to rain and I was persuaded into waiting for the Ilam bus by the other two members of the party who refused to follow my example in buying a pac-a-mac (price 17/4d).

It arrived eventually.

Now the Ilam bus isn't really a bus at all; it's a sort of rival time machine, say 50 years in reverse. Cold Comfort characters share their seats with a crate of fowls, an old sow or two, oblivious to eccentrics in anoraks.

We stepped back into 1957 and the rain at the Isaac Walton, and set off for the stepping stones and Dovedale (myself in pac-a-mac, value 20/-).

Just past the point where you always fall in the river we came across a group of huddled figures outside a cave. They spoke and pointed upwards to where Welbourn had disappeared in search of an old Valkyrie campsite.

Impressed at this well-deserved translation to a higher plane of existence, we retired into the cave and discussed the rival merits of a memorial on the spot, or at Stanage, but were relieved to have him back with us a few moments later in a most ungodly condition. The whole party proceeded to Halldale where tents were set up in high wind and heavy rain.

Sunday morning was fine and sunny. Moore, Geoff and myself setting off for Hartington, Welbourn and party pegging on Ilam Rock, and walking over to the Manifold. It soon began to rain again, Moore and Geoff eyeing my pac-a-mac enviously (value 30/-). We followed the usual path up Milldale and Beresford Dale, tried a scree run down the side of the valley, all going well until a short cut over a bridge which no longer existed, involved us with the serpentine bank of the Dove and brought us into a Hartington bar with a cloth on the pumps and all the farewell sadness of late Sunday dinner.

We ordered a pot of tea, eyed the polished horse brass on the walls and rafters, deplored the weather, and memories came back of previous visits to the Inn.

It is unfortunately possible to walk through Lathkill dale to Bakewell from Hartington. Moore and I were persuaded to do so against our better judgement, as it was still raining and I was obliged to refuse Moore's offer of £2 for my pac-a-mac.

I don't need to discuss the Hartington-Lathkill walk. Most of you have done it in your younger days. There isn't much to it really if you keep walking and talking - time soon passes and you find yourself walking downhill into Bakewell wet through and wondering what the hell you do it for.

The black wet misery of a winter evening stimulates the mind into activity. The night's particular fantasy took the shape of an Oread national Anthem, (tune - Jerusalem), something to sing in your bath at Bryn-y-Wern,

It might go in the following manner:

"And did those feet in Gibson's time
Walk upon England's mountains green,
And was the President himself
Upon the gritstone Edges seen?

etc. etc.

And was the Oread builded here,
Amongst these Welsh Touristic Hills?

Try it yourself and you'll probably get stuck on the second verse as I did.

We finally ended up in a Bakewell café where Moore was delighted to find that I was as wet as he was in spite of the pac-a mac, and, assuming his impeccable Yorkshire accent, shamed a number of walkers from Sheffield into silence.

That's about it, really, except that I had a day off on Monday to get over it. Healthy pastime, mountaineering.

LLANBERIS JANUARY 1958

A Bus Passenger   *(Attrib. Jim Kershaw)*

Surely such an occasion cannot pass by without a mention in the Newsletter. For the first time in many months a bus was being run and furthermore filled to capacity. All credit to the Meet Leader, Pete Gayfer and the many prominent and distinguished motorists who were to be seen mixing with their more pedestrian fellow members. No Bishop graced a tramcar with less condescension. No election candidate handled a noisome brat with as brave a smile.

A bus certainly fosters a sense of unity amongst its passengers. It could hardly be otherwise when thirty-odd individuals are confined together in a steel box on wheels for several hours in acute physical discomfort. There is a feeling of suffering nobly borne for the good of others, of a brotherhood sharing a common disaster. For a brief time Oread is fettered to Oread as inescapably as felon to felon in a Georgia chain gang. The hour of liberty and release is awaited with the same longing. Was America hailed by Columbus with any more joy than The Mermaid, Atcham, on a Friday night by the Oread?

One of the highlights of the outward journey was the distribution of railway travel literature by Moore at Lichfield. Most of it was converted into three-foot long paper darts, which sped about the bus to the danger of passengers. It brought to mind those travel analogies which are used to explain relativity to the layman.

Bolts of lightning striking a railway track simultaneously in front and behind a moving train. Observer A on the embankment, with a set of mirrors and Observer B precariously balanced on top of the train with a similar apparatus. When A is opposite B will the lightning flashes appear simultaneous to both of them? Knowing British Railways it all seems highly irregular, especially when the train is speeded up to 186,284 miles a second to simplify the problem.

What about the poor devil on the roof? Will not A be somewhat startled at the sudden speedup of the 8.10 to Dragthorpe?

I always like the one about the physicists in the lift falling freely down an immensely high building in accordance with Newton's Law of Gravitation. There is a degree of justice in physicists being used for the problem.

I admire the scientific detachment which they display in these alarming circumstances. They experiment with small objects from their pockets, and watch their coins and keys float around weightless in the air.

It is perhaps going a little too far to transport them (still in the lift) into outer space, and wind them on a cable by some supernatural force, or attach the lift to the rim of a huge merry-go-round. Deluded by the restoration of gravity they think all is well again, and eagerly await release on the ground floor of Steins Superstores. Even a physicist deserves some consideration.

To get back to the Llanberis Meet. The more affluent members of the party alighted at Pen-y-Gwryd, and those with historical interests at Pen-y-Pas. A considerable number of people also attempted to camp in this area, including Betty and Paul Gardiner, and Pete Gayfer. Phil Falkner stayed at Ynys Ettws, and Moore, Hatchett, Pretty and myself camped near Cwm Glas Mawr. John and Ruth Welbourn, John Bridges and several others went in search of the Chester Club Hut.

The erection of tents in pitch darkness and heavy rain, on a foundation of thawing snow was most unpleasant. I hadn't got a torch and spent a considerable time feeling around for aluminium tent pegs in the snow. When I had got the flysheet on I crept inside to find that the Lilo plugs were missing, and spent some time tying pieces of torn handkerchief around the nozzles. I was fortunately spared the necessity of making fire having remembered to bring matches. The primus stove was soon going full blast and drying out the tent. Before long I was warm inside a sleeping bag and eating chicken soup.

Saturday was fine with a glimmer of sunshine breaking through the clouds, although the bulk of snow had disappeared from the low-lying ground. Hatchett, Moore, Pretty and myself made our way up Cwm Glas and Parsley Fern Gully in soft snow. Frequent stops were made for the photographers in the party. What happens to these photographs? Only a small percentage of them find their way onto a screen. I suppose it is a modern twist to the time honoured "look at the view" method of regaining one's breath. At the top of the gully we met John and Janet Ashcroft and David Widdows who had finished a day on Snowdon and were descending. We followed their example but by a different route and after reaching camp and cooked a meal, were transported to Pen-y-Gwryd by Ernie Phillips. Here we found the campers from the Pen-y-Pas area, who had been washed out, and Geoff Thompson.

The return journey of the coach was rather uneventful. We learned that conditions in the Chester Club Hut were not quite up to Bryn-y-Wern standard, and that the one leak in the roof was over John Welbourn's bed. There was the usual stop at Shrewsbury for food and drink; the familiar few hundred yards of street which is all one ever seems to see of Shrewsbury. Wilfred Thomas Pinches was incredibly enough the new landlord at one of the public houses. The portcullis was lowered over the Gents in the square. The Bass house next to Gullet Passage had been modernised inside, but spared the accompanying jukebox. The one armed man was no longer behind the bar. The funeral white wash of an empty shop window underlined the ironic epitaph; "Dulleys Successful Seeds". Perhaps he has moved to less stony ground.

There is something about bus meets. When they are a thing of the past, which need not be for some time yet, the memory of them will linger on.

Some Flying Dutchman will flicker along A5 on a Friday night with Jack Ives at the helm, and a crew of damned souls in the seats eternally searching for the pure maiden who alone can bring redemption.

A phrase drifts on the air for a moment as they pass, ".....mysisterscats .....", a familiar haggard face with blood shot eyes looks out of the rear window.

THE HOUSE, HEBRIDEAN WANDERINGS 1957

Extract   *Jim Kershaw*

A sombre deserted land hemmed in by grey cloud and steep grass slopes, wet slabs of rock gleaming from loch and sea, to the west.

I turned the headland, crossing an old wall healed green into the hill and followed the track of cloven feet down to the tide. A mile away was the house, an empty walled croft, black wounds gaping in the slate roof of the barn, deer stealing away up the hill. I was alone with the cry of the gull that circled my head on the incoming breeze. Its harsh satirical laugh followed me as I dodged the paws of the sea lazily stretching between pink and white starved islands of turf, guarding mysterious bottles, bleached bones of wood, matted grass and seaweed, the drifted harvest of the spring.

At length I stood before a half opened green door, and, entering, found the usual litter of a deserted house, a tin or two, a scattering of fleece on the floors, damp lifeless ashes in the fireplace, names scrawled in pencil on the paintwork, nothing of interest except the yellowed pages of a newspaper pasted on a wall revealed by boarding stripped for the fire.

My interest grew as "The Scotsman 1902" promised the cure of alcoholic excess, drink and drug habits. "The Graphic 1899" advertised cigar cutters and sovereign purses. The "Graphic" was a Boer War issue containing early photographs; "Our men cutting off the retreat of the Boers from Papworth Hill, position 1,200 yds. from the enemy"; a drawing in a series of Heroes of the War, "The private who stayed all night with his wounded officer after the battle of "Elands Langte", the gentleman in question leaning back against a fallen horse surrounded by dead Boers and succoured by the private who was no doubt his butler in civilian life; "Life in a camp on the Mooi River which was lately shelled by the Boers; soldiers washing their "togs' on the bank"; gentlemen in topees, trousers rolled to the knees, a daring view of a shirtless man in long toms looking the other way; a curiously prophetic note in a satirical cartoon of infantry mounted on traction engines pursuing the enemy, a drawing of the Kaiser shooting at Sandringham with three companions, the ground littered with dead birds, two ladies looking on passively.

I left the house, fifty years dropping away as I climbed the zigzag hill path into the mist, and I thought about the Boer War, and my own war, and whether there would be a house somewhere in half a century's time treasuring a day from the past, lonely for the cry of the seagull, the step on the threshold that never came.

PANTHER REMEMBERS

Some of us have very definite beginnings to our climbing but mine was so gradual that I do not really know when it started.

As a boy, I was brought up, from the age of eight, in North Wales, so the effect of climbing and mountains on me was part of my growing process – hence the difficulty of stating when I really started.

After many years of reflection, I believe that one instance in 1946 was the event which has welded me to the hills forever ...

It was about December, 1946, I was just 14, and living in Llandudno in North Wales. From near my home I could see many of the hills of Snowdonia, including Carnedd Llewelyn and the cliffs of Craig-yr-Ysfa, although they did not mean a great deal to me then. On this particular morning in December, 1946, the air was fresh and clear. Much fresh snow had fallen on the mountains and the early morning sun shone with incredible brilliance. The dazzling white mountains stood out, sharp and clear, into a deep blue sky while the air was crisp and utterly invigorating. I had never experienced anything so beautiful, or exciting before – how I longed to be up on those snow covered mountains ...

That moment has gone forever but its vision often returns to me. But alas, I can never quite recapture the feelings I had as a boy. Then all was new and mysterious – now I know too much about mountains, and I am never surprised, even on rock climbs or on mountains which I have never seen before. A deeper appreciation however, more than makes up for this.

Trevor Panther, January 1958

. . . AND PERFORMS

FIRST ASCENT OF "FINGERTIND", LAKSELVTINDER, LYNGEN, ARCTIC NORWAY

Standing on Dick Brown's shoulders I felt around for some place to fix a piton. On my immediate left was the vertical, and part overhanging, north face falling in an unbroken bound of 2,000' to the Andersdal Glacier. On my immediate right was the wall of he "Fingertind", up which we had just come, and the upturned face of the third man, Bob Pettigrew, some 100' below. Beyond him, some 800' of slabs swept down to a small snowfield.

Unable to find a crack to take our thinnest peg I stretched up, and up, until my fingers closed over a small hold. A series of fierce fingerpulls, accompanied by quivering muscles and quick nervous breathing, followed.

Suddenly I was on top. We had succeeded and I could not stop myself letting out a violent shout. Screwed up nerves burst forth uncontrollably.

The descent was pure joy. A couple of fine abseils and a long trudge down in magnificent Arctic lighting saw us back in camp after 17 hours.

Trevor Panther

THROUGHOUT 1958, the committee, and others, were enmeshed in the developing crisis over Bryn-y-Wern, but other activities prospered in the Peak District, the Lakes, Wales and Scotland ..... and the first Oread boot was planted on Himalayan snow — *Editor.*

SUILVEN

FRED ALLEN   *Newsletter, June 1958*

After lunch we cached our sacs, uncoiled our two 120' medium weight ropes, tied our rubbers to our waists and walked over to the centre of the face, having decided to climb the first 200' to a grass ledge. At which point we would investigate the main face. Leading through pitch for pitch we found the rock dry, giving very good friction. The holds were rounded and the climbing similar to gritstone. The only disconcerting feature was the apparent lack of runners, we only used four on the complete climb.

The 200' took us about 2 hours and we arrived on a grass ledge, which appeared to encircle the face. At this point we should have decided whether or not to go on, but somehow the thought seemed to have been lost. We were on the climb and intended to reach the summit of the mountain via the remaining 600-700' of vertical face which now towered above our heads. The right hand side looked our best bet, apart from a line of overhanging rocks which we would have to turn, as we had no equipment to surmount them. However, the mountain seemed to look on us kindly, and we thought it would yield a route.

I led off, belayed, Peter[1] climbed, led through, on and on for hours, – the climb seemed never ending. From one of the few good belays we looked at three possible ways of climbing upwards, none of which looked very inviting. After trying the one I favoured three or four times, I asked Peter if he would like to look at it, which he did. After manoeuvring about for a few minutes he went up with a quickness which astonished me, and probably himself. Almost immediately he came to another impasse which he simply had to climb, as he could not reverse. After some ferreting about and dislodging a few lumps of grass he found himself a minute hold which enabled him to surmount a tricky mantleshelf, then he was away out of sight for another 70'.

The overhanging blocks which had caused us some misgiving were passed by traversing towards the centre of the face. After passing them on our right we gradually traversed back again to the right. It was getting on for 7.00 p.m. when Peter, with a shout, announced we were near the top. Another pitch, and we were on easy rock. After scrambling up another 100' or more we were on a grass dome, not very wide, indeed one could walk from edge to edge in a few seconds.

Grading this climb on the hardest pitch, we thought it mild severe.

[1] P. Janes.

Interesting, and perhaps typical of the time, that the route was climbed on sight with no previous or even subsequent interest as to whether it had been done before or whether any previous record even existed — *Editor.*

WASDALE

WHITSUNTIDE 1958

Postscript

I observe in Chris Martin's account that Ron Dearden was accompanied by "his wife". I wonder if Miss Ashcroft has heard about this? – or for that matter has Miss Dearden heard about Mrs. Ashcroft? No – that can't be right since Miss Dearden is now Mrs. Turner, and Mrs. Ashcroft was a Miss McHarg – hm! It is all very confusing and, what with all this intermarriage and the possibility of incredible permutations from future cross breeding, it is likely to become worse – I give up anyway – and so will Jack Ashcroft when Ashcroft junior (male) ups and marries a Miss Dearden and there is a progeny of second generation Ashcrofts – and what relation will they be to the first generation Mrs. Turner? – What a genealogical shambles! — *Newsletter Editor (H.P.)*

And response .....

..... Finally I was interested to read that I was camping in Wasdale with "my wife". My wife-to-be was even more interested as she happened to be in Wolverhampton at that time. Perhaps it would be a sound idea for the Oread to take out an insurance policy to cover the Newsletter against the risk of libel action.

Yours etc.
R. V. Dearden

ERIC BYNE'S ANNIVERSARY MEET
BIRCHEN EDGE

Newsletter, August 1958

Several Oreads made a recording for the B.B.C., Midland Region, during the recent weekend at Birchen. The emphasis of the short recording was amended by the Producer, when he heard of the reason why so many climbers had congregated at one place. He decided to include Eric in the programme and record on the spot rather than at Stanton-by-Bridge, which was the original idea. The recorded conversation very briefly covered the change that has come about in gritstone climbing during the last 30 years, and went on to discover what (theoretically) happens to youngsters when they first enter the orbit of a mountaineering club. Of the Oread, Ernie Phillips, John Welbourn (using his South Col voice), Malcolm Hunt, and Harry Pretty spoke. Laura Pretty, not to be outdone, contrived to drop a hard object onto a tin lid during the live recording. It was nicely timed to suggest a clanger being dropped in the background at the end of her father's peroration.

A NOTE FROM ALF

Newsletter, October 1958

Alf Bridge has been climbing in the Alps with Raymond Lambert this summer. The following is worth quoting from a letter received by Eric Byne:–

> "I have had some very good climbing in the Alps, though the snow conditions were far from good. On one out standing day we traversed the Dom and the Taschorn, and on another day I managed four 4,000 metre peaks in the day. In 12 days I managed 40,500' all above 6,000' level".

VOICE FROM THE EAST

Newsletter, April 1958

Returning from the Far East R. G. Pettigrew calls in on Kulu ....

My dear Charles,

I suppose you could call this a "news flash" regarding Oread in the Himalaya. I am very glad to tell you that Michael Thompson (Kings Dragoon Guards ex Ipoh) and I are planning to visit the Tos valley and attempt a mountain called Indrasan about which little is known. In fact survey work done in the 1920's has never been completed. According to the A.C., Indrasan is a high mountain (22,000 ft.), and a difficult one, that is unclimbed and not properly surveyed. Furthermore it appears that if this were our main objective, and we succeeded, we would have pulled off a harder thing than Deo Tibba (of which I have never heard) and done a useful piece of work withal.

From India I shall be returning gladly to the haunts of the Oread via Marseilles and Paris.

If I remain with the Trust it seems they might send me to Africa.*

Bob Pettigrew.

*They didn't, otherwise the history of the entire continent could have been different.

R.G.P.'s initial reconnaissance of this area gave rise to the Derbyshire Himalayan Expedition 1961, and his further exhaustive exploration of the area during the ensuing years up to and including the 1990's — *Editor.*

SAHIBS IN SHORTS

(*EXTRACTS*)

Newsletters 1958

However I decided to explore the approaches to Indrasan and Deo Tibba by way of the Jakatsukh Nullah, third down on the left from Manali. Everyone advised that I take a Ladakhi porter and thinking: "Harry Pretty will love this!" * I engaged a likely looking chap named Wangel who had had experience with the R.A.F. Himalayan expedition. He also accompanied Mrs. Dunsheath's party, of which Eileen Gregory of the Polaris M.C. was a prominent member. See "Mountains and MemSahibs". Originally he only wanted to carry 20 seers (40 lbs) – this included 30 lbs of his own bedding and food! However, when informed that Sahib, who tends towards the left, intended to carry an equal amount, he grinned acquiescence. We both staggered away from Manali bearing 70 lbs apiece and Lyngen days were only too vividly before my eyes. There followed four very interesting days of valley trekking in stages. The last stage in knee-deep snow from a fine cave bivouac, giving me one of the most strenuous days I have ever known and confirming my worst fears about Spring mountaineering in the Himalaya. Many Yeti-like tracks were seen, obviously made by the ubiquitous brown bear. To cap it all, during the return to Manali by a very high level Ibex high wire walk, contouring across apparently vertical grass of the worst order known to Vibrams, I was nearly erased by a well-aimed rock avalanche from a tottering face 600' above us. "Sahib, Sahib", shrieked Wangel through the dust cloud from a quickly attained vantage point. "Om mani padme hum" said Sahib emerging.

R. G. Pettigrew

* R.G.P. remembering his lowly classification as "the bloody porter", Lyngen 1951 — *Editor.*

Robert Pettigrew is once more among us and, on the slightest provocation, that hideous laugh together with an exhibition of the finest set of teeth in the Oread, can now be heard and seen (respectively) in the Bell of a Tuesday night. It is reported that the "King of the Arctic" and the Prince of Kulu (Designate) arrived in Paris in typical fashion. Only after he had been narrowly missed by a wide variety of missiles (he was, of course, standing in the back of a hired vehicle of unspecified make) was he persuaded of the hostile nature of the crowds in the Champs Elyseés and the Place D'étoile. He was apparently difficult to convince that the mob was not there to welcome him back from his mission in the East; and the news that he had been mistaken for a Gaullist Agent Provocateur, by left wing demonstrators marching towards the Arc de Triomphe, was something of an anti-climax.

Mrs. Pettigrew, who was there to meet him, recognised immediately his shocked condition and insisted that he go to bed for a prolonged period. He seems to have made a good recovery, and apparently was able to board the Channel Steamer without assistance.

Harry Pretty

"SIXTY GLORIOUS MONTHS"

DOUGLAS CHARLES CULLUM   *Newsletter (Extract), June 1958*

It will probably not be news to you that I have resigned from the editorship of the Newsletter and that after this issue the job will be carried on by Harry Pretty, and henceforth, that further issues will appear quarterly. It seems at any rate neat and orderly that this change should occur on the fifth anniversary of that historic day when Volume 1 No. 1 burst upon a startled Club. Five years is a long time, and I have to confess that during that time I have slowly lost most of the enthusiasm with which I first embarked on the task of editorship. All the same I cannot help regretting that my period of office should end "not with a bang but a whimper", as the man said.

DOUGLAS CHARLES CULLUM   *Newsletter (Extract), June 1958*

I am sure everyone will agree that Charlie has all along done a magnificent job. He does feel, I know, that he has not always had an adequate supply of news to work with, but any lack of stop press news has usually been compensated for by Charlie's own editorials. Whether serious, as when discussing threats to freedom of access, frivolous, as on the subject of flying whales, or romantic (e.g. Vol. 2 No. 2.) these editorials have always been first rate.

Space forbids an account of Charlie's other virtues, but for a profile, see Vol. 1 No. 9. The Club certainly owes Charlie a debt of gratitude, and also, I am sure, wishes his successor, Harry Pretty, good luck in the arduous job he has taken on.

P. R. Falkner

LETTER . . . from Marion Cooke

Newsletter (Extract), June 1958

But – and this is what has been brought home to me so vividly in these last few months – the Newsletter is a vital and significant part of the Oread, more so than the majority realise. It holds us together as little else ever will. To hear the silence in the Bell when it is distributed, should be sufficient alone, but let any of the active members try to be cut off for a few months. You will soon realise the necessity of the Newsletter continuing.

You complain that news is late – may be, but to at least 70% who do <u>not</u> get into the Bell, it is still News, accounts of meets are usually good and interesting and, after all, they form a large part of Club life.

THE RHINOG AFFAIR

The following contribution appeared in the Newsletter for October 1958 and is essentially a post script to the fabled Rhinog Meet, which took place earlier in that year. It was submitted anonymously under the attribution of "Special Correspondent".

An office in Derby:- the place of employment of those two professional gentlemen: Mr. D. Widdows and Mr. H.Pretty. Also to be found at the same address is Mr. Harry Townsend, who has only recently recovered from his ordeal on Win Hill (see Marsden-Rowsley 1958). The following conversation is barely audible above the din of mating pigeons in the roof space overhead. This particular office, occupied by Widdows is knee-deep in ancient tatty drawings, old clothing, overturned litter bins, empty matchboxes, technical pamphlets specialising in advice for the unmarried but virile young man about town, old racing calendars, and a healthy accumulation of pigeon droppings. There is an abominable smell of Sobranie Hashish, and what light there is shows the walls to be painted in a kind of creosote pink.

The characters in order of speaking: H. Pretty, D. Widdows, H. Townsend, and an unsavoury, 'though diminutive person by the name of Hawkins.

H.P.   *(Entering through matted undergrowth of old chair and table legs)*
            "Hey Widd., what about that article on the Rhinog Meet?"

D.W.   "— ah yes!"

H.P.   "What d'you mean 'ah —"
            (He is interrupted by a violent grating sound which turns out to be the voice of H.T.)

H.T.   "Rhinog meat – Good God, what's that!?"
            (He is ignored – as far as it is possible to ignore some-one 6'3" tall, with an ugly bullet head and a voice like a clapped-out steam-roller)

H.P.   "I was going to say – when am I going to get it? – Don't want too much, And nothing that's overdone"

H.T.   "Half a second mate – what is Rhinog meat, and where the hell d'you get It anyway?"

D.W.   *(a bit dim as usual)* "The Rhinogs are in Wales – Wales, y'know – hills and things, mountains ten times the size of Win Hill"

H.T.   *(Irritated by sneering implication)* – "I know all about that but what about these Rhinogs – thought they were extinct years ago"

H.P.   a kind of groan

D.W.   *(getting dimmer)* "Rhinogs – extinct! – just what are you nattering about Townsend?"

H.T.   *(wiping pigeon dropping off his blazer)* "No need to get chuffed Widdows – I meantersay – Rhinog meat – it's a bit thick"
            (During this outburst Hawkins enters, clad mainly in a large off-white topee which serves both as crash hat when mounted, and as protection from the pigeons during office hours)

Hawkins – *(who considers himself something of a naturalist)* "Rhinogs – ah! now that's interesting. That's what I would like to know where do they meet?"

D.W.   *(Now completely lost)* "Oh, for heavens sake what the devil are you on about – its bad enough already without ..."

Hawkins – "My dear chap – The Rhinog is a most interesting creature. They were thought to be extinct – the last recorded sighting is in a very old MS – around 1550 I believe, at a place called Caer Fadog on the Rhwng-y-ddwy afon"

D.W.   *(Incredulously)* – "What!?"

Hawkins – "Oh yes! – but you know they're not extinct at all. A pair were reported only last year by Franklin, – and his report has been confirmed by Welbourne-Smythe – not extinct at all old chap – In fact you want to keep your eyes open when you're off on these hiking trips of yours.

D.W.   "Really!?"

Hawkins – "You just keep your eyes open old chap – y'never know."

By this time H.P. has slunk away horrified by the realisation that all editors must have to listen to this kind of verbal muck.

Post Script

Some weeks ago Hawkins sent to the office a revolting post card – a violently coloured and grossly inaccurate painting of a train approaching the summit of Snowdon. On the back was a Criccieth postmark and a simple though moving message. "No Rhinogs seen as yet – but pressing on". I'm beginning to wonder – perhaps there are those in the Oread who could enlighten me?

Conclusion

The situation has subsequently deteriorated. An advertisement recently appeared in a Derby paper which announced that "..a few Rhinogs are now available for sale", and my name and address was given as the source of supply. I rather assume this to be a vindictive move by Townsend and Widdows who had not come out of the original encounter in very good shape. As a result of this ad. questions have been put to an eminent zoologist addressing a W.I.: arguments have raged in bars from Heage to Dalbury Lees; I have received enquiring letters from potential Rhinog owners; schoolmasters have been driven to the point of mental unbalance; a placard is said to have appeared in the Market Place announcing in bold purple letters "Rhinogs found in Wales" (which just goes to show); and Townsend in the role of agent provocateur, is said to have caused "wild scenes" in a local cinema by standing up and shouting in his normal cracked (slightly crazed) voice "They're out! – the Rhinogs have escaped!?" – whereupon people rushed into the streets in panic.

I really am beginning to wonder, for you know the word "Rhinog" has something in common with the notorious "Triffid"

    sic:– The Rhinogs and the Triffids
        were dancing on the shore
        And no man saw their strange delight
        For man – he was no more!

        It's all rather sinister ....

MOVING ON . . . SHAKING OFF THE DUST

When ye depart out of the house, shake off the dust of your feet.

St. Matthew (10: 14)

PURCHASE OF A CLUB HUT

Extract from Committee Bulletin 1958

Since the Club authorised the Committee to take steps to replace Bryn-y-Wern, the by-roads of North Wales have been well and truly scoured, and the estate agents of the area consulted at regular intervals.

The search culminated at Christmas (1957) when a "highly desirable" property was located at the south end of the village of Rhyd Ddu, 3½ miles from Beddgelert (Map ref. 571527, Snowdon 1" sheet.) It is a commodious house, somewhat smaller than B-y-W., in a good state of repair, with main water and electricity laid on. It could be put into commission as a Hut immediately, although we should naturally have to carry out minor alterations inside so as to make it suitable for our purpose, after which it should house about 25 Oreads.

The price quoted in the agent's "blurb" was £800, but this was negotiated down and an offer of £550 made and accepted, which seemed to be very reasonable at the side of other property that has been viewed in the area.

The method of administering the property has drawn heavily on the reserves of midnight oil in the cruses of the financial advisors, because the Club itself is not a legal entity and thus cannot own property; two alternatives have been considered. One is to set up a private Company while the other is to set up a trust. The original proposal to set up a Company has been looked into very carefully and although it is possible to do this there are considerable difficulties in the way, mainly due to the nature of the business it would transact. What is equally important, however, is the fact that expenses incurred over the period envisaged would be an appreciable proportion of the capital involved. It is considered that this money would be better employed in repaying that which is borrowed.

The recommendation is, therefore, that a Trust should be set up to enable the Club to own the property legally; the Trustees will sign legal documents on behalf of the Club, and also see that the terms of the loan are observed. Trustees are, of course, appointed by the Club, and may be changed from time to time, as necessary, in accordance with the wish of the members in the usual way.

The growing urgency of the situation may be underlined by the fact that on Jan. 31st. the Hon Secretary received a letter from the solicitors asking for the earliest date at which the Club can vacate Bryn-y-Wern.

By the time this circular reaches you, the Club will, in all probability, have made a deposit of ten percent on the property described above, the go-ahead from our solicitor being the only thing awaited, (in spite of the fact that the response to the first appeal was inadequate). The maximum effort is required on everyone's part so that we can be assured of a place of our own, free from the whims of this or that landlord.

It is essential however that the Hon. Treasurer should receive your contribution immediately, so that the Club is in a position to complete the transaction as soon as possible.

BRYN-Y-WERN . . . OBITUARY

Newsletter, January 1959

"Bryn-y-Wern " passed away quietly on Sunday 26th October 1958. Death took place at the time and largely in the manner predicted by our consultants some months ago. Emotional scenes were few among the family and friends who had come together to witness the old lady's passing on. Old lady she was, but game to the end, she showed signs of evident enjoyment when only twenty-four hours before death she was subjected to the irreverent high spirits of those who had gathered for the wake. A more detailed account of the events that preceded the quietus is given below.

Harry Pretty

BRYN-Y-WERN . . . VALEDICTORY

Newsletter (Extract), January 1959

We went down on the Wednesday. For the last time we enjoyed the quietness and the seeming isolation of Pennant. There was little stimulus to activity for cloud sat upon the wooded green depression around Bryn-y-Wern like a lid. So we sawed wood, walked a little, and ate our meals before roaring log fires in the lounge. It was utterly peaceful in a way that is not always possible today in other parts of Wales. But, as usual, the hour was constantly in question after supper on Friday – anticipation of that Friday stream of arrivals always produces its own kind of excitement. There is never any certainty who is going to show up, or in what order, and I enjoy that period of two hours when the house is full of clumping feet, whistling kettles, steaming cups of tea, and bodies relaxing after the drive. No other part of the weekend is ever quite like this – the weekend is yet to come – the atmosphere develops and suddenly is there.

I have noticed that among the regulars there is a pattern of behaviour; distinct and immutable. There is a feeling of permanence when Ernie Phillips descends into an armchair within a minute of arrival. You know that as certain as day follows night Ronni will be in with a cup of Milo five minutes later. An air of nostalgia will envelop Paul and Betty Gardiner on the corner sofa – Laurie Burns will be asleep within fifteen minutes of arrival. By midnight all will be quiet, but it is not likely that anyone familiar with the situation will have thought seriously about sleep – for this is merely the silence of anticipation. At 1.00 a.m. or thereabouts, there is sudden clamour that suggests the arrival of an armoured brigade. Organised marching and countermarching is taking place in the hall to the accompaniment of shouts and ringing oaths heard above the tumult of a Bacchanalian riot.

'On the morning of October 25th the Janes-Handley entourage were still under the spell of a fair in Bala where they had witnessed several exhibitionist forms of entertainment that hadn't improved Burgess's blood pressure, and required all of Janes' extensive vocabulary to describe.

Saturday was divided between preliminary "demolition" and the collection of wood for the evening's fireworks. Eccles cakes and beer were also procured – Cwm Silin was visited ".....we started on the bottom left hand side and finished on the top right corner" – according to Janes.

For many of us the bare inhospitable boards of the lounge were a sad and depressing start to Sunday's departure, but the mood could hardly last amid the shambles of loading the lorry. How it all went on we shall never know. When the overloaded vehicle lurched and swayed down the hill and over the bridge we watched it in fascinated wonder – it seemed as if the journey to Rhydd-Ddu might come within the class of "high adventure". However, despite their somewhat grotesque appearance, the lashing held. No unfortunate tourist in the Aberglaslyn was crushed beneath an avalanche of chairs, tables, steel bunks, cast iron boilers and stags heads – and by 2.00. p.m. Bryn-y-Wern had passed into Oread history.

Harry Pretty

CHANGE OF IDENTITY

At the present rate of progress our new hut will soon bear little resemblance to the property we originally purchased. This handsome establishment (Quellyn Arms 2 mins., Snowdon summit 2½ hrs.) was acquired under the name of "Snowdon View". In addition to being a complete misnomer (with the present window arrangement) the name is heavily suggestive of suburban mediocrity and is quite unsuitable for a mountaineering club hut. The Committee would therefore, be grateful for assistance in finding a new name. To be in character the name should obviously be Welsh. As some guide, the following names have already been put forward "Hafod Oread" (House of Oread), "Bod Oread" (Abode of the Oread) – there is also another which means "House in the valley by the water", but I can't remember what it sounded like in Welsh. Please send any ideas to Len Hatchett, 598 Burton Road, Littleover, Derby.

Harry Pretty

ANNUAL DINNER 1958

WHITE LION HOTEL – GREAT LONGSTONE

The Annual Dinner was, if anything, better than ever this year. A total of 112 sat down to Dinner and there were others in the bar who, not having booked a place early enough, were excluded from eating but who joined the gallery during the speeches. There was a record number of official guests from Kindred Clubs in addition to the three principal guests comprising Wynford Vaughan Thomas, Alan B. Hargreaves and Tony Moulam. All of these gentlemen spoke, and I have no fear of being contradicted if I call W. V. T's speech a tour de force which more than upheld the tradition of excellence that has come to be associated with after dinner speaking at Oread functions. Charles Cullum who, in the manner of his kind, had clearly carried out a lot of research from original sources maintained, if he didn't surpass, his usual standard of pointed wit – and moreover Bob Pettigrew's reply on behalf of the Club (delivered with clean-cut young Englishman back in the fold nuances) was not to be sneezed at, and nicely rounded off the polished performances of his predecessors.

Oliver Jones did not fail us and as usual Stan Moore was irrepressible when it came to the pinch. It was a pleasant surprise to find Clive Webb with us one more – and to see Eric Byne, – Cyril Machin and George Sutton in their proper places.

Geoff Hayes was not allowed to forget that it was his 21st birthday. Tankards were distributed as is the custom, but Geoff Thompson and Barbara (I must no longer refer to her as "his party") declined to return from Majorca to receive theirs. We were sorry that John Adderley was unable to be there to receive his.

For once the weather was magnificent on the Sunday and a surprising amount of climbing was carried out by what had only recently been described as "a club of rakes".

Alf Bridge, unable to attend the Dinner, sent a telegram to Alan Hargreaves advising him "to take a strong belay". It was noticed that A.H. did not ignore the advice.

Harry Pretty

OREADS IN SHORTS

Newsletter, January 1959

Bob Pettigrew has once more engineered his way out of a Bullstones Meet (there are some people who doubt whether he has ever been there). His attendance was eagerly looked forward to in November, but during the preceding week I received a note to the effect that he had been summoned to Dublin at short notice – allegedly to the I.M.C. Dinner.

Harry Pretty

GOLDEN OLDIES 1953 – 1958

FINALE

George Sutton elected to Honorary Membership 1958

At a recent Committee Meeting George Sutton was elected to Honorary Membership of the Club. In almost every way it is a fitting climax to Sutton's association with the Oread. It was George who really founded the Oread in 1949. He organised the first A.G.M., drafted the original constitution, and was the first Hon. Secretary. For many years he was the kernel of that small hard core of individuals to whom the Oread was not just a Club, but almost a way of life. Very few members of the Oread have ever read his first entry in the original Club Log Book. I remember thinking at the time (I knew very little of his character in those days) that he was rather overstating his case but, at the same time, I recognised what I thought to be a kind of hopeless idealism – stimulating and inspiring if you could take it seriously but not, ever likely to reach fruition. But how little I knew, and how many have been the persons who have reacted in a similar fashion since. The fact is that what he wrote expressed the idealism that has run through his life like a continuous thread and, more than that, has been translated into achievements that would have been considerable in a person trained to lead from infancy. His ability to organise, to lead both intellectually and physically; his skill in analysing difficult situations, and his readiness to take a calculated risk have been developed by the necessity of a spirit which has constantly aspired to things beyond the perimeter of the safe and familiar world. It is hereabouts that the explorer and the mountaineer find common ground, and few men have overcome greater difficulties in attaining it.

Harry Pretty

A Touch
of Class
1958-1970

With the acquisition of freehold premises in North Wales (Tan-y-Wydffa) the Oread took on increased responsibilities. But the period was mainly defined by a change in the characters who ran club affairs. The Golden Oldies of previous years, most of whom were either founders or very early members, declined in influence and a second wave took charge.

The first Oread Himalayan expedition (under the leadership of Bob Pettigrew) took the field and succeeding Presidents; Cooke, Ashcroft, Janes, Handley and Burgess, exerted a strong Alpine influence as becomes apparent from contributions to contemporary Newsletters. It is in this context that the late Geoff. Hayes distinguished himself. From 1963 to 1970 he edited the Newsletter and, with unrelenting energy, became the very fulcrum of Club activities both at home and abroad.

FIREWORK MEET AND OFFICIAL OPENING OF TAN-Y-WYDDFA, 5th NOVEMBER 1960

The period between vacation of Bryn-y-Wern, October 1958 and the opening of Tan-y-Wyddfa saw essential repairs and considerable structural alteration to the new hut all carried out by voluntary labour — *Editor.*

Everyone had a wet trip to Wales on Friday evening. However, the Ale was delivered intact and tapped with all speed. The hut was full and the lounge was used to accommodate the overflow from the bedrooms.

Saturday Started fine and several parties went out to climb. Fred Allan and John Brailsford swam up Eastern Arête in sock feet. The President spent the day thinking about the jobs which should have been done by the previous working party and, in consequence, a number of people beat it to the "Fleece" at Tremadoc lest they be detailed for a job.

Everyone arrived back at the hut in time for the opening ceremony, performed by Alan Hargreaves at 4.0. p.m. At 3.59 p.m. it was found that the front door knob was nearly off and a hasty repair was carried out. A.B.H. arrived on the dot, the rain came down in sheets and a tape across the doorway was speedily cut to the click of cameras.

Pettigrew introduced Hargreaves to the assembled company in the lounge and treated us to frequent displays of that fine set of 32 which it is understood, are at present being signed up as advertising material for Gibbs S.R. A tour of the hut ensued.

Everyone turned out in heavy rain the see the village bonfire and the fireworks commenced at 6.30 p.m. The proceedings got off to rather a slow start, mainly attributed to the unfortunate absence of R. (Rocket) Handley and "Burnt Jack" Burgess, until a Pettigrew special was used to put one of the hut dustbins into orbit.

Sunday was fine, but cloudy, and parties left the hut in every direction, some to Snowdon, some to the Hebog area, and a few to the coast.

Paul Gardiner

ALLAN HARGREAVES, in opening the hut, said: "Mr. President Pettigrew, and my very good friends you Ladies and Gentlemen of the Oread Club:–"

"I am very much gratified by being asked to do this official opening of Tan-y-Wyddfa – and, incidentally, what a delightful name – I feel it is an honour."

"Perhaps you intended the invitation to be a compliment to the Climbers' Club, which would be quite right having regard to our standing in North Wales, and if so, I thank you for that in my representative capacity. But perhaps partly, at any rate, it was intended to be a personal compliment, and I have wondered why, if that is so. For about my only contact with you, apart from the privilege of using Bryn-y-Wern as a Fell & Rocker – has been my pretty awful speech at your Dinner at Great Longstone a couple of years ago, when I completely forgot to propose a toast. However, you all seemed to enjoy that Dinner, nevertheless, and so did I, very much indeed. Indeed, until 2.30 a.m. when to my astonishment I discovered that the Landlord, when he was putting me to bed, had sparkling diamonds let into most of his teeth!"

Now this is not the first Hut opening I have been at – not by any means the first – for I have been concerned, one way or another, in the setting up of all the Huts of the Fell & Rock, Wayfarers, and Climbers Club except for the original Helyg which was just a couple of years before I began to climb."

"My first opening was of the Robertson Lamb Hut in Langdale way back in 1928 when I had been appointed the first Custodian. I didn't last long on that job, as a matter of fact, I had very little time to spare from climbing for the usual Custodian's chores. I was the world's worst custodian, so they sacked me and put in Harry Spilsbury, whom many of you will have encountered, as he is still there. But the opening I remember best was when we christened the Helyg extension in October 1932. That job was done by my most illustrious predecessor Dr. Tom Longstaff and we actually did break a bottle of champagne on the door, though it was surprising how much of the stuff got caught in both tooth mugs and other receptacles, without being wasted. That was an occasion of extreme bad weather, but nevertheless we did the job outside in spartan manner."

"So now, attempting to speak as an authority on Huts and the opening of Huts, I let my mind run over this one. And, if time permits, over your Club and its present doings and intended doings."

"As I take a look at Tan-y-Wyddfa, I recall with nostalgic regret that most delightful spot Bryn-y-Wern, a house of character in a beautiful setting and a convenient, if somewhat remote, location. But here, even though this is a pretty gory specimen of Welsh architecture – excuse me, but it is true, isn't it? – you have an even more convenient location, with nearly as much room to swing cats in; and it is your very own I understand and not held on the end of a short string by some old witch of a Landlord."

"I would be interested to know how and when this building came to be built, but I guess it was put up in the 1880's at about the same time as the Railroad – perhaps even it was a Railway House? Perhaps the Station Masters? If so, let's just work our imaginations for a moment on what the old Caernarvon, Beddgelert, Festiniog Railway was like in its heyday. I remember having a ride on it once when I first came to Wales, and it was quite fun. Emett in real life!"

"But however Tan-y-Wyddfa came to be built it is quite different, and pleasantly different now, after all you have done to it and I hope and trust you will be able to settle down happily here for a very long time. It has at least one amenity which Bryn-y-Wern had not, and that is Licenced premises only 100 yards away. I hope you are able to train them to let you in at the back door on Sundays!"

"Now I look at my watch I see I am getting 'long winded', so I won't go on to say much about your Club except that I have a high regard and respect for it as, likewise, has the Climbers Club. Small numbers, greatest average activity! But I would like to offer one word of Good Wishes for next year's Himalayan Expedition which, as I understand it, is mostly an Oread Show. The best of luck to them – and may they be borne up during their inevitable privations and harrowings on Indrasan with the thought that they have Tan-y-Wyddfa to come back to —"

"LADIES AND GENTLEMEN, I declare this hut well and truly opened, and I hope it never folds up or falls down upon you,"

Welsh Hut Custodians

Bryn-y-Wern	1955-1958	David Penlington
Tan-y-Wyddfa	1959-1961	Fred Allen
	1962-1965	Chuck Hooley
	1966-1967	John Corden
	1968-1971	David Appleby
	1972-1977	John Welbourn
	1978-1999	Chuck Hooley

OUTDOOR MEETS, U.K., 1959-1962
– OR THEREABOUTS

WELSH WALK 1959 (EXTRACT)

Compiled by Newsletter Editor (H.P.)

Phil Falkner and Peter Janes were behind Ashcroft and Hayes – Phil writes as follows:–

"Mike Turner and I were on Foel Fras 07.30 hrs., Foel Grach 08.00, Carnedd Llewelyn 08.20 hrs., Yr Elen 08.40-08.45 (5 min. halt), Carnedd Dafydd 09.40, Pen-yr-Ole-Wen 10.00, Glan Dena 10.30. Peter Janes was a few minutes ahead."

"Janes, Turner and myself set off for Tryfan at 11.00. The high speed over the Carnedds had taken it out of us, and we were not going at all well. We were hot, thirsty and Janes kept bemoaning the loss of his thermos of tea, which he had shattered on the Carnedds. About one third of the way up Tryfan Mike Turner dropped behind (I gather he omitted Y Garn, Elidir Fawr, and joined the Pretty group.)"

"Janes and I stuck together from here on. Summit of Tryfan 12.45. plagued by thirst. At Bwlch Tryfan we descended a short way to the spring for "gulpers" and washed our feet; great relief (13.15-13.25.)".

"Glyder Fach 14.00, Glyder Fawr 14.30; more gulpers at the Twll Ddu stream 15.00, and rest until 15.15. Y Garn 15.45, still thirsty, found another stream between Foel Goch and Elidir Fawr. Tom Frost and a friend joined us here and stayed more or less with us as far as Y Wyddfa."

"Elidir Fawr 17.00 descent mainly by "arsading" down steep grass. Timed our arrival at Nant Peris nicely. The Vaynol Arms had just opened. Pint shandies and biscuits and cheese 18.00-18.45 – road walk 18.45-19.15. Started up Cwm Glas 19.15. I was feeling ill, perhaps too much shandy. Grib Goch 20.45 – there I was sick and afterwards felt better. Carnedd Ugain 21.40 , Y Wyddfa 22.00, still open, thank God, mugs of tea."

"(I leave H.P. to describe the frippett). Descent rapid whilst the light lasted, then more slowly in the dark to Hut at midnight."

As for Burns, Widdows, and the Vice-President – they lounged in Cwm Tryfan, crossed Glyder Fach, and on the far side discovered a magnificent waterfall above Llyn Cwm-y-ffynnon. Some of you may have seen the results in a series of alarming photographs that were circulating in the Bell recently. It is possible that the Photographic meet might bring to light even worse indiscretions. In the Pen-y-Pas tea was taken in a leisurely fashion and the party, augmented by Mike Turner, eventually left for Crib-Goch – on the summit of which they joined up with Hayes and Ashcroft.

To most of us the traverse from Crib-Goch to Ddysgl had a dream like quality. Laurie was sick several times, everyone suffered from excessive weakness and over-susceptibility to exposure; and Pretty remarked that he remembered very little between the Pinnacles and seeing a young lady in a mauve jumper in the summit hotel. The same young woman immediately took us (in a metaphorical way) to her bosom – and there were those who could still resent the metaphorical manner of her taking.

Our descent to Rhyd Ddu paralleled the setting sun – it was one of those wonderful dull orange summer nights, but most of us were too far gone to really appreciate it.

The first 3,000 'anders to finish at Tan-y-Wyddfa — *Editor.*

WASDALE, WHITSUNTIDE 1959

The meet was attended by Mike Turner, J. (Gable)*, Ashcroft, J Bridges, R. Dearden, Paul Gardiner, P. Janes, and F. Allen with respective wives, sweethearts, camp comforters and families, also L. K. White, D. Chapman, S. G. Moore, R. Handley, and D. Burgess. Non-members on the meet included Kim Rumford, Nat Allen and wife, Ray Colledge and Wilf. White.

During the week-end the following routes were climbed:–

Scafell	– Scafell Pinnacle, Slingsby's Chimney, Pisgah Buttress, Moss Ghyll Grooves, Central Buttress, Botheralls Slab, (Sic.) Mickledore Grooves, Overhanging Wall, and Great Eastern.
Great Gable	– Eagle Ridge, Tychett Wall, Tychett Girdle, and Sepulchre Route, Arrowhead Arête.
Esk Buttress	– Medusa Wall and Bridges Route.

Derrick Burgess

*Pronounced "Garble".

OREADS ON MEETS

Re. D. Burgess   *Newsletter, October 1959*

Whenever women are discussed the name of Burgess is usually prominent. Be there a meet-less week-end and he is organising a social evening in the flat. Beware the Oread who thwarts his progress for we hear of two recent occasions when so called fellow travellers have been thrust aside.

There is the sad touching scene of that celibate fellow Janes, wending his weary way towards Bedgellert in car-less fashion while Burgess entertained some local Portmadoc piece in his recently acquired tin box. There is the more recent occasion when he was observed trying out the latest continental techniques in Coniston. Two young ladies lashed to the rocks, a sort of modern Greek Saga, while Burgess fought his way up a Mod. Diff.

Above stood Ashcroft gazing longingly out at Gable and wondering if he would ever get back to Janet before dusk when his peaceful reverie was disturbed by "I hope you don't mind old Chap". There was B in true Matterhorn fashion, shinning up Ashcroft's rope (to avoid the crux of course). As he disappeared above, faint mutterings, about Indian rope tricks and Ashcroft's chances with the two ladies were heard.

Tom Frost

CLOGWYN MEET – JUNE 1959

SATURDAY

Clogwyn D'ur Arddu

Curving crack, Sunset Crack climbed by 3 parties:–
   R. Handley, F. Allen, R. Colledge
   D. Davies, P. Janes, H. Pretty
   D. Hadlum and friend.

Route on Far West
> D. Hadlum, L. White, and friend.

Craig-y-Bere
Angel Pavement:–
> J. Welbourn, T. Frost, and Colin Hobday.

SUNDAY

Cloggy

Chimney Route:–
> R. Handley, R. Colledge and D. Davies.

Piggotts Route:–
> R. Handley, R. Colledge and D. Davies.

Sheaf Route:–
> D. Burgess, D. Chapman, N. Allen.

> These three climbed Lion and Ribstone Crack on Saturday on Carreg Wasted.

Nantile Y Garn

Eastern Arête – 3 parties.
> F. Allen, P. Janes, H, Pretty.
> J. Welbourn and Frank Davis.
> T. Frost, Colin Hobday, and Suzanne Harper.

Lliwedd

Route 2:–
> L. K. White and G. Hayes.

Ray Handley

SHIVERING MOUNTAIN, THE GREAT RIDGE

GORDON GADSBY

"Climb when you are ready". The words echoed from above the ice bound crags and were lost in the swirling wind. This was the moment of truth.

We were on the top pitch of Blue John Rib high up on the East Face of Mam Tor, the Shivering Mountain. Two hours earlier, much lower down on a frozen ledge of shale, we had witnessed an accident away to our left on the easier gully climb. A solo climber has slipped near the top then fallen, slithering from ledge to ledge for over two hundred feet, parting company with his rucksack on the way. He was one of a party of six on that climb and within an hour his friends had summoned help and he had been whisked away to Sheffield in an ambulance.

All this action beneath us had done wonders for my confidence, especially with the crux pitch still to come. Des Hadlum had led that steep thirty-foot pitch in fine style ten minutes ago so I was in good hands. He'd spent the time since looking for a belay on the snowy windswept summit. "Climb when you're ready". "You'll be fine Gordon", said Dennis Gray encouragingly, just take it steady and test every hold".

114

With a gulp I took the first tentative step up. Without crampons and with only one axe, I knew this final pitch would be for me a desperate climb. I'd not the vast experience of my two friends, but already climbing every weekend was becoming a way of life. Once I'd reached a position about ten feet above the ledge I felt strangely calm, my right gloved hand gripping the icy edge of the rib, my left swinging the axe into whatever snow or ice I could find in a shallow corner.

It was near the end of the day and bitterly cold, the sky was already tinged with pink from the setting sun. Most people would be heading for home by now I thought, or maybe even there already. The lateness of the hour spurred me on. If I didn't hurry, Dennis would have to climb in the dark.

I made another swing with the long wooden axe, the pick bit deep, but as I stepped up and carefully transferred weight onto my right boot, the shale beneath snapped off. My right leg slipped wildly into space. The rest of me almost followed, but luckily axe and hands held firm as I desperately scrabbled for a safe foothold.

With thumping heart, and after several more precarious upward moves, I was under the small cornice of snow that formed the top of the climb. Two more delicate moves, a final swing of the axe and I was on the summit dome beside a grinning Des Hadlum. I sat in the snow thrilled to have done the climb, certainly at that time the most difficult route I'd done. Ten minutes later the three of us were together once more.

"I was worried about pulling you off Des" I said, as the two lads gathered the climbing gear together. "No way that would have happened" replied a beaming crew cut Des. "Look here, my first ever snow mushroom belay. I could have held a car on that!"

The six foot across and nine-inch mound of snow looked good and stable, but I was thankful I hadn't put it to the final test.

A few minutes later we were on the crest of the Great Ridge and walking down to Castleton. Above the stone houses, the dark ramparts of Peveril Castle, and the shadowed gulf of Winnats Pass, a crescent moon had appeared to brighten the clear winter sky. The great adventure has lived long in the memory, for it was over thirty years ago on New Years Day 1961, the beginning of one of the coldest winters in living memory.

An Extraordinary Meet – Christmas Eve 1961

Gordon Gadsby and Dave Weston invite all Oreads to a one-night bivouac meet on Snowdon summit on Christmas Eve Sunday 24th December. Tents will be frowned upon except as bivvy sheets. We should arrive on the summit between 21.30 and 22.30. Good bed spaces can be found on the east face about 20 feet below the summit cairn, providing the wind is from the west. If conditions are anything like last year ice axes will be useful – also a rope, just in case – and of course, a poly-bag and food and drink.

Many Oreads are spending Christmas at Tan-y-Wyddfa, so we are hoping some will join us on what could be a very rewarding experience. We especially hope to see that Prince of the Duvet Brigade – Ernie (fire screen) Phillips, and that ace B.M.C. photographer – Hebog Jack ("Have you seen my crampons?") Ashcroft.

Postscript:

Gadsby, Weston and Doug Cooke did spend the night on the summit as planned, 'though the bivvy spot was changed from East to West face. The contingent at Pen-y-Pas, who saw them off, nearly got frostbite stepping out of their vehicles and those, who had been on Snowdon that day imagined they were seeing the trio for the last time. As the wind howled around Tan-y-Wydffa many cheerful comments were exchanged.

Geoff Hayes

Echoes from the Past:

During Christmas 1950 an Oread party of 10 (total membership 15) stayed at Tyn-y-Shanty (Ogwen). North Wales was snow covered to road level. On Christmas Day the entire party traversed the Glyders, descending to Pen-y-Pas. Most of the party walked or hitched back to Ogwen. Sutton, Pretty and Gardiner carried on intending to reach Snowdon Summit by way of Crib Goch. The sky was cloudless and there was a brilliant moon. Crib Goch defeated the party. There was much ice and no crampons. Some kind of high traverse was made to the P.Y.G. track and the summit was reached in the early evening. As was usual at that time a window of the summit hotel was left open (for emergency use) and the party sheltered for a while in a room wherein the snow was level with the windowsill. Eventually, still under a bright moon, they descended to Pen-y-Gwryd before midnight — *Editor.*

WELSH WALK – CYNWYD TO CWM COWARCH – MAY 1962

That people were loath to leave the pub at Cynwyd was indeed an understatement. The rain poured, the wind blew, I was dying with pneumonia. Then there was the blonde Wally saw at Llangollen. However Fred literally worked the oracle with a Welsh Farmer and shortly afterwards we were all installed in an empty farm house. The Hayes/Gadsby shouting team were confident that they had ousted Jack Ashcroft from their comfortable wooden floor, but Jack, wily old bird, was with Pretty, Dearden and myself amongst the straw in the barn. Yes even Dearden appeared on this meet, even if it was to prove that his feet are still as blister prone as ever.

We awoke on Saturday to the sound of rain on the roof and the H-G shouting team – (who appear to exist without sleep). After a ferry service had shuttled all the cars to Cowarch we were literally committed. That again is an understatement. Fred Allen, another wily bird, had generously brought all the drivers back from Cowarch in HIS car, crafty as ever.

We walked along the road for a midday pint and to see what the weather held in store. A rapid improvement soon tempted and we set off for the Hirnant, where the party arrived in dribs and drabs after a wet walk. I myself hurrying to make a considerable deviation to check that the H-G team were alright, and to sign their chit to continue to the Bwlch-y-Groes direct.

The evening was not without incident. Our comfortable barn was visited by an irate Welsh lady who, it transpired, owned the place and did not take kindly to our being there. Pretty, attired in pyjamas, assured her we were respectable. She however failed to see this and, objecting to being called 'madam', gave us the boot. A farmer down the valley was of a more friendly disposition and made us welcome. Sunday, in good weather, was spent in crossing over to Bwlch-y-Groes and then over the Arans to Cowarch.

Highlights of the meet;

TOTAL RETREAT by Fred Allen, Janes, and Handley.

Welbourn's celebrated 50lb rucksack quote; (a) "as you get older you can carry more." (b) "this is no country for a 50lb sack."

Derrick Burgess

LATHKILL MEET 1962

A vagrant leans upon the bar.
His vacant eye and empty glass suggest
Another round of drinks. The verse
He fails to write is much the best.

We spend the night in Rileys' barn,
Sir Laurence Burns conducts the snores
Of men and beast. He bows, The work
Receives a scatter of applause.

Welbourn leaves with torch in hand
To light the way around the bend,
Stretches on the Co-op porch
For bed-night with a dividend.

Ashcroft returns, his eye aloft
On nameless peak, the virgin snow
Of Himalayan scene, He leads,
But loses us on Arbor Low.

A crowd collects in Lathkilldale,
R. G. Pettigrew has gone
To sign his autograph, Denies
He spread a rumour of Sir John.

The Reverend Pretty eminent
Divine arrives with shovel hat,
Assumes this clerical disguise
For access to his Stanton Flat.

Hooley has a liquid lunch,
Unleashes Kim to spend the day
Retrieving empties from the stream,
I phone the R.S.P.C.A.

"Highlights of the Lathkill Meet",
Presumes it does no harm
To twist the metre or events,
And least of all the victims arm.

Jim Kershaw

117

THE 3,000 'ANDERS, 1962

Geoff. Hayes' times:

Start Aber	7.00 a.m.	Glyder Fawr	2.00
Foel Fras	8.30	Y Garn	2.40
Foel Grach	8.50	Elider Fawr	3.40
Llywelyn	9.25	Depart	4.00
Yr Elen	9.45	Nant Peris	4.30
Dafydd	11.00	Crib Goch	6.10
Penyrolewen	11.15	Crib-y-Ddysgl	7.00
Glan Dena	11.45	Snowdon	7.15
Depart	12.15	Depart	7.30
Tryfan	1.00 p.m.	Rhyd-Ddu	9.00 p.m.
Glyder Fach	1.40		

SEQUEL TO THE MARSDEN-ROWSLEY WALK 1962

Perhaps it would be as well to tell how I came to do the Chinley variant to the Marsden-Rowsley. It happened thus. Picking my way across the bog of Bleaklow Head, in absolutely first class bog condition, and idly musing about all and sundry. – Blondes, Brunettes, Beer etc., I looked around for the first time for half an hour or more and found it all unfamiliar. I fished my compass out of the rucksack and found I was walking Northwest. The compass refused to change its mind and even after several serious blows and kicks had been administered. So I reluctantly concluded I was on my way to Manchester. I took a compass course of 175° and found I had dropped into Yellow Slacks Brook, two miles from Glossop. Ascending the other side of the Clough I was on the Snake Road but rather late for Kinder and Win Hill in October. So crossing Featherbed Moss I made my way to Chinley, catching a train to Bamford and walking to the Yorkshire Bridge with a few minutes to spare before the first of the purists arrived. Just in time to consume a long visualised pint; and look a little self-satisfied.

Laurie Burns

BUTTERMERE 1962 (*EXTRACT*)

It was a memorable meet before it started.

There was a rumour that the meet, as re-arranged, was to be an engagement party. The Committee was so worried at the thought of 96 Oreads straining mightily that Fred Allen was ordered to buy a Bog Tent. Now Fred is mightily particular, as to the type of seat he uses, and was heard to say that this would cost the club a few hut loan repayments.

Luckily the National Trust said they were very sorry but even the Oread would not be allowed to erect a bog-tent at the north end of Buttermere. In a blind panic the Hayes mob wrote to Gates-garth farm for the use of their pigsty.

The atmosphere that pre-meet night at the Bell was tense as 96 Oreads argued between the north and south end of Buttermere lake. The President was in favour of taking the Dormobile up to Birkness Combe. Hayes maintained it was all a big mistake. Ashcroft arrived beaming, having washed his hands of the latest expedition aftermath. Pretty declared to all that it was a cock up. Janes said he was glad he was going on holiday. Welbourn threatened to resign unless he was allowed to take charge...

At 12.15 that Friday night (Sat. a.m.) all the cars, except Fred Allen's had their lights trained on Gatesgarth farm. The President triangulated the fields and reported that precedent had been established in the form of a solitary tent. A quick excursion to Buttermere village revealed no sign of the bog tent or Fred Allen, but only a "No Camping" sign.

At 2.0 a.m. 20 Oreads were well encamped near the original solitary tent with their own cars in close attendance in case of danger. The Hayes/Gadsby shouting team was in full session.

At 2.01 a.m. there was an eruption from the solitary tent, a car's hooter disturbed the peace of the night and a torrent of abuse, in French, descended on the ring. Attempts at appeasement, varying between being "terribly sorry" and an offering up of Margaret Lowe, were not very successful. An appointment was made for 6.00 a.m. the following morning and, at last, an uneasy peace descended.

The following morning was rather an anti-climax as by the time people woke up properly. The torrent of abuse had departed in a puttering Citroen having circled the field a few times looking for the English chicken.

Anon

OREADS IN SHORTS, 1959-1964

At Bullstones Cabin:–
Doreen Gadsby – "John do put your trousers on please.
John Welbourn – "As you can see I am well equipped." — *1961*.

RGP. Our new Vice President recently gave two lectures with slides in one evening at two Hucknall Churches. There was no audience for his first attempt. No wonder he didn't find Elsan the Throne of the Gods — *1961*.

On the winter Ogwen meet a watch was found by an Oread at the foot of Amphitheatre Rib. It was found to belong to a Dr. Houghton who was tragically killed when he fell from the rib two years ago. The watch is to be returned to his relatives. — *1961*.

John Foster has written on behalf of the Peak Park Planning Board to thank the Club for the effort in collecting litter from the Gardoms' Birchen area on December 3rd — *1961*.

The Derby Evening Telegraph will probably reduce its number of pages once Bob Pettigrew has left for India. — *1962*.

Stanage Meet:– Doreen Gadsby: "Of course I'm feminine during the week, and at week ends. You ask Geoff he's seen it".

"Clachaig Gully does not interest me". Jack Ashcroft — *Glencoe 1962*.

"I can't imagine Wally Smith as mechanically minded, he looks as though he serves behind the counter at Burtons".

After leaving his ice axe at home last year when going to Glen Nevis for the Easter meet, (not to mention the CRAMPONS episode in the Himalayas). Ashcroft did it again in Glencoe on the Easter meet when he and Pettigrew had been driven to the foot of the crag by their wives, (who soon drove off again), leaving these two hard men by the road, both thinking the other had the rope, when all the time it was in the boot of the car — *1962*.

Chuck Hooley to Doreen Gadsby – "Have you never been kissed passionately by a man with a beard?". "No Chuck, have you?" — *1962*.

"I don't consider walking meets of under 40 miles". A recent quote from Phil. Falkner — *1962*.

Quote on the recent Marsden-Rowsley walk "Do you know, this is the most expensive meet of the year for me? First I have to take my car to Derby, pay to keep it in a garage for the week end, buy a ticket for Manchester, then to Marsden and what with all those pubs we pass, I spend plenty on beer. Then of course I have to get a new pair of boots, and a taxi from the bus to the garage at the end of the walk, as I will have 'set solid' by then. Finally there is a week off work without pay and heaven knows how much a specialist will cost for the next few months!" — *1962*.

While Walking over Bleaklow one weekend quite recently, Burgess and party were almost blown off their feet by a blast of explosive. Yes, the rest of Yellow Slacks had just gone up in dust! The party rushed over to the scene of the crime to find the little dictator farmer gloating over his handiwork, supported by a crowd of locals, and the local bobby who had supervised the deed. The result of this wanton destruction is that a compulsory purchase order, for what is left of the rocks and the surrounds, has been made by the authority, a bit late, but action nevertheless. Let's hope it discourages other farmers from doing the same kind of thing — *1964*.

Just heard, the quote of the year from Doreen Gadsby: "If you want to be known in the Oread you have to do the unusual things at night" — *1964*.

Handley – "One of these days I'm going to go through all my slides and put them in a box". Ashcroft – "What a match box?" — *1964*.

".......Several of which (Oreads) even took baths and danced on the table-cloths...."

Letter from Devonshire Arms Hotel following Annual Dinner, November 28th, 1959.

ALPINE AFFAIRS 1959-1970

From the earliest days small groups of Oreads were visiting the European Alps but their activities received scant reportage in Newsletters and Journals. This scarcity of a written record was remedied, to some extent, between 1959 and 1970 — *Editor*.

DESCENT FROM THE PEIGNE (1959) (EXTRACT)

R. HANDLEY

We ascended onto a rib, only to be confronted by an apparent impasse. The rib dropped steeply into the mist and, descending a groove, I found only an impossible overhang. We cast to the left and tried to climb into the couloir below the steep step across its face. The time was 5 o'clock – it would undoubtedly be dark early. I prayed for clearance of the mist, and as often happens when things look bad, there was a sudden improvement. The mist twisted aside just long enough for us to see an abseil peg from which we could get back into the gully. We also saw Don and Chris about 400 feet lower down practically on the glacier. The rappel was steep but safe and we descended into the gully and down to the glacier, having been on our chosen small peak 12 hours.

It is usual when the green Alps are reached that one in able to relax and amble downhill musing over the days highlights. But this day was to have a kick in its tail.

After we got off the peak, Katerine, Ray C. and myself decided that rather than walk down we would take the teleferique. We were thinking of an early meal at the Café de Chamonix. In the event however, we were to be disappointed, and we nearly had to bivouac because of this decision. The teleferique had long stopped running and we had to return valleyward on foot. I saw Ted and the lads just disappearing past the Plan des Aiguilles and hurried after them. The track curved slowly round the hillside and slowly began to climb back to the other side of the teleferique. Ray C. said "This isn't the way", and I agreed. Seeing a path dropping down a little further on I said "That looks alright". With that, we embarked on our nightmare descent.

All went well for 1,000 feet until, suddenly the path narrowed, steepened and disappeared over a steep drop into the trees. The time was 8 o'clock and we had about ½ hour of daylight left. I proposed a rappel, which was reluctantly accepted. We seemed so near to Chamonix that I could almost smell the Beefsteak and Chips. But I had seriously clanged. The angle of the ground was 60°; loose, heavily vegetated and treed. We had descended into a kind of gorge with a torrent crashing down to the right suggesting steeper ground below.

To get out of this somehow onto more open hillside seemed imperative, but we were completely hemmed in by trees. On the left was a steep wall covered in moss which we climbed at speed because of the loose nature of its structure. The ground was still desperate and the last minutes of daylight were dwindling fast.

We gathered together looking longingly at the lights of Chamonix which appeared to be very near, but in our situation as far away as ever. We had been forced to rope up, and the only way to make any progress was to traverse in one direction, descend as far as possible, and then traverse again. This we did, but the ground was quite unrelenting and the torch was getting feebler every minute. Ray C. had the unenviable task of descending last with no torch, but he was using his axe well as an anchor. Katerine was getting very tired.

Out luck turned at last. I had already told Ray that if the next descent did not continue on a feasible line I wanted to bivouac as it was useless pressing on like this. But I had found a faint track, which went down and down. Even then we went wrong and had to retrace our steps 50 yards. The trees were thinning, the ground was less steep, and suddenly we came out into a little alp, and there was the moon. What a magnificent sight. Our spirits soared and I could not help bursting into song.

We stumbled into the hut at 1 a.m. after being out for 19 hours. We had expected a short day, but on reflection it had been worth it.

Others taking part: Ray Colledge, Ted Dance, Fred Boardman and a Greek girl, Katerine — *Editor.*

CHAMONIX (1959)

D. BURGESS

There are two main difficulties with a climbing holiday, one is the climbing itself and the other is writing it up afterwards. Last year the writing proved insurmountable.

The climbing party this year consisted of D. Chapman, R. Handley, R. Colledge and myself. Our first objective was Aguille du Fou by the S.W. ridge. This necessitated a 3.0 a.m. start from Montenvers, not exactly welcome after having travelled all the previous night, and a long trudge along the Plan-de-L'Aiguille footpath and up to the Nantillons Glacier. The Rognon was soon passed and we cramponed below the upper ice fall to the N. Ridge of the Blaitière. This was ascended to the third Brêche where a series of ledges and chimneys was followed across the west face to the Reynier Couloir. These ledges were not as continuous as the guide book implied and at one point a rappel was necessary to reach a lower ledge. From the couloir an obvious rake ran up below the Fou itself to the Col-de-Fou. Here we basked in the sun, ate some well earned snap, and gazed at the route before us.

The S.W. Ridge is not terribly long, only 150 feet, to quote the guide book, but it certainly looked impressive as we gazed at it. The first pitch appeared to be an overhanging layback crack, we were able to turn by climbing a steep slab artificially on some pegs already in place. Pitch after pitch followed, none particularly easy and all strenuous, a characteristic of the climbing, until at last we were all assembled beneath the final problem, a pear shaped boulder perched on the summit. This is usually ascended by throwing a rope over and using it as a hold for one hand. However, none of us appeared purist enough to worry over the last few feet and we considered the route done – the route no doubt considered us "done".

The view from the summit is fantastic, a forest of granite is an expression to describe the Aiguilles and how true it is. All round rock fangs stick in the air, the Caiman, Crocodile, and Plan next along the ridge seemed unclimbable from our position as indeed did the Blaitière in the other direction; until it dawned on us we had to bypass it on the descent. A vague traversing line led round beneath the N. summit of the Blaitière and the Bregault ridge was reached eventually and descended to the Nantillons Glacier, which we soon descended and reached Montenvers at 21.00 hours – 10 hours on the hoof.

We had a lay-in the next day, and after flexing aching muscles shelved the ambitious idea we had in mind and descended to the Coverche Hut. This we did, although R.H. descended to the valley to fetch Gloria to the hut, but was put off by a storm (and Gloria).

THE ALPINE SEASON 1962

D. BURGESS

This season has been the best of many years and consequently most routes were in excellent condition before the end of August. The many British climbers who were abroad this year were quick to take advantage of the good weather and many fine routes were done. The success of Bonnington and Clough on the Eiger was undoubtedly the finest British achievement, following, as it did, their ascent of the Walker Spur in record time. The harder Alpine routes all received their share of British ascents. But the emphasis certainly seemed to be on rock routes, and the Dolomites, Karwendal, and Kaisergeberge, were all well patronised. Chamonix was as usual the most popular centre and the campsite there was reminiscent of a bank holiday in Langdale. By the end of the season this was especially so as the rowdier elements had given the British a very bad name. Unfortunately there were many accidents involving British climbers, caused in the majority of cases through the folly of inexperience. The Eiger accidents should serve as a grim reminder that the mountains cannot be trifled with, and it is only due to the exceptionally good weather that the many parties, benighted or involved in extra bivouacs, escaped unscathed.

A few notes on the principle ascents (by British parties) that I have heard about, these are not necessarily complete or correct.

Chamonix Area

The E. face of the Grand Capucin was climbed by 5 or more parties, usually with one bivouac on the summit. The W. Face Aig. Noire de Peuterey had two ascents (B. Evans, I. Howell; Whillans, Bonnington), whilst the S. Ridge was climbed by R. Colledge and D. Davis. The Frontier Ridge and the Old Brenva Route on Mont Blanc were climbed by D. Gray, D. Hadlum, and E. Beard. Des at the time climbing with his arm in plaster following an accident in the Dolomites.

The Dru was in perfect condition and a multi-national procession wound its way up most routes. The Bonatti Pillar had an ascent by Crew and friend. Howell and Evans climbed the West Face, and the North Face had *at least ten ascents* before the end of the season. This was fantastic considering the second British ascent was by Oliver and Ruisson at the end of August. The other parties included Carruthers and Logan, John Brailsford, and L. Noble, I Clough, and J. Alexander.

The Aiguilles received their share of attention; the N. Face of the Plan was climbed by Carruthers and Les Brown. Several parties ascended the N. Ridge of the Peigne; the E. Ridge of the Crocodile, and the Ryan Lochmatter on the Plan.

Across the valley the Moine was climbed by its E. Face, and both the Petites Jorasses (W. Face) and Grand Jorasses (Walker) had their 3rd British ascents as also did the N. Face of the Triolet.

Zermatt Area

Heavy snow, left over from the winter was slow to clear and conditions were not good before August. The only notable ascent I have heard about was the Furggen Ridge of the Matterhorn (Clough, Alexander), and the Zmutt Ridge (G. Rhodes, L. Hughes, E. Beard).

In the Bregaglia many parties were active and the N. E. Face of the Badile has had numerous ascents – one report said that it had now been climbed by over 30 British parties and is now considered a voie normale.

A number of Oreads mentioned in this resumé, but what did Burgess do? — *Editor.*

AUGUST 1963

Contrary to reports, Colin Hobday and Geoff Hayes did get to the Alps. They wish it to be known that the only climbing they did was not in Munchen but in the Ortler – Seven peaks in all, including the Ortler and Konigspitz. Anne and Uschi send their best wishes to friends in the Oread but want to know if the club can offer anything better in the way of mountaineers than the above two so called Alpinists.

Burgess climbing with Ray Colledge had a good fortnight making the most of rather unsuitable weather. Route Major was one of their achievements. Theirs was the first ascent this year. A very fine show indeed.

Anne and Uschi eventually became Mrs. Hayes and Mrs. Hobday respectively — *Editor.*

EDITORIAL (EXTRACT)

Newsletter, September 1964

Tragedy struck the happy group of 15 Oread members and friends who were camping and climbing in Saas Fee.

On Wednesday July 29th, Guy Lee, Chris Culley and Martin Jarvey left the village and walked up to the Mischabel Hut where they bivvied the night. They started up the North East Face of the Lenspitz (a fine looking snow-ice cliff). At approximately 7 a.m. stones falling from the summit ridge were falling very close to the party and it was while this was happening that Martin slipped, pulling Chris off backwards, and Guy was unable to hold them both on his belay. All three fell and cleared the bergshrund, landing on the snowfield. Martin was killed and Chris suffered cuts to his face and legs, Guy was only bruised. The body was taken down to the valley by helicopter and Chris followed after a considerable time and was taken to the hospital at Visp. Guy was able to walk down.

The rest of the party were up at the Brittania Hut when they heard the news of the accident. Chris was visited every day by his friends and after a few days discharged himself from the hospital. Martin's body was flown back to England for Cremation at Mansfield at which the Oread was represented. Martin, although not a member of the Oread was a friend of the Sutton and district group of the club. He had been out on club meets at Glencoe and the Dane Valley as well as having climbed with club members.

Our deepest sympathy goes to his parents and family.

Geoff Hayes

STORM ON THE BIANCOGRAT – 1966

RAY HANDLEY

When the Oread decided to hold a meet in the Bernina group last year, Derrick Burgess and I decided we should give the more popular Alpine centres a miss and and join it. We were particularly attracted by the nearness of the Badile and the chance of breaking new ground.

We arrived in St. Moritz in time to hear that England had won the World Cup and we knew at last why at every village we drove through we received the "thumbs up" sign. The weather had been and still was very indifferent, one day fine the next snowing. We did a few training climbs, one being the Piz Morterasch which gave a very impressive view of the Biancograt ridge of the Piz Bernina.

We set off as a large party towards the end of the second week bound for the Tschierva Hut, from which we intended to attempt the traverse of the Piz Scerscen and the Piz Bernina, ascending the Ice Nose on the former and descending the Biancograt on the latter. When we arrived at the hut, there was a mixed school party in residence, who were to keep us awake most of the night until Digger Williams, unable to contain himself any more, sat bolt upright in bed loudly mouthing foul German oaths. With much grumbling we all tumbled out of bed at 1.00 a.m.; this is the time on any alpine meet when I wonder whether it is really necessary, and ask myself why I am not lying on some sun drenched beach surrounded by glorious females.

Derrick, who is always anxious to be away first, set the pace, and forcing a dry crust of bread down a dry throat we stumbled off into the cold darkness. I slowly became aware that the stars were out, but this did not help my temper as I staggered from one boulder to the next. After an age of going up and down and skirting a large rognon we stepped thankfully onto the glacier. Suddenly it was light enough to see the way ahead and trace the route; to the right lay the Piz Roseg to which the rest of our party were making their way. Our route lay straight ahead for a quarter of a mile over the Tschierva Glacier, then to rear itself abruptly on to the ridge and flatten out again before rearing steeply up to the Ice Nose. Beyond that, all was hidden.

Even so, this is the time that one begins to enjoy the thought of the climb. We strapped on our crampons, bid *bon voyage* to our friends, and stepped out across the glacier. We quickly reached the point where we had to break to the left to climb steep snow to the ridge. This proved quite straightforward, and after a bit of mixed work we found ourselves at the foot of our first difficulties, the Ice Nose. This is of a most peculiar nature and is the only reasonable way on to the summit nevé of the Scersen; some years it overhangs, but this year we were lucky as it was only vertical for a section of about 100 feet, and then lay back at about 70 degrees. However, this was not what we were thinking when we stood at its foot, and Derrick prepared himself to attack while I found a convenient stance and clipped on to a peg. One of the snags of ice climbing is that it takes a long time to cut hand and foot holds, the ice cut away usually hitting the Second, and this was no exception. I spent a very cold twenty minutes or so dodging ice chippings, alone with my thoughts, which weren't very pleasant. Suddenly there was a sickening crack and groan under my feet. I shouted up to Derrick. "This thing's collapsing – let's get off!" He looked at me without speaking and carried on. There is always a time on a alpine climb where the wrong decision means the difference between failure and success, and the choice is so marginal that a piece of paper will not go between. This to me is what makes a good alpinist, particularly on big climbs, and this is why I like climbing with people like Derrick and Ray Colledge, who make the right decisions. Derrick had found a stance, clipped to a peg, and I moved up, balancing from hold to hold. It was cold on the hands and the footholds seemed wide apart, the pegs he had placed seemed reluctant to come out and one channel just refused to budge. After some interesting climbing I joined Derrick at the top of the steep section on a small stance he had carved out of the wall. We quickly changed places, and he moved up another sixty feet to where the angle relented. I quickly followed, leading through to the lip of the plateau.

We were now in the sun and had to tramp across the plateau for some distance before climbing steeply up snow on to the crest of the ridge. The views were magnificent, and we could see the route on the Piz Roseg where our friends were climbing. In the still atmosphere we could distinctly hear shouts and yodels. The weather was still fine with a light trace of cloud. Before us stretched our ridge leading to the Piz Bernina and behind us lay the summit of the Scerscen. Examination of the ridge was not encouraging; it was a tightrope between heaven and earth. Vertical on one side and about 60 degrees on the other. The snow had the consistency of icing sugar, but the big problem was the gendarmes. These stretched one after the other like a switchback and were covered with powder snow. However, to rest was not to conquer, so with some misgivings we pressed on.

The first section was not too bad, but at last we reached the first tower. To get to its foot meant a steep descent on the crest of the ridge with variations on the vertical side where our axes were practically useless. We descended and moved one at a time, stopping only when a rock poked its head out. The ridge proved to be the very devil, as for every tower passed there was always one worse immediately after. I remember one place in particular, a descent into a brèche of about a hundred feet coupled with the ascent of some 250 feet to the top of the next tower. We accomplished this by tying two 120-foot ropes together. I clipped into a piton at the top of the tower we were on, Derrick then descended down a steep wall of tottering snow and then climbed the gendarme, which was rock finely sugared with snow. We were really gripped.

However, all good things come to an end, and finally only a short descent and a difficult traverse lay between us and the col leading up to the Piz Bernina. It had taken us four hours.

What we had not noticed during all this time was the steady deterioration of the weather. We now noticed the ominous clouds about and pressed on quickly up a steep ice slope to the ridge, which is the ordinary route on the Piz Bernina. When we did this ridge some days earlier it was covered with people but today we raced to the top, skirting the gendarme from which two Germans had fallen a day or two before.

We reached the summit at 5 p.m. From here we could easily retrace our steps and stay the night in an Italian hut. Or, as we wished to do, descend the Biancograt. This ridge consists mainly of a snow arete, but the top section was again rock towers. We had had good views of the route from our other ridge, and as people had been going up it during the day steps would be available. I felt we should go to the Italian hut, but Derrick was for the Biancograt. The weather was threatening, and it was late.

If there is a difference of opinion and you give way, you must always throw yourself into the decision. This we both did; the rock was not difficult, just time-consuming. A few hundred feet below the summit we met a belated party of three going up, but we did not stop as they had time and we did not. Ten minutes later, hell broke loose; I have only been in an electrical storm once before and that was on Scafell. I have always been afraid at even the thought of one, but here we were in the middle. The air became deadly still, a phosphorescent glow seemed to enclose us, when flash! bang! it had started.

Our immediate reaction was to get below the ridge, leaving the axes where they were, as we clung to our tower. Common sense then returned. We could not stay there, as darkness was not far off. We decided to move down as fast as possible, the storm lending wings to our feet. We quickly descended first one then another gendarme, the storm seemingly receding as we concentrated on the job in hand. At last we dropped on to the snow at the top of the arete; the storm had passed, leaving in its wake quietly falling snow, with visibility down to five yards. We cramponned up and moved quickly to the top of the arete, where we found footsteps which we followed, moving together and at speed. As darkness approached, we knew we were safe, but not off. We missed a slight detour in the route which cost us a valuable half hour, and my cartilage had jumped out.

Rough treatment soon put the latter right, but we could not regain the former. We thought of a bivouac, but decided to press on while what light there was remained. I slid down a chimney and thought I could see the col. It looked a long way off, but after traversing for fifty feet I found myself above it. The time was 8.30 p.m.

The descent of the couloir was interminable. My torch packed up and we had to move one at a time, but we were happy, and very tired. We had made the right decisions, how right, who can tell?

Originally printed in the M.A.M. Journal 1967.

Their arrival at Pontresina was not the end of the story. Burgess, insistent on ale, made for the station bar whereas Handley, focussed on getting back to the camp site at Silvaplana, jumped on a train. Unfortunately the train was heading over the Bernina Pass to Italy. At some point, realising that something was wrong, R.H. jumped off the train and made his way back to Pontresina where Burgess was still relaxing. They both had to walk back to Silvaplana – Some day — *Editor.*

GOING TO THE ALPS?

Newsletter, June 1967.

The Alpine Club have requested that all British Mountaineering Clubs notify their members of the situation in Chamonix this year. Because of trouble with English climbers and campers in the past, particularly last year, the police in Chamonix will ban all English climbers from the area if there is a recurrance. If you do intend to go to Chamonix please set a good example.

Geoff Hayes

The North Wall Club, Alpine Meet 1969

Editorial Extract   *Geoff Hayes*

I am sure very few climbing clubs of the size of the Oread can boast so many good routes in one short season. Congratulations to all those who did these climbs. There will be a special edition of the Oread Newsletter devoted to these ascents when you will be able to read the personal accounts of Ray Colledge on the Walker Spur of the Grandes Jorasses and the North Wall of the Eiger. Ray Handley who, with the President, Derrick Burgess climbed the North Face of the Dru; Pete Scott who did the Matterhorn North Wall and the Pear Buttress, (Colledge also climbed the Pear on the same day). I also hope to be able to print an account of the Cassin Route on the North East Face of the Piz Badile which Nat Allen climbed. Finally an account of the first ascent of Ali Ratna Tibba by Chris Radcliffe, who was a member of the successful Scottish Himalayan expedition 1969.

Hayes was, as usual, optimistic in his intention to publish a special edition of the Newsletter. I can find no trace of it. Doubtless accounts of these various ascents were published in "other places". More detailed references appeared in *Climb if you Will*, an earlier Oread commentary on Geoff Hayes and the Oread M.C., published in 1974 — *Editor*.

LETTERS . . . TO THE EDITOR 1958-1970

33, Tailo Street,
Tiger Bay,
Cardiff.
July 1959.

Dear Editor,

My situation at the moment is adequately described by the caption on a poster outside the Cardiff Labour Exchange. "They got me back to work". The happy, smiling figure in a natty trilby which it portrays, unfortunately bears little resemblance to myself at 7.45 a.m. However, in one of the brief intervals of rest from beating my brains out for meagre reward, the occasion of my first meeting with the Oread came back to me.

In November 1953 I wrote to the Secretary and learnt that a number of members would be meeting at Bullstones Cabin during the weekend. I set out from Strines Inn on Saturday afternoon and made my way via Dovestones, Abbey Brook, and Howden Edge to Margery Hill. It was almost dark by this time, and Bartholomews ½" gave no information on Bullstones Cabin. I had unfortunately forgotten to bring a torch so there was little I could do except find a suitable place to doss down and wait for morning. Morning arrived, and with it an introduction to those rarely seen figures, Ron Dearden and Jim Winfield who had spent the night on the bosom of Margery Hill. Together we made our way to Bullstones where Gibson, Clive Webb, Laurie Burns and a new recruit (who later became of note by his possession of a MA. Walking certificate) were preparing breakfast.

We were soon bound for Bleaklow, a single file, in drizzling rain on a narrow path above Derwent Valley. It was here that we met a search party from Bamford who were looking for an old shepherd lost on the moor during the previous night. We reached the Snake via the Alport, skirting round Kinder on the Roman Road, to Edale and the Church Inn. The outstanding event of the journey being the collapse of the holder of the Walking Certificate, on the last quarter mile.

127

Walking meets in Derbyshire such as Bullstones, Marsden-Rowsley, and Five Inns have always seemed to me to be one of the most characteristic Oread activities, and it is in connection with them that I shall always associate Gibson, who now leads a shadowy existence somewhere remote from the weekend world. Many people in the Oread knew him better than myself, and it is only as a result of their silence that I put forward the suggestion of doing something in this tenth anniversary year to honour his memory. Gibson the man, is dead. Gibson the symbol, lives on.

Two projects have occurred to me as a means of commemorating the occasion. I humbly put them forward for the consideration of the members and the Committee. Firstly, the purchase of one of the Bullstones Cabins, and if this proves impossible, the maintenance of them in a reasonable state of repair.

Secondly, the erection in the Peak District of a suitable memorial to Gibson. This could take the form of an engraved tablet, or a likeness of the man, in stone or metal, placed at the scene of some memorable Gibsonian incident. A well-known sculptor could be given the commission if sufficient funds were available. The thing should be in conservative taste I suggest. I don't, somehow, fancy a Gibson with holes in, or done as an abstraction in wire. Failing this there is a lively market in second hand sculpture nowadays. North country Aldermen are two a penny, pillars of the Empire are put down to base use, and late Queen Victorias fetch little more than aspidistra pots. A rough likeness could be bought and knocked into shape with little expense. There is Fergus O'Conner in the Arboretum Gardens for example. Nobody wants him and he could be moved away for the mere cost of transport on a quiet evening.

An equestrian Gibson? Gibson with a scroll? I think not. I remember him, a tall spare figure, cap at a jaunty angle, knee length cords, cigarette nonchalantly hanging down from lip, finger pointing with absolute certainty to the Derbyshire earth;

"I know this rock"

Yours in exile,
Jim Kershaw.

It seems entirely appropriate that Kershaw should first encounter Ron Dearden resting "on the bosom of Margery Hill" — *Editor.*

Re. HOLDING OF ICE AXE:

Most members of the Oread are forced by "Rubber Face Whymper" to purchase a copy of *Mountaineering.* Read Sept. 1961 page 26. – "Adze blade points forward".

I Agree,

J. Ashcroft – March 1962.

I can't agree with "fall-out" in his letter, when he recommends the ice axe to be held pick forward. On his next fall out he will most likely wish he had held the adze forward.

Unfortunately a number of professionally trained mountaineers in the Oread have been taught "Fallout's" method.

No less a mountaineer than George Band feels strongly on this subject. A letter from him is printed in an article by Humble in the Sept. 1961 issue of *Mountaineering,* from which I quote: –

"When a climber is on snow or ice slopes he should hold his hand over the head of the axe in such a manner that the adze blade points forward and the pick points to the rear and not vice versa". Then later in the letter – "I believe it well worth cultivating this habit even when using the ice axe as a walking stick on easy terrain."

I recommend anyone who has not read the article by Humble to do so as it gives some interesting information and useful tips on snow work in Britain.

Geoff Hayes – March 1962

CLUB SPIRIT

The Following extracts are included since they are exemplars of a recurring theme in the Club's history, and similar arguments have arisen time and time again during the last fifty years. Doubtless the divisions engendered in climbing versus huts will have its protagonists in the future. May the following be some guide to balanced thought — *Editor*.

"Pride goes before destruction, and a haughty spirit before a fall".

Proverbs (16:18)

TO THE COMMITTEE: 1960 *(Extract)*

Dear Friends,

This is to tender my resignation from the Oread Mountaineering Club. Apart from a few scattered weekends I have never really taken any part in the doings of the Club since the end of my first year in climbing, 1955, and I think this is an opportune moment to resign. However, I should like to express a few thoughts, which come to mind.

Unfortunately, I agree with all the newsletter's spasmodic comments about characteristics of the Club such as "chique-ness", insensitivity, and misplacement of effort. From my earliest days with the Oread I have sensed this barrier which surrounds the nucleus of the Club. And definitely repels exploratory advances of all but the most brash and extrovert new members to gain admission. Other people have mentioned this to me, so I am not the only one to have suffered from the insensitivity of several of the inner circle to the plight of an eager newcomer in the Bell for the first time.

It seems to me that far too much effort is expended on building a posh club hut. Doubtless there are several superficially powerful arguments in favour of this policy (notably reciprocal rights) but to get down to fundamentals, this is a CLIMBING CLUB. O.K.. So a hut at the foot of the hills is a good idea so that folk can spend a dry night in Wales as a change from pitching tents in a storm at 1 a.m. on Saturday. O.K. so we can buy or rent a HUT, and the deal takes one month. At the end of one month (when the hut is "sure") can we start visiting and climbing from it? Oh no. This weekend is a working party! We have to spend this and many other weekends pulling down walls, putting in grates, tiling, plastering, plumbing. Some members spend the weekend climbing and are roundly castigated in the next Newsletter, and accused of lack of club spirit. Surely a climbing hut should stay a hut and the energies of members should be expended in climbing from the hut instead of making it a 5-star hotel for "Pretend members" who are the type of people largely attracted to the Oread of late, it seems.

Brian N. Richards

Newsletter (Extract), November, 1960

Dear Sir,

I read with some impatience the reproduction of Brian Richards letter of resignation.

The hoary spectre of extra-climbing activities is produced as a sign of human decadence.

The criticism always stems from those who least participate in the Club's organisation and activities. Naturally people who can only seldom enjoy visits to mountain country have little time for administration or working parties. I do not think that anyone has expressed an opinion that they should so waste their time, nor has the use of facilities available been in anyway begrudged by members whose labour has made them possible.

The matter is fairly clear. There is the individual and the Club. The Club augments and supports the individual but you can climb without being a club member – many do – but if you enter into association with an organisation of this character you find many additional facets of enjoyable companionship and enterprise. To the many who make the Oread M.C. a part of their leisure life, there is much to give and much to take, and most find it gives life an additional flavour. But above all they find no attenuation of activity. The reverse is true, the most active members are also the working members.

Regarding cliques. It is a logical corollary of members. When Homo Sapiens are gathered in number, they nucleate, and smaller intimate groups form. But the wider activities and interests overlap and integrate the individual to the whole. Above all they are essentially nice people and, although they have most in common with intimates, will not rebuff a stranger or little known member. We are constantly adjured to make entry into Oread circles easier, but something more than a purely negative approach by the novitiate is required. Otherwise only time will bring confidence which is probably the best way.

Laurie Burns

Newsletter, November 1960

Sir,

I expect that there were a few tongues in cheeks when it was decided to seek the approval of Brian Richards to publish his letter. There is hardly any need to invite discussion, indeed very much of the same things have always been discussed within the Club as long as I have known it, and I remember recently swopping a few ideas on the subject with our President.

It is always regrettable to receive a resignation and it is always regrettable to tender one. How many such letters begin: Dear Sir, I regret?

It is a pity that Brian's criticisms, which he himself declares to be well meaning and (he hoped) constructive, were not more energetically and practically applied by him for some of the time since 1955 when he became a member.

Roger Turner

Newsletter, August 1963

Dear Sir,

There are 100 or so members in the Oread, who are so because they enjoy mountaineering of varying degrees of activity. It would be unreasonable to expect all 100 to be wildly enthusiastic about the hut at Rhyd-Ddu. Some are quite happy to spend their time in the mountains voluntarily improving the hut to a standard well above that which is sufficient for the more active mountaineer who may regard the hut as a refuge for the night, i.e. in the Swiss Alpine tradition.

I think it is important for those interested in, and responsible for, the hut to realise that there is this division. A natural enough one and not a situation which should cause any strife within the club but one which must be accepted by those interested in the club for it's own sake

I have helped finance the hut and, despite a lack of enthusiasm for it's structure and location, I have, in the past, helped to establish it; for a hut is a good focal point for a club. On the rare occasions when I can now spare the time from establishing my own home I prefer to go mountaineering.

It is very noticeable that on Saturday evenings the hut is deserted after 8.00 p.m. in favour of the pub and dance hall. The installation of the bath for instance must be regarded in the light of this social, or anti-social phenomenon.

Let not the Oread subscription chain the mountaineer to the hut if he does not wish it.

If Tan-Y-Wyddfa burns tonight the Oread should still survive.

Yours etc.
Tom Frost.

Newsletter, August 1963

Sir,

What is happening to the Oread? Is it just becoming a pile of dead wood waiting for someone to put the final match to it and destroy it forever? Over the past year members seem to show less and less interest in the club and if it was not for a few active members, most of whom come from Nottingham, the Oread would fade away.

That, I'm sure, members would not want to happen. After all why not change the Tuesday evening meets in the Bell to Nottingham where the most active section is at the moment. If you go to the Bell it's a waste of time. It's impossible to make arrangements for the weekend and those who do go out seem to have their own private meets.

I know it is difficult for people who live away from the area to take an active interest, but it would be nice to see and hear a bit more of them, than their names just being on a list in the handbook. Well I have had a moan, so let's have a bit more enthusiasm for club activities. Maybe some of you will agree, others not, so why not write to the Newsletter and express your views. But let us remain a club and not become an association, which I think we are fast becoming.

An Active Member

I must admit that I agree with much that is in the above letter about the Bell. If people get there much later on Tuesdays it will be drinking up time before I see anyone. However, I believe that the club has been never more active on meets, although those attending are mostly from my way.

Geoff Hayes – Newsletter Editor

Indrasan (6,221m), Kulu Himal.   *Photo: Jack Ashcroft.*

Derbyshire Himalayan Expedition 1961. D. Gray, D. Burgess, S. Read, R. Handley, Balgit Singh (liaison), R. G. Pettigrew (leader), J. Ashcroft.   *Photo: Indian Press.*

Summit of Konigspitze, 1963. C. Hobday, Geoff and Anne Hayes.   *Photo: Uschi Hobday.*

L. Burns, Margaret Hooley, Bernina 1961. *Photo: C. Hooley.*

Engadine 1966; G. Gadsby, Doreen Hodge, G. Reynolds, P. Janes.   *Photo: J. Aschcroft.*

Alpine Games: Fred Allen and Tinsel Allen, Digger Williams and Pattie Carnell, Peter Janes and friend. *Photo: D. Burgess.*

Alpine Meet, St. Moritz 1975.   *Photo: G. Gadsby.*

Newsletter, January 1964

Dear Editor,

Through the medium of your newsletter may I seek advice on some climbing matters, which might be of general interest.

Is it possible for some avant-garde member to offer suggestions as to which nailing patterns are most highly thought of this year? The tricouni edge nail appears to enjoy popularity but some new types of clinker are available so possibly someone has some useful experience to impart on this most interesting subject. Illustrations would be a splendid idea although difficult to reproduce in the newsletter.

A Further recent innovation too, is the lighter type of Beales' Hempen Alpine line, which seems to be a great improvement upon the heavy manila in use at the present time. Does this give satisfaction?

Whilst reading the letter of "active member" in the most recent Newsletter it is difficult to resist the temptation to ask if, to some degree, he is confusing vociferousness with interest, and is this partly responsible for the absence of some members on meets?

Yours sincerely,
John Fisher

Newsletter, August 1963

Sir,

On the recent Marsden-Rowsley meet, a magnificent day on Saturday was followed by a sorry display of decadence when Yorkshire Bridge was reached. Of the ten participants, two were spirited away by their wives on Saturday evening. On Sunday all sorts of specious reasons for not continuing the walk were advanced. The walk down the Edges was contemptuously dismissed as dull and pointless. Urgent reasons were found for catching early trains to places like Liverpool and Coventry, and, most insidious of all, one member of the party had left his car in Grindleford, with malice aforethought.

As a result, I was left on my own from Fox House onwards; but cheered on by meeting Laurie Burns in Longshaw Park, and a large Oread climbing party at Froggatt. I eventually reached Baslow under my own steam. Here I succumbed to an unexpected offer of motor transport by two former Oread stalwarts of earlier days, Mike Turner and Ron Dearden.

Looking back, I recall that something rather similar happened in 1953, when I started from Colne, and did most of the walk on my own. After 1955, the Marsden-Rowsley meet was rested for a while and was a popular success again when reintroduced a few years later. After this years' performance, may I suggest that it is again dropped for a year or two, and then perhaps, when it does reappear on the meets programme, there may be a party with sufficient enthusiasm to complete it.

Yours etc.,
Phil Falkner

TO THE EDITOR – RE. MARSDEN-ROWSLEY 1963

Like many another exile I am occasionally seized with nostalgia for the region where I was born. I long for springtime in the rhubarb fields where the dark rivers meander through the spoil heaps of the West Riding. In the greener hills to the west, the grimy minarets of Marsden beckon the pilgrim on. I was not alone among the faithful as I left a

Huddersfield tram and enquired the way to the Pettigrew Memorial from a wandering Sikh. Erected on the site of the Marsden Gas-works the plaque is inscribed

"In gratitude from those who knew
Robert Gavin Pettigrew".

The 9.40 train from Manchester discharged a select company. (as Welbourn says by invitation only). Burgess, Pretty, Falkner, George Sutton, Janes, Ashcroft, Dave Williams and Wes. Haydn. A screech of bath chair tyres began to race down the incline to the Ramsden Supper Rooms and the Tetley House next door.

I will not weary you with the details of the Marsden-Rowsley route itself. I think Phil Falkner is missing the point a little when he complains that nobody finished the walk. The thirty or forty miles of desolate moor between Marsden and Rowsley are merely a canvas on which a series of incidents and characters are painted. The picture varies in quality and size from year to year.

These are the highlights of 1963, A fine Saturday, (many of those present had never before seen Black Hill). Dave Williams' Instant Soup, which exhausted all fuel supplies. The despatch of Janes by Burgess down Crowden Brook, to perish in machine gun fire – he survived however to provoke an incident with the Landlord at the Yorkshire Bridge. Pretty abbreviates; "Ashcroft really does know the way across Bleaklow". Falkner threatens to write to the Newsletter about the lack of enthusiasm. I retire at Fox House to give his case greater weight.

I really most complete this walk some time.

Jim Kershaw

THE DERBYSHIRE HIMALAYAN EXPEDITION 1961
(Patron: His Grace The Duke of Devonshire)
FROM *CLIMB IF YOU WILL*, PUBLISHED 1974:

"The Derbyshire Himalayan Expedition comprised eight members, five of whom were Oreads, including the leader Bob Pettigrew. The others were Derrick Burgess, (Deputy Leader), Jack Ashcroft (Surveyor), Ray Handley and Trevor Panther. Dennis Gray, as a Rock and Ice Club member joined the expedition with Steve Read of the Summit Mountaineering Club (Nottingham). The eighth member of the expedition was Nick Smythe, who, at the time, was working in India, a temporary expatriate of the Mountain Club of Stafford (at the time Harry Pretty was President of the Stafford Mountain Club). The expedition was fortunate in obtaining as Patron the Duke of Devonshire and the help of Sir Jack Longland and Robin Hodgkin was ever present. It is difficult to itemise the individuals and organisations who supported the expedition, but two men within the Oread who had worked conscientiously until the moment the party left U.K. were Harry Pretty and Dave Penlington. It was their original intention to join the expedition but they both had to withdraw before the expedition left".

"The expedition left Manali in the eastern Punjab on the 2nd June 1961. The main objective was to climb Indrasan (6,221m). Burgess and Gray reached the highest point by following the west ridge[1]. However the length and technical difficulties and resources available at the time, enforced a retreat some 200m short of the summit. The nearby peak of Deo Tibba (6,002m) was climbed by two parties, (4th and 5th ascents)".

"The east ridge[2] of Indrasan was also probed but found to offer no easy alternative. Pettigrew wrote "the only route offering any hope of reaching the summit would be a frontal attack in a diagonal line, before taking the steep snow of the south face". This was accomplished the following year by a Japanese expedition[3]".

"From 9th July for two days Pettigrew, Burgess and Ashcroft trekked over passes between the Manali Glacier and the Bara Shigri, setting up plane table stations, and taking photographic panoramas, thus adding to the work done by Snelson (1951), Dr. A. E. Gunther (1964) and Joss Lynam, who had essentially surveyed the Bara Shigri side. On the return journey they snatched a peak, and made the second ascent of White Sail (6,446m), first climbed by Lt. Col. J. O. M. Roberts in 1941".

1   Climbed by Tony Johnson, Roger Brook, John Brazington, Geoff Arkness, Geoff Tabbner, Bryan Pooley, 1971.
2   First ascent 1973; H. Day, G. Owens.
3   Koyiro, Tomita, Yasumasa, Miyaki.

"Simultaneously Handley and Gray reconnoitred the nearby peak of Ali Ratna Tiba (5,492m). They explored south of the peak and made two first ascents in the cluster of aiguilles known as the Manikaran Spires. Onset of the monsoon precluded any serious attempt on the Ali Ratna Tibba[1]."

1   First ascent by a Scottish party in 1969, which included an Oread sassenach by the name of Chris Radcliffe.

Trevor Panther had to retire early from D.H.E. 1961, due to illness — *Editor.*

ON THE OTHER HAND...

Sometimes expeditions, with serious intent, are better exemplified by incidents that are not included in the official report, and I am grateful to Dennis Gray for providing some insight into the private life of Bob Pettigrew and his fellow apprentice expeditioners — *Editor.*

ON THE HIGH SEAS WITH COLONEL BOB

DENNIS GRAY

1961 is a long time ago and memories of the Derbyshire Himalayan Expedition of that year, which was very much an Oread initiative, are distant. But not too remote to still raise a smile when I think on them now and then.

On the boat going out from Liverpool to Bombay, we established a reputation for ourselves as a team of live wires, and even, on occasion, eccentrics. Younger mountaineers who are used to modern communications, will probably be amazed to learn that as recently as the sixties, most expeditions to the Himalaya had to travel to Pakistan/India and back by passenger liner. Imagine a team of Oreads let loose amongst a boat load of bun-eaters, with the odd wealthy tourist aboard and a few young unaccompanied females, plus many British staff members going out to the various High Commissions, with unlimited amounts of cheap booze available day and night. This created an environment for fun in the sun, which allowed many an adventure, both above and below decks.

I experienced something of a *faux pas* at a fancy dress evening, for I went as Susie Wong. I borrowed a dress which was so tight I had to be cut out of it with a pair of scissors afterwards. Wearing rouge and eye shadow, plus falsies I must have appeared desirable to some, for a large Sikh gentleman pursued me around the boat deck pinching my bottom whenever he caught up with me.

Gaylord Handley had a fine boat trip, the highlight being when Thunderthighs, tired of his usual chat up line; "I'm an executive with Rolls Royce you know, travelling out to India on top secret work. Cannot tell you more", became so frustrated with the waiting she threw him onto a bed and dived on top of him. Gaylord obtained his nickname from the exclusive restaurant/night club in New Delhi, where he liked to spend his days and nights rather than on Colonel Bob's outings to ancient Indian relics.

Ray and I had met Thunderthighs and her cabin mate Khakiteeth on about the fifth day out from Liverpool. Up to then the old tub we were sailing on, The Cilicia, flagship of Glasgow's now defunct Anchor line had been behaving like a bucking bronco, and many of the passengers had spent their first few days confined to their cabins. Included amongst them was our youngest member Steve Read with whom I was sharing accommodation. Tired of being an invalid, and listening to my tales of four course meals, he insisted on coming up to the dining room one evening to try to force some food down. He managed to do this, but promptly brought it all up again, all over our table.

Back to Khakiteeth, who, apart from her nicotine stained molars was actually very petite and attractive with ginger hair. She turned out to be just as agile and strong as her friend; and, having seen what had happened to Ray, proceeded to throw me onto her bed with similar results. As Gaylord remarked afterwards, "It was like a scene out of a French farce". I cannot recall which one, but in case any Oread feels that Handley behaved like a cad, as was his habit in those days, he did offer to marry the girl.

Colonel Bob was our leader, and I still recall Burgess's amazement one night in Manali, when, after a few beers, he discovered that this was in all truth only an Honorary rank. In fact Pettigrew had never risen higher than an AC plonk when he had done his national service. But he has never let that stop his progress. I always think of him as a high ranker myself, for he has such military bearing. Bob's finest hour was when he out drank the Purser, glass for glass, on his own poison, gin! To realise the enormity of this feat, you must understand that this sailor was a dipso and drank several bottles of the stuff each day. He had invited us to his cabin one night for a session and Burgess, Handley, Steve and myself were all pissed as farts within half an hour. But Colonel Bob, with stiff upper lip, kept on drinking for the glory of the Oread, putting away doubles and trebles as if they were water, whilst trading stories with the alcoholic Jack Tar until the Purser was also blathered. As I passed into oblivion I realised what our leader was up to. Sitting at the side of a sink, he would divert our attention with a story, tip his drink down the plug-hole, then raise his glass to his lips and pretend to knock it back. "Aye your man Pettigrew is a fine drinker", admitted the Purser to Ray and myself, once he had recovered the next evening. I have kept quiet about this subterfuge until now, but it should be obvious to any reader why Colonel Bob has gone so far in British sport, despite being known in his youth as "Half a pint Pettigrew".

Do not be misled however, by his establishment image. In 1961 Colonel Bob was as capable of kicking over the traces as the rest of us. He might have been cast by the fates as out 'Great Leader', but he was still up for it given the chance. This came about one night in the shape of Brigadier Billy's perambulator. The Brigadier was on his way out to New Delhi to take over as Military Attache to the British High Commission. A huge florid fellow, he was a rather odious, upper class twit, and was accompanied by his younger wife who had recently presented him with an heir. They spent their days pushing this baby round the deck, being rude to any of the other passengers who might get in the way, and demanding instant attention from the Goanese waiters. They used to leave the perambulator after its daytime use tied up on deck. So. Late one night, after all the other passengers had retired, under the influence of alcohol and the direction of our leader, we decided to hold a pram race. One of us sat on this contraption, whilst another of our number raced around the foredeck to a course set and timed by Gaylord. He of the H. Samuel Everight. The pace became hotter and hotter, and the pram was subjected to even more extreme treatment until the inevitable happened as Burgess was hurtling around the deck full tilt with Pettigrew sat like a huge baby in the Silver Cross. When the thing collapsed two of its wheels came squealing off. There ensued quite a pile up, so we simply stuck the wheels back on as best we could and crept off to our respective cabins as if nothing had happened.

Early the next morning Brigadier Billie and his wife set off for their morning constitutional, pushing the perambulator with their pride and joy inside. They only managed a few paces before the contraption collapsed once more and its front wheels went spinning off in different directions. At which the officer's roar of rage could be heard even below decks. But despite his anger he never did discover that it was a fellow officer, Colonel Bob, who had been the one most responsible for the buggering of his pram.

There are many more memories from that boat trip. We saw a blue moon over the Nile, some dirty postcards in Port Said, and a little of the devastation caused by the Suez conflict of a few years previous, The canal was still partly blocked by scuppered ships and we had to gingerly pick our way round and through, but it was in Aden that Handley and myself nearly met our nemesis.

The boat berthed and Ray, Thunderthighs, and myself jumped into a taxi to go to Krater City, for it was there one could then find the cheapest cameras, electrical goods, hi-fi's etc. Unfortunately the taxi driver, who turned out to be a rogue, kidnapped us out of the Aden Protectorate and into South Yemen, taking us to a camel market. We only realised this when, instead of taking about the thirty minutes normally required to reach Krater, one hour later we were still rolling over the desert. Thunderthighs became alarmed and Ray and I furious, and we all three shouted at the driver. But to no avail. On arriving at the market in South Yemen he demanded large sums of money, or threatened he would dump us. He also suggested to Ray that he exchange Thunderthighs for several camels. It appears that young ladies with very large thighs were very sought after in the Yemen. Anyhow as we had not the kind of money he was demanding we had a stand-off and slowly it dawned on the hapless driver that instead of well heeled tourists, who normally fell for his scam, he now had to deal with Gaylord Handley of Rolls Royce. No less that Skylon himself. A deal was struck.

Yet, even when we arrived back at Krater, we nearly did not get back to the safety of the ship. A large Nubian armed with a knife jumped Ray and myself as we emerged out of an electrical goods store, carrying the hi-fi system that Gaylord had treated himself to. The chap had us pinned against a shop window and was waving the knife under our noses, demanding with menaces the hi-fi and money, when salvation came in the form of Jerry. Physically a huge chap, a missionary, (from off our ship) who was on his way to India to carry the Christian message. He immediately sized up the situation and calmly walked up to the mugger and shouted at him loudly in English, "Put that knife down and go away you naughty man". And amazingly the Nubian did just that!

When we finally arrived in Bombay, having taken a month over the journey from Liverpool, it was with real sadness that we bade farewell to the Cilicia, her crew, and our fellow passengers, some of whom had by then become firm friends. In all truth I could have made a career out of being a cruise guide, going back and forth from Liverpool to Bombay. I had almost forgotten by then why we had set out in the first place. But waiting for us on the dockside was out Parsee agent, Freddie Buhariwallah, who was to shepherd us through customs (it took several days to clear our mountain of gear), and who introduced the rookies such as myself to our first sights and sounds of India and the realities of everyday existence on the sub Continent. An introduction that was to have a profound effect on my own life and for which I will always to grateful to my friends in the Oread who made it possible for me to share in such a mind expanding adventure.

Visit Chatsworth and see the room in which the Duke of Devonshire met RGP. All proceeds to expedition funds.

Oreads in Shorts. Newsletter, January 1961.

THE KULU WARRIOR

During 1962 Bob Pettigrew took up a teaching appointment at Rajkumar College, Rajkot, and between 1963 and 1967, visited the Kulu, Spiti, Lahoul area, with various parties, no less than six times.

Extracts from his frequent reports to the Newsletter follow.

KULU PUMORI (21,500') 1964

We left Manali on May 12th and, after a day's delay due to a storm on the pass, entered the Chandra valley. The valley porters were paid off on May 17th in a camp near the snout of the Bara Shigri glacier. Thereafter the work of ferrying stores and equipment was borne equally between the four climbers.

Base camp at Concordia, the junction of several glaciers, was finally established on May 28th, despite prolonged bad weather, with food supplies for a further 21 days including caches at intervals on the glacier.

Two days were spent in reconnaissance after which the routes selected by Lynam's party on the Northwest ridge, and the eastern approaches to the mountain, were both ruled out. We decided to seek a route on the south-west ridge, the foot of which seemed accessible from a small nevè draining the south face of Pumori. Accordingly, Advanced Base Camp was sited on the main southern tributary glacier of the Bara Shigri, near the junction of the nevè icefall from the south face of the mountain, and beneath the impressive rock spire of Lal Qila (Red Fort) 20,839'.

Two ridge camps were successively established on the crest of the southwest ridge at 19,000' and 20,000'. From the latter at 6 a.m. on June 6th Wangyal and myself climbed to the summit via the south-west ridge, making a diversion onto the steep snowfield of the south face to avoid a rock step a few hundred feet above Camp 2, and regaining the ridge just short of the summit. This, a perfect snow cone, was sited some way to the northwest along a spectacular and corniced snow ridge. The time was 9 a.m. and, for once the day was clear – permitting the identification of many mountain groups and their individual peaks as well as a round of photography. We commenced the descent at 9.30 a.m., and reached Camp at 10.45 a.m.

Three days later, June 9th, Franz Mohling and Ang Chook repeated the ascent.

We withdrew from the mountains on June 13th, heavily laden, and re-entered Manali on June 20th.

RECONNAISSANCE OF ALI RATNA TIBBA (18,013') 1965

Ali Ratna Tibba, 18,013', and its fore-top known respectively as Paptula and Dramtula to the local paharis (hillmen) is a formidable mountain resembling the Aiguilles des Drus. Aiming to carry out a close reconnaissance Langford, Pettigrew and Wangyal circumnavigated the base of the mountain by ascending the Ali Ratna Tibba East glacier, a tributary of the Malana glacier, and descending the Ali Ratna Tibba West glacier which emerges in the upper Malana, on the true left bank of the river, just below the snout of the Malana glacier. Two camps were required, one on the new pass we made immediately south-west of Ali Ratna Tibba, and one above the lower icefall on the descent glacier. The pass was named the pass of the Obelisks, 16,000'. We consider that once gained the south-west ridge offers the best chance of an ascent. But it would have to be reached by a route traversing the steep ice fields of the south face, which would require considerable resources and prolonged preparation.

The party withdrew from the area down the remarkable and precipitous gorge of the Malana river, reaching the motorable road of the Parbati valley at Jari, (5,260') on June 17th.

BRUCE'S SOLANG WEISSHORN (19,450') 1966

Base camp (11,500') was established in the remote Upper Manalsu valley, three miles south of Seri on May 27th beneath a spectacular rock wall some 3,000' high, and close to a spur inhabited by a herd of ibex containing some splendid heads.

Subsequent days were spent reconnoitering a route northwards and establishing Camp 1 at 14,500'. Beyond the camp the route soon climbed out of the Upper Manalsu valley, over its west containing wall, and across the Kulu/Bara Bangahal by easy but exhausting nevès to the foot of the South face of Hanuman Tibba. Camp 2 was duly established at 16,500' on June 2nd.

From this camp on June 3rd two ropes consisting of Pettigrew and Pasang, Ang Nima and Rinzing, set off at dawn to make a summit bid by a route which weaved through the triple-tiered ice-cliffs of the south face.

Progress was encouragingly swift as far as the upper tier of the ice-cliffs some 600' below the summit cone. The snow condition was just beginning to perplex the party when suddenly, with a load report, a quarter-mile wide wind-slab avalanche split off at the exact level of the leading rope and swept the two ropes helplessly down the slopes for 500' only to discard them on the narrow terrace above the second tier of ice-cliffs. A later examination of the debris showed that the avalanche had continued for a further 1,500' below the second tier, and had come close to obliterating Camp 2 before it stopped.

Uninjured but bereft of an ice axe, the party quit the South face and traversed eastwards to gain the crest of the corniced East Ridge. Climbing steeply past small outcrops of vivid yellow rock, the snow summit was reached at 11.30 a.m.

Bruce's Solang Weisshorn (19,450') also known locally as Hanuman Tibba. First ascent 23.06.12 by Swiss guide Heinrich Fuhrer of Meiringen and a Gurkha soldier. Second ascent as above on 03.06.66 by Indo-British party organised by the Bombay Climber's Club — *Editor.*

HIMALAYAN NEWS – PAPSURA (21,200')

Newsletter, June 1967

News has just arrived of an accident in the Himalayas to a party, which included Bob Pettigrew. Climbing in a rope of three, the last man slipped and in a fall on snow of approximately 2,000'. Pettigrew sustained a dislocated hip. He was carried by stretcher for many days and subsequently had the hip attended to in a hospital in North India. He is now convalescing.

The best wishes of the whole club go out to Bob, and we trust that he will soon recover and be able to lead his usual full and active life.

Geoff Hayes

Here is an extract or two from a letter written to the Newsletter Editor.

"You will be surprised to hear that I am lying here convalescing after my first serious accident in the mountains. It occurred during reconnaissance of Papsura. We were three on the rope, descending a steep couloir. The lowest man slipped out of his steps, the second man's steps collapsed and the two of them dragged me off. We fell about 2,000' and came to rest in the bergschrund. The other two were dazed but unhurt, but I fell across the lower lip of the 'schrund and dislocated my left hip. Ultimately I diagnosed this myself. John Ashburner got me installed in a tent just below the couloir that night. The next day they shifted me to the highest camp on a stretcher, improvised from skis and aluminium pickets. There I lay for seven days while they organised a stretcher team of Porters from Manali. The journey across the mountains took eight days (I'm claiming a stretcher record!). It was 16 days before I was X-rayed in Manali hospital and the diagnosis confirmed. By then I'd got used to seeing my left leg 2 inches shorter than my right!"

"By a lucky coincidence a professor of orthopaedic surgery was holidaying in Manali. He decided to try and replace the joint under spinal anaesthesia – thus averting a serious operation, which is the usual course after such a lapse of time. He was successful and I am now encased in plaster from chest to left big toe for six weeks".

"I'm glad to report that a determined final bid for the peak by Colin and Geoff was successful".

Salaams to the Oread
Bob Pettigrew

R.G.P. had further surgery in 1998 as a result of the fall in 1967 — *Editor.*

ALI RATNA TIBBA (18,031') – FIRST ASCENT – MAY 1969

Ali Ratna Tibba had been superficially reconnoitred by the D.H.E. 1961 and its approaches more thoroughly examined by Bob Pettigrew in 1965. Not a high peak but of some technical difficulty akin to classic Chamonix aiguilles at altitude. A Scottish team (Fred Harper, Marjorie-Anne Harper, Jim McArtney, Dave Nicol) invited Chris Radcliffe (Oread) to join them when Ian Clough had to drop out.

Radcliffe arrived at the base camp only five days after leaving U.K. having been assisted by the RAF who flew him to Bahrain in a Transport Command V.C.10.

The base camp was above the village of Malana (10,000') and directly beneath the west glacier of Ali Ratna Tibba. During load carrying to establish a camp on a high col, Jim McArtney had a serious crevasse fall, and with damaged ribs, had to retire to Malana. From this high col (partially established) camp the rest of the team pushed on;

Extract (from *Climb if you Will*) by Chris Radcliffe:

Late in the evening we saw two figures returning to our camp. We were surprised but pleased to find that these were Fred and Marjorie-Anne. They had accompanied Jim to base camp where he had insisted on continuing without their assistance. As the arduous part of the descent was behind him they had let him have his own way and returned to join Dave and myself.

At 4.00 a.m. on May 25th we set out across the hard frozen glacier. Soon we reached the foot of the ice ramp. We moved in ropes of two and steadily, pitch after pitch, we climbed the ramp, 4,000', to the point where it joined the west ridge. Below us vertical granite walls dropped to the glacier, above us ice-plastered walls. We crossed frequent avalanche runnels and had no doubt about the consequences if an ice field should break loose from the walls above. Dawn arrived and revealed a new panorama of peaks, but we pressed on and encountered no problems so that by 10.00 a.m. we had reached the notch in the west ridge. Here we rested and enjoyed the view. A fantastic sight greeted us. These rock and ice aiguilles seemed to belong more to Patagonia than to the Himalayas. Facing the east ridge of Ali Ratna Tibba across the Pass of Obelisks, one aiguille presented a face as big as the west face of the Dru. All seemed more serious than the training peaks we had expected of them.

Above us 4000' of climbing separated us from the summit. A series of granite buttresses were separated by snowfields. The climbing was superb. Chamonix type granite gave us the familiar strenuous type of crack climbing of. Grade D-Sup, but now we also had the insidious effect of altitude to contend with. Every move demanded a special effort; we gasped breathlessly over even the easiest moves. We had only one thought in our minds – to reach the summit. But as the shadows lengthened it was clear that we were not to reach the top that day.

Now we started looking for a bivouac site, but on this mountain they were hard to find. Pitch after pitch and still no ledge appeared big enough to accommodate us all. Eventually we found a site. It was well enclosed on three sides and would afford us some protection in the event of a storm, but the main disadvantage was that we had to sit on snow. We donned all our down gear and after an unsatisfactory meal settled down to bivvy at 17,500'. So far we had been lucky with the weather; there had been no afternoon storm, but now thin wisps of cloud were sweeping round our bivouac place and we were apprehensive about how the weather would turn out for the following day.

We were very fatigued but we slept little as the cold penetrated our clothing. However it remained fine and as soon as the sun reached us the next day, we hastily prepared for the final ascent. Five hundred feet to the summit and no great difficulties in our way. Two hours later only a thin blade of rock remained to be climbed. – a fine summit to a fine mountain. There was not room for all of us, so one at a time; we climbed to the highest point to be photographed in turn. The time was l0.00 a.m., the day May 26th. Ali Ratna Tibba had finally been climbed.

There was no great feeling of achievement. The views were breathtaking, yet not perhaps as fine as lower on the mountain where there is nearby perspective. There was no time to relax as the storm clouds were building up and we had no wish to be trapped on the mountain. The descent began uneventfully as we descended by an interminable series of abseils. We followed the ridge as far as the notch. But we had no intention of reversing the ramp because of the objective dangers. Instead we descended the south face by yet more abseils. As we feared a storm broke over us, but we reached the site of our half-finished col camp safely. After collecting the gear we had left there several days before, we descended the icefall. The surface if the glacier was in a terrible state after the effect of the sun and it was wearying work crossing it. We finally stumbled into camp at 8.00 p.m. Our ropes and gear were carelessly dumped and we collapsed into the tents totally fatigued.

Chris Radcliffe's contribution to the successful ascent of Ali Ratna Tibba concluded Oread involvement of Himalayan climbing during the period 1958-1970 — *Editor.*

THE SOCIAL WHIRL

During the years 1958-1970 the Annual Dinners attained a standard of excellence which unfortunately has not been maintained through to the present. Distinguished mountaineers from other clubs almost competed to sit at the Oread top table once a year, to have their characters delicately "done over", and to enjoy the privilege of answering back. Character assassination by panto, song, and mimicry left few unscathed.

"the imaginative and outrageous Saturnalia which it inadequately describes as the Annual Dinner" – Jack Longland in his foreword to *Climb if you Will — Editor.*

THE GREEN MAN, ASHBOURNE

November 1960

Shamed by last year's debauchery in Baslow, 120 Oreads and associated friends, guests etc., sat down to a chic-chic dinner in more opulent surroundings than usual.

And in more distinguished company than usual, for among the guests, including the youthful Miss Sue Hunt and the Countess Gravina, (remembered for her example and leadership on Cho-Oyu) was at last seen that elusive flamboyant representative of the Brazilian Ladies Alpine Club, Carmello O'Higgins. Her entrance, reception by an outwardly startled, though obviously prepared Pretty, and subsequent speech of welcome must rank as the peak of Oread humour for many years to come.

What is also so commendable is that the whole hoax was one of the most closely guarded secrets of the year, for not even Gringo Handley knew of it, though from the speech of welcome he was obviously well known in O'Higgins' shadier haunts. Much suspicion must rest upon our Assistant Secretary, for the ebb and flow of O'Higgins presence was in complete harmony with his own movements. One is therefore bound to enquire as to whom paid for whose ticket. If our Assistant Secretary then his wife must feel a little non-plussed. If our lady, then Pete Janes is a bigger rogue than we have previously realised.

The speeches from R.G.P., Harry Pretty, Douglas Milner and John Jackson (the two chief guests) and Doug Cullum were consistently good. The President must be admired for his non-stop survey of Oread affairs, idiosyncrasies of individual members etc., which left Ashcroft muttering "I'll get that fellow Pettigrew yet", in a quite venomous tone. Pretty for reading out a letter from Canon Janes, and giving a graphic account of Douglas Milner's arrival at the Alpine Club. Douglas Milner for some of his subtle jokes and account of a nailed boot ascent of the Grepon. John Jackson for some common sense at last, and Doug Cullum for some doubtful jokes. The speeches from our members must be almost incomprehensible to many guests unfamiliar with the tight circle of the Oread.

Tom Frost

THE GREEN MAN, ASHBOURNE

November 1962

The Annual Dinner was of course a great success and is now, according to one member, "The event of the Mountaineering Year". The Green Man once again provided a fine meal, which was followed by the usual crop of good speeches. Brian Cooke in his last year as President gave a good account of the club's active and social life, and then he was followed by the two chief guests. Dennis Davis and Gwen Moffat. Jack Ashcroft and Phil Falkner spoke on behalf of the club. The evening was particularly merry because Wally Smith, who was celebrating his 21st, provided a very large barrel of 'E'. Wally was presented with a sleeping bag and hut key from members of the club. Oliver Jones once again put on a fine show with the pipes and led the singing, which, with the aid of the extra beer, went on for the rest of the evening. The quote of the night came from Jack Ashcroft who was presented with a toy elephant on a plaque, surrounded with all the gear he had lost during the past year. Later Jack, asking why he had been given the elephant, said "Is it because I am thick?"

Geoff Hayes

THE GREEN MAN, ASHBOURNE

November 1963

It seems a long time since the dinner but here are a few details. Ashcroft, (President), spoke at great length about marriage, children and babies. The only thing he did not suggest was that the Club should be turned into a day nursery for large Oread families, both actual and planned! Burgess also spoke at length (45 min) and very successfully pulled all the guests to pieces – he has been ignored by most of them since. Chris Bonnington, one of the chief guests, talked about Stanage and not the Eiger. Rafe Jones told one or two of the most recent jokes. He was overheard asking members for some new ones just before the dinner. Jack Longland took great delight in quoting from the newsletter, tryping mastakes, grammatical errors and all. The Editor wishes to inform Jack that he was educated in Nottinghamshire and not Derbyshire. Oliver Jones again put on a good performance. It was a shame we did not hear more from Oliver as he was cut short due to lack of time. For many Oreads Oliver's little one-man show is one of the highlights of the dinner. Mugs were presented to Mr. & Mrs. Burgess and Mr. & Mrs. Caris.

Geoff Hayes

THE GREEN MAN, ASHBOURNE

November 1964

LETTER FROM INDIA – A taped address from R. G. Pettigrew

Short sequence of Indian music...

"Good evening, I hope you enjoyed my rendering of the Indian version of "Eskimo Nell". My accompanists were: Pete Janes on the Sarangi, an instrument designed to express sensuality, pleasure and love; Ray Handley on the Sitar, conveying the peaceful atmosphere of a starry night in Belper; and Harry Pretty on the Vina, this instrument is made of a long pole of bamboo to which two spherical resonators have been attached – an admirable emblem of Pretty the Man."

"I was going to entitle this letter from India "Some Good Men I have Known", when I realised that, to the new "Beatle" set in the Oread, I might as well be speaking of my forefathers, who were, of course, good men."

"When this keen young set write to me, as they occasionally do, to complain of nameless persecutions that go on in that Colditz of the Oread, Tan Yr Wydffa, they sometimes refer, in a puzzled way to the shadowy power group as the "Bathchair Brigade". These must be none other that the good men of my youth and of the Oread's Golden Era."

"To these young lads and lasses on the threshold of life, bursting with energy, even jumping off the Lenspitze for thousand foot slides to show they are 'with it'; and bringing a delightful hint of Mods and Rockers into the Oread, but, amazingly still uninformed as to the facts of life in the Club, I have decided to reveal the hitherto carefully concealed fact that the Oread has an establishment."

"You might ask: is the time ripe to reveal this fact? Is it opportune? And, above all, since you are speaking from India, is it auspicious?"

"The answer is that you must judge from one whom can best be described as an exiled Oread Pundit who is sick for a pint in the Bell, and has the Club's interests at heart."

"For you are about to witness an event unprecedented in the long and glorious annals of the Oread – perhaps, then, you will permit me to interpret for you its full significance."

"When, with a creaking of arthritic joints, frantic tuning of hearing aids, adjustment of crutches and a good luck pinch of snuff, Janes and Handley are at last ready to stand and face their eager young audience, a collective question will arise in the minds of all:"

"Who are these men?"

"There they will stand, blinking nervously at the prepared statements, caught finally and irrevocably in a situation they have avoided for so long. On them will be riveted perhaps, as many as two hundred blood-shot eyes."

"The silence would be pregnant if they were not, clearly, both passed it."

"I cannot predict what they will say, with what new clarion calls they will inflame Oread hearts and inspire young initiates to scale bigger and better things. Perhaps, with Conservatives they will merely cry, "up, up, up!" My task now is to disclose history."

"The truth is that there never has been an Oread Committee free from the influence of Janes and Handley or the Manipulators, as they are popularly known to generations of Oread Committeemen. Ah! Say some – you are wrong. What about the Pretty era?"

"Now, my children, when the young, adolescent Pretty launched the Oread as his peacetime answer to the Fleet Air Arm, all the crags and moors of Derbyshire were controlled by a large, powerful empire called the Valkyrie, (the name alone still excites wonder and gets Janes and Handley slobbering in their beer). By payment of large sums of protection money the Oread was permitted to climb in special reservations like Birchen Edge, and even write guide books."

"However the external affairs of the club were, naturally, controlled by the Valkyrie who deputed two notorious ex-cyclists, who worshipped a God called "The Murk", as gauleiters of the Oread Committee, with Pretty as a front Man."

"The decline and fall of the Valkyrie Empire, like the decline and fall of the British Empire, has never properly been explained, but some say that the secondment of the two key men of the Valk was instrumental in extinguishing this bright start of the climbing cosmos."

"Their future in the Oread was, of course, assured. After all it was a mixed club – even those hardened warriors of the Valkyrie needed a change – they had shared a tent with Nat Allen long enough."

"From then on – for an unbelievable period of 15 Oread dinners they have been at the helm. The front men have come and gone. The facts speak for themselves."

"*Pretty.* Loaned indefinitely to the Mountain Club at a ridiculously small fee, then recalled, and submerged in rural Holbrook."

"*Sutton.* Banished to the back streets of Liverpool to found small protectorate clubs in the Oread orbit."

"*Pettigrew.* The last of the Kipling Breed – exiled to India in exchange for Maria Handley – and so it goes on. Where are the Bynes, the Falkners, the Cookes?"

"But the present man is alright, I hear you say. The man with eyes like traffic lights gone berserk; Hebog Jack Ashcroft. Surely he was sent to Coventry in his prime, just when he had all but completed the greatest cock-up of his career, the diversion of the Derby ring road into the main Derwent sewer to clear the congestion of Roll-Royce traffic. His last, defiant words were, "It was the best place for 'em!"- agreed but, like his predecessors, he was quietly eliminated."

"Normally only seen stalking smoothly from one delicacy to another at the refreshment period of Committee Meetings, pausing only to pinch the bottom of their hostess, what had brought these two away from the backrooms where the decisions are taken? Is it senility? A last crazed bid for popular acclaim in recognition of their long vigil over the affairs of the club? Or is it final proof that Fred Allen has at last seized effective control in the Kremlin of the Oread, and you are about to see the new front men flushed from their holds by a new and noisome wind of change?"

"And Spherical Resonators to Pretty!"

"We send out best wishes to you all at this great annual celebration which we hope to join next year (if we can persuade the Committee to delay it nearer Christmas) and we salute the Oread Mountaineering Club."

Bob Pettigrew. Written and recorded 27 September 1964.

THE GREEN MAN, ASHBOURNE

November 1967

As sung by the three belly dancers (Handley, Burgess and Wes Hayden).

Tune: 'Hang down your head Tom Dooley'.

Rescue me Chuck Hooley.
For I'm gonna scream,
Rescue me Chuck Hooley
With the Alpha Alpine Team.

We're stuck up on this mountain,
Our lives not worth a cent,
Bring up Johnny Corden
Not your dirty President.

It was in the Bell one Tuesday
We met your climbing club,
There was Pretty, Janes and Williams,
Now we're in the pudding club.

Hurry up Chuck Hooley,
We're lying on the scree,
Hurry with your coolies,
Or there'll soon be six not three.

Tune: 'Its Foolish but it's fun'.

I love to go in Janes' car,
And drive round to some shady bar,
And slap him when he goes too far,
It's foolish but it's fun.

147

I love to go out for a ski
And wrap my boards around a tree,
Then Dennis Davies rescues me,
It's foolish but it's fun.

With Trevor Jones out on the rocks,
My sweaty hands upon his chocks,
Jamming his nuts behind the blocks
Its foolish but it's fun.

The Green Man, Ashbourne

November 1968

With over 140 members and guests this was the biggest gathering of the club ever. The Oread was once again fortunate in obtaining two excellent guest speakers and the high standard of previous club dinners was once again maintained. It was a happy occasion with an excellent meal, good speeches and entertainment.

The Green Man once again provided very good eats, which were followed by a number of entertaining speeches. President Ray Handley opened with a short preview of the years' meets and the present state of the club. For a change Bob Pettigrew appeared live to propose the toast to Guests and Kindred Clubs. Although we missed the usual Pettigrew 'Tape' it was good to see Bob back at the top table.

Al Alvarez, of T.V. and Observer fame, replied on the behalf of the guests. McNaught – Davis followed with the toast to the Oread, and Geoff Hayes replied.

Further entertainment was provided by Nat Allen who introduced three Oread Virgins who gave a song and dance act. Chris Brasher also put the boot in. (Fairly prescient of him — *Editor.*)

George Reynolds who did most of the graft for this year's dinner deserves everyone's congratulations on a job well done.

Geoff Hayes

Presumably "graft" included selecting the Oread virgins... of dubious qualifications, they should remain anonymous. Handley denied that they were on a free transfer from the Pinnacle Club — *Editor.*

Newsletter, February 1966

At the first committee meeting of the New Year it was decided to change the Tuesday night rendezvous from the Bell to the Wilmot Arms, Borrowash.

Borrowash is a little nearer to Nottingham, which is tipped to be the new seat of power. But keep your eyes on Coventry Hebog Ashcroft who is spreading the gospel loud and strong in that area.

Geoff Hayes

So began a long association with John Fredericks who eventually moved from the Wilmot to the George at Hubberholme in Wharfedale. Many subsequent ex officio gatherings of Oreads took place at the George during the '70's and '80's — *Editor.*

THOUGHTS ON MRS. MALAPROP AND THE OREAD ANNUAL DINNER

JOHN FISHER

The fear of being asked to speak at the Annual O.M.C. dinner must be a sort of unpleasant dream for a good number of the club. What to say and how to say it in the full knowledge that few have such ability are the disturbing essentials of that dream.

Should one be puritanical and set about a discourse on the modern climbing scene? Items for savagery could be the unnecessary and repetitive magazine articles reminiscent of the inane babblings of wine pundits, self-promotion, gear freakery, gross commercialisation, and ravings about the great outdoors. What on earth does this last item mean? As a speaker you could only take this approach if you had the stature of a Longland or a young hard member who could readily deny fogeyism.

Exploration of the philosophy of climbing is, in my view, largely phoney. Climbers simply like the risk, gymnastics, companionship, technology, mountain natural history, literature or any combination according to taste. Seeking a philosophical basis for an inclination to climb is like looking for reason in love. Forget about the spirits behind stones and character building. As for the latter, just reflect on climbers you know. Having said all this, climbing has given most of us experiences, pleasures and sometimes solace, which I doubt could have come from other endeavours.

Reflections on the nature of the club and its doings over the years risks sounding like too much of a list and, of course, to best do that you need to be recognisably mature, even old. Clearly there needs to be some pep and probably only the extremes of determined supercritical review, or something funny, are likely to succeed. No one has done the former because it hazards a catastrophic failure when addressed to a society conditioned to accept half truths from self seeking politicians, media, advertising and other purveyors of the illusion of benefit. Kindly do not accuse me of prejudice because I shall tell you that my prejudices are simply a honed up combination of insight, experience, the ability to see and read and, of course, a natural ability to recognise a rogue a mile off.

Turning back to the theme, something funny and possibly new could be in the form of Malapropisms injected into a climbing subject. An audience takes pleasure in recognising these 'isms', laughs and congratulates itself on doing so. This self-congratulation is said to be a basis for much successful English comedy. To give an example one's effort could go a bit like this:–

"That northern youth with climbing ambitions said he was interested in that Eigerbond issued in Carey Street. I'm told his wages are good but the expenses of living in the Old Rectumry must mean he could do with a few more pounds per anum. His girl friend won't help because she is something of a woman's bib and got so mad at his overtures that she spilt Bonjolais all down her new Grottex, or was it Prattex, jacket. She feels she needs sexual uplift and thinks the Indian Congress Party could help. She could combine that with a high mountain trip since this year that organisation is meeting in the area of the Ram of Krutch (sorry, Rann of Kutch) near the Indo-Pakistan border. I must say I find a dose of Vino Barbitone is more useful to quieten such ambitions."

As for myself, I'm staying at home with my eyes on the Faecal Ridge of Cairngorm next winter.

All this, I suppose, is rather lacking in taste and rather biological, but, if padded out a bit, would entertain both the serious diners and drunken oafs and get you, the speaker, something of a reputation.

A WEEKEND WITH RAWHIDE, TODHUNTER, AND OTHERS
(*EXTRACT*) SUMMER 1961

HARRY PRETTY

Stafford-Williams is of the opinion that all this "slice of country" jazz really finished when, in trying to lead us through the "trackless wilderness" to Hebog, Rawhide had to accept out topographical advice in order to prevent the party from inadvertently taking in Mynydd Drws-y-Coed and Moel Lefn en route... I am inclined to agree but, as I started to say earlier, it was for all practical purposes R. Todhunter who some time later emerged at our feet upon the northeast shoulder of Hebog.

I suppose that by this time the situation was a bit out of hand. Stafford Williams and I simply accepted the fact that we were climbing with Todhunter and eventually the whole set-up began to feel quite normal.

There was a small incident, slightly unnerving to one having some affinity with early days. We were climbing a particularly disreputable series of pitches; all vertical heather loosely connected by minute areas of clean rock, which has, I believe, been included in the guidebook as a rock climb. Todhunter said it was called Caterpillar. I was tied in the middle of the rope but, at the time, was in the lead – a situation not uncommon when climbing with Stafford-Williams and the ghost of Todhunter. It was noticeable that Williams had not quite assimilated the circumstances although those ancient breeches were providing plenty of atmosphere. He never looked Todhunter in the eye – always a nervous sideways glance. Williams was definitely jumpy and when, during his negotiation of a particularly nasty stretch of heather, Todhunter addressed him quite clearly and firmly as "George" – he fell off, to be pulled up shortly by an adeptly applied shoulder belay and the cry of "jolly hard luck George, old chap!" There was something very odd about it, and it wasn't until sometime later that I remembered the name of the man with whom Todhunter had made the first ascent of Yellow Buttress on Craig y Cwm Du. It was, as I say, very odd indeed.

With reasonable expectation I thought that a night in the streaming fleshpots of the Port Madoc British Legion Hall, a few hours of stomping with the cats, would remove all trace of Todhunter. It might well have worked but for the fact that every time he showed promise of getting real way out his partners would insist on enquiring after the health and strength of "the tall dark 'andsome man – surely you remember?" Janes said they were talking about Welbourn – anyway it didn't do his condition any good, and he had a relapse.

Not until we scrambled up to the small ledge at the foot of Curving crack, at some hour of the following day, did I see the change. Todhunter quite suddenly was no longer with us.

But even at the end you can't win – not with Janes. He stared at the long slit of a first pitch and, jumping up and down in a curious excited way he began to claw at the rock in the manner of a hard man. "Come on Pretty", he boomed "Get on my shoulders, I can easily throw you up".

I turned sadly to Williams. "If he calls you Maurice or Colin, take no notice".

ROCKS, RAILWAYS AND THE ARENIGS
LIMESTONE MEET, JANUARY 1961

DES HADLUM

The Peak District has some of the finest Limestone for climbing in Britain, and not all routes are peg routes. So if you have not got the necessary pegs, krabs etc., don't be put off from turning up on this meet.

Camping will be at Black Rocks, a quiet place in the winter. Permission has been obtained for parties to climb on High Tor during the weekend, so I expect we will make use of this. Free climbing can be had in plenty at Willersley Crag at Cromford. This fine high cliff was recently discovered and now gives many routes with or without pegs.

See reference to R. A. Brown climbing on High Tor on Coronation Day, 1953. This was probably the first official Oread Limestone Meet — *Editor.*

WELSH HIGHLAND LIGHT RAILWAY

Newsletter, September 1964

Rumour has it that a certain member of the Oread (one who sports a beard and lives at Rhyd Ddu – well almost) has applied to be issued with a black peaked cap and whistle. It is quite likely that this rumour has some foundation. The old railway track from Caernarvon to Bedgellert is in the process of renovation and it won't be long before our hut is the half way station! Are the committee to discuss the idea that Tan y Wyddffa be once again opened as a snack bar? This sounds quite an idea to help the club finances. Upon seeing progress on the railway outside the hut recently, Welbourn was heard to state that the time would soon be here when Oread members would be sitting on the wall outside the hut, waiting their clients to alight from the early morning train, eager to be guided into the fantastic world of Snowdon. Get your ice axes ready chaps and don't let the guides from other valleys step on our ground. We have a right to keep our Hornli Grat.

Geoff Hayes

First reference to proposed re-opening of the Welsh Highland Railway, in an Oread publication, and very light hearted at that — *Editor.*

Newsletter, June 1965

According to a report in the Liverpool Daily Post of 17/4/65, the sceptics who said that the narrow-gauge railway line past Tan y Wyddfa could never be opened are a little nearer to being confounded. The news item stated that "Russell" a twenty ton narrow-gauge locomotive has been given to the Welsh Highland Light Railway Ltd., who are planning to re-open part of the line which closed in 1937. Saved from the scrap yard by the Birmingham Locomotive Club, the loco is now undergoing an extensive refit at Shrewsbury. She was built in 1906 for the North Wales Narrow Gauge Company, a forerunner of the Welsh Highland, and ran for many years on the line through Rhyd Ddu, until she made the last trip to collect the remaining rolling stock from Portmadoc in 1937.

If that part of the line which runs past the hut is re-opened, and there now appears to be some doubt if that particular section will be the first, we shall be able to claim the somewhat doubtful honour of having the only climbing club hut with a railway within touching distance!

Ronnie Langworthy

151

BURGESS GETS ABOUT A BIT
EXTRACT

Newsletter, November 1965

The main climbing on Arenig Fawr is situated on the crag to the West (behind) Lyn Arenig Fawr. Approaching from the campsite at Bryn Ifan, the main mass of cliff is on the left as the buttress bends back to form the side of a valley. A feature being a White Streak, this provides a route of that name for 300', approximately H.V.S. A series of grooves leads to the foot of a steep slab. This is climbed on the left-hand side with a hard move right across the top to enable a large grassy ledge to be reached. From the left side of the ledge a chimney leads to the top of the pinnacle whence a short groove leads to the top of the crag.

D. Burgess

FROM OUR JAPANESE CORRESPONDENT

Newsletter, November 1965

Mountain climbing enthusiasts now practise scaling rocky slopes on the façade of a building in the hustling entertainment and shopping district of Shibuya Tokyo.

When the Taiyo Industry Company, makers of mountain climbing equipment, had a new building constructed, they had the façade, from the second floor to the roof of the six-floor building, constructed of concrete so as to duplicate the appearance of a rock face.

This structure has been named "Tokyo Rock". It is 65 feet 6 inches high and 32 feet and 7 inches wide, and has been built at an angle of 84 degrees.

In addition to a few channel-like chimneys and overhangs, 130 hankens, the special spikes used in climbing, have been fastened to the façade.

The Tokyo Rock was designed under the supervision of leading rock climbing experts. A safety net has been spread along the lower edge of the rock.

The Tokyo Rock is open to the public for Y200 (4s) an hour. Trainers are always available at the site to help beginners, while members of the Japan Alpine Association and other mountain climbing groups hold regular training sessions on the rock.

A DISTANT APPOINTMENT

In 1966 John Fisher had the opportunity to visit Tristan Da Cunha. By now Fisher, after army Service in the R.A.M.C. (a real captain, none of that honorary stuff), was on the teaching staff of the Dental Faculty at Birmingham University. His visit to Tristan concerned the dental condition of the local population — *Editor.*

TRISTAN DA CUNHA (*EXTRACT*)

The island of Tristan Da Cunha and its two uninhabited satellites lie just north of the "Roaring Forties" on latitude 37°S, 1,500 miles from the Cape of Good Hope and 2,000 miles from Buenos Aires to the west. The remoteness of the group is very obvious, more so I suppose in some respects than the South Pole. The island is one of the visible manifestations of the submarine Mid-Atlantic ridge running from Greenland in the northern hemisphere to Bouvet island in the south; throwing up Ascension and St. Helena. With its typical volcanic structure, some cynical observers have likened Tristan island to an ash cone with grass on the sides supporting a population of 250 souls. So much for the romance that has always been a feature of Tristan commentary, misplaced though it is at the present time. There is of course some considerable justification for the aura which surrounds the place but I suspect this is partly reminiscing from a distance and partly, the very real fact, that prior to the last war, Tristan and its people were unique, the inhabitants possessing at that time some of the desirable social characteristics which are rapidly disappearing in our materialistic urban society.

Enough of the background save to say that when the opportunity came to go the temptation was impossible to resist. A two minute decision, a couple of months waiting for grant authority to come through, and a desperately hectic five weeks organising equipment, found the writer exhausted on the liner to Cape Town.

Eventually all good things come to an end and the reckoning time arrived when I took passage in the M.V. Gillian Gaggins, 600 tons, for Tristan da Cunha. The "G.G." as she was called. is one of the two fishing vessels that twice a year visit the Tristan islands from South Africa for two periods, each of six months, to fish for crawfish.

Eventually Tristan appeared and, in the words of A. E. Baker, a chronicler of the Peak District, showed as "a prospect of unmitigated gloom"; cloud, rain, a heavy swell and much to the chagrin of the writer, no possibility of landing that day owing to the heavy seas. The ship therefore retired to what lee there was to await improvement.

Improvement there was the next day and the cargo including myself was off-loaded with a sense of profound relief on my part. On the whole, my stay of three months on the island was interesting but the fact remains that it is a small and rather limited place. Not only is the island small, about seven miles across, but has a singular sameness in its features as would be expected of a volcanic cone. It is, in general, treeless, often wet, almost always mindlessly windy, and with a high humidity which has a devastating effect on metal equipment. The variation in land flora and fauna is very small, relieved to some extent by the profusion of sea birds and fish, including whale and shark. To be perfectly objective, Tristan is not much of a place except in three respects, – its rather unusual and romantic background described by Brander in his book "Tristan da Cunha 1506-1908", the impressiveness of the combination of mountain and sea emphasising the remoteness and, finally, and most interesting of all, the people who have jumped from the 19th to 20th century in a very short period of time.

Hence they are interesting from medical and sociological points of view, notably in relation to the effects of isolation. Especially interesting is the fact that since the population is small and their genealogy completely known, such a group readily lends itself to the study of some aspects of human genetics. My own interest lay in the dental condition of these people.

It hardly needs saying that one of my personal objectives was to climb the peak. This did not prove possible and will always be regretted. Unfortunately the authorities insisted that to ascend the peak one must be accompanied by a capable islander and these were never available, in spite of promises, on the very few days when an ascent might have been a prospect. An ascent of the peak in fact would have presented no technical problems, being really an exhausting walk. The real problem was that of assessing weather since this was extremely erratic and frequently bad, especially at that time of year. Further, any mistake in route finding could have been catastrophic because of hard going through tree fern and the high prevalence of gullies, steep deep and shattered, which radiated from the ash peak. Half of the island periphery even now has not been traversed by land. My job anyway was to obtain co-operation of the authorities, not alienate them, so the temptation to go off on my own was resisted. Nevertheless on the quiet the padre and myself went up about 3,000-ft, almost to the edge of the ash, to gain a good view of the top itself. Even this we found quite a performance.

Newsletter, January 1967.

John Fisher, now on Tristan da Cunha, has recently been joined by a lady rat catcher – a Miss. Is there any connection?

Geoff Hayes

Fisher has always refused to comment on lady rat catchers. His lips have remained sealed for over thirty years — *Editor.*

OUTDOOR MEETS U.K. 1962-1970
EDITORIAL (*EXTRACT*)

Newsletter, Summer 1962

Last October a party of Oreads arrived at the Cat and Fiddle en route for Edale from the Roaches. It was a typical winter's day in the Peak, bleak with cold windy rain, but we had been heartened by the hope of a cup of tea after the long plod up.

On arriving at the inn at about 10.00 a.m. the inmates refused to serve us, a party of twelve, with tea or anything hot. On leaving, a little dejected and rebuffed, we passed a front window of the pub containing a single worded placard "LUNCHEONS".

Luncheons for whom? For those who are unwilling to ascend a mountain except on mechanical legs, for those who are unable due to infirmity? Luncheons for those with a shine on their shoes, a shell round their souls, and stupor in their limbs; by those who proudly claim to be the owners of the highest pub in England and yet refuse a hot drink to a group of people who love heights but not at luncheon tables.

Geoff Hayes

Not a lot has changed at the Cat and Fiddle even though there is now a walker's refreshment room. Recently in 1998, on a bad summer's day (wind and rain) they "ran out of tea" in mid afternoon and declined to provide a fresh supply — *Editor.*

OGWEN 1963 (MARCH) (*EXTRACT*)

I can't report much about the Ogwen meeting this year. Although I did get to Wales – just. The van was in collision with an 18-ton coal lorry about half a mile over the border. The meet leader was also in the van so he won't be able to give his usual report. I'm pleased to say that the Nottingham Team who ended up in Shrewsbury Hospital is almost back to normal. We are having to tie Doreen Gadsby down with her climbing rope to stop her throwing herself back on the crags, broken ribs and all.

Geoff Hayes

BULLSTONES 1963 (DECEMBER)

Perhaps the largest number ever of Oreads were on Bleaklow for this meet. The unfortunate thing was that there were two separate groups, which never actually managed to connect.

Harry Pretty led the Friday night group in triumph from Poltergeist Barn to Lower Small Clough. The party was about twelve strong and included Gibson (returned from the dead). Apparently the hut was over full and the Vice President was sent outside to sleep (he is the fattest of the group). The Hooleys and Langworthys tried to connect with Pretty's Mob, but after wandering about somewhere near to the correct Clough and, later at the head of the Derwent, they managed to get into Bullstones Lower Cabin about Midnight. Welbourn, Hobday, Rod Craddock and Margaret Lowe also arrived late in the evening at Bullstones top Cabin, after doing a double trip of Derwent Edge etc. I have to put etc. because no one knows where they went, not even themselves. I was in the other party, twelve strong, consisting mainly of the Nottingham Ice Rink Section, which left Yorkshire Bridge at 7.30 p.m. and only just managed to arrive at Bullstones at about 2 a.m. (Welbourn was pleased to receive us!)

Various route were used to get back to Yorkshire Bridge, some went over the tops, in thick cloud and others took the road back beside the Dam.

Geoff Hayes

This was probably the first use of Lower Small Clough cabin on a Bullstones Meet — *Editor.*

Bullstones 1964 (December)

The annual epic managed to take place once again despite the rapidly deteriorating condition of the aged participants. The theme this year was "It's not so much a walk as a way of life". I hope that Pretty may give a full and revealing report of this meet and the subsequent downfall of Janes and others, but meanwhile here is a short report.

The scene opens at the Nags Head, Edale. Eventually after much intake of ale by the older members the group set off in the dark for Poltergeist Barn. Within 100 yards Pretty, who is leading the gallant few, does a purler on some ice on the path and manages to wet his beard, and other parts, in the local stream. The Barn is found with ease and those in the know get the best kipping spots, leaving the others to do as best they can with the rest of the shelter. Pretty declares that he has only brought his airbed for a ground sheet and does not intend to blow it up! Eventually everyone settles down. The first disturbance is when Ashcroft and Bob Gill arrive about 2 a.m., and, shortly after Pretty is heard inflating his airbed, (just got his breath back from the walk). Eventually the cold cruel light of dawn rouses those who managed to sleep and Frost is observed complete with North Wall hat heating his breakfast over a candle! Cold limbs are dragged up the slopes of Kinder Scout and after about two hours in an icy rain everyone gathers in Ashop Clough Cabin. Here the eclipse of Janes, mentioned by Pettigrew at the dinner, takes place. In an unusually quiet voice he asks who is going with him to the Barnsley Club Hut in the Snake. He and his chief rucksack carrier – Williams depart. A sorry sad group of supporters trudge off down the path, leaving a young virile group with a drooping Pretty at the rear to continue the pilgrimage to Bullstones. By the time Grains in the Water is reached the condition of Pretty is evident to all, and it is decided, as most of the walk is completed, to go down the Alport to see if the others managed to get to the Barnsley Hut. The hut is locked and empty. Luckily whilst having a drink in the Café next door a couple of Barnsley lads arrive and the doors are thrown open to us. A pleasant evening is spent around a magnificent fire and all clothes are dried out. At this time the Janes group, having found the Hut locked, are trying to sleep in a barn about two miles further down the road. The two parties were not to join again until the completion of the walk to Bamford. Here Jim Kershaw is found. He was drinking in the bar of the London – Manchester train when it stopped at Coventry, where he should have joined Ashcroft. Jim spent the night on Manchester Station and made a solo route to Bullstones where he spent a lonely night in Lower small Clough cabin without light or paraffin!

"Its not so much a walk as a way of life".

Geoff Hayes

Valkyrie, Froggat Edge. J. Fisher and "Unknown" (who subsequently fell and was held by J.F.)   *Photo: Gordon Gadsby.*

Harding's Super Direct, Stanage: Derrick Burgess (leading) and Andy Oakden.   *Photo: Dave Guyler.*

Above:
Yew Tree Wall, Tissington Spires, Dovedale,
Dave Knighton climbing.
Photo: Gil Male.

Above right:
Jitter Wall, Stanage, Doreen Hodge climbing.
Photo: Gordon Gadsby.

Right:
David Penlington, Rainster Rocks, 1949.
Photo: Harry Pretty.

C. Radcliffe on the Old Man of Storr, Skye.
Photo: J. Ashcroft.

Abseiling off the Inaccessible Pinnacle, Skye.
Photo: J. Ashcroft.

Elliotts Buttress, Gardoms Edge,
D. Burgess and Hank Harrison climbing.
Photo: Unknown.

Valkyrie, Roaches.
Photo: J. Ashcroft.

Welsh Walk 1968: Abergwesyn to Pumlumon: G. Gadsby, C. Hobday, M. Clark, P. Gardiner, J. Crosse, H. Pretty, P. Janes.   *Photo: D. Williams.*

Marsden to Heathy Lea (Baslow) 1969: M. Clark, P. R. Falkner, C. Hobday, M. Hayhurst, R. Squires, J. Crosse, D. Williams, P. Gardiner.   *Photo: H. Pretty.*

21st Bullstones Meet, 1970: Holden, Kenny, Russell, Squires, Weston, Linney, Williams, Gregson, Ashcroft, Janes, Allen, Winfield, Johnson, Reynolds. In front: Scott, Foster, Radcliffe.   *Photo: H. Pretty.*

Bullstones Meet, 1968: Meet leader (H. Pretty) assembles troops in Blackden Clough (awaiting D. Williams adrift on Kinder overnight). Troops: P. Gardiner, P. Janes, J. Welbourn, C. Hobday, R. Handley, M. Hayhurst, S. G. Moore, F. Allen, D. Burgess.   *Photo: C. Radcliffe.*

BULLSTONES 1965 (DECEMBER) (EXTRACT)

Just a short report to tell you that the meet was a great success despite no one getting within miles of Bullstones. I'm hoping that Pretty will come up with the full details of this epic. It deserves being reported in full detail, being a meet of the "Vintage" type.

After gathering in the Nags Head, the party was called to order and marched swiftly around the village following Pettigrew on the bagpipes. Unfortunately he took the wrong track to the Barn and ended up at the rear of the file. This was to be Bob's finest hour. How he managed to play the pipes all the way to Poltergeist Barn no one will ever know. It was a fantastic effort. Although by the sounds of his breathing during the remainder of that long cold night Bob must have blown a gasket in his right lung! Everyone slept in the snow that night because the barn was inches deep in churned up mud etc. I expect all were pleased to see a fine sunrise over the Mam Tor Ridge.

Geoff Hayes

Editorial comment might provide further enlightenment...

Bob Pettigrew was on leave from India where he had (inter alia) been undergoing instruction in the art of the bagpipes. His achievement, in playing this instrument without pause from the Nags Head via the steep slopes of Grindslow Knoll to Poltergeist Barn, remains unique in the annals of the Oread.

It was a cold clear night with deep snow cover and the sound of the pipes was heard from one end of Edale to the other. The mystery of it engaged the locals for many a day.

As Geoff Hayes noted we slept in trenches excavated in the snow. Pettigrew, attired only in sports jacket, cords and deerstalker, hung his jacket on a clothes hanger (sic) to a nearby tree. Next morning the jacket was iron hard with frost. When the main body departed north over Kinder, en route for the Barnsley M.C. cottage, R.G.P. returned to Edale. There was a rumour that Sir John was looking for him.

Reference Poltergeist Barn: In the 1950's it became the haunt of the then Sheffield University M.C. (R. A. Brown, J. Clegg, D. Wooler, P. Wilkinson, Chalky White etc.) and it was so named following a curious incident when a rucksack self ignited during the night. No logical explanation ever transpired.

After early Gritstone Guide Committee meetings at Manchester University (1950-1), I used to return by train, with Eric Byne, Dick Brown and George Sutton to Edale where R.A.B. would conduct us to the barn after the usual hospitality of Fred Heardman at the Nags Head. It was there that I first met Phillip Falkner in 1950.

By the late 70's the barn was a wreck and incapable of providing any shelter. A sad result.

Editor

CRAIG CWM COWARCH

Newsletter, August 1963

Cowarch is possibly the most secluded and beautiful of the Welsh valleys. We were all made very welcome by the friendly farmer on whose land we camped. Possibly this was because his dogs had the best weekend's food supply at our expense. – Yes the "Dogs of Cowarch" are still there, as crafty as ever. – Is it true that they can really climb trees for food? The moderate climbers of the party found the rock not to their liking. Harry Pretty led a successful assault on North Gully. Crampons would have been useful, as they had to kick steps – in the moss. Burgess and party had a good day on Sunday, climbing what was possibly the only ascent since 1956 of a Harding V.S.

Geoff Hayes

I rather doubt Geoff's remark regarding the Harding V.S. The tigers of the Mountain Club (Stafford) had roamed all over the crag in the late 50's. While still occupying their original hut in the valley — *Editor.*

161

ESKDALE, WHITSUNTIDE 1966 (EXTRACT)

Saturday morning saw feverish activity, as everyone left early to make the most of the good weather. Many good climbs were done, the pick was "Speedy" Smith and Des Hadlum's (Rock & Ice) ascent of the Central Pillar of Esk Buttress. One of the Lake District's hardest climbs and Derrick Burgess's fine lead of Hell's Groove.

Sunday dawned just as good as the previous day and another rush was made for Scafell, with routes such as Gremlin Grooves, Yellow Slab, and Botterills Slab, and a heroic lead by an Oread on Moss Ghyll Grooves in an Anglo-Summit, Rock and Ice, Oread Party, comprising "Big George" Potts, "Oxfam" Tabs, and R. J. Cummerford who were all rescued by George Reynolds on the crux. Brian Cooke "clocked in" with the meet leader on Mickledore, explaining that he and Jack Ashcroft could not camp with us due to the lack of traffic lights on the farm track. The day finished with nude bathing (all male), several brass objects being observed in the stream. Whilst the men retired to the Bower House, the Ladies had a rowdy Hen Party for Ronnie Leeson in the George. She is of course about to take on a great weight in the shape of Johnny Corden.

Monday again saw a rush for Esk Buttress and Scafell. Handley and Ray Colledge did Great Central on Esk, and Geoff Hayes completed the demise of Moss Ghyll Grooves. Messieurs' Corden and Appleby ascended Pillar via the Wasdale Head Hotel, and Burgess led the steep and difficult Gormengast on Heron Crag. All hands descended to the superb swimming pool, just above the campsite, for fun and games.

Nat Allen

WELSH WALK (14 PEAKS) (EXTRACT)

Newsletter, June 1966

In Retrospect maybe the Meets Circular was presumptuous. Of eleven members and friends who left Aber on Saturday morning only two did the 14 three thousanders – and they bivvied the Saturday night on Crib Goch.

Gadsby and Reynolds did the whole walk having left Aber at 9 a.m. The main party left at about 5 a.m. (Gadsby and Reynolds were late starters due to car trouble). They arrived at Rhyd Ddu in time for breakfast on Sunday morning.

Paul Gardiner, Colin Hobday and Dave Weston did their walk missing out Y-Garn and Elidir Fawr, arriving Rhyd Ddu 11 p.m.

Jim Kershaw, Dave Penlington, Matt O'Brien and myself finished at Nant Peris 6-7 p.m. (Saturday). Dave Williams and Mike Watchers added the incredulous element arriving on Snowdon Summit at 11 p.m. Williams led the weary novice walker into the summit café to coincide with arrival of the train. It had come up from Llanberis to evacuate the staff after a report to the police of a planted bomb. Mike departed for Llanberis on the train and, under the watchful eye of the constabulary, found room in a police cell for the night. Williams descended to Rhyd Ddu solo, arriving at 1 a.m.

Pretty walked by himself throughout the weekend turning up at the hut to voice his disapproval at this year's variance from the traditional nature of the Welsh Walk.

Burgess, Nat Allen, and Handley camped and climbed in the Gwynant – another voice of protest from Burgess.

Jack Ashcroft

First ascent of Ram Chukor Peak (5,500m) above Malana Glacier, Kulu Himal, India.
In background Deo Tibba (left), Indrasan (right).   *Photo: Bob Pettigrew.*

Derbyshire Himalayan Expedition 1961: Camp 2 on Indrasan.   *Photo: Jack Ashcroft.*

British South Georgia Expedition 1954/55: Allardyce Range including Three Brothers (2,050m) across un-named glacier.   *Photo: I. M. Brooker.*

The Isle of Arran Ridges.   *Photo: Gordon Gadsby.*

Monte Rotondo (2,670m), Corsica.   *Photo: Gordon Gadsby.*

Glencoe, towards the Buachaille.   *Photo: John (Rock) Hudson.*

An Teallach from Sail Liath.   *Photo: Colin Hobday.*

Peter Scott on the Schaligrat, Weisshorn.   *Photo: Chris Radcliffe.*

Descent from the Grandes Jorasses (after ascent of Walker Spur),
Paul Addison in flight.   *Photo: Robin Sedgwick.*

Kharcha Kund North Ridge, Day 4, Robin Beadle climbing, Garhwal Himalaya. *Photo: Peter Scott.*

Derwent Edges – Chris Radcliffe in action. *Photo: H. Pretty.*

Day Walk – above Gratton Dale 1998 – too many to name.   *Photo: Colin Hobday.*

Annual Dinner Entertainment 1986. Helen Griffiths, Dawn Hopkinson, Peter Scott, Sharon Russell, Lisa Welbourn.

After ascent of Pear Buttress (Mt. Blanc de Courmayeur behind), 1969. P. Scott, Ron Lake, Dan Boon, (J. Fullalove).   *Photo: Ray Colledge.*

North Wales, October 1966 *(Extract)*

The Ladies meet was combined with an unofficial Men's Welsh Walk at least as far as Cerrig Druidion. Here, after the pub had closed, the ladies motored on to the hut for two days whilst the men trudged on for a night under Pretty's fly sheet. Many a good meet has started under this old fly sheet and this was no exception. Of course it was raining very hard in the morning, but eventually a start was made for Cefn-garw, the objective for the following night. Some interesting un-pathed country was traversed which was completely new to everyone. A fine night was spent in Cefn-garw with a magnificent fire and endless tales from Pretty and Janes with Williams and Handley taking most of the raps, and Hobday and myself, as insignificant observers, perched on our airbeds.

It came as something of a shock to everyone when looking at the map on the Sunday, to realise that only one third of the walk had been completed. However in brilliant weather everyone reached the Gwynant for the evening, to the welcoming arms of the ladies and so back to the hut for a communal bath (men only I'm afraid).

Geoff Hayes

Once more across the mysteries of Migneint and the Moelwyns — *Editor.*

Tranearth (Lakes), October 1966 *(Extract)*

Mention Dow Crag to anyone who went on that meet and they will still show you the sodden car floor coverings. The highlight of this meet apparently when the stream near Tranearth rose rapidly overnight and it was "as wide as the Trent" the following morning! – With the cars in the middle. Tales were told of waist deep wading, and boots floating level with steering wheels (inside the cars), also of water rushing out when doors were opened. I hope someone took a photograph. Wallerbarrow was visited and climbed upon on the Saturday before the rains, but Sunday was spent baling!

Geoff Hayes

Beeston Tor, Manifold, June 1967 *(Extract)*

Yes, to the cheers of the onlookers, a dashing rescue was carried out on Beeston Tor, which proved to be the highlight of the meet. A fair damsel, marooned by her compatriots in the huge cave midway up the Tor, was deemed in need of rescue. With little ado team Alpha sprang into action. The Thorn had its first mass ascent and bodies hurtled into the cave; the resulting melee hardly likely to placate our fair maid. Chivalry prevailed and some Cairngorm patter saw the terrified look fade from her eyes. She was quickly lowered off into Hayes' waiting arms.

Derrick Burgess

Pembroke, August Bank Holiday 1968 *(Extract)*

Sixty-one Oreads and friends encamped on Mr. Jones' splendid site above White Sand Bay. We clocked 230 miles from Nottingham. Hayes and his gang managed to cover 269 miles via the Birmingham back streets. Jim Kershaw walked it from Dolgellau, in two weeks, and looked very fit.

Climbs done on Saturday: Craig Garn, Porth Long: Reptilian by Burgess, Handley and Colledge. Our youngest members, Tom Green and David Brady also climbed Reptilian, Barad by Chris Radcliffe and Peter Scott.

Sunday morning: Forty Oreads assembled on the Life-Boat slip-way, Porthstimiam. Hard bartering with boat owners and eventually twenty-five set sail for Ramsey Island (15/- return).

Tuesday was beach day: surfing, football, swimming and climbing. Radcliffe did the lot including the 2,000' girdle of St. David's Head. Mr. True Form, (Reg. Squires) made an appearance, having walked a mile and a half along the cliff top in alpine fashion (roped up and carrying coils). All tourist operations were halted to observe this caravan.

Those on the meet:- Jim Kershaw, Mike and Meg Moore, J. Dench, Reg Squires, Ann Thornhill, D. Carnell, Pat Carnell, Allan Squires, Robin Green, Judy Skinner, D. & J. Burgess, Gary B., Joan and Andy Oakden, D.Gadsby, J. and G. Reynolds, R. Colledge, P. Craddock, Christine Brady, David Brady, Tom Green, Ron and Kath Chambers, Stew Bramwell, K., B., and C. Clark, Mat and Maureen O'Brien, C. Radcliffe, P. Scott, C. Culley, Ray and Maria Handley, Bernice Heason, H. and M. Marshall, John Crosse and family, Geoff Hayes, Colin Hobday, Wendy Bottomley, Rosie Grayson, Marke Clarke, John Fisher, Mike Berry, and various other unidentified friends.

Gordon Gadsby

This is the first mention of Chris Radcliffe and Peter Scott on an Oread meet (not to mention Wendy Bottomley and Rosie Grayson) — *Editor*.

WELSH WALK, JUNE, 1969 (*EXTRACT*)

What stands out most about this meet is that those present were subjected to yet another series of Williams' culinary fiascos.

The fact that, on Friday night, he was encamped nearer to Rhondda than he has ever been since his miss spent youth had the most wayward effect.

On Saturday's walk up the Towey we were afflicted with renderings from William Shakespeare and, at the lunch break, by his Consommé Ospiz, which dissolved Chris's cup on contact.

By the time the watershed above the Elan reservoirs was reached we were being regaled by Churchillian speeches. It is well known that William's ability as a map reader is, to say the least, suspect, and he engaged in his usual terrier-like diversions whilst the rest of the party pursued a straight line. However, he later admitted that, as Bombardier Williams. D, C.M.D., he had spent all map reading training sessions in a public bar. At 4 p.m., when all food had been consumed, Janes was still asking for a lunch stop.

On Saturday night we bivvied above Cwmystwyth where Williams, surveying the "job lot" of ex WD food he always carries, decided to build himself up with Pretty's tinned fruit whilst H.P. was engaged elsewhere.

Anon

"Engaged elsewhere" describes the long drive back to start point at Abergwesyn by Betty Gardiner, her support team, and drivers, in order to ferry cars to Cwmystwyth; thus minimising further driving at the end of the walk somewhere north of Pwmlumon Fawr, even as far north as Machynlleth. At this period long distance walking across the Cambrian "Empty Quarter" was a serious business — *Editor*.

TAN-Y-WYDDFA, WHITSUNTIDE 1968 (*EXTRACT*)

Prospective members, Peter Scott and Chris Radcliffe, climbed Narrow Slab on Cloggy. The remainder (22) spent the day at Morfa Nefyn – footballing and swimming.

Gordon Gadsby

Although not yet members perhaps this meet gave some impetus to the hard-hitting Editorials by Radcliffe and Scott when they took over as joint Newsletter editors in February, 1970 — *Editor.*

BULLSTONES 1968 (DECEMBER)

Quite a large crowd of Oreads staggered out of the Nags Head in Edale on the Friday night. Ashcroft and Chambers were in such a state they slept the night in the pub yard. Two others only made the foot of Golden Clough. Dave Williams and a prospective member[1] led off at a hot pace over Kinder and were not seen again that night. The rest of the team eventually arrived at the Barnsley Club Hut in the Snake. By now Williams had found what he thought to be a stream leading down to the Snake, followed it, and found himself back in the yard of the Nags Head after two hours of walking.

On Saturday a rescue party was sent out to round up Williams. He was found and had a public dressing down by H.P. the meet leader (who was wearing full ceremonial dress and medals for the occasion) After demanding that Williams should resign from the committee, everyone left for a good trog over Bleaklow.

Ron Dearden and Mike Turner returned from the dead and walked over Kinder to attend the meet on Saturday. Geoff Hayes and Jim Winfield arrived in the Nags Head on Saturday night, Just before closing time, a 'phone call came through for a certain Harry Pretty, it was the one and only Pettigrew on the Hot Line from Tunbridge Wells! Pettigrew has taken to attending club meets by telephone.

Geoff Hayes

[1] Prospective member was Brian Hayley. I don't think he aspired to full membership. In 1969 he left for Africa; probably safer than Kinder on a dark night in the company of Digger Williams. This was the first (and only?) time that anyone failed the night crossing of Kinder from the Nags Head — *Editor.*

THE CZECHS ARRIVE

Newsletter, June 1967

A party of Czech climbers will be spending two weeks in the U.K. during October as guests of the B.M.C. and various British Clubs who are being co-ordinated by John Hunt's main Reception Committee.

I am representing the Peak District and am responsible for organising the activities of the party during their visit to the Peak District from 11th-13th October.

A number of "tigers" in the Oread have already been forewarned that their services will be required on the 12th and 13th October. This group will also be responsible for transporting the Czechs to North Wales on the 13th where they will be handed over to the C.C. (C.C. North Wales Dinner).

I shall be organising accommodation (in homes) for the party and a Sausage and Mash supper at a Derbyshire pub on Thursday night (12th October) at which all club members, who are interested, can meet our guests.

I shall be pleased to receive any offers of assistance.

The visit by Czechs is of course in direct line with the previous visits by the Russians and the Poles – but this is the first time that Derbyshire has been included in the itinerary. I would like to think that the Oread will be the mainspring of a successful first visit by an away team who normally climb in mountain areas so little known to us.

Harry Pretty

The Czech team: Dr. Ludek Koupil (leader), Dr. Josef Kupec (political relations). Dr. Jindrich Steindler, Vratislav Fibinger, Michal Lichy, Jiri Tomcala, Marie Kasalicka, Milan Kucik. Koupil, Kupec, and Steindler were from Prague. The remainder came from Ostrava to the east.

The nucleus of the Oread climbing team: Ray Handley, Peter Janes, Derrick Burgess, Geoff Hayes, Nat Allen, Speedy Smith, Des Hadlum, George Reynolds.

The Czechs arrived by rail at Sheffield (after visiting Glenmore Lodge) were met by the Oread team and transported to a welcoming party at Jack and Peggy Longland's house, Bakewell.

The Oreads provided accommodation for the Czechs in their own homes (Handley, Janes, Pretty, Hayes, Allen). This was the only time during their stay that the Czechs were not accommodated in either hotels or institutional establishments. This fact made a great impression on them.

John and Joy Hunt joined the party for a day's climbing on Stanage. There was a sausage and mash supper at the Spotted Cow, Holbrook, to which many other Oreads came.

On the second day the whole party was entertained at White Hall and from there a cavalcade of cars drove to North Wales (an arranged tea stop at the Fox, Overton) and the Czechs were handed over to the C.C. at Pen y Gywrd.

Subsequently the Oread team, plus wives, attended a quite lavish reception at the Czech Embassy in London (everyone occupied spare beds and floor space at Dick Brown's substantial town house in Putney) before seeing the guests off from Heathrow.

In 1970 (after the Russian re-invasion of Czechoslovakia) Janes and Pretty (with wives) were invited back by the Prague and Ostrava groups. During a hectic two weeks (by car and frequently under close Russian observation) Prague, Ostrava, the Betskydy Mountains, and the High Tatra were visited. The Tatra ridges were reminiscent of Skye, the scale being multiplied by two. Only in the mountains did the Czechs feel free and the difference in atmosphere between city centre and mountain hut was remarkable.

Further visits occurred in later years and contact with the Prague Czechs is still maintained in 1999.

Harry Pretty

BURNS TAKES A SWING

Newsletter, January 1967

Sir,

The love of wandering in the hills springs from a desire for the serenity and contentment that is the rich treasure found only in the beauty and desolation of upland country. Also in some great measure to the individual enjoyment of this, a way of life that requires no organisation of teams, no requirement for companions for whom you need to adjust your intentions. Pick up your rucksack and go – where you please, how you please – alone. To the tree lined river and pastures of the valleys, or the windswept desolation of the high moors, or the more trodden paths of the Peak – preferably in winter. You carry no number on your back, you report to no check point, nor are you directed to go here – or there – and you leave behind the decrees and regulations that stifle your life in alleged civilisation.

Those last bastions of solitude and freedom are now being assailed by laws of authority and organisation. We now have the official rescue teams. The hills are hideous with the shrieks and whistles – the Army – Police – Fire Service – uniforms, and all dressed up "in a little brief authority" with all that ill-considered interference of authority. To my dismay, this is being introduced with the connivance of alleged hill lovers – a treachery condoned by the insidious voice of those people who plead safety, in defence of the indefensible, and who wish to have some measure of control over those who wish to be free. Recently two arm-banded protectors had to be rescued from the comparative safety of Alport Dale on a mild October night because it had turned dark.

Laurie Burns

. . . AND GETS A REACTION

Newsletter, March 1967

Sir,

Whilst appreciating the wish of Burns that the last bastion of solitude and freedom in hills should not disappear (letter in last Newsletter) times are changing and so are peoples' approach to mountaineering.

The increase in the number of people, young and old, taking up the sport has been fantastic during the last decade. Ten years ago there was barely a small track below Stanage Edge, the road at it's foot only wide enough for one car, and without a surface. Nowadays there is a wide track around Kinder and almost one over the very summit of its plateau. This was not so in the 1950s.

Whether we like it or not this upsurge must bring with it more accidents, more access problems, more litter. There has to be some sort of organisation for all this. It is something to be proud of to find that clubs such as the Oread are willing to give up some time to organise a rescue team. Litter hunts have been organised in the past on club meets.

I offer this advice to Burns. Go to walk the Arenigs, or Radnor Forest this summer. These are the places you love. They are still not the "done" areas and I'm sure that you will be almost alone and away from "arm bands" and whistles; but you may find me going along as well.

Mountain Oread

The years between 1959 and 1976 were marked by the loss of the Oread's first two Presidents. Cyril Machin (C.B.M.) succumbed in the early part, and Eric Byne towards the end.

An Appreciation of both men appeared in the relevant Newsletters and extracts are given below, together with E. B.' write up of his 38th and last rock climbing anniversary at Birchen Edge in 1967.

Editor

CYRIL MACHIN, AN APPRECIATION – 1963
(EXTRACT)

Cyril Machin died in Bedgellert on Saturday 14th September whilst attending the M.A.M. Anniversary Dinner. For those of us who came under the influence of this remarkable man in the very earliest days of the Oread it may seem characteristic that he departed suddenly and without fuss – in the company of some of his oldest friends, and close to the mountains which had been at the very core of his life.

In 1949 he was old enough to have been a grandfather to most of us, but he climbed with more panache, greater technical skill, and a higher determination that many of us even dared to aspire to. He climbed and caved with what at times seemed almost a ferocity of purpose as though in regretting his relatively late start as a climber he was determined to compensate for the "lost years". This he surely did.

He never understood our inveterate bawdiness, nor our brash ebullience in pubs and on buses. Retrospectively it is difficult to understand how he tolerated our uninhibited ways.

For my part I shall always remember him for the way he unaffectedly welcomed Molly and myself, complete strangers, to his 1949 Skye Meet. Anyone who had the good fortune to join one of Cyril's legendary parties on Skye, Fort William or, more latterly, in the Dolomites, is never likely to forget the warmth, humour and excitement of the occasion – for the atmosphere of his parties was invariably an extension of his own unique personality.

The first anniversary number of the Oread Newsletter, June 1954, carried the news of Cyril's serious fall from Castle Naze. Only his determination and unquenchable spirit brought him through. He never climbed again. To walk at all, his limbs artificially supported, often extended him to the limit, but few, if any, of his closest friends would have dared to express vocal sympathy. Independent and wilful as ever, gentle and courteous despite all the pain and stress, self effacing to the point of embarrassment when his friends kind heartedly invaded his amazingly self sufficient world – he devoted his latter years to working and organising on behalf of others.

Not only did he continue to organise meets in the Dolomites and Skye with the same efficiency and attention to detail which always gave his parties a very special atmosphere, he continued to attend them. Ubiquitous in his little motorised chariot, (as M.A.M. Hut Warden), he commuted to N. Wales in all weathers, living on his own for long periods, organising work parties, climbing ladders into the loft, and lending to committees far and wide that very special gift he had of getting things done.

In company with all his friends I remember his determination and courage though the years since 1954. His gentleness and patience will be remembered by hundreds of White Hall youngsters who tied themselves to his rope. At an age when most men have taken to carpet slippers and the melancholy of remembering only the past, Cyril lived vividly and urgently in the present.

When the founder members of the Oread made him their first President, and subsequently their first Honorary Member, Cyril was at the very height of his powers. These were the days of C.B.M. in his prime – the period during which so much of the legend had its origin in fact.

Cyril going out for a solitary walk from Glenbrittle House and going on to complete the entire Cuillin Ridge Traverse in well under twenty-four hours. "I had a pair of plimsolls with me for the harder bits" was his only significant comment.

Cyril patiently tunnelling his way through a massive Nevis cornice- a task that occupied him all of a long night and which will never be forgotten by those of his companions who were normal men.

Cyril abroad on the Terrace Wall with a frightened plumber who had merely called at Glen Dena on business, and was unfortunate enough to find C.B.M. alone and raring to go.

Cyril wandering solo across steep Welsh rock – he probably lost count of the times he'd soloed Pinnacle Wall, which was one of his favourites. I don't know just how much solo climbing Cyril indulged in – he always talked of it with the same deprecating nonchalance that enlightened most of his climbing stories. But I suspect that during the long periods he spent on his own in Glan Dena he enjoyed more than he admitted to.

On one occasion he fell down No. 3 Gully accompanied by a large cornice. "I knew it was safe by then...so I went back up and it was easy". He was climbing solo of course, and I remember that others, who met him on the plateau and had no idea of the toughness of this apparently frail balding old man, showed signs of being outraged by such flagrant non-observance of the rules.

Cyril clawing his way up President's Wall barefooted on a raw, foggy winter morning. These were special years for some of us and much of the fun, and discovery, and the excitement was the gift of Cyril Machin.

Not long ago I came down from Tryfan to find Cyril in sole occupation of Glan Dena. I was returning to Rhyd Ddu, but for a while we sat outside and talked of this and that. Desultory gossip about nothing in particular, and about which I remember very little. He said that he'd been in the loft and was a little tired, but he emphatically insisted of making tea and bringing it out. I do remember that we talked about Derbyshire and, among one thing and another, I remember chaffing him, as I had done a dozen times in the past, about the time he got lost in a Derbyshire cave with a mutual acquaintance – and how he'd sat all night leaning against the small hole that eventually got him out. And I remember thinking that he did look tired, and that I didn't possess one decent photograph of him. So I took several – and he sat very still and asked several times whether I wanted him to move – Cyril always seemed to get what I can only describe as a young person's enjoyment out of being photographed. Eventually when Tryfan was a dark wedge against the evening sky I drove away and it never crossed my mind that I would not see him again.

H. Pretty

BIRCHEN EDGE, JUNE 1967
(*Extract*)

After nearly ten days of continuously fine weather I began to wonder if the conditions would hold out for this 38th rock-climbing anniversary of mine. However my week of effort on the family prayer mat proved successful and the whole weekend was nothing else but fantastic. After counting two hundred and twenty people I knew, either by name or familiar face, I gave up, but roughly estimate that about two hundred and fifty people turned up from such sources as the Oread, Mountain Club, M.A.M., Peak C.C., S.U.M.C., Harrow Mountaineering Club etc. Amongst these were such pre-war climbers as Harry Dover (whom I hadn't seen for thirty years) and Fred Jones the original founder of the S.U.M.C. There were also many odd bods from such far-flung places as London, Lincoln, Leeds, etc.

As near as I could work out there appeared to be about fifty Oreads plus their offspring, which is a confirmation that "tradition plus fine weather plus the Peak District" is an unbeatable combination.

Unfortunately I can no longer identify every face by name – I easily get confused these days, especially when I am having such a happy time greeting everyone. Janes was there of course, looking as leathery as ever and still full of those caustic flashes of humour which have always been such an essential and individual part of him. – Nobby Millward was nursing him along making sure he didn't get into serious trouble, – and keeping a wary eye on both was Judy Millward. What a wonderful woman, and that's saying something, for I've seen a few in my time, and the Oread has always been noted for fine looking wenches from Molly Pretty onwards. Needless to say Molly and Harry were there. It wouldn't have been so good if they hadn't been, for Birchens and Pretty's are part of my life.

To see Paul and Betty Gardiner gave me a great kick – John Welbourn too. Strangely enough I saw him do more climbing this time that previously. One mustn't forget Jack Ashcroft, looking as well as ever although somehow we never seemed to get together for a chat properly – and Dave Penlington, growing grey, and in shorts. I don't think I've ever seen him in shorts before – and Janet Penlington, looking as young and charming as the day Dave first snared her.

Somewhere I caught a glimpse of Laurie Burns. Doug Cook was there, and Jack Leeson. Jim Kershaw let me buy him a drink in the Robin Hood, which was indeed a privilege.

These are but a few of the names that come to mind. I hope the others will forgiver me for not mentioning them. I ought really to have had a register at Nelson's Monument. The signatures would have proved interesting and informative.

One last thing – believe it or not – I did climb. I led all those mods and diffs who's every hand and foothold I know off by heart. I even brought the great Frank Fitzgerald up Left Ladder Chimney, on a rope. He swears he slipped off one move! It's hard to believe. Anyway he retaliated by dragging me up Emma's Dilemma and another severe and, thus bolstered up; he began a slanging match with Pretty. He should have known better, if only from past experience. It's not surprising therefore to find that a little later he had to be rescued by a top rope on Crow's Nest. He finally departed leaving me with a final message for Pretty – a brief but telling – "Bugger off".

If this were, for any reason, to be my last Birchen Edge Meet. (God forbid) then it has been a glorious one.

Eric Byne

This was E.B.'s last Gritstone occasion and, in the following January, he died. The Newsletter for January, 1968 carried the following.

ERIC BYNE, AN APPRECIATION, 1968
(*EXTRACT*)

Eric Byne was not a founder member of the Oread. He became a member in 1950, largely due to his previous association with George Sutton and Cyril Machin, and the club's acceptance of his invitation to work on the Baslow Edge's Section of the Sheffield Area (volume 2, Climbs on Gritstone), which was published in 1951, under his editorship, and during his term (1951-1953) as President of the club. He was elected an Honorary Member in 1953.

Up to 1960 he was an extremely active member of the Oread and exerted great influence during those years that the Oread developed from a small group of friends into an well-organised club.

His sudden death on the 2nd January 1968, at the age of 56, when many of his friends had not realised he was so seriously ill, has left a space that nobody will ever quite fill.

Eric Byne was born and raised in Sheffield, and came of age at the height of the thirties depression. From the hopeless situation of industrial Sheffield, with a small group of friends, he set in motion a social revolution in the climbing world.

Eric was a founder member of the Sheffield Climbing Club which consisted principally of young men like himself, without work, without money, who walked their native moors and climbed on the Edges in workman's overalls or cast-off plus fours purchased for a song in the city rag market. They were the real prophets of the egalitarian principles, which have become the tradition of present day climbing society.

He was a fine rock climber and many of his first ascents are still classic Gritstone routes. But Eric had a quality, which translated him from the good climber of the thirties to a man of real stature in the post-war years. He was a man of incredible determination, with the perception to realise that what was happening on the moors and outcrops of the High Peak was more than casual recreation. He recognised the real value of this wild country wedged between the massive conurbations of Sheffield and Manchester. While many of his contemporaries were making reputations in more exotic mountain areas, Eric Byne devoted all of his energy to fostering the interests of those who lived and took their recreation in the Peak.

Throughout his life he displayed intense feeling towards freedom of access to open country and took part in both individual and mass invasions of Kinder Scout during the years of prohibition, police protection, and frequent physical violence.

The most assiduous and authoritative chronicler of Peak District affairs, he was the first editor of the first serious volumes to describe and classify the Gritstone outcrops. It was entirely typical that he was still improving the early excellence of the 1950's as editor of the new *Rock Climbs of the Peak* series right to his death.

It is difficult to describe how great was our delight when *High Peak* was published in 1966. Many of us witnessed Eric struggling with the MS of this book for nearly twenty years, and it is a further tribute to his fantastic determination that, at long last, he found a solution in association with Geoff Sutton. But, for me it will always be Eric's book – not so much as a record of physical activity but, more significantly, as a carefully observed record of social change.

In the post-war years Eric climbed in the Alps and frequently in North Wales and the Lakes. He discovered a number of new routes on Tryfan all of which exemplify his early flare for picking a splendid line of great character between established trade routes. But it is his association with Derbyshire that was the core of his life.

He was deeply moved by the number of people who went to Moorside Farm and Birchen for his June 1967 Anniversary Meet. Perhaps as many as two hundred old friends, with their numerous progeny, came from far and wide to talk and climb, to drink gallons of tea and a fair amount of ale, and those, who recognised the seriousness of his malady, wondered at his energy and his ability to still lead an awkward severe. Maybe he recognised it as possibly his last Gritstone occasion for certainly it was. But he gave no hint and, his new beard lending substance to his features, I could still think of him as indestructible.

Older members of the Oread will member Eric's obsession at every AGM concerning the acquisition by the Club of a hut in the Peak. He considered a hut in Wales to be of secondary importance. It is ironic that he should die in the year that we are on the verge of attaining this objective.

I can think of nothing more proper than commemorating the name of Eric Byne in the cottage that the Oread will eventually acquire in the area that he loved more than any other.

H. Pretty

SELECTIONS FROM OREAD VERSE

Between the years 1959 and 1970 Jim Kershaw's muse went into temporary retirement but the flame still flickered amusingly elsewhere.

Newsletter, September 1962

Ode Oread

Once upon a time we're told
All stories thus begin -
But many, many years ago
Is this one's origin.
Pretty then, was in his prime
And even Falkner used to climb,
And as we gaze around the Bell,
We see the others there as well,
The Druids and the Climbing Bard,
With faces weatherworn and scarred,
The mainstay of the club they are,
The ancient bearded crew
Who rest on laurels earned in days
When mountaineers were few.

A name among the famous few
Is that of R. G. Pettigrew,
It wings our thoughts to distant lands
Of turbaned chiefs and Sherpa bands.
"What's in a name?" new members ask,
"Who is that man behind the mask,
Of legendary and talked-of feats,
Why don't we see him on our meets?"
But now they find to their dismay
The Pettigrew of yesterday
Is busy climbing social routes,
Hard V.S. in dinner suits!

There's that old timer Hebog Jack,
He used to be a climber
In countless ages back,
Though now alas, from all reports,
We face the bitter facts –
Old Hebog went to Scotland once,
He left behind his axe.
Old Hebog went to higher peaks
And trailed around for many weeks
Searching – as so well we know -
For his lost crampons in the snow.
But Hebog hadn't cooked his goose,
He made it all a good excuse
To stay at lower altitudes,
For photographic interludes,
While hard men struggled ever upwards

Hebog's plans were all laid cupwards.
Old Jack is now beyond all hope –
In Glencoe forgot his rope.

The Oread holds out arms
To friends from far and wide,
Among its members
Proudly claims a real Italian guide.
His name is Guido Gadsby,
His fame has spread abroad,
For taking swims while fully dressed,
A cure for feeling bored,
A menace to the club one fears,
For circulating mad ideas,
Like bivouacs on Christmas Eve,
With only frostbite to achieve,
Or quite unnecessary feats,
Like alpine starts on Ogwen meets.

The President himself appears,
A climber still, though many years
Have not quite gone without a trace
Of household cares upon his face,
But still the twinkle in his eyes
Conveys that keenness never dies.
Herr Turner gazes past them all,
Dreaming of the Trolltind Wall.
...And great new routes that he will do,
With pale-straw filtered photos too.
And wond'ring how the holds will grip
When boots are cleaned with Molyslip

If your name does not appear
Within this weird epistle here,
Take heart – you're either in your prime
Or else I just can't make it rhyme.

Anon

Newsletter, October 1968

Newsletter, April, 1970

MY BILL

My Bill's a climbing man you know –
'E's always tellin' people so,
I met him in a lovely caff
Down by the road at Matlock Bath.
'E likes to dress up smart does Bill –
it gives me ever such a thrill
to see 'im in 'is mother's coms
all sewn up tight wi' leather thongs,
and tucked inside 'is jungle boots.
'E's made 'is shirt from parachutes –
'E says it's Spanish terylene –
it's yeller, black and olive green.
'E's got a lovely 'at 'e took;
'E found it 'anging on an 'ook.
It's orange, shinin' like the sun –
I think it's aluminium.
'E's borrowed my suspender belt
and covered it wi' purple felt,
It looks a treat when it's all laced
And pulled in tight around 'is waist,
'E uses it to 'ang things on
like nuts an' bolts an' a funny prong
what 'ammers into solid rock.
('E's clings to it or else 'e'd drop.)
Sometimes 'e takes me for a walk –
I think it's nice to here 'im talk
To other climber men, and say
"It's nice for tyin' off today"
and "what a lovely abseil thrutch",
or "do you oil your runners much?"
'E keeps on shoutin' all the time
about the crags 'e's goin; to climb.
Before 'e does, I really 'ope
'E's goin' to buy a bloody rope.

Anon

ROCK

No I wouldn't say he was a dangerous climber
but he'd lose control of himself, get all worked up
With the rock, almost personal, as if he reckoned
that if trusted, it might let him down.
He'd uncoil the rope at the cliff's foot and
banging his hammer on the crack shout "brainless bitch
You're as proud as eternity, you've helped
Twenty of my friends drop to their deaths,
Yet you can't move around like we can and you can't climb up"
– then, scrabbling and grunting, he would make a jump
and land at the top so fast there just wasn't time
for the rock to act; for his logic was simple,
if he could fall off a cliff, he could also climb it.
Not like another I know, who'd coax black rock
For hours, as a royal lover
will stroke a girl's hair half the night (and only then
dare make what in most men's repertoires
are the opening moves). He'd fondle the crack
with the palms of his hands, lowering each wrist in turn
to feed the fingers with blood; finally when the rock lay
most relaxed, glide softly upwards like a dancer.
A queer thing, but the rock was almost like a woman,
forgiving this one his seduction (he died
not by striking, but in a snowstorm, peacefully)
– and punishing that one's rape by breaking him.

Ronnie Wathen

Ronnie Wathen, although known to many Oreads, was not, to the best of my knowledge, ever a member of the club and I am not certain how an example of his great gift came to appear in an Oread Newsletter.

This remarkable man; poet, climber, part clown, and player of the pipes, died well before his time, in September 1993 — *Editor.*

MEMBERS

In an Editorial (Newsletter, 1967) Geoff Hayes noted that membership was increasing slowly (thirty new members between 1959 and 1970). The Newsletter for November 1967 included the following applicants:–

Ronald George Chambers	*Proposed:* J. Corden	*Seconded:* D.Williams
Roy Horatio Sawyer	*Proposed:* D. Williams	*Seconded:* P. Janes
Tom Green	*Proposed:* J. Welbourn	*Seconded:* G. Hayes

An interesting trio and good evidence for the theory that fancy plumbers always come in pairs, complete with the apprentice — *Editor.*

ENTERTAINMENTS
BONFIRE, PANTO, DOVEDALE DASH – NOVEMBER 1967

The weather did it's best to stop this meet. The few hardy Oreads who camped almost drowned in the mud on the field. No one managed to get to the bonfire in the Hall grounds on the Saturday night; all were trying to keep warm and dry inside.

For once one did not have to fight the queue to get into the Pantomime. Tinsel Allen and her magnificent cast did their best to warm up people with a fantastically well-costumed and performed panto. The club was well represented in the cast with Wes as "Blames Jond" in the lead. President Handley seemed quite at home playing the part of the villain. Burgess played alongside a slick blonde who turned out to be his wife Janet. Pretty was made for the part of the big fat sheikh. He was well attended by Digger Williams who was the only Welshman of coloured extraction in the cast. Big John Corden took the part of the big beefy henchman. Tinsel took the part of Harry's first and favourite wife – who treated all the lads to a fantastic belly dance. The ladies of the chorus have never looked lovelier – or more naked! All were introduced by 'Uncle Nat' complete of course with topper, which becomes more battered each year. Keep it up team it was a terrific evening.

Geoff Hayes

For many years the Ilam Hall Bonfire party, followed by a home made panto, preceded the Dovedale Dash. The occasion was invented by the Derby Mercury RC in the mid '50's. By the mid '60's Tinsel Allen was not only the chief scriptwriter, she was also producer and principal costumier. Occasionally Oread and Valkyrie members were invited to make guest appearances until, by 1966, they were playing the major roles. The scripts were freely amended on an ad hoc basis by Peter Janes both during rehearsals and the actual performance. They invariably played to a packed house. The more exhibitionist of the cast occasionally wore their costumes for the Dash on the following day to loud applause at the Stepping-Stones. At this time the number of runners rarely exceeded 200 — *Editor.*

Quote from Pete Janes to Les Langworthy – "When are we getting these bloody side boards off? I'll be glad when the panto season is over".

"I've got to get a few pints of beer inside me before I get rid of my shyness".
From that Oread Amoré – D. Burgess

"NOWHERE TO STAND"

"Nowhere to fall but off,
Nowhere to stand but on".

Ben King – The Pessimist

Swanage, Easter 1969 (Extract)

Ron Chambers

I set off up the slab, nonchalantly flicking a MOAC behind a flake as I went. After a further twenty feet the slab steepened into a wall completely void of suitable nutting cracks. I decided to place a peg and review the situation. The peg went in with a thud and I then realised just how much the quality of the rock had deteriorated during the last fifteen feet – the peg was useless in the event of a fall.

In retrospect I should have turned back at this point but a good corner crack beckoned a further fifteen feet higher and to the left and the rock friction was very good – I pressed on.

After about ten feet of diagonal traversing on very small and sloping holds I put in another peg runner, then made another delicate move leftwards and was relieved to find a really good undercut handhold at about shoulder height.

"Ah! The secret jug" I told myself, but as I moved across to bring myself into balance, the hold and a large flake suddenly came clean away from the cliff hitting me on the forehead. I instinctively glanced across at the two pegs as I fell over backwards, as my weight came onto them they flashed out as if fired from a bow. Everything went black.

A few minutes later I regained consciousness to find myself lying on my back staring up at an angelic figure hovering over me with outstretched hand doubtless sent to escort me to the "Promised Land". Then to my relief the hazy figure announced that he thought I was still alive and I immediately recognised the impeccable elocution of Ray Colledge.

A crowd of willing rescuers soon arrived and I learned that as the rope came tight as I was approximately six feet from hitting the ground, and that thanks to the nut runner and Nat's ability to hold me, I had escaped with comparatively minor injuries. No bones appeared to be broken as I could move both arms and legs, but I couldn't raise myself off my back. A human "caterpillar" was formed along the "Ruckle" and a spectacular stretcher raising exercise up the two hundred-foot cliffs organised by Don Whillans. I was rushed off to Poole General Hospital where it was found I had a couple of cracked ribs and a compressed spine.

Colledge writes, "Ron lay there moaning and mouthing "My back, my Back". I put my hand under his back and found a bunch of pegs. When I removed them he said "That's better". The coastguard produced a stretcher and ropes and we hauled him to the top. But just as the stretcher was nearing the last few feet I noticed that one of the two ropes has almost worked through – two of the strands having broken. So Ron was in danger of going back down again whilst strapped to the stretcher, but it didn't happen – a remarkable escape".

NEVIS, CHRISTMAS 1954

NAT ALLEN REMEMBERS . . .   *Newsletter, April 1970*

There was a great snatch as I took the strain and I was pulled sideways from my steps in the near vertical ice. The ice peg, which was my belay, went next and I was catapulted into space as if on a sling. I remember the gully walls coated in ice rushing past, then a sickening thud as I apparently landed with one leg driven into the deep gully snow and the other boot full of tricouni's in the left side of Joe's face. This was his second bounce and I had stopped him in his tracks. Out I catapulted again, a further hundred feet. When the rope pulled me up I was semi-conscious and upside down. Painful cries from above and it eventually occurred to me that I was strangling the "Baron Brown" as he was wrapped up in my spare rope. Somehow I scrambled back up a little, my dislocated right leg swung back into its socket and I passed out again. Later I sat with blood running past my eyes; I felt around for "holes and bits" but, apart from the leg and a nose bleeder, I seemed to be OK.

We had been stanced at the top of a hundred foot ice wall pitch on the major difficulties of Point-five Gully, trying for the first ascent. My stance was two footholds and a long channel ice-peg at nose level. Joe traversed leftwards to gain a steep ice rib, which, in turn gave to a nasty bulge of water ice. He had placed two ice-pegs for protection to his right, about three feet apart, and was on the tip of the bulge trying to gain lodgement in the snow runnel above. I was thoroughly gripped as I watched the struggle, then there was a sharp "CRACK" and the whole bulge, Brown ice-pegs and all left the "hill" en-bloc.

Nip Underwood in steep snow at the foot of the ice-pitch, a hundred feet below me, was third man on the rope. He had a good snow covered rock spike and for a second effort a loop of rope round an ice axe that I had dropped to him. When he took the strain the sling flew off the rock spike and he rolled over, but the axe held us. Below us the gully steepened and then ran out in about seven or eight hundred feet into the corrie. Nip was unhurt, but Joe looked as if Nat Allen had kicked him in the face! I was sitting there with a "gammy" leg so they tied my legs together and slid me pitch by pitch on to easy ground at the foot of the gully, then towed me sledge-wise down to the C.I.C. Hut – a case of frost bitten "bum".

In conclusion, I suppose if Joe Brown had been a better climber we might have made it!

DESCENT OF SPENCER COULOIR (AIG. DE FOU) (*EXTRACT*)

Newsletter, April 1970

DON COWEN REMEMBERS . . .

Our deliberations were brought to an end when lightning struck the ridge. We risked the couloir.

After fastening on crampons we descended in order: myself, Eileen, and then Pete as backstop. We were off the ridge and felt a little happier as, by now, the ridge was being continuously struck. Darkness, hastened by bad weather, was almost upon us. It began to snow.

I began cutting steps into ice below the snow but almost as fast they were filling up. We had no ice-pegs and our belays were extremely poor, and I was all too conscious of this fact as Pete started to climb down towards us. He was having great difficulty in finding the steps and was well above us when a shout from Eileen and a swishing sound from up above announced that Pete was on his way down and pretty fast at that. He streaked by me, feet first, lying on his back. My thoughts at the time were why doesn't he turn over and start braking with his axe, but before I could turn my thoughts into words he'd vanished down the couloir. Almost immediately, the strain came on Eileen who hadn't a chance of holding him. She was plucked straight from her stance and went by me in a flurry of snow; there was only a relatively short length of rope between Eileen and the axe from which I was belaying her. But the shock, when it came, tore the axe from the ice, and before I could do anything about this, the strain came upon me. – Strain is perhaps the wrong word – it was more like being ejected from a catapult. I left my stance and described a great arc before crashing onto the floor of the couloir. I then started to slide when, wham; I was launched into space again, as the rope between the other two and myself snapped tight once again. How far I travelled before I hit the deck I'll never know, but the bang on landing knocked the breath from me. I was now sliding down the coiloir at an incredible rate without an ice axe. This had gone, but precisely where it and I had parted company, I cannot remember. In some respects the fact that I lost my axe might have been a good thing, as I suppose I could have been impaled upon it. Ah well, that's my leg broken – surprising how the thoughts run through one's mind – no sense of fear, just one of annoyance at being so stupid as to get killed in the Spencer Couloir at the end of a holiday. Killed I was sure I would be, as I had few illusions of a gentle run out at the bottom of the couloir. If I didn't bash my head in on the way down the couloir, the ice cliffs of the Nantillons Glacier would soon rectify that.

My progress down the couloir continued in a series of slides and flights through space, whilst all the time I was waiting for the bang on the head that would put me out. I've heard it said that some people see their past flash before them under such circumstances; this was not so in my case, but all the same my mind was very active and I clearly remember thinking "Well I suppose my friends will read about this in the newspapers".

Suddenly a tremendous bang and oblivion. That's it I thought, I must be dead. The sliding, flying sensation had gone; everything was still, no sound – no light and black as hell. No pain even. So this is death – Hell, I'm still thinking, you can't be dead if you're still thinking. Dead of not, it was still black and silent as the grave, and I couldn't move. How long this lasted I have no idea, in reality probably a short time. A shout, it was Eileen's voice. I couldn't be, surely we'd all been killed. Another shout, this time "Don, where are you – are you alright?" My addled brain began to clear, and I began to realise the reason why I couldn't move, and why it was so dark. I was buried, obviously not very deep; otherwise I would not have heard the shouts. I managed to free an arm, and instinctively probed above my head. The snow above yielded and I saw a lighter shade of darkness and felt the fresh air on my face. It was incredible – I was still alive – after falling some seven hundred feet and what's more, I was not alone.

The rest of the story is a boring one of doctors and hospitals.

Footnote:

There can be no credit for sustaining a fall, yet it is in the nature of climbing that the finest achievements are separated from disaster by a razor sharp margin. For instance, on Bonatti's solo first ascent of the SW Pillar of the Dru: The crux came at the great overhangs above the red slabs. With insufficient gear to peg over this barrier, his last resort was to lasso an outcrop of rock above the overhang and pull himself up to it. Would the outcrop itself support his weight? "One last poignant hesitation. One last prayer from the bottom of my heart, and then, as an uncontrollable tremor ran through me, before my forces grew less, I closed my eyes for a second, held my breath and let myself step into the void, clutching the rope with both hands. For an instant I had the feeling of falling with the rope, and then my flight slackened, and in a second I felt I was swinging back; the anchorage had held!"

D.C.

177

"Climb if you will, but remember that courage and strength are naught without prudence, and a momentary negligence may destroy the happiness of a life-time. Do nothing in haste; look well to each step; and from the beginning think what may be the end".

Wymper: Scrambles Amongst the Alps

NOTHING TO LOSE

"If you don't spent owt, you lose nowt".

Derrick Burgess

TWO HEADERS

Ray Colledge

In 1963 Derrick Burgess and I climbed Route Major on the south face of Mont Blanc. The main difficulty was the upper rock buttress split by a strenuous chimney crack, ably climbed by Derrick. On top of the buttress was the ice cliff and my turn to lead.

This ice wall had two indefinite cracks leading upwards and, climbing up a little, I was able to hammer my ice axe shaft into the right hand crack. The wall was not too high but it was vertical. After borrowing Derrick's axe and with a hand jam in the left crack, I was able to mantle shelf onto the axe. Standing on the axe, I could use the other axe to step up onto the snow slope above. Derrick followed.

Now we had the problem of retrieving my axe. It was a new one, about ten days old, and I was distinctly worried about Derrick's lack of will to take recovery seriously. It was rumoured that Derrick never actually bought any equipment or food either, relying on his companions to provide what was needed. As he did most of the leading, it must be assumed that he carefully checked other peoples' racks before climbing with them.

However as I lowered him headfirst down the vertical ice, he was probably more worried about my ability to hold the ropes than anything else. A few gentle taps and the axe was safely recovered. We gained the summit of Mont Blanc and on the descent to the Grand Mulet hut we caught up with Ray Handley's team. They had done another route on the face.

In 1969 I was part of two teams on Mont Blanc. There was Peter Scott and Ron Lake followed by J. Fullalove (Dan Boon) and myself. This time it was Pear Buttress and again we descended from the summit to the Grand Mulet Hut.

Next morning we continued the descent over the dry glacier towards Chamonix. At one point we made a stop, where Pete put down his axe onto the ice next to a pool of melted glacier water. The axe slid into the water.

Pete rolled up his sleeve and reached down but not far enough. Using another axe he could hook it, but it always slipped back. Now Peter is known to frown on the very idea of releasing the moths from his wallet and so we knew what he had to do to avoid buying a new axe. He would strip to the waist and be lowered headfirst into the water. Cameras would record the event. He was thought to be a hard man who would not hesitate.

Alas, to our disappointment he refused and left the axe to its' fate.

Now, if Derrick Burgess has passed that way later on, and seen the axe, he would have dived in fully clothed to retrieve it.

The Welsh Hut: Tan-y-Wyddfa, Rhyd ddu. *Photo: Colin Hobday.*

The Derbyshire Hut: Heathy Lea (Sawmill) Cottage, Chatsworth. *Photo: H. Pretty.*

Bryn-y-Wern 1956: Janes, The Smiths, Marshall, Thompson, Berger, Welbourn, The Wrights, Phillips, Prettys, Cullums and Parsons.   *Photo: H. Pretty.*

Panto at Ilam Hall – the 1970's, includes Janet Burgess, Rita Hallam.   *Photo: D. Burgess.*

Bullstones 1968: Paul Gardiner, Derrick Burgess, Don Chapman.
Photo: C. Radcliffe.

Annual Dinner, Devonshire Arms, Baslow 1956: Dr. Norman Cochran, Alf Bridge, H. Pretty (President),
Molly Pretty, Showell Styles.   *Photo: Mike Moore.*

Cyril B. Machin – Opening of R. O. Downes Hut,
Froggat, 1961. Ernie Phillips at rear.
Photo: Harry Pretty.

Effervescent Bob Pettigrew with Margaret Lowe.
Photo: Jack Ashcroft.

Contemplative George Reynolds.
Photo: Harry Pretty.

Eric Byne and Harry Pretty. (E.B.'s last Anniversary
Meet at Birchen Edge, June 1967. *Photo: Molly Pretty.*

The Czechs arrive, 1967: Spotted Cow, Holbrook; J. Tomcala, D. Weston, G. Smith, V. Fibinger, R. Handley, M. Kucik, P. Janes, J. Steindler, D. Hadlum, M. Lichy, E. Wallis. Seated: H. Pretty, Nat Allen, M. Kasalicka, J. Kupec, L. Koupil, D. Burgess. *Photo: Derby Evening Telegraph.*

Working Party Weekend, Heathy Lea 1995; lunch break. The Hobdays, Tony Raphael, Eileen Gregson, Keith Gregson, Chuck Hooley, Kevin and Margaret Sarson, John Shreeve, Margaret Hooley, Brian West. *Photo: J. Hudson.*

Ski-ing in the Cairngorms, 1969. Standing: Peter Janes, Arthur Hawtin, John Crosse, Ron Chambers, Colin Hobday. Crouching: Dave Appleby, Dick Brown, Dougie Godlington, Gordon Gadsby. *Photo: Harry Pretty.*

Annual Golden Oldies Meet, Tan-y-Wyddfa, 1980's. Jack Ashcroft, Ken Hodge, Meg Moore, June Telfer, Janet Ashcroft, Mike Moore, John (Rock) Hudson, Charlie Cullum, Nat Allen, Ruth Allen, Colin Hobday, Doreen Hodge, Mary Cullum. *Photo: Chuck Hooley.*

Opening of Eric byne Memorial Cottage, Heathy Lea, Chatsworth, by Ivy Byne, October 1970. Alf Bridge and Derrick Burgess (President) in attendance. *Photo: H. Pretty.*

Evacuation of Bryn-y-Wern, October 1958. Lorry leaves for Tan-y-Wyddfa, Rhyd ddu. (B.-y-W. behind). *Photo: Jack Ashcroft.*

President's Meet (Brian West) 1996: Heathy Lea, Chatsworth; Derrick Burgess, Janet Reynolds, Brian West, George Reynolds, Ruth Allen. *Photo: H. Pretty.*

Nat Allen.
Photo: J. Ashcroft.

Molly Pretty: en route Coulags to Torridon, 1984.
Photo: H. Pretty.

Shirley Wainwright, Hon. Secretary 1999.
Photo: Julia Willson.

Uschi Hobday and friend.
Photo: Colin Hobday.

A HUT IN DERBYSHIRE

Well, some people talk of morality, and some of religion, but give me a little snug property".

Maria Edgeworth – The Absentee

The period 1958-1970 opened with the purchase of Tan-y-Wyddfa and closed with the successful effort to acquire a base in Derbyshire.

AGM, March 1967 (*Extract*)

Then followed some heated discussion on a proposal by Geoff Hayes that it was now time that the club should look into the possibility of obtaining a hut in the Peak District. Others thought the upkeep of our hut in Rhyd-Ddu was difficult enough without taking on further work. Nat Allen said that if it were not possible to get a hut in the Peak then a field should be purchased close to the Edges for an Oread campsite. Sites are becoming very scarce in that area. Harry Pretty said that from the earliest days of the Oread it was always hoped to obtain a hut in Derbyshire. Eventually a proposal was carried by a substantial majority, that the committee should look into the possibility of obtaining a hut in the Peak District sometime in the future.

In 1967 a Derbyshire Hut Sub-committee was formed comprising Pretty, Penlington, Nat Allen and Paul Gardiner — *Editor.*

A Home in Derbyshire

Newsletter, June 1967

By now many Oreads will have heard of the idea. What are the views of the members? As editor I have the chance to speak out first.

When I voiced my opinion at the last AGM I had in mind the kind of place that would become the active centre of the Oread in the Peak, with members gathering there, not only to stop overnight, but to meet friends at anytime. It should be a place that would not always have to rely on visitors for an income, so that one could go out whenever one wished and expect a bed.

What do others think? I hope that everyone thinks the same as Bob Pettigrew who writing from the Himalayas says, "Your idea of a Derbyshire Hut is an excellent one. The club must move forward".

Geoff Hayes

That Derbyshire Hut

Newsletter, November 1967

Due to the efforts of Harry Pretty, who has spent considerable time and corresponded with many people, the Oread are within an ace of obtaining a Derbyshire Hut. After meeting the agent of the Chatsworth Estate, Harry was offered a small cottage close to Chatsworth Edge, just off the Baslow-Chesterfield Road. The property, which includes two good barns, was offered to the Club at a most reasonable rent and with quite a long lease. The building is in a good state of repair and would sleep approximately twelve people. Close by is a large pumping station.

After discussing the find with the members of the Hut Committee, Harry and others called an Extraordinary General Meeting of the Oread in September. The club were shown plans of the property, and all the advantages and disadvantages were pointed out. The meeting overwhelmingly gave its approval and told Harry and the Committee to continue negotiations for a long lease. All seemed well.

On almost the same day that Harry contacted the Chatsworth Estate, the Water Board had let it be known that they wished to do one of three things. Either to extend the pump house into the cottage, or to extend the pump house across the stream away from the cottage, or finally, to remove the pumps and build in another place. It would of course be ideal if they decided on the latter course. All that we can do now is to wait and see and hope.

If the deal falls through it will be a blow to many members who were prepared to do their bit, but I'm sure that Harry and the others on the Committee of the Derbyshire Hut will not despair and that the search will go on.

Geoff Hayes

THE DERBYSHIRE HUT

Newsletter, October 1968

The Club has now taken possession of Heathy Lea (Sawmill) Cottage below Chatsworth Edge. For the first year (until March 1969) the Club will use the cottage on a trial basis. If the Estate and the Club agree a lease, it will run for approximately fifteen years. Until that time it is not intended to spend much on improvements etc. At the time of writing the Hut is not ready to use but within the near future there should be limited bed space available. The Hut Custodian is Harry Pretty.

Geoff Hayes

PREPARATIONS

Between taking possession in late 1968 and the official opening in 1970 a great deal of work was required to make the cottage basically habitable – it had stood empty for many years. On one notable Saturday an army of Oread navvies dug out the wet marsh at the rear and eighteen tons of limestone hardcore was brought in and consolidated (existing rear car parking). Sodden plaster was stripped off walls and Nat Allen created the "exhibition wall". The cottage was re-wired under the supervision of Derek Carnell. Paul Gardiner installed basic kitchen fittings, and a new water supply established. The matrazzenlager was constructed in the bedrooms and basic work to establish the Barn was started. But the Elsan stayed.

It was a sad irony that E.B. never knew that we had acquired Heathy Lea for it was only months before, at his last Anniversary Meet (1967) that he'd told me how in the 1930's the cottage was occupied by a rather aggressive gamekeeper who kept vigil over the Chatsworth Edge. E.B. and his Sheffield lads considered it something of a victory when, on rare occasions, they contrived to bivvy overnight in one of the Heathy Lea barns without being discovered.

So, in the occupation of this site, the Oread is returning to and sustaining some of the earliest history in gaining access to Gritstone — *Editor.*

OCTOBER 11TH, 1970

3 p.m. Official Opening of the Eric Byne Memorial Hut by Mrs. Ivy Byne and Mr. Alf Bridge.
7 p.m. General Meeting, Royal Oak, Bakewell.
8 p.m. Photo Meet, Royal Oak, Bakewell. Judge: Mr. Douglas Milner.

(Newsletter announcement, September 1970)

It was a major day in the Oread Calendar. Over one hundred members and guests attended, including many representatives of kindred Clubs – Fred Piggott, Douglas Milner, Eric Byrom, Ron Townsend, Don Morrison, Dave Gregory, Larry Lambe, Bert Heap, Peter Wilkinson, Tony Moulam, Dick Brown, Dennis Gray, Fred Williams, Duncan Boston.

Also present was Charlie Ashbury and several surviving members of the original Sheffield CC., together with E.B.'s brother Wilfred.

Derrick Burgess (President) introduced Ivy Byne, Alf Bridge spoke about Eric, and the slate plaque (organised by Nat Allen) was unveiled outside, before being hung over the fireplace.

Paul Gardiner had organised a fine barrel of ale and old friendships were renewed, in an around the cottage, on a fine Autumn day. Digger Williams (adrift as usual) arrived to cheers on his bicycle shortly before the barrel was drained.

It was a wonderfully informal day and no record was kept of the various speeches which perhaps is the way it should be — *Editor.*

ODDS AND SODS FROM THE 60's

The (Great) Gadsbys knowing that the hut would be full one weekend decided, because they would be later arrivals, to send their sleeping bags with friends to be placed on beds thus making sure of a place to sleep, and to force the editor and others to sleep on the floor. However justice was done. It turned out to be a foggy night and halfway to Wales they were faced with the decision to turn back or risk a night in the van without Bug Bags – they returned home. Everyone else had a good time in Wales.

Quote at a recent Committee meeting – "We must keep a close watch on this man Gadsby, Hitler started out as a painter".

Ray Colledge was recently reprimanded by the President, Ray Handley, whilst lagging behind on a mountain walk. "The trouble with you Ray is that after a couple of routes in the Alps you are burnt out for the rest of the season".

CHRISTMAS AT TAN-Y-WYDDFA 1969

Quote of the holiday came from John Welbourn, fresh from burglar prevention activities in Bangor is y Coed, when he announced "You know really I'm the chief screwer in our village . . ."

TAN-Y-WYDDFA 1968

The Committee have decided that the Welsh Hut shall always have one spare room reserved for club members every week and, that other clubs who use the hut, can only have other spaces on two weekends per month. The idea behind this new rule is to give members more chance of finding room in the hut at any time. Previously other clubs were able to take the whole of the Hut.

I understand that this rule is still applicable in 1999, vis a vis guests who attempt to use the Oread room when they have booked the entire hut. There was a minor incident in this context as recently as 1998 — *Editor*.

"SPATZ-M" AT THE DERBYSHIRE HUT

Those enjoying "deep sleep" comfort at Heathy Lea should have the greatest admiration for Harry Pretty's powers of persuasion. The "Spatz-m" has been provided by K-foam in recognition of the important part Heathy Lea plays in the mountain rescue activities of Team Alpha!

The foam was delivered to H.P. at home and on Boxing Day he took a load to the hut strapped to the top of his car. It was freezing hard and when filling up at the local garage, the attendant cynically commented: "You're a bit of a pessimist aren't you?"

PATTERDALE 1968

Clive Russell reports various activities, "on the other side of the valley. Ray Colledge made a rumoured first ascent with Honor".

(Honor . . . , well remembered and much admired by red blooded Oread males was elected a member in January 1969 — *Editor*.

Lower Small Clough Cabin interior.   *Photo: Colin Hobday.*

The Moderns

1970-1990

Re-inventing the wheel

During the late 1960's Chris Radcliffe and Peter Scott had blossomed into Oread hard men and, in their wake, came a string of like minded enthusiasts so, when Geoff Hayes, (after seven years) retired from editorship of the Newsletter, it seemed wholly appropriate that Radcliffe and Scott should jointly take on the job.

They were at the height of their powers, ready for the ultimate mountain challenge, and simultaneously irritated (if not angered) by an apparent torpor that permeated club activities. Their early Editorials made their point .... and there were those who did not agree.

> "Stiffen the sinews, summon up the blood,
> Disguise fair nature with hard-favoured rage"
>
> *Henry V*

STIFFENING THE SINEWS
EDITORIAL (EXTRACT)

Newsletter, February 1970

"The Oread? You want to steer clear of them, they're a cliquey lot" said this character we met in the pub. Undeterred we visited the Wilmot and after a few weeks we managed to get a foot in the door. Soon we began to appreciate the very considerable depth of experience and variety of outlook which characterised the Oread. We found that this unique club comprises climbers whose mountaineering experience extends over many years and at the same time many whose ambitions do not extend beyond a few rigorous walks; many members who are prepared to devote hours of time in the thankless tasks which are necessary to make the club tick; a lively social life; an original approach to meet venues. All this contrasted strongly with the "hard-man's" club we had come from. That club was a 'clique' personified – venues were limited to the current vogue areas, social life limited to beery confabs. The collective experience of the Oread mounts to a living tradition. Whilst we have the greatest admiration for this tradition, it seems fitting to ask if it is one that will live on into the seventies and is it an appropriate tradition for the new era?

The Oread was formed in 1949 and thus it bridged two famous eras in the history of British Mountaineering. Members are still active, whose associations were with the pace setters of the pre-1960 era: Arthur Dolphin and Peter Harding and the pace setters of the era that followed; Brown, Whillans, and the Rock and Ice. The link the Oread has with the Development of climbing in the Peak District is an essential part of its character and it is fitting that the club included among its members the late Eric Byne, whose unparalleled contribution to Peak District climbing began in the pre-war era. Within two years of its formation the Oread formed an expedition to Arctic Norway, in a period of post-war rationing, long before expeditioning became as straight-forward as it is to-day. Other expeditions followed to Arctic Norway, Spitzbergen and South Georgia, and ten years after the initial expedition the club was organising a major expedition to the Himalayas. In spite of the virile way in which the club has contributed to the British climbing scene, it is nevertheless true that it has played no part in the modern era of climbing.

Chris Radcliffe, Peter Scott

The implications did not pass unnoticed and there was a response – *Editor.*

LETTERS TO THE EDITORS

Newsletter, March 1970

The 'Modern Era' is considered by some to have started in 1949, with Brown and Whillans, or with Crew's downfall. How wrong they are. It is also said by our equally modern Editors, that the OREAD has played NO part in the development of this 'Modern Era'. How wrong are they? It seems to me that some backroom historian should do something to put the books right, and if this article seems to 'shoot the bull', may I be excused on the grounds of provocation.

The sixties started for the Oread with the full task of putting a fairly sizeable expedition into Kulu early in 1961, and whilst it only concerned five members, it required the efforts of several Oread backroom boys to launch it.

1962 was a quiet year, the majority of Oreads seemed occupied with repeating Brown's routes, especially those at Tremadoc. In the Alps the East Ridge of the Crocodile and the West Face of the Petits Jorasses were the pick of the season.

1963 Saw three new routes on Baslow Edge, two on Curbar and three new routes on limestone in the Manifold. Pick of the Alps in '63 were Route Major and the Old Brenva on Mont Blanc.

1964 saw the completion of the Froggat-Curbar-Baslow Guide for publication. Two new routes were climbed on Chatsworth Edge and one in Dovedale. In the Alps the East Ridge of the Pain de Sucre and the Scarfe Arête were ascended. Our man was active in Kulu.

In 1965 the Manifold Guide was undertaken and seven new climbs were found in the valley. Elsewhere 'Light' in Gordale, a HVS on the Ruckle at Swanage, and one in Dovedale were climbed for the first time. The Brassington Area Guide was completed with three new routes. In the Alps the North Face of Lyskamm, the Caterinagrat on the Monte Rosa, and the Zmutt Ridge of the Matterhorn had Oread ascents.

In 1966 Oreads put up two HVS and two VS routes in the Manifold, one Dovedale VS, and two routes on the undeveloped Guillemot Ledges at Swanage. The Chatsworth Edge section of Vol. 4 Gritstone was handed in. During a bad Alpine season the Scerscen-Bernina was traversed. Another good route on the Ruckle at Swanage was put up and our man was at it in Kulu again.

In 1967 one new Dovedale VS and one Manifold HVS led to the completion of the Manifold Guide Script for Vol. II Limestone. Two new Swanage routes were knocked off. The pick of the Alps included the S. Face of the Meije, S. Face of the Aig. Dibona, S. Face Punta Guigliermina; and don't forget our man in Kulu.

In 1968 two more HVS Manifold routes were put up and another VS in Dovedale. A C.C. Guide to Cader Idris was written and in the poor Alpine season the traverse of the Schreckhorn, the Bonatti Pillar of the Dru and the N.Face of the Doldenhorn were climbed.

So ends this quickly sorted, potted history which I hope will at least stop our young climbers joining the local rambling club. Not a lot you may say, but every little helps.

'Clinker'

.............on a less sanguine note ....

To the Editors!

E. Byne, A. Bridge, G. Sutton, D. Penlington, E. Phillips, P. Gardiner and H. Pretty – names such as these earned the Oread recognition as one of the top clubs in the climbing world in the late 40's by their pioneering on Derbyshire Gritstone, whilst more recently the names of Burgess and Nat Allen have maintained our position by their magnificent efforts on Derbyshire Limestone.

What have the 70's in store for us? – or more to the point – what has the Oread in store for the 70's? Perhaps another Himalayan expedition or a trip to the Andes, it is entirely up to us: especially we younger members full of the spirit of adventure!! Or are we? Come to think of it, what has happened to the spirit of adventure of the Club generally? Are we entering a phase devoid of enthusiasm and achievement? Let us not bask in the reflected glory of the past.

Every member is or should be aware of the hard work that has gone into building the Oread into what it is to-day, but it is no use sitting back thinking, "Well, we've made our mark, we needn't do any more". On the contrary, we must continue to maintain the standard set by the earlier members. Are we younger members really bothered about this? I am beginning to doubt.

There are too few members striving to keep the name of the Oread to the fore front and all too many content to go to the weekly ale-up and to do plenty of waffling about what they are going to do but, come the weekend, and it is the same few climb-any-weather members who are keeping the flag flying.

Is this good enough for a club that used to be so active? For the last two years attendances at meets have declined, although the club membership has increased. Why? Amongst other things I fear that the membership could be exceeding the limits and straining, perhaps too greatly, the much coveted Oread bond. People do not seem to want to make the effort. There are too many relying on too few, and when the few cannot make it, the unfortunate meet leader finds he is spending the weekend on his own. Which brings me to the subject of huts.

We have a Welsh Hut used more by other clubs for meets than ourselves, and a Derbyshire hut also neglected by all except the usual crowd. Much hard work went into the landing of this hut and it is up to us to keep it going.

This is the Club's 21st birthday year, let us younger members try to do as much for the Club in the next twenty-one years as was done for it in the first twenty-one years by the founders and the earlier members.

Ken Hodge

The new Editors were not over impressed by Clinker's C.V. and in April kept the pot boiling ....

One of the more remarkable features of the Radcliffe/Scott editorship was the introduction of a fairly regular contribution by Tricouni. The identity of this anonymous commentator has, to this day, never been divulged and, despite much discussion during the intervening period of nearly thirty years, still remains a mystery. Tricouni employed a sly wit, often in a serio-comic vein that displayed an intimate knowledge of club affairs which, on occasion, could lapse into embroidered fantasy. His first contribution, in the form of verse, was directed at the crisis in club climbing activities as alleged by the new editors — *Editor.*

THE PROBLEMS AND SYMPTOMS OF A THREATENED AND DECLINING IMPETUS TOWARDS THE PHYSICAL ATTAINMENT OF GEOGRAPHICAL SUMMITS

Tricouni . . . Newsletter, March 1970

It was during a short walk in the lower British hills, that the memory of the following discourse came to mind, touching a major problem affecting to-day's climbing world............

It is true that old climbers go septic,
That the gleam in their eye tends to fade;
That piton and rope are considered a joke,
When the debts owed to time have been paid?

Or do they in turn take to ski-ing
To cover their lessening skill;
Adopting a pose and wearing flash clothes,
And pulled by a motor uphill?

Many old climbers were going this way,
But now it's beginning to spread,
With all the young Tigers deserting the rock
And acting like penguins instead!

There's Handley and Hayes and now Weston;
Appleby Dench and old Pete;
Forsaking the edges from Birchen to Stanage
In favour of those on their feet.

Perhaps it's a sign of rebellion
Now that climbing has lost its mystique,
Due to Whitehall, Prince Philip, and now 'Mac the Tele',
On the box on every new peak.

Or is it the lure of the dollies
That brings these fine men to their knees;
of Rosies and Wendies and discotheque trendies
To fill up those hours apres-ski?

I wonder where all this will lead us?
With what joy will father tell son.
That the pride of his youth was no Dolomite roof,
But descending Mam Tor on his bum!

So 'alas and alack' for the climbers,
Who's hearts must be aching full sore;
No gear in the shops, just queers on the tops,
We're second class beings once more.

Tricouni

EDITORIAL (*EXTRACT*)

Newsletter, April 1970

British climbing clubs are many and varied, but basically they can be grouped into four main categories. At one end of the scale are the senior clubs such as the Climbers Club or the Fell and Rock club with large scattered memberships, excellent facilities, considerable resources, and an unquestioned, but possibly undeserved authority. At the other end of the scale are local clubs such as the Nottingham C.C., Rimmon M.C., which have an essentially informal structure, offer little in the way of facilities but, composed of small groups of climbers with like interests, they survive on a surfeit of enthusiasm. Thirdly there are the specialised clubs – in the Universities, the Services and other institutions, which have an essentially transitory membership and an equally chequered history. Somewhere between the first two groups comes the somewhat nebulous fourth category which we can call the Area clubs. The Oread, having of course started life as a local club, has, after 21 years, now outgrown its role and belongs properly to this fourth category. Its survival up to now is evidence enough of a healthy development, but can we look forward to an equally prosperous period in the seventies and eighties? Or are we, in our twenty-first year, going to indulge in a self satisfied bubble of complacency which when pricked will reveal a skeleton of a club composed of faded heroes, supported by a plethora of beer drinking, peak-bagging, piste-bashing, fair-weather socialites; a sterile community in which any emergent talent is still born?

There can be few clubs in the country which boast of two huts. On the one hand this is a credit to the stalwarts who have done all the work to put us in this fortunate position. On the other hand it spells danger when people join to take advantage of the facilities rather than contribute to the spirit and fibre of the club. We also count ourselves as a senior Peak District club. Why is this? Presumably on account of the work done by the club in the development, fifteen years ago, of a few overgraded beginner's crags, in the vicinity, appropriately enough, of the Derbyshire Hut. Also, as "Clinker" told us in March, this vestige of authority is attributable to the development work done on some vegetated limestone outcrops on the southern fringe of the Peak. Sterling stuff, but can we rest on such laurels? Modern developments make all this seem as ancient as the Gully Era. The Peak District moderns generally operate outside the club context anyway, which begs the question, whether the club is an appropriate institution now that everyone is mobile and T.V. has put climbing alongside soccer as an attraction for armchair enthusiasts, and whether the club is in fact a hindrance to a climber's progress – the antithesis of its original concept.

Radcliffe/Scott

Editorial note 1998: – Interesting that many of the climbs on these "overgraded beginner's crags" have gone up several notches in grading in the 1996 Chatsworth Area Guide, in a period when climbers are using a plethora of protective aids. In the 50's we led most of these "overgraded" routes straight through without much in the way of intermediate protection (no harnesses, no friends, no nuts, no wires), frequently in boots and, at the very best, a pair of Woolworth's plimsolls. A quick comparison between Climbs on Gritstone (1951) and the Chatsworth Area Guide (1996) in respect of Birchen Edge, indicates that at least 20 routes have been upgraded in the 1996 edition – a number from V.D. to H.S. Since the Derbyshire Hut was not available until 1970 the reference to it seems largely irrelevant, except in the pejorative sense.

Newsletter (Extract), March 1971

Many of you will be reading this Newsletter for the first time at the AGM, hence this is an appropriate time to take a critical look at the health and spirit of the Club. Last November we celebrated twenty-one years of existence as boisterous as ever at the Dinner and many fine phrases were flung around looking forward to equally fruitful years to come. We hope that this will indeed be the case and that the Club will move from strength to strength. It is clear that the Club as we know it comes from the farsighted enthusiasm of it's older members who spurned the conventional framework of climbing communities. As Eric Byne wrote in "High Peak", referring to the early expeditions organised by Oreads; "It is perhaps difficult to realise nowadays what a psychological and social breakthrough this was, or how much character it required."

Fine though these achievements may have been, it is equally clear that conditions have changed so radically that the essential character of the Club must change if we are once again to be seen as pace-setters. The privations of earlier days which tended to throw fellow climbers together have largely disappeared and as with life in general the sport has become too comfortable. Is the age of the extrovert personalities who did so much to kindle enthusiasm now lost to us? Perhaps the concept of a club is the antithesis of vitality – certainly the front runners of today's climbing scene tend not to be club types. However we believe that this outlook is far too narrow-minded and that the club retains a place to foster a true spirit of the hills and a belief in mountaineering as very much a way of life.

Radcliffe/Scott

Newsletter, March 1971

Dear Sirs,

I have read with interest your comments on the state of the Oread in past Newsletter Editorials. Since you are obviously hoping for replies, here are my observations for what they are worth.

In general I do not agree with you when you denigrate the past of the Oread, but like yourselves I am afraid for the future. At present the Oread is a club to be proud of; but will it be so in a few years time?

If a climbing club is to retain its 'hard image', I believe it must retain within itself a nucleus of keen young climbers. The age group of the nucleus must normally be 16 to 25 (which lets you out Pete) since these are the years of comparative freedom from responsibility (polite word for wife, children, home, garden etc.) and nearly all one's spare time can be diverted to climbing. The size of the nucleus must be such that an element of competition creeps in between individuals and I think this means a minimum in the nucleus of 8 or 10 people. Since by the laws of nature individuals are continually leaving the nucleus from the top end, it is obviously necessary to recruit into it preferably at or near the bottom.

Climbing clubs are normally formed by such groups of individuals, but if a club fails to continually replenish its young nucleus, then a form of creeping paralysis sets in. For a few years all will seem well on the surface and the hard image will remain for a while, but eventually it is doomed to become what you so aptly described as 'a skeleton club composed of faded heroes'; a joke among the more virile clubs of the day.

How does the Oread fit in with this picture? When I first stepped through the doors of the Wilmot to meet the Oread, my eyes were greeted by a bevy of beautiful birds.

To digress for a moment; for a while I was amazed at the way the Oread managed to attract them unto itself, though I now appreciate this is entirely due to the magnetism of certain senior members. When I looked round for the young men who ought to have been hanging round these birds, I could see very few – no more than a few glowing embers in a once vigorous fire. Admittedly a "not so young as it used to be" group were and still are putting up a pretty good smoke screen which tends to hide the trouble underneath. Unless something happens, however, I believe the Oread is doomed to obscurity in not too many years time, at least from the climbing point of view.

Trevor Bridges

So, an outsider was brought in to have a look, and consider the verdict.

GREENER GRASS (*EXTRACT*)

TIM LEWIS *Newsletter, March 1971*

These days it's no good moving from one climbing area to another and expecting to have an effect like Prometheus bringing fire down from Olympus to the mere mortals. You're more likely to suffer his fate – drinking all night and having your liver pecked out next day by the local vultures (or something that feels like that). The days of Gods descending from the clouds in climbing circles are gone. Climbing has now reached the communist ideal – a classless society where no-one's impressed by anyone else's status. Now don't get me wrong. The only reputation I have to precede me is best left behind.

The editors asked that I point my trumpet Derby-wards. Now if I blew it a hundred times more often than the seven times that fixed Jericho, Derby and Rolls-Royce wouldn't bat an eyelid. First things first. I've seen them play often now; Mackay is still impressive, Macfarland's learning well, but who are the pygmies at the front and back? As a forward line they make a good circus act – with Shetland ponies and followed by sea-lions. What next? Oh yes. The clubs. This town's got more than Arnold Palmer. It took me some time to work out the difference between the Mercury and the Oread and why they were connected. I've got it sorted now, I think. This old guy told me in a pub. He said, and I've no reason to believe he lied, "A long time ago the Gods came down from the North (I think he meant Manchester) and gave three gifts to us, water, the wheel, and iron. We'd no use for the first, having found better brews ourselves, so one took the wheel, and the others iron. Now the lot with the iron needed some means of moving so they conned the lot with wheels into letting them join. The lot with wheels didn't want iron so they felt aggrieved and eventually both sides had recourse to water substitute to sort out their problems. That's the way it's stayed. As I said, I've no reason to believe he lied; an extraordinary story for an extraordinary set-up. Finally then, I was warned before coming to Derby about them: I was prepared to believe it, but the truth was worse. They don't think they run the town, they just ignore it.

Then there's another party; I call him that because the first time I met him, he was a one man celebration and asked me the second time what I'd said. God bless you sir, and your penguins. The rest of the Club seems to have remained uncontaminated; do yourselves a favour and remain that way.

Well, I've nearly done and I've not said much about climbing in this climber's newsletter. Disregarding the cries of "That's because you've not done much", he passed on. I think, I hope I'm right, that the reason for this is the diversity I feel in this club. It has more opportunity for becoming inbred than most other clubs, because of its nature and the area it operates in. The climbers seem to climb, the ramblers to ramble, and both to discuss anything other than that when not in action. It also seems to have a healthy sense of inter-personal vituperation – gossip to you madam – which does not prevent it from being friendly. Thanks to all who have helped ease my entrance to a new area, especially those I've had a swing at. I've only one criticism to make: in the breathalyser age; why does the club meet so far out of town? Not good thinking for good drinking.

This is only 1971 – and it's going to run, and run and — Editor.

For example – later in 1971

Dear Sir,

As to the general gloom and despondency expressed in your editorial, and other letters, I cannot see the Club "doomed to obscurity in not too many years time". It must be agreed that a regular intake of the young is essential to the virility of the Club but the totally rational approach of the nucleus outlined by Trevor Bridges does not quite workout in practice. To take as an example; the great alpine routes in Rebuffat's 'Starlight and Storm'. In recent years the record of Oreads in this context is equal I'm sure to any club of similar nature. The age spread of climbers is the significant point, 27 to 47 (at a guess). Admittedly the climbers involved have joined the Club by various routes but this only serves to reinforce the point. Might I be so bold as to suggest the "faded heroes" image and "wittering on about passes", image is not yet on our doorstep. The reference to a club composed of "faded heroes, a joke among the more virile clubs of the day" is rather a joke in itself. The most virile clubs of the day are notorious for only surviving the day. The A.C.G. have acknowledged this basic fact and deny club status.

Yours, a witterer
Triple Hob

Despite the Alpine record of 1971[1] the Newsletter Editor was still worrying away in 1972.

[1]see Alpine Affairs 1970-1980.

EDITORIAL (EXTRACTS)

Newsletter, July 1972

Judging by the attendance on recent meets, perhaps it is not surprising that nothing is being written since nobody is doing anything to write about. Surely attendances cannot have been as bad at any time in the history of the club, especially considering the nominal membership of 120 plus. The weather has of course not been good, but this in itself is an insufficient explanation. No meet (apart from the 14 Peaks walk) has been well attended for many months; several attendances have dropped below ten and, on one occasion, the meet leader himself didn't turn up. Even the best attended meets are usually swollen in numbers by non-members. As a whole the picture is pretty pathetic. In the past I have attempted to write some reasonably vitriolic editorials, but the response has been staggering in its indifference. So I continue to despair as to what is happening to the club.

In the April 1970 issue of the Newsletter I attempted to analyse the Oread M.C.'s position in terms of British Mountaineering and questioned whether in fact we would look forward in the seventies and eighties to the same fruitful development we had enjoyed in the first 21 years of our existence. I concluded that this would depend on the encouragement given to the younger members, but that in essence it depends on the overall enthusiasm of the club. Now, only two years later, I can see little to provide much optimism. I see little to change the view expressed in the March 1971 Newsletter that we still owe too much to the older members, who increasingly are fading from the scene.

Chris Radcliffe

COMMITTEE MEETING DISRUPTED . . .

Newsletter, March 1970

During the meeting of the Oread Committee at Dave Appleby's in February, the numbers were suddenly reduced by the call out of Team Alpha. Messrs. Weston, Hodge and Appleby departed to Ashbourne, leaving the remainder of the committee lounging in front of Appleby's fire, enjoying Judy's excellent cuisine. The business of the evening was nevertheless completed. Dave returned about 11.30 p.m. and quote ...."to find the rest of the committee tossing up to see who should leave last".

The rescue involved the recovery of two young lads who had fallen at Tissington Spires.

MANIFOLD VALLEY

Newsletter, March 1970

It was reported in The Guardian (18/2/70) that 'defenders' of the Manifold Valley, which the Trent River Authority plans to flood as a reservoir, are to invite an all-party group of MPs to tour the valley.

Jack Longland has pointed out, however, that no definite plan has yet been put forward by the Authority. They are scheduled to do so in a few months time. Depending upon where the dam is to be built more or less of this valley will be flooded. In any case this will not be effected for some years to come.

It would seem fairly ineffective to protest at this stage if no plan has yet been submitted. Nevertheless if such a plan is forthcoming and the amenities of the valley are to be drowned, then is the time to write your protest letters.

This proposed scheme seems to have died without trace, or does it still lurk in the files of Severn Trent ..... or was it overtaken by Carsington? – *Editor.*

ERIC BYNE MEMORIAL FUND

Newsletter, April 1970

Eric Byne Memorial Fund/Campsite

The official closing date for sending contributions to the Eric Byne Memorial Fund was April 1st. The Peak District lacks good camp-sites and it is hoped that a permanent camp-site will be purchased and equipped in the vicinity of Gardoms and Birchen Edges. This is a most important development when the general trend is towards restriction of casual camping in the Peak District. No doubt the trustees of the fund will only be too pleased to receive further contributions, especially from members of one of the senior Peak District clubs. — *H.P.*

The E.B. Memorial Fund was set up in May 1968, largely due to initiatives by R.E. (Larry) Lambe, Jack Longland, Alf Bridge, Harry Pretty, and Nat Allen.

The Trustee Group comprised: Nat Allen, John Hunt, Don Morrison, Geoff Sutton, Alf Bridge, Jack Longland, Fred Piggott, Larry Lambe, Joe Brown, Tony Moulam, Harry Pretty, and Eric Byrom (Treasurer).

Negotiations with the Water Board and Peak National Park were mostly conducted by Longland, Pretty, and Lambe. The Fund was not heavily subscribed but by late 1970 the Peak National Park Board had agreed to take over land at Moorside Farm, below Birchen Edge, to establish a "wild" camp-site.

The campsite was officially opened by (then) Sir Jack Longland in October 1976 — *Editor.*

FOREWORD TO NEWSLETTER, DECEMBER 1971 *(EXTRACT)*

PAUL GARDINER *(PRESIDENT)*

I am sure that members and friends will understand the mixed feelings with which I put pen to paper in an endeavour to write some appropriate words on Oread events of the past five months.

The feelings range from pleasure in the club's outstanding Alpine achievements to heartfelt despond at the loss of two members to whom the Oread owes so much.

My intention in late August was to write a foreword recognising the outstanding performances of Chris Radcliffe, Peter Scott, Ray Colledge and others during the Alpine holiday.

However, the events of September 1971, the loss of Geoff Hayes in an accident on Dow Crag, the injury to Lloyd Caris, and the untimely death of Alf Bridge, transcend all other thoughts, and this numbing effect is felt by all. I extend to the relatives of Geoff and Alf the sympathy of the club, and wish a successful and speedy recovery to Lloyd.

GEOFF HAYES, 1938-1971

AN APPRECIATION *(EXTRACT)*

The first Oread meet which Geoff and I attended was at the Roaches, some time in 1955. That meet saw the genesis of the person who was to become, without doubt, the "Complete Oread".

In all aspects of his mountaineering activities, Geoff exhibited a high level of competence, although it was typical of the man that he did not always set his sights so high that this standard was required. One felt that whatever the occasion, Geoff would always have something in reserve. It was unlike

Geoff to train seriously for long walks or Alpine meets. We all know that he did not need to and that on a given occasion he could have walked probably any of us into the ground, although that would have been the last think he would have wished. The walk that gave Geoff the greatest retrospective pleasure was when he and Bob Pettigrew were the only non-stop finishers of an epic trip from Penmaenmawr to Bryn-y-Wern, our old club hut in the Pennant valley. This walk included Drum, Yr Arran and Moel Hebog as well as the 14 Threethousanders. Their time was around 19 hours and I remember Geoff saying that this was the only time he had been really tired. It has been voiced by many experienced Club members that Geoff seldom seemed extended on rock, indeed he was proud of the fact that he had never peeled, either when leading or on a rope.

There is no doubt that in his rock and Alpine climbing his family responsibilities had an inhibitory affect upon his performance. It was only in recent years that Geoff began to realise his potential on rock and was well known for climbing in boots quite hard routes in inclement weather.

Due to his overall competence and ability to make the correct decision, Geoff often became, by general consent, a leader of small groups in the hills. It was fitting that he chose to communicate his knowledge to a multitude of beginners both on Oread meets and through the medium of his Ilkeston College night school classes. That these classes were effective can be vouched for by a number of the younger Oreads. It can scarcely be doubted that Geoff introduced more people into the Club than any other member and willingly spent very many days in the mountains, helping beginners when he could have been doing harder and perhaps to him, more interesting things.

From soon after his election as an Oread member in 1956, Geoff showed his willingness to perform any official duties asked of him and served on the Committee for many years, as well as in the offices of Meets Secretary and Indoor Meets Secretary. He is best remembered in this context however, for the ten years he spent as Newsletter Editor. I am sure that those who have performed this office will appreciate the enthusiasm necessary for so many years of hard labour. There is no doubt in the minds of many members that Geoff would eventually have become President of the Oread Mountaineering Club, perhaps in the near future.

Mike Berry

IN MEMORIAM

Stricken with grief,
Tears run down the gully of my cheeks
Shattering my world of calm.
Why?
Snatched from the joy of living,
A life so glorious as the mountain air
Of a September day.
Why?
The chance to live, seized by the crags
He loved so dear.
Why?
He gave so much to many,
Expected nothing in return,
But only the freedom of the hills.
Why?
We shall never know.
Farewell loved Mountaineer,
Your memory will linger on.

John Crosse
13th September 1971

It has not been editorial policy to include a compendium of obituaries but I have felt compelled to include (inter alia) Geoff Hayes since he was a very special Oread. His abiding modesty provides a suitable counter point to other inclusions that seem to suggest that personal status can only be enhanced by unrelenting attention to so-called Club Status — *Editor.*

OUTDOOR MEETS, U.K., 1970-1973
21ST ANNIVERSARY, PRESIDENT'S MEET 1970 – RHYD-DDU *(EXTRACT)*

King Grot, alias Geoff Hayes, led a large party up Lockwoods Chimney. Wendy Allen came back with bruised knees and elbows and was reported to have stood on Tom's head which may have prompted his remark "you have to be married to get anywhere in this club". Geoff, being the traditionalist, finished up Geoffrey Winthrop Young's climb on Teyryn Bluffs. (The last man was still in Lockwoods!) The veterans were jolted into action by the younger extremists for a winter ascent of Lliwedd. Once in the mist, they were soon lost, taking Don Cowen with them, leaving the plodders, led by 'Eigerwand' Colledge, to search for Horned crag. The sight of the route turned Ray 'whiter than white' and he immediately hid behind a snowflake whilst R.H. and I climbed the easy gully to the ridge. Needless to say, we were soon followed by Colledge who promptly accused us of cowardice, to which we agreed. Lliwedd was traversed and the stragglers picked up on the col (is this Tryfan they asked?) and brought to safety over Snowdon to the hut.

Teams did go out on Sunday and were rewarded by a glorious late afternoon. Chris, Don, and Ray C. climbed Angels' Pavement without getting shot; whilst Martin Harris took Pete to snatch his first ascent of Tryfan taking in Grooved Arête en route.

There was activity elsewhere; the Grey Man was on the Carnedds with a team; a member of the Lightcliffe Harriers was there, a Kiwi passed by; it all added up to a good weekend.

Derrick Burgess

CHRISTMAS, TAN-Y-WYDDFA 1970 *(EXTRACT)*

No doubt, John Fisher was looking forward to a juicy steak after a hard day in the hills, but his luck was out. The steaks and the sausage, which he had so carefully hidden under a slate in the garden, (why, we shall never know, because the kitchen was like a refrigerator), had been found by an equally hungry dog and instantly devoured.

CHRISTMAS, KESWICK 1970 *(EXTRACT)*

Christmas dinner at the Watendlath cottage, the largest of the frugal dwellings, was it's usual riotous occasion. The climax was a hand written Appleby song, toasting the ladies, which seemed to be stealing the limelight from a noisy 'Gaylord Handley', whose face took on a most peculiar expression. He shuffled away from the table like a China man in tight shoes. Later a search party found him gazing hopelessly at the shattered remains of his distinctive underpants. It appears that in trying to trump Appleby's ace song, he overstrained with disastrous results.

Nat Allen

LANGDALE, 1971 *(EXTRACT)*

Rusty, out to prove that one can survive without the five star luxury of Arctic Guineas and Mountain Tents, was ensconced in the remnants of a kiddies (15/- plus 2 Kellogg's tops) play tent, with the added luxury of two lilos (one to keep the place afloat).

THE PEAK HORSESHOE, JUNE 1971 – *(EXTRACT)*

Eric Byne in "High Peak" wrote at some length about the epic Peak Horseshoe walk, first done by Sumner and Lambe of the Mountain Club of Stafford in 37 hours in 1953. Long before this book was published, the Oread had attempted the same marathon walk. The first attempt started fromthe barn at The Roaches early on Saturday morning in '59 (I think). It ended for some at Buxton in the foulest of weather, with Gordon Gadsby being transported from Whitehall seated in a wheelbarrow. Ashcroft, Frost and myself did get as far as Edale, but a night at Poltergeist Barn in pouring rain put paid to us and we got the train to Grindleford before limping to Rowsley.

After a twelve year lapse I decided in a weak moment to lead the meet once again. A few weeks before the date, I was regretting the decision, but lived with the belief that no other Oread could be interested in doing such a slog. It was therefore with much surprise that on Friday evening, 19th March this year, that I saw assembled at Trevor Bridge's home in Derby the following young and not quite so young Oreads and friends: Dave Williams, Paul Gardiner, Clive Russell, Chris Radcliffe, Trevor Bridges, Neill, Doris and Dog!

Geoff Hayes

The following is a brief extract:

Left Upper Hulme 21.30 for barn near Three Shires Head. The barn reached at midnight after Williams encountered "The Black Horsemen"

Late start on the following day via Cat and Fiddle, A6 close to White Hall, Combs Moss and descent to Dove Holes (Hot drinks from support party: Jean Russell and Shelagh Bridges). Doris and dog retired to the relief of Williams. Route continued to Sparrowpits, Brown Knoll, Kinder Low. The party became separated in cloud and rain before crossing Snake summit (Support party waiting). Hayes, Radcliffe and Bridges pressed on for Lower Small Clough. "Remnants" sought refuge at Barnsley Wood Cottage and/or Heathy Lea.

Lower Small Clough reached at 22.00. Don Cowen in residence. Next morning the main party continued south over Bull Stones, Margery Hill, Derwent Edges to Ladybower road, where Rusty suddenly appeared with support party. Heathy Lea was reached at 18.45, a total of 25 hours walking. What happened to Williams and his "remnants" is not known. Hayes makes no further reference to them in his extended account — *Editor.*

OGWEN, FEBRUARY 1972 *(EXTRACT)*

Sunday dawned fine and clear, but mist rolling up the valley drove everyone to a relatively early start. The ascent of Tryfan brought everyone above the cloud into warm sunshine and spectacular views. Various routes brought the party to the summit. Chris Radcliffe, Pete Scott, Pete Holden, Trevor Bridges, Derrick Burgess and Don Cowen ascended Grooved Arete – but not without incident. Pete Scott dislodged a "grand piano" on the lower reaches of the climb and petrified people standing on the eastern terrace. Chris Radcliffe was later heard to remark "I was more frightened than on the Eiger".

Radcliffe in an attempt on the world record Gribben Ridge descent, was believed, over a section of about forty feet, to be accelerating at something like thirty -two feet per second, even collecting a bruised shin and a broken rucksack strap on the way.

Dave Guyler

THE INFAMOUS CRATCLIFFE MEET, DECEMBER 1972

*(Meet Leader Designate:******** Derrick Burgess)*

This meet must surely stand out, for the leader at any rate, as the biggest "NON-event" of the year, for, having described in glowing terms his intentions in the Oread Circular, to wit: "There is camping at the farm". — Mr. Burgess turned up at Black Rocks on the Saturday afternoon without venturing into the meet area at all.

His attendance at Black Rocks not withstanding, those regular acquaintances of the Meet Leader should have been forewarned, for is it not a fact that Mr. Burgess has already reached maximum points in the 'One-Day-Only-At-The-Weekend' stakes for 1971, and could possibly be forgiven for forgetting that in this era of easy, comfortable, pluto and auto-cratic living, there still exist those people who have to rely on "Shanks' Pony" or the "Thumb" to achieve their destination.

It must also have been refreshing for the prattlers of outdoor keenness and enthusiasm to find that in this day and age a prospective Oread could travel from Chesterfield to Cratcliffe by these methods – passing comfortable Heathy Lea on a Saturday forenoon, and arriving after lunch at the designated spot. Unhappily, he was the ONLY ONE THERE ....!!! What thoughts did he have then, Dear Member, as he retraced his weary steps under the racing cloud and the darkening evening sky to reach at last the succour of the Derbyshire Hut and a 'Chamberspot' of tea?? What dark thoughts suffused his brain as he bathed his reddened feet in the plastic bowl, or turned uneasily upon the Kayfoam bed? We may never know, but suffice it to say that, while his victim of the first debacle was nursing his wrath and aching feet, the perpetrator was setting in motion the chain of events that was to lead to further scenes of human endeavour. Read on....

At the party (I did mention there was a party in Derby that Saturday night, didn't I?), the Meet Leader (CRATCLIFFE), after his afternoon on the rocks (BLACK), was feeling expansive (BEER). With several pints under his belt and a crooked smile on his lips, the fateful words flowed smoothly: "If you all come out in Dennis and Ken's cars tomorrow, I can bring you back and they can go straight home to Manchester. (Denis Davies and Ken Beetham were two friends from the Karabiner Club who were to climb with the team on Sunday). The die was cast and the happy, inebriate Players left, their cups o'erflowing and their pint pots empty, to the various homes that awaited them, secure in the knowledge of the 'morrow's plan.

Fate, however, in the guise of a four hour cloudburst delayed an early start next morning into the beginning of the afternoon. One member, one Hon. member, and their guests duly arrived at Cratcliffe and, for three hours, amused themselves on the crag and the various boulder problems that abound. They saw no-one, but several cars parked on the top road in the distance testified that a number of people were about. "Probably all gone for a walk into Bradford Dale, seeing that it was raining this morning", they decided. The Manchester team left and the remaining Derbeans walked over the fields to find the Meet Leader's car in the gathering gloom. IT WASN'T THERE – IT NEVER HAD BEEN!

"He'll be waiting down on the bottom road", said the All-Time-Believer devoutly, so back they rushed. An hour later as the second rainstorm lashed into his winter woollies, the All-Time-Believer shuffled his feet, his facts, his opinions, and became blasphemous. "God rot him, we'll walk", was the decision and the trio set out in an increasingly damp wind for Wirksworth. Space does not permit a full description of their suffering or language during this time, but it is sufficient to say the journey was not without incident.

The five-to-seven was, happily, a bit late starting out and, as the trio grasped the handrail and swung aboard, the memories of bygone aeons flooded back: the upper deck full of climbers, the back seats piled high with Ex-WD rucksacks, the front ones being used for brewing, the inevitable clashes with conductors and letters to the press. They mounted the stairs eagerly, the ghosts of yester-year panting at their heels. A red-faced man in a pacamac gazed at them stonily from the back seat. A callow youth with spots placed his arm protectively round an overweight girl and the rest of the seats were moodily empty. So much for memories. The trio moved to the front and gazed bleakly through the steamy windows. The conductress punched the tickets and took Hank's name and address because he was two bob short and, finally, the One-with-'Flu reverse-called wife, who collected them from the Derby bus station and tried not to smile.

Those attending the Meet, in order of suffering were:- Billy Beveridge, Derek Carnell, Nat Allen, Hank Harrison, Denis Davies and Ken Beetham. Burgess stopped home and made himself ill at yet another party on Sunday afternoon.

Anon

I consider the above to be a minor classic of Oread reportage, The author has remained anonymous but a distinct whiff of gunpowder in the style of Nat Allen – Derek Carnell is self-evident. — *Editor.*

LANGDALE, MARCH 1973 *(EXTRACT)*

The morning dawned with Handley opening his eyes and muttering "Who's ringing that bloody till?" – he'd pitched next door to the shop. On looking outside, the bag was down and the rain was falling; and so it was for the weekend, – rain and quite cool.

Sunday was the same if not worse. Fisher came out of his tent at 10.30 a.m., grinned and uttered, "Il faut que nous avons l'amour." Gritting his teeth he went back in for his breakfast.

Penlington ate Ashcroft's breakfast; Carnell went back to Derby to play golf; Handley threw a brick in the shop and quietened the till; various parties went for short wet walks; Fred wasn't to be seen, although a report came through that his van was seen leaving at 7.30 a.m. with Fred driving, still in his pyjamas.

Why on earth we don't go to Eskdale I do not know. Perhaps now Burgess is off Committee, we might stand a chance.

David Appleby

MARSDEN-HEATHY LEA (BASLOW), JUNE 1973 *(EXTRACT)*

Those doing the complete walk were Nat Allen, Pete Janes, Paul Bingham, Roy Sawyer, Dave Weston, Clive Russell, Ron Chambers, Les Peel and Tom Rogers. Those "on and off" the route, part timers, etc. were Jack Ashcroft, Dave Appleby, and Derek Carnell. Phil Falkner, the old man of the party, came out for the Friday night and Saturday. He was last seen heading over Kinder by himself, in a wet and bedraggled state, for Edale. It's his 50th birthday this year.

This year's meet was the 21st anniversary of this favourite Oread bog trot. The first was on October 24th-25th, 1952. The party then consisted of Phil Falkner, Geoff Gibson, Mike Moore, Harry Pretty, and Dave Penlington. The party slept the night at Marsden gas works, and in the back parlour of the Nags Head (Fred Heardman). Edale had been the original objective, but they continued down the Edges to Baslow.

Jack Ashcroft

Week-end prior to this meet Ashcroft, Penlington, Winfield and Darnell completed the Pennine Way (North to South) in seven days — *Editor.*

DOVEDALE, JUNE 1973 (EXTRACT)

The sun still shone brightly as we forced our way through the jostling crowds on the George's field. I tripped over one of Reg Squires' boots, barely hidden by the long grass, and subsided heavily into the Oakden's nest of billies. My heavy rucksack held me floorbound and I was uncaringly trampled by the quartet returning from Beresford Dale. A plethora of wives, occupying sundry camp beds, lilos, spats, and chairs were spread over the field like "pearls byfore the swyne", and Chambers was trying to fit himself into a Whillans' jockstrap that was obviously too small. The Oread had arrived, and from my prone position by a teacup, I surveyed it all with pride. Bare-footed children and dogs played frantically round the tents: reddening anatomies rotated sunwards, and tea bubbled on the stoves. The President arrived back from Cummerbund with our K.C. friends, Shelagh Manning and Denis Davies and much wine was spilt replenishing old friendships. As the sun set and the sky darkened an aura of respectability crept over the scene as numerous people dressed for dinner at the George and surrounding hotels. It was about this time that 'Nitelite' Burgess arrived and set off for his one route of the day (Venery), and London-based Charlie Cullum was savagely scouring the country round the Isaac Walton for traces of the club meet.

Derek Carnell

BLENCATHRA, WINTER 1973 (EXTRACT)

The level of activity was about normal for a club in the last stages of decadence. Various groups on Saturday approached Blencathra by different routes, many continuing to Skiddaw House and beyond. Reg Squires, Simon Crosse, Sabina and myself opted for a short but interesting day by descending Sharp Edge. Lounging in a sheltered spot besides Scales Tarn, we discussed most of the world's problems and solved none(an irresistible crib from Whillans' ghost writer, whoever he may be). Saturday evening's boozing was most competently carried out and afterwards the bladders of Messrs. Williams, Janes, Burgess and Co. pointed out the error of their ways when I locked them in the bicycle shed where they were domiciled for non-payment of fees and general insubordination.

In conclusion I must agree that the Oread is dying. Panther said it in the Newsletter in August 1955, Radcliffe said it again in 1972, but with a turnout of 49 adults on a winter meet, 160 miles from home, we at least have the consolation of an uncommonly healthy corpse.

Clive Russell

This report on a winter meet did not appear until July 1973 — *Editor.*

LIMESTONE, ETHICS, AND STOPPERS
DABBLING IN DOVEDALE
(NEW GUIDE TO LIMESTONE) (EXTRACT)

Newsletter, July 1971

Already our first line of defence is breached. We have surrendered such fortifications as Campanile Pinnacle, the Col du Turd, Silicon, John Peel, and Simeon. The pristine whiteness of these areas reverberates with shouts and the clink of alien gear. Foreign hands clutch at unworn holds, Moacs bite at sharp-edged cracks, rucsacks cluster together for safety, and equipment lies in bright-hued heaps. We are forced higher and higher into uncharted country in our search for seclusion.

With aching hearts we turn to the areas that are left us – green, mossy walls, slimy cracks, and shattered rock. Were all those other routes once like THIS before we came? We scrabble on, seeking to excavate a niche for ourselves; mindlessly, but with an awareness of the others far below, we hack and hew and dig and pray, seeking our own individuality; seeking to carve from the jungle a route worthy to be done by the future generations of 'Guidos' – seeking to finish before we are overwhelmed by time and the inexorable pressure from below.

Hanging from a rose bush by one hand, and with a grass sod in the other, spitting out soil dislodged from above and twisting sideways to avoid the limestone block that is about to fall on your knee, you shake your head sadly, and promptly fill your eyes with dirt from your hair. Centipedes scurry across the back of your hand, and a snail drops from nowhere down your neck. "Could do with a helmet if only to keep off the soil, "you think, and then your spirits soar as the rock (which missed your knee) lands with a crash on to the spare coils of your rope far below, breaks into several lethal chunks, and smashes on to your second's shin-bone! Good job you'd got him tied to that tree – he might have been able to get out of the way otherwise!

Derek Carnell

EDITORIAL (EXTRACT)

Newsletter, July 1971

At Stoney Middleton, which has seen more activity than any other limestone crag, most of the routes have become quite safe and old peg routes are now led free, some at quite a reasonable standard. Even so, another problem is the polishing of holds on the most popular routes – Windhover comes to mind as an example. On the other hand certain routes on other crags are becoming positively dangerous with increasing use. The detached flake on the first pitch of Debauchery on High Tor, and a similar feature on the first pitch of Campanile in Dovedale, are both getting very loose. It seems extremely likely that sooner or later there will be a serious accident.

What can be done about this? On the continent, where climbers are far more organised than in this country, many of the pegs on outcrops such as the Ardennes in Belgium or the Vercours in France, are real "stoppers" that have been cemented in place. These would be considered very major crags indeed if situated in this country and the operation of cementing in pegs must be quite an undertaking. Surely it would be quite justifiable for a similar practice to operate on routes such as Debauchery? Perhaps it cuts across the grain of normal British thinking, but with the increasing popularity of such routes a change in attitude in this respect could be timely.

Chris Radcliffe

EDITORIAL (EXTRACT)

Newsletter, July 1972

There is (inter alia) another incident in which the Vice-President (who is also a co-author of the guide to Chatsworth Edge) discovered a youth placing a peg by the crux on High Step at Chatsworth. An argument ensued in which Mr. Burgess maintained that a 20' route, albeit a highly technical one, which was originally led without protection (none was available) should not be debased in this way. If the climber was not sufficiently confident to make the move, he should retreat. This argument had no effect on the youth who maintained that as he knew several people who had injured themselves on this route, some form of protection was justifiable. He was clearly the sort of person who was prepared to fall off Cloggy (which is steep enough to keep the rock well out of the way of falling climbers) quite indiscriminately. The gap between their two viewpoints was wide and remained unbridged, but perhaps the final comment lies in the fact that the peg so placed (and left behind) was removed easily by hand! Perhaps to-day's climbing clubs have a role in bridging this kind of gap and providing some kind of sense about ethics.

The Mountain Schools, Outdoor Pursuits Centres and other 'authorities' who provide 'instant adventure' have a heavy responsibility to bear for introducing people to the hills without weighing in the balance the consequences of doing so. The position is well expressed by Gwen Moffat writing in the Sunday Telegraph recently about the Cambrian Way, the proposed way-marked path between Cardiff and Conway, now under consideration by the Countryside Commission;-

> "we inveigh against hydro-electric schemes, mining, widened roads, conifers (all in the national parks), but the people who love the hills, yet travel only on designated paths, are themselves wearing them away. Already parts of the Pennine Way have had to be closed to prevent further erosion by feet – and now there is talk of a Cambrian Way: signposted, way-marked, official...."

Chris Radcliffe

TRICOUNI STRIKES AGAIN
British Varasham Expedition 1970

It was during a short walk in the lower British Hills whilst the men of the OREAD were away in the high Alps, that the bizarre nature of the whole adventure set-up became so evident. The wild, excited eyes and open mouths of a devoted climber faced with new and exciting peaks, gives credence to the maxim that:

> "The only difference between a goldfish and a climber is that one mucks about in fountains....."

Not that climbers are alone in their peculiarities. Speliologists are undoubtedly worse. Mind you, I wouldn't say that all potholers are perverts, but they do put those rubber things on and stuff themselves down little holes in the ground!

Surely though, it is the expedition more than any other activity of "civilised" man, that destroys the barriers of reason, establishes pseudo-religious fervours, and inevitably makes a Patrick Moore out of the most reticent participant. Throughout modern, and not so modern history, the human animal has rallied with relish to the "call to arms", where service in far distant lands is promised. Perhaps this instinctive need of organised man for battle – for life as a hunter in a hostile environment, encourages the unmistakable flavour of the Colonial Force in expeditions of all sizes and all degrees of formality......

> Pettigrew as Caesar of Rome.......
> Radcliffe as Gordon of Khartoum.........
> Squires as Horrible Hannibal the Heliphantine Hun........

So it was with the most recent of British expeditions. As members will know, Mr. Janes and Mr. Pretty have just returned from a long absence from the British climbing scene, purportedly from a mid-European state of dubious political motivation. In fact, this news letter is able to reveal the true unexpurgated facts concerning their leadership of a small, but highly organised expedition to the little known mountains of the Varasham in Central Asia. Brilliantly formulated, but unfortunately unsuccessful, its concept, organisation, and untimely demise are well summarised in the first hand account of our Asiatic correspondent, which is reproduced below........

One day, Handley was sitting in his bath, contemplating his lot and the achievements of the Oread. All of a sudden he jumped up and called to Janes (who was holding his runners at the time) "I've just had a thought", he said.

"Oh yeah?" cooed Janes cautiously.

"Yeah; well you know how we feel about expeditions and things and how pleased we are now that we've conquered the whole world and everything?"

"Here's your runners, Ray".

"Well, what I mean is, we haven't; I mean we've forgotten Varasham – Pretty isn't going to like this you know!"

Word spread, and a couple of days later Pretty was at a first division drinking match between Oread and Rock and Ice United, when a lad called Hodge, who had heard the news, felt that the time was right to break it to Pretty (OREAD were 3 pints up at half time and an orgy was scheduled for after the match).

"Er, H old pal, er, you know this expedition business and all that, and how we've done the world over?"

"Yeah", said Pretty, picking up another peanut.

"Well, we haven't actually, we've forgotten somewhere!"

"Where, for Chucks sake?", cried Pretty, sitting up and spitting nuts at Colledge over the bar.

"Varasham", said Hodge, looking uncomfortable.

Far from being angry, Pretty was delighted, so that was that. Pretty was soon on his way to Varasham at the head of his good old army. Europe was nice, and although they had a bit of trouble with the Deutsche Bundespost over food parcels, the trip went fairly smoothly. When they reached Varasham, not unexpectedly they had a few stiff passes to climb, and not unexpectedly one or two natives to coerce, but within a very short time the area was fully Anglicised and Pretty was marching up and down the country looking for hills to climb.

Anyway, to cut a long story short; one day our lad was marching along at the head of his army on his way to visit a "daughter" of his in Vodrograd, when he happened to glance up at a hill he'd been thinking of bashing up for some time, and there, standing on top, as large as life – blow me down if there wasn't a Mercury Man, complete with bicycle clips and Ramblers Club card. The Mercury Man coughed, and shifted from one foot to another. Now a bit further down the line, it suddenly occurred to Under-Bergsteiger Thomas Green that they hadn't actually climbed that hill, and that the Mercury Man was obviously determined to defend it at all cost. He passed this information on to Ober-Bergsteiger Burns, who was picking his nails with his ice axe at the time. Burns passed it on to Janes, and Janes told Pretty, who was very angry at the cheek of the chap, and yelled "Oi, what do you want on our 'ill?"

The Mercury Man cleared his throat and yelled back "One OREAD, one MERCURY and a wet slab!"

Now Pretty allowed himself a chuckle, and called up one of his best wet rock men to knock-off up the hill and "sort that bloody cyclist out!"

Scottie smiled to himself as he sauntered up the hill and over the brow. Pretty lit his pipe and confidently awaited the return of our hero. To his surprise, however, it was Scottie's tissue in bits and pieces that came back, rolling down the hill and coming to rest at his feet. When Pretty looked up, there was the Mercury Man, as fresh as a daisy.

One MERCURY, Ten OREADS, Pegs at ten paces", he shouted down.

Well, Pretty was astounded. "You cheeky billiard player", he shouted back, and immediately despatched ten of his best peggers up the hill. The fight lasted about fifteen minutes. All that Pretty could do was listen to the furious sounds of battle from above. To his utter amazement one by one, the burps and clogs of his lads came rolling down the hill followed by their battered helmets. After a while the noise ceased and the Mercury Man reappeared over the brow of the hill, his peg hammer bent and his helmet all dented. He was definitely still in one piece as he called down to the speechless Pretty –

"One MERCURY, a hundred OREADS, Ice Axes and Ice daggers at arms length."

Well, night was drawing on, so the OREAD made camp. Pretty had long since forgotten all about his "daughter" up the valley.

"I'll be a laughing stock", he thought. "I'll never be able to look the committee in the face again!" He went right off his food, even refusing a plateful from Wendy A. who was serving the blokes that night, though she was supposed to be in Switzerland.

Come first light, there was the Mercury Man standing patiently, axe in hand, waiting for the hundred OREADS. When Pretty ordered Janes' mob up the hill, he got very little response. Most of them pretended to talk amongst themselves or look in the other direction and fiddle with their crampons. At last after a bit of backside kicking by Pretty, they all shuffled up the hill, each one doing his best to keep at the back of the line. The battle that eventually took place was horrible to hear. The carnage lasted all morning, while Pretty stood at the bottom of the hill with his hand over his ears. One by one, axes, daggers and such-like came rolling down the hill, followed by battered OREADS.

A sobbing Pretty counted them; "Ninety seven – Oh no! 98, I can't believe it, 99, it's all over."....... But wait, – a ray of hope?" Pretty looked anxiously up the hill. Only ninety-nine. Dare he hope – could it be? At that moment, a bleeding Janes appeared at the top of the hill, staggered a little, and groggily made his way down to Pretty clutching the shaft of an axe, that all too evidently to our 'Arry went straight through him.

"Harry, Harry," he groaned, pulling up his Y-fronts with his free hand.

"What is it man, what is it?" screamed Pretty (who was pretty much in a state by now), as the unfortunate man sank to his knees before his beloved leader.

"Harry,- Harry mate-, It's a trap, there's two of the bastards!"

The Mercury R.C. or "the Murk": The Derby cycling club of distinguished lineage (60 years old in 1996) which, together with the Nomads and Valkyrie M.C. gave many Oreads their first taste of adventure in the Great Outdoors. This rich mix of cyclists (national and Olympic record holders), senior walkers, bog trotters, mountaineers, and rock climbing tigers established Derby as a centre of excellence for many years. The Derby Ski Club, and events such as the Dovedale Dash, all started from this alliance of youthful enthusiasm and, although some have sadly departed (Eric Thompson, Nat Allen), others such as Janes, Burgess, Handley, Welbourn, Weston, Hank-Harrison, Oakden, Godlington, etc. are still with us — *Editor.*

ALPINE AFFAIRS 1970-1980
CHAMONIX ROUTES 1970

Mont Blanc – via Gouter Hut	J. Ashcroft J. Dench D. Reeves	L. Burns R. Sawyers D. Williams
Mont Blanc – Old Brenva	Peter Scott Ray Colledge	Chris Radcliffe Dennis Davies
Aig. du Midi – Frendo Spur	Peter Scott	Chris Radcliffe

210

Aig du Chardonnet – Forbes Arête	Trevor Bridges	Mervyn Sarsons
	Howard Johnson	Geoff Hayes
	Ron Chambers	Andy Oakden
	Peter Scott	Chris Radcliffe
	Don Cowen	
Traverse of Les Dorées	Trevor Bridges	Mervyn Sarsons
Aiguille de L'M – NNE ridge	Trevor Bridges	(+friend's wife)
Les Courtes – traverse	Geoff Hayes	Howard Johnson
Tour Noir – W-ridge	Ron Chambers	Andy Oakden
Aig. de Tour	Don Cowen	Dick Saw
	Paul Bingham	Digger Williams
	Lol Burns	Jack Ashcroft

DAUPHINÉ 1970 (EXTRACT)

An 'odds and sods' team, comprising Oread, Rock & Ice and Summit members, spent a pleasant holiday in the Dauphiné this summer. We camped near Briancon, a historic walled city of Vauber fame, at a delightful 4 star camp site. From our base we had relatively easy access to the Ailefroide and La Grave areas, with delightful open air swimming pools, numerous bars and clubs popular with Tinsel's jet set.

Routes climbed:

S. Face Pavé	D. Burgess	T. Lewis
	S. Smith	Nat Allen
Trav. Salaoize	S. Smith	Nat Allen
	T. Lewis	D.Burgess
	R. Handley	
Agneux	D. Burgess	R. Handley
	S. Smith	Nat Allen
	P. Brown	'Tabs' Talbot
Pelvoux	D. Carnell	L. Peel
Ailefroide	M. Talbot	P. Brown

Compiled by D. Burgess.

MONT BLANC TRADITIONAL 1970 (EXTRACT)

DIGGER WILLIAMS

To commemorate the virgin ascent made in those stalwart days of 1786 by Jacques Balmat, it was considered fitting that the Oread, albeit some of the venerable members together with some young blood, should try to capture a little of that past glory by repeating the venture.

The ring leader for an abortive start was Ashcroft ably supported by that old codger Burns. We set off for the Tête Rousse Hut 3hrs. guide book time away. The weather was holding despite some thundery cloud and it was good to be alive.

After the usual wrangles about where the route went (sic.) – my instinct pointed the way and we set off at a cracking pace of 1 mph. The snow was softish but we arrived at the hut around 2 pm. and promptly ordered soup for the six of us. This simple culinary request sparked off a little dispute between Burns and myself , the gist centring on quality not quantity and the rights of the individual to have the soup the way he wants it. The altitude was beginning to tell.

The route to the Gouter Hut lay across a snow basin which crosses a small couloir which is prone to stonefall, especially at this time of day. We met no real difficulty but from all accounts a sharp look out is necessary; we learned later that a fatality had occurred that same day.

We arrived around 4.30. pm, in various degrees of "knackeredness".

Ashcroft was interested in a female of about fifty, well preserved, but accompanied by a tough looking character. The rest of us were admiring the two young au pair girls, particularly attractive in their knee-length tight breeches. We experienced no more trouble with Burns.

The dreaded hour soon arrived and by two-thirty a.m. the place was like the black hole of Calcutta. The whole hut was seething with bodies all intent on filling any blank floor space and it was every man for himself. From this chaos we emerged like Neolithic throwbacks and set off in exemplary fashion, some with crampons, and some without.

The route was straight forward with no crevasses and we soon topped the Dome du Gouter.

Ashcroft now took the lead as I was slowing down, almost into reverse. Roy Sawyer was surprisingly fit, almost running for the top.

A very fine ridge led up to the summit providing a magnificent situation along the narrow crest for the last 30' or so. By 7.00 a.m., six of us had made it and, although only by the facile ordinary route, felt a great inner satisfaction and joy at being there.

GROSSHORN NORTH FACE 1970 (EXTRACT)

RAY COLLEDGE

Next day being August 1st and Swiss National Day, we were reluctant to leave the valley. However, the weather, though very doubtful all day, was not bad enough for an excuse and so off we went to the Schmardri hut.

The hut is one of the best I have seen, and far from the madding crowd. Here at least, I thought, no other OREAD member had penetrated: until we saw the hut book.

D. Carnell, N. Allen and others had slept here, and done the West Ridge of the Breithorn in 1968.

By 2 a.m. when we left the hut, the sky was clear and with head torches made good progress to the foot of the Grosshorn North Face.

The initial slope took us to the first bergschrund which presented the usual difficulty but was crossed at first light. A steep slope of thin soft snow, then ice, went up to the second, somewhat easier bergschrund. The slope above steepened appreciably and consisted of bare hard ice, except for a ribbon of thin soft snow on the ice to take us most of the way to the overhanging rock nose in the centre of the face.

Cramponing together up the thin layer of snow, we ran on to hard bare ice towards the rock overhang. At this point we had a choice. Either the original Welzenbach route to the right of the nose, or the Feuz/Von Allmen direct route to the left, through a belt of icy rocks, with a pitch of V. We chose the Direct route.

From now on it was to be hard bare ice, very difficult to crampon. But the Direct route was preferable if only because it was shorter. In the event we at once found a way through the rocks by an icy gully and perhaps a rock pitch of III, although the gully required step cutting and took time.

Having broken through the rock band we were now on the great ice slope beneath the summit tower and we began to think that we might have cracked it. Another ribbon of snow took us up about a hundred feet, then a length or two of crampon work before the ice became very hard.

The great slope was endless. Behind us the usual dense black clouds obscured the Lauterbrunnen but always the Grosshorn was clear.

At last we arrived at the side of the summit rocks, only to find another three rope lengths of steep hard ice up the side, easing off into snow.

We climbed the snow with head torches to arrive at the summit at 10.40 p.m. The summit was so pointed, and covered with soft snow, that care was needed in the darkness. Once balanced on the point, one carefully turned round, then moved backwards with equal care until able to step down on to the South Ridge ten feet lower. A hundred and thirty feet or so down the South Ridge we found a small rock platform and here we made a comfortable bivouac for the night.

NEWSLETTER EDITOR'S NOTE: Grosshorn North Face – 21 hours in difficult ice conditions – probably a first British ascent – (if Talbot has done it with Martin Epp, that would be an Anglo/Swiss ascent).

Colledge also climbed the west ridge of the Nesthorn in 7 hours.

IMPRESSIONS OF A NORTH WALL NOVICE
PIZ BADILE (EXTRACT)

PETE SCOTT

"Yes, we've been up, but it's pretty bad on the Badile." ......hearts sink; so it's out of condition; disappointment floods in but quickly changed to apprehension when.....

"We tried it yesterday, but there's a body up there; we came across it and couldn't face the thought of going on; retreated from the snow patch; there was a big rescue a week ago, steel cables and everything ..."

At the Sciora Hut a day later the Piz Badile raises it's huge shield of granite slabs 3,000', gleaming dully in the morning sun, soon to be cast into shadow for the rest of the day; the snow patch is just discernible; we are very impressed. The day is spent lazing in the sun at the hut, our gaze forever being drawn to the slabs of the Badile. Suddenly our minds are made up; a hurried meal – don't feel like eating it though – force it down. Food, water, bivy equipment, pegs, krabs, two ropes, torches: all are thrown into one sac; going to be heavy, should have brought two really, still – can't be helped. The others wish us good luck and we stumble off across the moraine in silence, each with his own thoughts .....

.....across the moraine and up the glacier. The foot of the wall is sheer where we walk under it; could get three Malham Coves in that little lot; not a fracture or natural line anywhere. We move gingerly along the glacier at the foot of the face and come to the yawning bergschrund: Corti's mate fell down this, better be careful. We don crash helmets and rope up for the crossing of the bergschrund: Exclamation from John .....

"There's blood on the snow here, and a fragment of bone too." Bits of tattered equipment lie scattered around the snow. Hell! This place is 'the absolute berries', better not turn out like this for us. We kick up the last few feet of hard snow and step across the gap onto rock; that's better. We wander up the first easy pitches looking for the bivouac spot, instead we find a torn rucksack and a boot, raisins lie scattered on the rock; more jitters; too late to turn back now before it gets dark; where's this

213

bivouac spot? A shout from John and I traverse across to find him standing down behind a large flake; perfect spot for two; looks safe enough from stones, can't fall out either. We don duvets and crawl into sacs as the sun sinks in a blaze of colour behind the granite needles of the Bregaglia. Silence .... the body gradually relaxes ..... suddenly we hear them coming; a high pitched whirring heralds the arrival of some big stones; nerves scream and remain taut long after they have gone past, many feet out from the rock; only a trickle of dust and gravel remains. We try to settle down and gradually drift off into a fitful sleep only to be awakened again by a hideous crashing and rumbling ......silence again .....I look at my watch, the luminous dial reads one o'clock; getting cold now; I wish dawn were here. Another three hours of alternate dozing and waking follows.....

.....half past four! Dawn IS here! We scramble stiffly to our feet. A cloudless sky. Well, this is it. Excitement grips the whole body; I shiver violently. Could it be nervous tension as well as the cold? Breakfast is forced down; don't feel like climbing, in fact I feel decidedly rough. Still, who does feel like climbing at this time of the morning?

John leads the first diedre. I haul myself after him with the sac; hard going. I climb clumsily across the slabs; don't feel any good yet. An overhanging groove; my lead, must force myself to lead it, although it's agony at first. But as the blood begins to flow I warm to the climbing and soon arrive at the first Cassin bivouac, feeling better now. Away we go across now sunlit slabs, pitch after pitch; slabs, grooves, diedres, threading out way up the wall. Apprehension gives way to elation, driving us every upwards; like a sunny day in Wales this; then we remember the drop below us and take a bit more care ...... but the driving force is there and we settle down to climbing the great Alpine classic.

The above account appeared in a Newsletter in 1971 but describes an ascent made in or around 1964 and is therefore chronologically misplaced — *Editor.*

TRAVERSE OF MONTE ROTONDO – CORSICA (*EXTRACT*)

GORDON GADSBY   *Newsletter, March 1971*

The silence and grandeur of Mountain Corsica is hard to describe but, like the Alps, once seen is never forgotten. We were soon crossing large snow patches, and then up the steepening slabs on the right hand side of the Restonica river. Just before the final steep rocks guarding the plateau where the lake lies, we noticed avalanche debris below us and to our left, (where the usual route would go in summer). This consisted of large and small blocks of ice and also some broken trees.... a sobering sight! The tourist pamphlet to the lake and environs warns walkers not to take the route by the slabs, but after heavy snowfalls or early in the season, it is the most enjoyable route. The lake was still in shadow and was almost completely covered over with snow to a depth of over two feet. On the left, falling ice or rocks from some steep cliffs had broken through the surface snow and a slow thaw was spreading its way across the lake. The view was very impressive. Beyond the lake a wide snow basin curved upwards, flanked by the rock towers of Punta La Porte on the left, and the sweeping snow and ice of Mt. Rotondo on the right. At the head of the coomb was the snow peak of Punta Mozzello, 2,342 metres and behind these peaks the backcloth of sky was the deepest blue I have ever seen.

The French guide books on climbing in Corsica contain accounts of summer routes only, when the peaks are free from snow and ice. Any routes therefore in winter or spring have an aura of real adventure about them. This, coupled with the lack of rescue facilities, and the fact that in two weeks mountaineering we saw not another living soul beyond the tree line, give a certain seriousness to the climbing.

We decided to climb more or less direct up the wide concave couloir and to traverse right on the steep upper section to reach the gendarmes of the South Ridge. The slope was still in shadow as we cramponed up, moving together for about a thousand feet. We then made a rising traverse to the right above some steep rock butresses. This section, although now in full sunlight, still contained many large patches of bare ice and was very exposed, and it took a good hour and a half of step cutting and belaying to reach the pinnacles. The rock here was excellent granite which provided an enjoyable route along the ridge of mod/diff standard in places and plenty of scrambling over minor summits, until the main rock point, 8,750' was reached.

OREADS IN THE ALPS – 1971

The Club Meet this year was held in the Zermatt valley from 24th July to 7th August, with about 25 members, friends and children camping at Zermatt and a further 10 camping at Tasch. The weather was generally excellent, although the late snow that had accumulated during a poor June was very much in evidence.

A list of the routes followed:

PENNINE ALPS
Mischabel Chain

SPITZE FLUH, 3,260m	Janet Ashcroft, Brian Cooke, Anne Hayes
ALPHUBEL, 4,206m	Jack Ashcroft, Pete Badcot, Gordon, Gadsby, Geoff Hayes
	Derrick Burgess, Don Cowen
TASCHHORN, 4,490m S.E. Ridge (Mischabelgrat) DOM, 4,545m Traverse by the Domgrat	Derrick Burgess, Don Cowen
NADELGRAT:- (LENSPITZE, 4,294m) NADELHORN, 4,327m STECKNADELHORN, 4,242m HOBERGHORN, 4,219m)	Pete Badcot, Geoff Hayes

Monte Rosa-Breithorn Group

DUFOURSPITZE, 4,634m	Derek Carnell, Les Peel
LYSKAMM, 4,480m (W) North West Spur	Nat Allen, Derrick Burgess, Don Cowen
BREITHORN, 4,165m S.S.W. Flank	Derek Carnell, Dave Guyler, Les Peel

Matterhorn-Dent d'Herens Group

MATTERHORN, 4,478M N.E. (Hörnli) Ridge	Tony Hutchinson, Frank Yeomans
DENT D'HERENS, 4,171m North Face (Benedetti Bivouac, 3,469m)	Ray Colledge, Dennis Davies
	Derrick Burgess, Don Cowen

Zermatt West

POINT DE ZINAL, 3,791m N.E. Ridge	Gordon and Margaret Gadsby
OBERGABELHORN, 4,063m E.N.E. Ridge (over WELLENKUPPE 3,903m)	Pete Badcot, Geoff Hayes
ZINALROTHORN, 4,221m S.E. Ridge (via Gabel Notch)	Jack Ashcroft, Pete Badcot Brian Cooke, Geoff Hayes
– Kanzelgrat Variation	Ron Chambers, Andy Oakden Pete Scott
	Doris Andrew, Chris Radcliffe, Frank Yeoman
(East Face)	Ray Colledge, Denis Davies
TRIFTHORN, 3,728m South Ridge	Ron Chambers, Andy Oakden
	Terry Lowe, Mervyn Sarsen
WEISSHORN, 4,505m S.W. Ridge (Schaligrat)	Chris Radcliffe, Pete Scott

BERNESE OBERLAND

ALETSCHHORN, 4,195m S.E. Ridge	Ray Colledge, Dennis Davies
EIGER, 3,970m Eiger North Face	Chris Radcliffe, Pete Scott

SILVRETTA ALPS

DREILÄNDERSPITZE, 3,197m	Gordon and Margaret Gadsby
SILVRETTAHORN, 3,244m South Ridge	Colin and Uschi Hobday
OCHSENKOPF, 3,057m	Colin and Uschi Hobday
SIGNALHORN, 3,210m Traverse S.W./N.E. Ridge	Colin and Uschi Hobday
PIZ BUIN, 3,312m Wiesbadener Grat	Colin and Uschi Hobday

GERMAN ALPS

ZUGSPITZE, 2,964m (Klettersteig)	Colin and Uschi Hobday

GRAIAN ALPS

GRAN PARADISO, 4,061m	Nat Allen, Don Cowen
LA TRESENTA, 3,700m	Dave Guyler, Les Peel

MONT BLANC MASSIF

GRAND FLAMBEAU, 3m559m	Nat Allen, Dave Guyler, Les Peel

ARDENNES – FREYR

Nat Allen, Derek Carnell, Ray Colledge, Dave Guyler, Andy Oakden and Les Peel, climbing in various combinations, did 3 routes here on their way back to the U.K. The buvette at the top of the climbs seem to have been the major attraction, but the climbing is good although very polished.

BREGAGLIA/BERNINA

John Fisher and Len Hatchett are known to have been shambling around the region, but are totally reticent about routes actually climbed.

I have thought to include the above listings since, contrary to contemporary Newsletter Editorials, it provides some evidence of "Club Virility" in the 1970's — *Editor.*

EIGER NORTH WALL (EXTRACT)

PETER SCOTT   *Newsletter, December 1971*

The Brittle Ledge was a heap of "tot". Crampons were removed and as we climbed the Grade V pitch it began to snow. The Traverse of the Gods was a wilderness of black scree covered ledges disappearing over a sickening drop, technically easy but, with virtually no protection, a slip was awful to contemplate. Four ropelengths and we again cramponed – up onto a good bivouac ledge at the foot of the White Spider.

"And there the spider waits"

A few rocks crashed past on their way to the valley, but Chris (Radcliffe) undeterred front pointed out onto the Spider. Soon we were both suspended from its icy back.

This is what we had come for, The White Spider, a grey icy slide surrounded on all sides by wild vertical screens of rock streaming upwards to the sky. The view downwards almost made me giddy, Chris 150' below and our two friends climbing out from the Traverse of the Gods on the edge of nothing silhouetted against the meadows of Alpiglen. We steadily made progress and after four ropelengths I entered the black and gloomy confines of the Exit Cracks. The others were still down on the ice and Chris dropped a rope to Bernard who was finding the lack of steps a little trying. An ice peg suddenly came out and Bernard with a yell of fright hurtled down the Spider only to be held in a second by Chris. He was lucky that time as he was a full rope-length above Jean-Pierre.

The ascent of the Exit Cracks was relatively uneventful, but what places of climbing history we trod. It would have been pleasant to linger at the bivouac of Rebuffat and Buhl, the epic Quartz Crack, and the Corti Bivouac, but the traditional Eiger storm was brewing. The rock was nearly free of ice and snow but nevertheless the ascent was completed in crampons. After the abseil pitch four steep rope-lengths followed up smooth black wet grooves. Pitons appeared at about hundred foot intervals but further protection was impossible. Water showered down numbing fingers and slowing progress. Just as we exited from the grooves the storm burst. Thunder echoed in the crags and snow whirled into our faces. A wave of snow and rocks from the summit slopes hissed past and rattled down the cracks up which he had just climbed. Four more rope lengths over 'tiles' and gravel and suddenly it was there – the summit ice field, now bathed in evening sunlight, the storm having passed as suddenly as it had arrived. We cramponed up the gleaming slopes and along the ridge to the summit. An icy wind was blowing as evening approached.

The dream had been translated into reality.

PULMONARY PANTING IN THE PENNINE ALPS (EXTRACT)

D. CARNELL   *Newsletter, December 1971*

The weather breaks. Parties return from the Matterhorn in a stupendous electric storm, rain like glass rods, hailstones big as marbles. We sit in the campsite – boozing – until it passes (2 days). We fail to get up the Weisshorn when half the party's' legs develop punctures. We return, and the social life takes yet another pasting. Dennis Davies, the suave and debonair member of the Karabiner Mountaineering Club, throws himself wholeheartedly into the social whirl and the net covered pool at the Theodule, his dripping moustache more eloquent than his French as the manageress makes off with his clothes. Ray Colledge, getting more dances than peaks this year, has the party in hysterics telling jokes in a high, wine-cracked voice. Pete Scott threatens to take on the whole might of the American hippies before leaving for Grindelwald, but they are finally destroyed and overwhelmed by the little men from the other side of the world – the Japs!

We sit and remember climbing ropes with minds of their own, frozen fingers, and sweating armpits, the snoring German in the next bunk in the hut, the early morning search for the elusive sock. Candles flicker, forming pools of light, their weak rays swallowed up by the dark pine interior of the hut. Tousled heads bent over bowls of steaming liquid, and the pinch of frost in your nostrils as you step outside the hut. The head torch that fails, and the ever-present stars that compensate. The toiling up the darkened slopes, the agony of placing one foot in front of the other, again, and again, and again. The sunrise striking the summits with its' attendant warmth. Watch the light spill over into the dark, still, sleeping valleys thousands of feet below, softening the outlines, and promising a glorious day. The exultation of the summit ridge, all the masochistic effort forgotten as Happiness is paramount. ....

PIC DU MIDI D'OSSAU, PYRENEES 1973 (EXTRACT)

D. CARNELL

We set off at 5.45 a.m. for the Col de Peyreget and the start of the route. We saw plenty of lizards but nary a bear. We climbed the Peyreget ridge after a false start keeping pace with a French party on the adjoining Flammes de Pierre arete. Grade II, with pitches of III, both led to the summit of the Petite Pic (9,139'), on perfect granite all the way. The temperature by now was hotting up and, after a quick drink, we descended the slabs on the east side, and abseiled into the Fourche and welcome shade.

Nat led across the Dalle Blanche and round into the chimney. Seen from the other peak, this section had looked steep and unnerving, but proved in fact to be very pleasant climbing, the holds and angle perfect. A succession of short walls, chimneys and grooves led to the summit of the Grand Pic. A large fat man in sagging vest grabbed me by the hand as I emerged from the final groove onto the summit, helped me belay, kissed four pretty girl walkers who arrived with their escorts, and burst into song. When Nat arrived on the summit there was a full scale choir going, the quality of which deteriorated as the cognac flowed.

GETTING THERE . . . "UMLEITUNG"

COON TRIKEY   *Newsletter, July 1973*

Oreads going to the Zillertal this year may, in Germany or Austria, encounter the sign "Umleitung". This is not a direction to the home of Chinese girl of easy virtue but a device to prevent motorists from entering their cities. My first experience of this Teutonic trap resulted in a whole series of misfortunes.

Entering Augsburg a large yellow sign pointed left. "Umleitung" it said. Turning into a side street, we found another sign, smaller and less obvious; "Left" into an even more "side street". Another sign; straight ahead took us into what appeared to be a cross between a Wimpey building site and a terminal moraine. No more signs. Leaving by the only exit possible to a wheeled vehicle we found ourselves on the eastbound carriageway of the Stuttgart-Munich Autobahn and had to do a total of 58 km. to return. Re-entering Augsburg; there it was again "Umleitung", turn left. Not willing to do that sodding lot again, we went straight on: an unwise decision as it was a one-way-street and we were reversing it. After staring into the accusing headlamps of a large Benz bus, we hurriedly backed out, nearly maladjusting the o/s front wing of an opulent black Mercedes.

The driver, a miserable looking b....... in rimless glasses, came to give us the benefit of his comments. However justifiable, they were not welcome. Our "love thy neighbour" spirit was a bit tattered at the edges, but our best collection of Anglo-Saxon four letter words was wasted as he understood not. Then he was reinforced by his Frau – a granite faced bitch of great superiority. She didn't address us personally, but whatever she said was relayed verbatim through Herr. From his obsequious manner he was obviously afraid of the old bat and expected us to wither in consequence. But he retired defeated to his car, where he and the Queen stared at us through the windscreen like two frustrated hens.

Then the law arrived, highly polished, both doors opening simultaneously in true official style. Now was the time to try the Falkner technique. However multilingual these characters may be it does not include Welsh – the fact that you yourself can't speak it either is immaterial, so long as you think of some good Welsh place names like Penrhyndeudraeth or Llechwedd Byniau Defaid.

They stood back a bit, decided on the evidence of our GB plate that we were English, and with great deliberation said, "DRI-VING LI-CENCE". But this, when produced, was of little help as it was a W.D. licence and with great economy bore the legend "31 BVD WST COMD – return if found to MOD". Then the old saw took a hand, and after perusing at some length a "Book of Useful Phrases" made us understand that Herr Complainant was a member of the Deutsche Automobile Touring Club and, in consequence, of some importance. This we countered with an R.A.C. membership card (expired). Then they said in Deutsch equivalent, "P-ss off while you are still free", and, discretion still being the better part of valour, we went back on the Autobahn. But this time we went to Ulm instead.

The writer is now more experienced, and mature, and does not admit to mistakes, so he prefers to remain anonymous.

Monte Disgrazia, G. Gadsby on N.W. Ridge.
Photo: K. Bryan.

Mont Blanc, 1970. D. Williams and Lawrie Burns.
Photo: J. Ashcroft.

Morterasch Glacier, Bernina and Bianco Grat – Janet Ashcroft.   *Photo: Jack Ashcroft.*

R. Sedgwick and P. Addison, bivvy at Hörnli (North Face of the Matterhorn).   *Photo: R. Sedgwick.*

C. Radcliffe, bivvy on Croz Spur. *Photo: P. Holden.*

R. Handley on P. Scerscen ice nose.   *Photo: D. Burgess.*

Peter Holden on Mt. Blanc, Grand Pilier d'Angle, East Face (Bonatti-Gobbi Route, Eckpfeier Buttress). Traverse from top of Chinmeys, 1974.
Photo: Chris Radcliffe.

Peter Holden on Central Pillar, Mt. Blanc, Frêney Face. Climbing the Chandelle, The Crux, 1973.
Photo: Chris Radcliffe.

Croz Spur, Grandes Jorasses, Peter Holden climbing.
Photo: Chris Radcliffe.

Croz Spur, Grandes Jorasses, Peter Holden climbing.
Photo: Chris Radcliffe.

Paul Addison, Frendo Spur, Aiguille de Midi, 1978. *Photo: R. Sedgwick.*

Aiguille Dru, West Face. Peter Holden climbing. American direct route – rock profiled is "Niche" on North Face, 1974. *Photo: Chris Radcliffe.*

Paul Addison above the first icefield, North Face of the Matterhorn, 1979. *Photo: R. Sedgwick.*

Petit Mont Collon, North Face. (C. Bryan and J. Hudson just visible near top of face). *Photo: G. Gadsby.*

223

Igneous Fezoff Does it Again *(Extract)*

J. Linney *Newsletter, Winter 1977*

Phew! It's warm! I'm not going very well, my sack feels heavy and I must tighten my right boot next stop – next stop? At last we move into the shade of the Trift Forest. Cooler now, we march onwards and ever upwards. All too soon we move back into the open and the oppressive heat. Houses appear ahead. "Trift hamlet" I declare. The sound of running water greets us and we stop. "No! Mustn't stop, got to keep moving!" Igneous cries. The rest of us ignore him, after all he is a prat at times. He again preaches the Gospel, looking at his watch and muttering something about guide book time. No one is listening, we are all too busy drinking the cool refreshing water. The inevitable happens of course. We are all ready to move off just as he decides to have a drink. Soon we settle back into the monotony of walking, minds wandering aimlessly, moving one foot infront of the other

Not as many zigzags as I thought. Wonder what Marge is doing now? Then a certain doubt starts to creep in. This is too easy. Wish bloody Beverley wouldn't dash off in front. I check the map with Igneous. Puzzled we continue on. Bloody hell! What are those people doing there? Through the trees can be seen several cars parked and people picnicking. A sign post confirms my suspicions. We are lost! "Didn't think we were right. Not enough zigzags". "I thought that" said Igneous, looking at his watch. We retrace our steps quickly, embarassed by the stares and obvious comments made by the people we had so professionally passed earlier. We seek refuge and find somewhere quiet to read the map.

Sentinelle Rouge *(Extract)*

Chris Wilson *Journal 1978*

Midnight, and first to leave the hut. At Col Moore the confusion of old footsteps ensures a false line and enforced retreat, but soon the long exposed traverse to the Sentinelle's rock commences. No obvious line to follow either. Simply cross a couloir, heart in mouth, go to the next arête and repeat the process, fighting terror all the time. Usually the 'line' goes up and across, sometimes down, and always snow or ice. Snow covers everything, making identification difficult.

"Is this the Red Sentinelle?"

"No, because this isn't the Great Couloir".

Up and across, nothing difficult, and body now almost enjoying its unroped freedom. At last the Sentinelle Rouge and the start of the long diagonal traverse, hugging Mummery's Rib, pretending to be shielded from avalanche. Up and up and then across the subsidiary couloir. It's a long way. Shapes loom up from lofty heights above. On towards the couloir's centre.

sh......sh.....sh.....shush.

The sound was almost imperceptible. A slow timeless river, un-ending. Gentle rivulets flowing slowly and smoothly down, down, down into the narrow beam of torchlight. There a change occurred. Individual particules madly cascaded down, bumped into one another, and accelerated one another, bomber cars bent on destruction. Just like a river in full spate.

A brief hesitation. long enough to grasp that anything larger than these grains of snow might also follow the same course. And then again long enough to realise that this might not be a pleasant view-point. Merely time to regain lost rhythm – hammer in, crampon in, right crampon in, axe in – only now with increased tempo. Later, a slight lessening of tension as body and mind emerge unscathed from the tumult. But the rib is still far off; adjust course for the snow arête at its base, trying not to look up at the menacing shapes far above. On the arête aching lungs and weariness catch up, as does slightly harder climbing, so it's on with the rope and up again. But at last safety has been reached, and none too soon as the early morning sun wakes a previously sleepy face.

The ground changes to snow-covered rock, not hard, just 'interesting', and the sweet curves of snow on the right look more appealing.

Long pitches follow one another until the Rib lies below. Meanwhile the sun, despite the wind, is getting warmer, and all the while throats are becoming drier. A water bottle would have been appreciated on this route, especially as no ledges are forthcoming on which to brew up. A respite from the wind, gaining strength with every metre in height, would also be appreciated. The 'difficult rock chimney' mentioned in the guide and leading to the upper slopes, is enclosed in an ice wall and this calls for more skill than the usual run of the mill 'advanced snow plod'.

"Scottish Grade 4?" enquires a croak from above.

"Tight", being the standard reply in such situations, is croaked back.

Above, the wind increases, inducing a strong desire to be done with the route. But on it goes, through the windslab, ever upwards. As Route Major recedes below the climbing and angle ease until it becomes time to unrope, and struggle up the last few feet to the top.

There, in the screaming, numbing wind, a thought gets through – "Still nearly 3 weeks to go, and we've got one off the list already!"

PETIT DRU, NORTH FACE (*EXTRACT*)

ROBIN SEDGWICK   *Journal 1978*

We say farewell as the Scots move off right, en route for the hole leading through the Bonatti Pillar to the descent route on the S.E. ridge. Paul and I continue, up and left, drawn by the glinting lodestone of the Summit Madonna, now visible in the afternoon sunlight, seemingly beckoning from above the final ramparts of the face. A straightforward snow and mixed gully leads me inexorably upwards to the base of an appalling-looking squeeze chimney, walls glistening with verglas, back crammed with rotten ice. I clip into an in-situ ring peg on a long belay and bring Paul up. It's 4 in the afternoon and the sunshine has deteriorated into thick, cold, all-enveloping grey cloud. Forcing tactics are the order of the day. Paul takes both Terrordactyls, the etriers, and most of the hardware, and moves up 20 feet to the base of the chimney where a peg provides welcome protection.

"Leave your sac on the peg, I'll bring it up".

He acknowledges, removes his sac and clips it in. Moving up, he realises the rope is tangled round the sac, so reaches down and unclips it again.

The next half second runs through with the clarity of slow motion as Paul's crampon points shear out of the ice and, oh so slowly for the senses, but much too fast for any action save reflex, he's off and down. We both yo-yo to a stop on the ropes; he 15 feet below the peg, still holding his rucsac, me swinging on the belay rope in the middle of the gully, pulled off the stance. We clamber back to our previous positions. Paul clips his sac into the peg and tiptoes on up, terrors biting rotten ice, crampons grating on ice-glazed granite. An aid-nut, a struggle, into a sling, another nut, and finally a pull out from the icy slit into a gully and easier ground. I bounce up on jumars, towing a sac, impressed with the lead as I swing into the chimney to clear the pitch. As I crampon off into the mist on what we both hope will be the last lead, Paul's voice floats up behind me;

"Shout Geronimo if you get to the top."

Ten minutes later, he emerges into view to find me sitting smugly on a square-cut block, topped by a small gold-coloured Madonna:

"What was the name of that Indian, Paul?"

ASHES TO ASHES

DUSTIN KRAPPMAN   *Newsletter, April 1975*

Since 'our mans' last visit to that most celebrated of mountains, the Matterhorn, certain facts have come to light. It appears, on talking to an official from the Ministry of Tourism in Basle, that he has set them a bit of a problem causing much confusion as well as some considerable cost. It all revolves around his last ascent of the Hornli ridge. So much congestion was caused by his habitual and selfish 45 minute stint that something just had to be done. Consequently, the ministry have poured thousands of francs into a rare convenience – a fully functional gas-powered lavatory which converts human waste into dust. It is situated just below the fixed ropes above the shoulder. As most of you know (either by actual ascent or by guide book) there are seven in number, therefore, the Loo has been situated at the side of the rope that is popular with the Americans (he never has liked them since the day they entered themselves into the last war).

Recent statistics show that on a good day some 150 climbers attempt the peak so you can imagine the problems, the hold-ups 'our man' causes on that knife-edge ridge. So after many months of research and development they came up with the gas-powered loo. A trial run was made in the latter part of the '74 season but the loo was not an unqualified success due to a temperamental burner setting, a rarefied atmosphere, and failure to supply operating instructions in several languages.

An official explained "as soon as you have finished you put down the seat lid and the contents start burning – there's an electric battery, a cylinder of compressed gas and a 7 foot chimney. We are using this type of loo every day in the valley, and have done for many years but since your man's last visit to the mountain the ministry had to do something". He went on: "It took the International Environment Corps seven weeks to get it up there and a further two weeks to get it going". He looked at me with a pained face – "We've heard he's coming back this year, can't you suggest that he goes to another area".

"I'll see what I can do", was my reply, "But he has this thing to prove, something to do with the older generation and all that".

The official mopped his brow and then raised his head and looked up at the mountain. "Then there's the telephone", he said. "What telephone?", said I, enquiringly. "What's this about a telephone?"

"Well, a couple of years ago a violent storm hit the ridge and blew away his pigeon loft (used for world-wide communication), It was situated just behind the Solvay Hut, pigeons were scattered everywhere – in all directions. It was a disastrous affair. Well, your man came along and insisted that we make amends or offer an alternative system of some kind. He kept on shouting, "Do you know who I am?" and started mentioning names like Herr Petigashen and Frau Welbunz. Are they politicians in your country?" he asked.

"No" I said, "but they can be just as amusing".

From the last report, instructions in seven languages have been fitted to the loo (under the seat) and may be used by all, but the telephone is for the use of "our man" only, unless someone returns the last breeding pair which were last seen in the bar at the Lady Bower Inn.

Todhunter is ever with us ... but I am pleased, if only for the record, that he mentioned the last known evidence of the celebrated R.H. Pigeon Post Communication System. I was privileged to be present when that exhausted bird fluttered in through the window of the Lady Bower Inn bringing confirmation of yet another coup (or coop) — *Editor.*

MONTE DELLA DISGRAZIA 1975 (EXTRACT)

GORDON GADSBY

We set off at a steady pace on a good undulating track past the old stone cottages of the Preda Rossa Hamlet (long since deserted but still in good condition). Our destination was the Cesare Ponti Hütte situated above the lateral moraine of the Rossa glacier at an altitude of 2,559 metres. On our right from the track, above the forest, we would see a spectacular ridge of red granite leading up to the summit of Corni Bruciati (3,114m), whilst on the left rose the equally impressive ridge of the Punta Della Averta (2,853m). Ahead of us the track climbed steeply alongside a series of delightful waterfalls, stunted pine trees and masses of azalea with butterflies in such abundance that we had to watch where we trod.

Thirty-five minutes later the ground levelled off to another idyllic valley with a small tarn. Soon we passed the last of the trees as the track turned sharply to the left and ascended a steep rock band in a series of zigzags. The hut was hidden from view until the last ten minutes. As we approached, it looked like an outpost from the Alamo, with dirty cement walls offering little contrast with the rock surroundings. We were pleased to step out of the hot sun and into the cool dark interior of the spacious hut – the walk had taken two and a half hours.

"Arrividerci, Grazia, Buona sera" – that was about the limit of our Italian and the three teenagers in charge knew no English. We soon gathered, however, that we were the only overnight visitors in a hut of forty beds, a welcome change from the overcrowded conditions in the Bernina Alps. It was a lovely evening with a delicate pink sky over the shadowy hills of Italian lakeland on the horizon. Across the Rossa glacier snout were the impressive twin summits of the Cima Di Corna Rossa (3,250m) just catching the last rays of the evening sun.

We decided on a three o'clock start. The cold grey light of dawn was slowly easing across the sky as we fitted our crampons on the upper moraine of the Rossa glacier. We had left after a torchlight breakfast in our room.

The first hour had been a stumbling process with no real track across boulders and creaking snowfields. It was real pleasure now to lead off at a steady pace up the long and fairly steep Preda Rossa glacier. A chilling wind was whining across the snow-ice from the North East and the dark morning was bitterly cold. About half an hour later a cry from Stuart "Look behind, Gordon", stopped me in my tracks and, on turning, I saw the first rays of the morning sun changing the dark tower of the Cima Rossa into a red fiery light. Slowly the light spread along the ridge, dancing from rock to rock; a breathtaking spectacle of nature that never fails to enthral. This was our third sunrise of the holiday and by far the most memorable.

The sky above us was filled with small fast moving clouds, a true herring bone formation, and a sure sign of bad weather on its way. Ken reckoned we had twelve hours, but Disgrazia is noted for attracting bad weather and we were worried.

At five-fifty a.m. we reached the lowest point of the North West ridge at the Sella di Pioda (3,387m) after crossing several large crevasses and a bergschrund without incident. On our left the satellite of Disgrazia, Mount Pioda (3,431m) swept up to the heavens like a missile. On our right the very sharp N.W. ridge of Disgrazia rose up in a series of towers and snow crests into a deep blue sky. The views northwards into the Valley Sissone was all peace and beauty with green meadows and tiny villages dotted on alps thousands of feet below us. In the middle distance was a band of haze and mist with the enormous backcloth of the main Bernina massif rising above.

The snow was in excellent condition as we traversed the base of the first tower and then climbed steeply to the crest of the ridge, a short exposed snow arête followed, then another rock tower taken direct. the rock was very sound and we climbed in crampons. "This is the best route I've done!" shouted Stuart as he followed up the rough red granite. It was certainly a fantastic ridge with spectacular views on both sides.

After an hour we reached the base of the steep curving shoulder of the forepeak. The first thirty feet was a delicate traverse across icy slabs above a sheer drop of three thousand feet, then a direct ascent up very steep snow glazed with ice for about two hundred feet. Eventually the slope eased and we stepped onto the almost level snow summit of the forepeak. Ahead of us the main ridge dropped slightly then was blocked completely by an unusually shaped hunk of granite – The Bronze Horse!

Beyond the block the imposing summit tower, reared to the heavens, so near, but could we get round the Bronze Horse?

I approached the impasse carefully. The guide book said traverse left or right low down, both very exposed. I decided on a direct ascent and surprisingly climbed the impostor without difficulty. Ken and then Stuart followed with comparative ease and at 8.15 a.m. the three of us stood on Monte Della Disgrazia's highest point, at 3,687m.

A few days later Ken, Stuart, Chris Bryan and I were descending from the long snow ridge of Piz Fora. As we emerged from the pine forest in the upper Fex Valley above Sils Maria, we met two German Alpinists who were descending from the rocky peak of Il Chaputchin.

They had a good command of English and we walked down together in the evening sunshine, chatting away about our various mountain adventures and other things. They made an unlikely climbing team, one very slim, the other tall and heavily built, "What jobs do you do in England?" asked the latter, adjusting his spectacles as he spoke. When we told him that we were two decorators and a toolmaker, and that we were camping at St. Moritz with our families, the two men expressed surprise. "We thought only the rich people in England could afford holidays abroad, especially in Switzerland", exclaimed the slim one, whilst his friend nodded in agreement.

Ken closed that conversation by assuring them that workers at home were not the poor relations of Europe, and that climbers in Britain came from all levels of society. Our group for instance has been visiting the Alps since the early sixties. An hour later as we reached the cars at Sils Maria we exchanged good wishes for the future. Just before getting into their car, the slim man turned to us and said, "My friend, Helmut, will soon become an important man in German politics; remember the name – Kohl, Helmut Kohl.

Also taking part; Stuart Bramwell, Ken Bryan, Chris Bryan — *Editor.*

TRICOUNI REVEALS
THE GREAT GARDINER GUNGEY

It was during a walk in the lower British hills that the chance sighting of one of those large blue fertiliser bags that you see here and there in the great out-doors, caused my companion to reveal to me an episode and resulting saga, which has lain carefully concealed in the minds of a chosen few OREADS for many years ..... the saga of the Great Gardiner Gungey.

It started in Scotland, just ten years ago,
and by chance to an OREAD man,
when Paul, who'd been ill
was out on the hill
with his wife and a new lad named Sam.

Being strong walkers; in those days quite hard,
they were soon quite high on the Ben,
with no-one aware
of the secret they'd share,
or the thing that they'd bring down again.

The phenomenon known as the Great Gardiner Gungey
was discovered by innocent Paul
as he stopped for a pee,
at the top of a scree,
in the lea of a tall dry-stone wall.

In the clear mountain air it shimmered and shone,
as it drifted down into his sight;
like a sack filled with gas,
a candle of glass,
or a coral pink rubber clad kite.

It fluttered to earth, not making a sound;
one end of it right at his feet,
while the other came down
all bulbous and round,
at a distance of twenty-three feet.

Now Paul is a miser as everyone knows,
and just can't resist a few bob,
and the sight of this thing,
and the cash it could bring,
seemed rather like Manna from God.

So quick as a flash, when he'd finished his slash,
he set about rolling it up,
It was into his sack, and onto his back,
'fore anyone knew what was up.

They stopped for a breather at three thousand feet
when Sam took a fancy to food,
and before Paul could stop him he'd found it; eyes popping,
at the sight of a Gungey so huge.

Sam wasn't convinced by the tale that Paul told
of how it came down on the fell,
and he said so that night
in the pub, when quite tight,
though he swore that he never would tell.

The thing was produced for all there to see,
the men thought it funny and lewd,
while the female reaction
was one of contraction
at the sight of a Gungey so huge!

The trouble then started for innocent Paul,
now the fame if this Thing was unfurled,
and plots they were made,
and schemes they were laid,
in the night by the women and girls.

Paul woke with a jerk at a quarter to two,
and could see as they parted the flap,
the two hungry women
intent on their sinning,
disturbing his nocturnal nap.

He leaped from his bag like the star of a 'drag'
thinking thoughts that were carnal and rude,
but the look in their eyes,
and their languishing sighs
were too much, and soon changed his mood.

The women advanced on innocent Paul,
who retreated as far as he could,
not sure if relieved
or thoroughly peeved,
that Betty had slept at the pub.

Now Paul is no chicken as everyone knows,
but the two rampant nymphs were too much!
He fled past the pair,
though indecently bare,
to escape from their ravishing clutch.

The glen was alive with a feminine hoard,
some were just curious to see,
while others desired
to be fully en-sired,
and were willing to pay a stud fee.

All night Paul was running from pillar to post
pursued by the petticoat hounds,
till at last he fell spent
at the door of his tent,
on his face, on the warm summer's ground.

The women encircled; a quivering mass,
each one of them dying to view
what filled out the Gungey,
which made them so hungry,
for posture three hundred and two!

Paul was rolled over: the women all gasped,
the colossus they'd hoped for was missing.
He was quite well endowed,
with a right to be proud
But not at all what they'd really been wishing.

In deep consternation the women searched round
for the Gungey that started the trouble.
They found it at last,
with this label stuck fast
to the base of that wondrous bubble...

    "Will the finder return to the address below
    post-paid by ourselves on receipt.
    To N.A.S.A.,
    Department D.K.
    Houston, Texas, East 43rd Street."

Post Script:

Letter to the Editor, Newsletter, November 1971

    Dear Sir,

    Reference to the Gungey; it is time the truth is revealed.

    In fact it was a large bag of wind which I subsequently sold to Tricouni, who is apparently still using it.

                            P. W. Gardiner

MID SUMMER MUSINGS (*EXTRACTS*)
TRICOUNI

Newsletter, July 1972

It would seem then, that a truly Freudian urge could well be the binding factor which draws the mountaineer from so many walks of life. As yet, however it is undefined; equally identifiable as a homo, or heterosexual drive. Consider though that, in general, climbing is accomplished by pairs or teams of the male gender. This in itself suggests interesting relationships; relationships which have been so eloquently summarised by our old friend Raymond Colledge, who despite all our efforts, must again be quoted by 'Tricouni', but in this instance however, I assure you, only because of his profound knowledge of Latin!

    "Nec vidisse semel satis est:
    juvat usque morari, et conferre gardum,
    et veniondy discere causas!"

("Nor is it enough to have seen him once; it is a pleasure ever to linger by him, and to come to close quarters with him, and to learn the causes of him coming".)

Swallows Nest 1969

It is further recorded that once upon a time, in ages past, George Reynolds used to climb. His contemporary activities can only be guessed at however, when records reveal that on one occasion he spent two hours and forty-three minutes belaying a totally inadequate gentleman on the first pitch of

Ordinary Route at Brassington. His eventual arrival at the stance was greeted with these most suggestive words of Mr. Samuel Pepys......

> When I at last beheld thee,
> Mine heart did leap within me,
> And the bonds about my loins were greatly loosed!"

Of course he could have been dying for a slash!

Such a discourse would not be complete without due regard being given to the state of affairs as it stands between the long, the short, and the tall, namely Rot, Scabcliffe and Phew! Not content in throwing a huff whenever 'she' puts the mockers on a weekend with Rot, old Scab (an affectionate nickname from his horny and thick skinned character!) elected himself giver away, best man, and chief bridesmaid for the May festivities, and threatened to stand as chief objector on the grounds of breach of promise made in the exit cracks (where else might I ask). In view of this, how else could one conclude, but to quote the lyrical free adaptation of Wordsworth's "Lines above Tintern Abbey" which were discovered watered into the snows of the Second Icefield....

> "The tall rock, the mountain, and the deep and gloomy Scottie,
> Their colours and their forms were then to me an appetite, a feeling, and a bottie."

FOR SALE

Shortly after the successful ascent of the Eigerwand by Radcliffe and Scott in 1971 the following advertisement appeared.

B.B. 'EVEREST' RUCKSACK
This is a large frame sack in excellent condition. Large zipped front pockets; two large side pockets; features include quick release buckle for easy lifting, chrome leather straps throughout.

| | A first-rate buy: | £3.00 |

McINNES-MASSEY ICE AXE (24")
The hinduminium alloy shaft makes this the strongest axe in the world, Forged head; polythene sleeve covering shaft. Excellent condition.

| | A fantastic bargain: | £3.00 |

STUBAI 'ASCHENBRENNER' ICE AXE (85cms)
A conventional axe, although it has a curved adze. Cost new £6.00

| | Ideal for winter hill walking: | £2.00 |

STUBAI NORTH WALL HAMMER (50cms)
Proved on many north walls, but equally useful to include in your sack, just in case. Cost new £5.95

| | Great Value | £1.25 |

FISHER'S WATERPROOFS (No connection with "Parsimonious John")
Cagoule and overtrousers of the oiled fabric type. Needs re-proofing (Fishers provide this service) but plenty of life left.

| | Can't be bad: | 25p |

LEATHER OVER MITTS, Good quality buckskin, unused: 25p

LEATHER OVER MITTS, as above, used 15p

1 PAIR GOGGLES (tinted brown)	5p
1 PAIR GOGGLES (tinted yellow)	5p
1 PAIR STOP TOUS	5p
SUPER BLEUET CASE – this holds your gaz stove, 2 spare cartridges and acts as a windshield in use. Little used	50p
MISCELLANEOUS CAMPING ACCESSORIES – including two sandwich boxes; two 2-egg containers; tin opener, a polythene mug and misc. K.F.S.	10p
Total	£10.65

All available from: Chris Radcliffe,
21 Avondale Road
Chesterfield, Derbyshire.

It is alleged that Burgess acquired the job lot for £ 9.50 and, after some judicious asset stripping, made a decent profit. After compensatory payment of bus fares to Nat Allen, Hank Harrison and Derek Carnell (See Infamous Cratcliffe Meet 1972) he was said to have maintained a healthy surplus — *Editor.*

THE DERBYSHIRE HUT
HEATHY LEA COTTAGE

After the death of Geoff Hayes in 1971 it was decided that the barn should be brought into use and should stand as a memorial to him. This work was completed during 1972 and the early part of 1973 under the supervision of the Hut Custodian, Ron Chambers. As previously, in the cottage itself, much of the graft was carried out by Nat Allen, Derek Carnell, Fred Allen, Paul Gardiner, and George Reynolds — *Editor.*

OPENING OF THE GEOFF HAYES BARN

March 3rd 1973

This function, the culmination of eighteen months of decision making and effort was marked by the presence of Anne, Mr. & Mrs. Walter Hayes, Geoff's sister Barbara, and Mrs. Kall, Anne's mother.

Five minutes before the opening a steady drizzle began much to the annoyance of those present and the photographers amongst them in particular.

The simple plaque was unveiled by Anne, who then, having said a few words, opened the Barn door officially and everyone managed to squeeze inside for shelter and to hear a speech of appreciation from Mr. Hayes.

The final working party had put the Barn in splendid order, the newly lined roof making a vast improvement and everything appeared clean and shining; a fine tribute to the man commemorated and a credit to the Heathy Lea Warden, Ron Chambers, his sub-committee, and all who have turned a hand to the numerous jobs.

Mr. Hayes generously donated the new gas heater which gives heat at the turn of a tap; better than the cottage where one has to chop the wood and forage for "kindling"!!

233

Tea and biscuits were dispensed efficiently by a team of Oread ladies, principally Margaret Johnson, Tinsel, Kath Chambers and Janet Reynolds. The visitors book was passed round and a count up showed some seventy-five in attendance.

P. W. Gardiner

As the Oread were opening the Geoff Hayes Barn, there was a death in Edale and Nat Allen (President) contributed an Appreciation to the July Newsletter:

FRED HEARDMAN 1896-1973

Fred Heardman of the Rucksack Club and living in Edale, died at the age of 77 years at the end of the first quarter of 1973.

Fred, for many years licensee of the Church and Nag's Head hotels in Edale, was a pioneer of many of the now famous Peakland walks, earning himself the nickname of "Fred the Bogtrotter". His marathon walks, often made in the company of such characters as Cecil Dawson, Harold Gerrard and Eustace Thomas, began after the 1914-18 war. In 1922 he invented, and walked, of course, the Three Inns walk, which in modern times has been varied to include four or even five. In 1926 he walked the 73 mile "Colne to Rowsley" in a time well inside 24 hours.

The 1930's saw Fred Heardman on the Rural District Council, fighting a successful and almost lone battle, to stop the building of a giant steelworks in his beloved Edale valley – an act which placed him "in Coventry" with the locals who were strongly in favour of the idea. He was an outstanding worker with the C.P.R.E. and was a mine of information from behind the Bar of the 'Nags' when it became the Peak Park Information Centre.

For the 1952 Rucksack Club's Jubilee, Fred invented the Tan Hill – Cat and Fiddle walk, which five of their members completed. He compiled the booklet Walks Around Edale and in later years became the BMC's Peak Committee man on the spot, rarely missing a trick when the vandals or planners stepped out of line.

For his work he was awarded the O.B.E. The late Alf Bridge would always refer to him when talking of walking, as his "mighty yardstick". Peakland walkers and climbers have indeed lost a champion and friend.

See Eric Byne's Appreciation: Bloody Bill the Bogtrotter, Newsletter, February 1955 — *Editor.*

SOME OUTDOOR MEETS, U.K., 1974-1990
PEMBROKESHIRE, EASTER 1974 (*EXTRACT*)

GORDON GADSBY

I joined some of the children in a walk across the Island (Ramsey) to join up with Hobday at Foel Fawr. Goldsmith and Hobday had rigged up a rope across easy sea cliffs so that the youngsters could be taken down for a closer look at the grey seals. From the bottom it was possible to make an exposed traverse into the cove, with a sloping shelf, then down to a boulder beach and two fine pinnacles.

Hobday, Craddock and Ken Bryan climbed the east face of the further pinnacle – possibly a new route; Lost Arrow. I climbed the easier but more spectacular tower (moderate), belayed by Shirley Goldsmith (later Wainwright), who bears a remarkable resemblance to Thor's Hammer on the Kvanndalstind ridge in Romsdal, Norway.

Perhaps a subordinate phrase is missing here – Thor's Hammer indeed — *Editor.*

ESKDALE, MAY 1974 (EXTRACT)

DERRICK BURGESS

"Will you write up the meet? Handley's organising the campsite and we don't really need a leader for a Bank Holiday meet." The President's words came to mind as I stared blankly at the "NO CAMPING" sign on the gate at Brotherkeld farm, our venue ("idyllic" raved Handley) for the weekend. The headlights picked our numerous scraps of paper pinned to the gate; surely someone had left a note, but no word of the Oread, although Fred and Dave (?) were at Wasdale, and half the other clubs in the land seemed to be featured. A hard word from inside the car jolted me back to reality. The image in my mind of Handley stretched on the rack faded and I was faced with finding a campsite – quickly. Like the majority on the meet I drove back down the valley and was very pleased to locate Ray and the rest on the campsite at Spout House, and all worries soon disappeared over hot cups of tea.

SKYE, WHITSUNTIDE 1976 (EXTRACT)

JOHN DOUGHTY

That evening heralded the arrival of a few more Oreads and it was decided, yet again, that a walk along the cliffs would be a good idea. this time to go looking for rare wild flowers. After a day's exercise I was feeling a little more human and tried to encourage one or two of them to go with me to Corrie Lagan and, if weather permitted, do a climb. Alas, this was not to be, so our bumptious botanists and yours truly started the search for the elusive orchid. After a while, I became rather bored and decided, as it was a nice day, to soak my feet in a stream and look at the mountains I had travelled 700 miles to climb. When the fancy returned to join the others it wasn't long before I found them sitting in an orderly circle. I assumed they were having their lunch and did not pay much attention to Hodge lying on his stomach with his camera to his eye. I thought this was how he always spent his lunch breaks. The friendly atmosphere soon changed as I strode into the centre of the circle. It's a good job there are no trees around or else I think I would still be hanging there. I had just stepped on the only Skye wild orchid in existence! Anyway, we splinted the poor thing up and left it looking somewhat dejected and bent. After this unfortunate episode, I spent the rest of the day on my own as no one would talk to me. I walked on to the peninsula jutting out into Loch Brittle and soloed one or two routes on the cliffs. The reason I mention this is because on they way off this peninsula I noticed thousands of these rare orchids and you just could not help stepping on the dammed things!

After completion of the Cuillin ridge:

Absolutely finally, I would like to thank W. D. and H. O. Wills for their support because without them I don't think the expedition would have succeeded. If anyone asks how long it took, I tell them about 50 fags long!

'Half a lung, half a lung, half a lung onwards'.

GLENCOE, JANUARY 1977 (EXTRACT)

ROBIN SEDGWICK

The moon is already high and still rising. It's light in the west above the cold, grey wastes of Loch Leven and the dying sun highlights scattered innocuous looking black clouds. Puffing and panting settles into a steady rhythm in picking a way up the steep broken slopes to the right of Clachaig Gully. Gaining height quickly, the grass and earth is seen to have a feathery white dusting. Soon the heather is starting to struggle under a white blanket and I'm crunching a satisfying trail in half consolidated snow, moving well and wondering if this is going to be third time lucky. A quick stop to put on crampons and then back to the rhythm of movement, weaving round shadowy rock outcrops and up glimmering snow ramps, trying all the time to keep to the ridges where the wind will have stripped off the recently fallen powder. Occasionally floundering in knee-deep sugar, rhythm broken and gasping, making a bee-line for the nearest rock outcrop. Easy scrambling and snow-slope plodding, sliding past larger outcrops, climbing the smaller ones, until the angle drops back and leads to the plateau below the summit. A little voice in my head appeals for time out and a hastily taken cigarette and handful of nuts gives time to contemplate the weather. The black clouds are still floating across but don't appear to be harbouring any hostility. So it's up and off again, across the top of the sgurr and onto the ridge of Aonach Eagach.

OYSTER CLOUGH, MARCH 1977 (EXTRACT)

BRIAN WEST

Habitues of the Bleaklow cabins will know only too well how these nights of adversity arouse the baser human instincts and this night proved no exception. On these meets you soon get to know your place in the Oread hierarchy. Exercising his Presidential prerogative (Beryl averted her eyes), Hobday, resplendent in his apres-ski gear, was soon into the optimum position nearest the fireplace and furthest from the door. The rank and file were left to sink to their respective levels; David Cheshire in the spilt sugar under the table, and myself as reluctant door stop. Incontinent Mike Wren showed his native cunning by trampling everyone but the President whilst rushing to and from the door. This despicable exhibition of blatant boot licking was rewarded by a number two spot under the President's wing. Beryl, of course, was spoilt for choice...

CEFN GAWR, APRIL 1977 (EXTRACT)

COLIN HOBDAY

A small hand-picked group of Oreads decided to make the pilgrimage to Cefn Gawr on Migneint on Friday, April 22nd 1977 to relive some of the delights first introduced to the Oread by Harry Pretty way back in 1965. The group consisted of myself "leader", Chris Bryan, apprenticed to John "Bruno" Welbourn, Brian West (Fire Lighter, first class) and Beryl Strike (Bronze Medal Life Saving).

It was now 4.00 pm and still the last part to complete. We set off and crossed the Trawsfynydd – Bala Road. There, in front of us, the great expanse of Migneint. In the true traditions of Migneint we were soon wallowing in bog and thigh-high heather. In the distance, perched on the side of the hill, we could see Cefn Gawr. In an endeavour to find easier walking, we made for the higher ground, only to get mixed up in "Turks Heads". There appeared to be no choice but to plod in a direct line for Cefn Gawr, which slowly grew closer. The sky became darker and in a matter of minutes we were enveloped in the full fury of the storm. Upon reaching the Afon Gerw, one look at the depth and width told us there was no chance of crossing. Cefn Gawr seemed so close, but so far, as we turned upstream into the driving rain. Chris saw the black horseman for the second time that day and complained that Bullstones would be a piece of cake after this.

Welbourn's pipe went out, which demoralised all the party. Brian who had been out in front had found a possible crossing place, a rather dubious looking island in the middle of the river, about twice the size of a dustbin lid and in much the same condition. The first section to the island was comparatively easy. Brian completed the second part safe and dry. The rest of the party gathered on the island, whilst I made a safe landing on the far bank. John, however, in a flurry to get across, threw his rucksack and, at the same time, was attacked by severe cramp and fell into the river, taking on the appearance of an obsolete submarine with his pipe just above water. I think it was on the third time he surfaced that he muttered between obscenities "Pull me out". Beryl who was quite overcome by the drama taking place before her eyes, leaned over the bank and looked into John's glazed eyes, his trilby hat floating away downstream.. Realising it was for real, we pulled him onto the bank. The final insult being that he was back on the bank from which he had started! Chris showed no improvement when crossing the river and, falling short of the bank, was pulled out dripping wet. What followed was like a scene from Monty Python. John, after ten false starts left the island, failed to gain sufficient height, fell short of the far bank and once more disappeared into the murky water to be pulled out by Brian and myself. Beryl quite disillusioned by all that had been happening, made a half hearted effort to get across the river, failed, and sank slowly.

Does the painting of the ram still exist? What is it really like at Cefn Gawr? Only those who go there, will know the secrets of Migneint Moor.

BIVOUAC OF THE YEAR 1978

"I could stand the thought of a night
on Angel Pavement. I could stand
those silly buggers waking us up
every hour. I could even stand the
thought of 'em jugging it up at
the Tan Ronen. But all these fags and
no matches .... "

J. Doughty

On December 26th, Dave Cheshire and John Doughty were benighted on Angel Pavement on Craig y Bere. They were unable to retreat and spent 18 hours sitting on a small ledge without bivi-gear, whilst the remaining Oread Team enjoyed their Christmas Dinner at the Tan Ronen. The following morning they were rescued by a strong Oread team led by Chris Radcliffe — *Editor.*

TAN-Y-WYDDFA, JUNE 1984 (EXTRACT)

RUTH CONWAY

We make the Prince Llewellyn by 10.28 and the rest of the team are already ensconced, Colin Barnard, Richard and Dawn Hopkinson, Helen Griffiths, George Fowler, Alistair Gordon, John O'Reilly, and Martin Roome. I stop worrying about living and start worrying who I'm going to climb with. I seem to have done nothing but pester people to be third on a rope recently. To my unutterable relief Helen says she's on her own and why don't we team up? The Pinniclub had better watch out, the most unlady-like ladies team ever is about to hit the crag.

237

Well, as I told you, Saturday dawned fine and fair. By the time I got up John and Martin had already disappeared with mysterious aims in mind and our numbers had been magically swelled by Roger Larkham who chose to drive overnight and arrive at 7.30 a.m. (no accounting for taste). Weather like this it has to be Cloggy, but what to do? Richard and Dawn are already established on Boulder, everywhere is busy, so Helen and I set off up Sheaf after George and Alistair. She makes short work of the first pitch, I lead through, but eventually we are both defeated by the beastly overhang. We try amazing contortions, turn ourselves backwards, sit in the groove, bridge out at alarming angles . . . we just can't do it. We begin to realise that as a climbing team we do lack that certain something – basically inches. Eventually George returns from aloft and offers advice on how to leap up and throw wires into cracks. Thus emboldened I merrily aid it until I grab the jug that they could reach standing. Alistair says we can't help it, it's not our fault if we're stunted from birth – and to think I rather liked him!

The following pitch involves stepping out wildly right-wards onto the arête. The elongated bean poles in front leave us an aid sling without ever being asked – what price Womens Lib? Well, it was too early to go home and too late for another major performance so we dithered and watched Richard and Dawn on Diglyph. Eventually George and Helen decided they'd had enough while Alistair and I, little puritans at heart, did Sunset Crack for our sins.

TAN-Y-WYDDFA, CHRISTMAS 1984 (EXTRACT)

In the evening a knock at the door was heard and upon opening it two Dutch lads appeared. These were immediately recognised by Ruth as the same two who had arrived five years ago to the very day, perhaps to the very hour. That time they were cold, wet and much fatigued after traversing Snowdon (in clogs, carrying rucksacks bulging with daffodil bulbs), but were now suitably clad. In minutes with typical Oread hospitality, tea, cakes and places by the fire were provided. In those five years they had often recalled the friendliness given and the pleasure of the North Wales hills.

DERBYSHIRE BARN MEET 1987 (EXTRACT)

RICHARD COGHLAN

The British Legion club was not yet open (Parwich). We did the obvious and went to the pub just down the road. As more and more Oreads converged on the same spot, what had happened to Rusty eventually became known. Three of his cattle had 'escaped' (we never found out whether this was by tunnel, glider, or the vaulting horse trick), with potentially horrendous insurance consequences. In the darkness Rusty had to give up the search.

We all piled into the British Legion club for more beer before setting off up the road to what was clearly someone's music room annexe for an excellent meal of stew, with a sweet course and coffee to follow. The setting and cuisine was a cut above the rough company ravenously devouring food. Mike Wren had a go at playing the harmonium in the centre of the room. The set of songbooks used for the music provided the official version of the words. The Oread choir, led by Dave Weston, invented their own, "not recommended for young children or people of nervous disposition".

On then with the rucksacks, out with the maps, and up we went, following Rusty's direction to Two-Dale barn about a mile north of Parwich. Rusty had obviously prepared the way by laying a thick layer of clean hay on the floor. Some barn this, it even had a built-in hay strewn matratzenlager which looked purpose built, except that there was no ladder up to it. This taxed the technical ability of not a few people. The worst ascent was made by someone during the night who climbed up the wall at the wrong end of the barn, embarked on a lengthy traverse on the inside wall and fell off, landing on Gordon Wright, sleeping on the floor below. To save unnecessary nocturnal preambulations, there was a hole in the matratzenlager down which one could urinate as one wished. It was not obvious where the liquid ended up. Sleeping below, I'm sure I felt something splashing onto my face during the night, but in my drowsy state I didn't think too hard about it. Before settling down to sleep there was a short, sharp burst of much promised "outrageous repartee" one classic example being "Last time I saw one that size, it had a harpoon in it!." Draw your own conclusions.

BULLSTONES, DECEMBER 1987

Compiled from Extracts   *Editor*

Nags Head – Edale (Friday night) present: West (Meet Leader), Jonson, Hudson, John Green, Helen Griffiths, Bingham, Coghlan, Amour, Phillips, Burt, Hopkinson, Pretty, Williams. Overnight to Jubilee Cabin, very dark, but dry.

Departure Saturday a.m. for Cat Clough cabin, all except Pretty and Williams who went north west following some ancient Oread songline.

Main party split at Bleaklow Stones, Party A (Amour, Bingham and Jonson) headed for Lower Small Clough. Party B (remainder) arrived at Cat Clough to find only a neatly stacked pile of timber and corrugated iron, so turned south towards Lower Small Clough in stygian darkness (and gloom). At junction of Stainery Clough with main valley they encountered Scott, Larkham and Radcliffe, all heading north for Cat Clough. The united teams reached Lower Small Clough at 19.00 (Radders actually went past and had to be brought back). Additional arrivals were Gadsby and Bramwell.......

Extract from 1987 Journal   *Anon*

The cabin (Lower Small Clough) had been repaired – a new window and renovated walls, but some of the wooden benches had been removed, while grotty plastic mini tables, quite out of place, had been installed. Along the back wall people sat in duvets. Some had balaclavas on, some were gloved, while others cupped their hands around a hot drink. From nails or just perched on protruding sharp stones, hung removed gear; various designs of rucksacks could be seen by the flicker of candles or the search-light activities of head torches. Boots and gaiters caked in mud stuck our from beneath the table. The table was littered with all manner of things, many of which in any normal household would have been removed to the refuse; all shapes and sizes of plastic containers, plastic bags, with knives and spoons lying in congealing food, witness to some culinary failure. Loaves of bread were hacked apart by blunt knives, and clusters of tins, their contents of garden peas, chunky steak, baked beans or curry mix indicating what was in an adjacent billy. Bluet, primus and meta burners produced a steady roar and the steam rose upwards past concentrating faces which peered into the boiling cauldrons.

In one corner Rock stood in his sodden gear, for there was no seat available. He stirred some revolting mess. A second course was tipped into the remains of the first; this was to produce a sauce! After a while a mucky handkerchief was clasped around the billy, so that he could lift it towards his mouth and tilting it at a slight angle towards him he shovelled the overloaded spoon fulls down with greater ease. While licking the spoon, the billy was returned to the Bluet and a tin of cream-rice tipped into the left over soup, greens and meat. The warmth of the meal obviously reached his legs for he stopped trying to get warm by stamping his feet.

On the Saturday night Pretty and Williams descended from Oyster Clough Cabin to the Snake Inn where they came upon Janes, who had arrived by car. They all returned to Oyster Clough for the night.

The main party returned to Edale on Sunday. En passant they spotted Chris Burt in the vicinity of the Jubilee Cabin. Had he been there all week-end? But no – he had reached Cat Clough on his own, had proceeded downstream from the vacant site and found a newly renovated structure which he occupied alone. Brian West was not impressed by this revelation. All parties re-assembled at the Nags Head, Edale by 13.30 on Sunday.

Janes and Williams walked over Kinder from the Snake; Pretty drove Janes' car back to Edale. As Westy would say "Just another Bullstones really".

A MESSAGE FROM MOULAM – JOURNAL 1978
(EXTRACT)

A. J. J. MOULAM

The club spirit has been held high over the years. The early Lyngen expeditions and the Oread book are just two of the many notable accomplishments for a 'local club, but the Oread is strong because of its local connotations, rather than in spite of them.

Having been banished to the southern flatlands for nearly ten years, and having other commitments at weekends, most of my recent climbing has been at Oread evening meets. I'm not yet sure whether I make the Wednesday evening pilgrimage to Derbyshire for the rock, or for the beer in Jonah's pub. It's probably a bit of both, and at least it keeps my consumption of routes and ale at an acceptable level.

Certainly I begin to live, as opposed to exist, at the Derby exit from the M1. There is a change in my metabolism, when I enter Oread country, and sparks of joy as I meet the members at different crags, all well set up in a rosy glow brought on by kindred spirits. Either struggling up a few feet from the ground, or sitting on it chatting, I feel I have come home.

The high spot of 1977 was not an official meet but it was one of the best attended. Nat Allen's 49th (oops – perhaps he'd meant to keep the number secret) was the occasion, a week after the season had officially ended. I arrived at Black Rocks, scene of my youthful endeavours, and thus dear to my heart, complete in city suit. A bite or two of this nourishment fortified us for a flying visit to Dukes Quarry, and Great Crack; as Nat put it: "the best gritstone crack you've never done".

Keen to get back to the meet we did it quickly and descended. On the quarry floor we met the eternally youthful Peter Pan figure of Nobby Millward, and his wife Judy, who had come to see us in action. They were too late as we declined to do it again, and so back to Black Rocks for a work-out until dark. Birch Tree Wall, (LH) Stonnis Crack, The Ravage – how often is it done? I'll swear Harding's buttons still lie in the dark depth of the crack, and they have been there since they fell from his cut down Mac in 1945! Queen's Parlour Slab as the last light faded took me back to the old Stonnis days when Harding first top-roped it, and then led it – with a handkerchief round his eyes. The result of a youthful boast in the Greyhound that he could do it blindfolded.

The great days of our formative years culminated in the Superstitious start on Lean Man's Buttress, the easy exit from Promontory Cave, and Demon Rib, the latter an early forerunner to the extreme and unlikely gritstone routes of today. These were all done on a Friday 13th, and apt it was, too, on Demon Rib. I gave Harding a top rope so that he could learn the early moves and thought he shouted 'haul away!' As I did so he jumped for the ground, having really said 'all away!' and to his surprise floated upwards drawn by the rope manipulated by my strong young muscles!

However, the Promontory was our 'piece de resistance'. Members of the Polaris had witnessed our early tries and told us, gratis, that "better men than you have tried and failed". The nose was relatively easy to reach and one Thursday, (after school!) Harding and I stood in the cave. We had confidence in one another, and no belay. A little tension ensured my exit down the eastern side, my feet searching for the hidden foot crack. My toes slipped in and somehow I made the few feet to the abseil spike. A descendeurless abseil on a single line deposited me in Prom Gully, and left Peter to make these few difficult and unprotected moves before he could join me, and we knew then, at least we could completely girdle our home ground.

It seems we were blind to the limestone possibilities that have now become the normal routes, aping climbs on bigger cliffs. We did try one or two things but were indoctrinated to believe it was all rotten, steep and unclimbable. Our ascent of High Tor Gully, full of debris, was not inspiring, although I well remember the struggle shared with Harding, Horsfield and Herbert up pitch after pitch of rubbish, after the first clean little wall. The park police were not so active then, or years later when I did the Original Route on High Tor with Don Whillans. They wanted to take our names but they didn't believe us when we said that we were both called Brown!

A MESSAGE FROM BRAZIL – 1979

Editor

The 1960 Annual Dinner had been distinguished by the appearance of a representative of the Brazilian Ladies Alpine Club. Sen. Carmello O'Higgins. This lady had been in communication with the Oread some years previously, when D. C. Cullum had made some scathing reference to Brazilian lady climbers in a Newsletter Editorial.

Relations with the Brazilian Ladies A.C. had not entirely withered and there were stories of an alleged encounter with Major Bob's 1961 Himalayan team in the Manali Orchards. "A Latin-American formation dancing team" was referred to deprecatingly by Burgess and others, when questioned, but Ashcroft's spectacles steaming up at the mere mention was not convincing.

The 1979 Annual Dinner (President: Chris Radcliffe in charge) brought some enlightenment in the form of a letter from the legendary lady. The letter was addressed to H.P. who, only recently, in the company of David Appleby, had met an O'Higgins lady journalist at an International Ski Congress at the Coylumbridge Hotel, Cairngorm. The letter was read out to the assembled members and guests among whom was the celebrated New Zealand mountaineer/explorer Mr. George Lowe, himself only recently returned from a long attachment in Santiago, Chile.

Villa Santos

My Dears

How sad it is I am not able to come with you at the Dinner in Derbyshire. Me and my now fast groping son Roberto Gavino, truly an O'Higgins, but with the big ruptured mouth of his father, we was much anticipating your unstuffed shirts and your well stuffed breeches. I often tell him of those days 18 years ago when me and my Brazilian ladies made the 5th ascent of the world's 35th highest peak. He likes to hear how I met Major Bob in the Manali Orchard with his English tuffs. My Dorita has said sometimes that she has never felt so many hard men in their English vests and horse riding shorts. As my pictures tell me, they have all been so flashing, and I am always remembering Major Bob's teaching me the long English words about how he has always been reaching the culminating points.

I am always thinking about my visit to your Dinner many years ago now I think, and all this noise from the bog pipes which I am not hearing till then.

241

Will you remember my French friend Esmé who was with me. She is still wondering about this story that your friend she says is Pierre was telling her in the bath room about an Octopus and the bog pipes. We have never been understanding it but as my Esmé says "this Pierre he is the man who has the big parts in your entertainments". She is not understanding that he is not round shouldered.

And how is the funny man with what he calls the Welsh dragon on his espadrilles. He always reminds us of our Patagonian Patron who has all the sheep on his pampas. He tells me when he takes me to see his big glass instrument and his special paper on the walls of his hut that looks like real bricks that he has had his privates in the Welsh Dragoons when he was young. My Esmé says this English word 'privates' is a funny word and I must be careful what I do with it. Perhaps I am not understanding too well.

You have the new El Presidente, Senhor Ratsniff, and I am trying to remember him in the flesh as you say in English. We have looked at the old photographs but we are not able to see him. Esmé thinks he is the one who wears the Velcro chest wig with the Vaseline finish. He is I think what the American gringos call the Big Apple.

It is nice that you meet my second cousin Elizabeth at the ski-ing in Scotland with her Belgian friend Henri. She is often laughing about your little dark skinned friend Davvid Applestrudle – she tells me he has the face that the skis have run over. Henri says he should have been run over by one of the trains that my great grandfather, the General, was running in 1835. I think that your friend does not know that Elizabeth is high caste O'Higgins and is not like her Brazilian cousins. When we next meet I think we give him the Brazilian wax treatment.

Please remember me to all my English friends
with love
Carmello

P.S. My cousins in Chile tell me that they have met a long time ago an English Colonial man called Geog Lowey who has climbed some mountains. He tells them that he knows the English climbing boss, my Roberto, but my cousins think he has all the bull – they do not think Geog is that important a man.

Historical Note: Bernado O'Higgins (1776-1842) Soldier and Statesman, head of first permanent national government of Chile, born at Chillan (20.8.1776) the natural son of the Irishman Ambrosio O'Higgins, Governor of Chile (1778-95), and Viceroy of Peru (1795-1801). A cavalry general in many South American campaigns against the Spanish supremacy. Also a great railway engineer celebrated throughout South America — *Editor.*

ALPINE AFFAIRS 1980-1990
LES GRANDES JORASSES

The 1,200 metre North Face of the Grandes Jorasses, rising above the Leschaux Glacier.

W   – Point Walker, 4,208 metres
WH – Point Whymper, 4,184 metres
C   – Point Croz, 4,110 metres

The lines of the Walker and Croz spurs are marked and white dots indicate the bivouac sites mentioned in the articles.

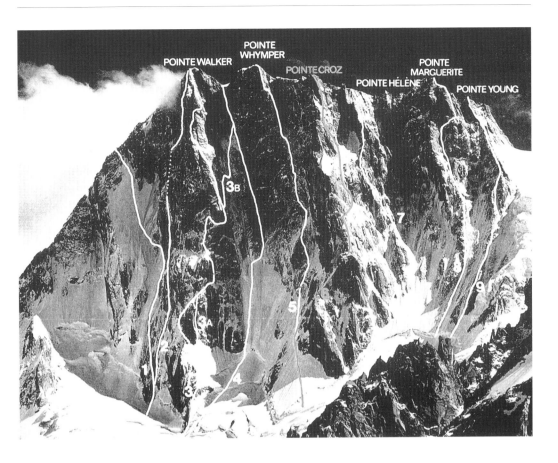

DOUBLE TOP 1980

This year saw two notable Oread successes on the North Face of the Grandes Jorasses in the Mont Blanc Massif. Firstly Pete Holden and Chris Radcliffe made an ascent of the Croz Spur over 6 days at Easter, an ascent which, while outside the period for the recognition of Winter Ascents, was probably the first time the route had been climbed by a British team in winter conditions. It was Chris and Pete's third attempt at the route.

Later in the year Paul Addison and Robin Sedgewick made a storm bound four day ascent of the neighbouring Walker Spur.

The following are extracts from the Journal 1980 — *Editor.*

LES GRANDES JORASSES PAR L'EPERON DE LA POINTE CROZ, 5TH-10TH APRIL 1980 *(EXTRACTS)*

PETER HOLDEN

As a most generous act Howard Lancashire and Pip Hopkinson carried some of our gear and deposited it beneath the Leschaux hut as an extension of their ski-descent of the Valleé Blanche – this act most probably saved us a further bivouac on the glacier approach to our climb.

Chris and I had made two previous attempts on the climb, both over the Christmas period, but the highest point attained on these had been the top of the rock barrier beneath the middle ice-field. These attempts had cost us enormous effort and had been great experiences – but of course to retreat twice from the same climb had left a very deep impression of an undertaking unresolved. So for a third time we faced the mountain; it looked the same majestic bastion, but were we this time sufficiently determined to overcome our weaknesses and it's strengths?

After the two weeks of storms which had preceded our attempt, the glacier was covered in deep, fresh powder snow; but whereas the Mer de Glace had been quickly transformed into a regular firm ski-piste, the Leschaux Glacier before us was virgin and soft. On a slight easing of the slope we decided to make our bivouac and proceeded to stamp out with ease a large platform in the powder snow.

Next morning the sky was clear and we turned our eyes and thoughts to the steepening glacier which we had to ascend for 1,500' to reach the foot of the face. Three hours of strenuous plodding. The last few hundred feet of ascent had been a battle against wind slab crust which had formed and threatened to break off in large slabs. It was a great relief to take a stance beneath the first ice-field, to gear-up, and to take off the snow shoes.

The ice-field was covered in deep snow. The good snow-cover over the ice continued up into the couloir behind the 'first rock tower'. Immediately above us we knew that the serious climbing began. On our last attempt we had been involved in a near bizarre epic in the company of Patrick Valencenne only 150' above where we stood and we had all retreated from that point. Thus we were quite happy to make an early stop and prepare a bivouac at the foot of the rock wall.

The next morning we resolved to avoid the steep rock tower which we had climbed on previous attempts and we opted for the steep ice gully on it's left hand side. It was very difficult (Scottish Grade 5 for 300'). We were forced to take extreme care with the soft unstable snow which terminated in the most amazing knife-edge arête atop the 'second tower', which gave us a 75' sky-walk along its fine crest. Two strenuous pitches up snow plastered rocks led to the clean, near vertical, 150' wall which bars access to the 'middle ice-field' We knew that there was no good bivouac site to be found above the wall, so we resolved to make the best of the poor site where we stood. Now in the last light of a fine day, we hacked away two acceptable ledges from the hard grey ice. To sit on this vast wall in winter is an incredible experience – the feeling of isolation being compounded by the intense cold which was intensified by the strong wind.

We warmed to the next day by prussiking up the rope fixed on the previous evening and above a tiny stance we contemplated the huge expanse of hard grey ice which forms the "middle ice field" and up which we would have to climb as a diagonal line for eight pitches. Very often the shattering of the brittle surface skin would cause a foot to skid off and one's whole body heaved with the strength of the reaction which powered front-points back into place. (It took two months for our toes to recover from this mal-treatment!) A very dramatic moment occurred when I asked Chris to make a pendulum across the ice because an in-situ piton had tempted me too high onto the ice glazed rock wall. The back-up piton, which I had placed, moved under load and the existing one began to bend slowly down. I cried to Chris to off-load the rope and in those agonising seconds, as I watched him quickly regain security, I saw Chris fifty feet below, splayed out on the vast sheet of mirror-like ice above the impending void. The upper rim of the ice-field was followed with sustained effort until at the highest point of the ice the rock band had to be taken to. After this pitch we were one again briefly in the evening sun, but the rigors of a steep ice crack and chimney absorbed the last remaining minutes of light and the expected ledge could not be found and eventually a desperate bivvy place was fashioned where we stood.

The dawn came red and fiery and we knew that the storm which had been building up for the last few days was about to break. The pressure to find a route up was great because of the swirling grey clouds sweeping in. We scanned right across the wall and decided to make a traverse on the steep, brittle ice at its foot in the hope that something would turn up! Eventually the ice gave out to bold granite ten feet before a groove which promised a way up and out. The ascent of this pitch in the swirling snow without crampons was something which demanded full use of the skills of delicate bridging on both rock and ice, combined with cunning deployment of curved axe-picks until the ice-field was reached and crampons were strapped on whilst standing in a sling. Avalanches cascaded down the face and we became buried on belays and everything rapidly became covered in 6 inches of freshly fallen snow. Progress was slow. We swept our way slowly upwards until we reached the next rock band and there we searched for a place to bivvy. An obvious bivouac site did not materialise before the ice loomed again so we applied creative ingenuity in the form of a two hour hacking session at a hard, grey ice-boss atop a rock flake to produce a couple of meagre sloping ledges.

The first pitch on that next morning was 150' of total concentrated effort on four points, cruelly unreliable on brittle glassy ice. Further ice led into a rocky couloir which acted as a perfect funnel as, with only a few seconds warning, we regularly found ourselves completely enveloped in rushing, pouring snow. A narrows formed a steep technical pitch up a chimney and an icy crack which led to easy but very unstable snow which we followed to the crest of the spur. We tackled the steep rocky crest above. After 150' of this climbing a crisis of confidence occurred on a band of shattered rock which defied all attempts to place a secure belay. The wind was up again and chilled us to the bone as it blasted in from the north-west. So yet again we began the search for a bivouac place – but this ground promised none and above us reared the summit headwall. A descent had to be made from two pitons placed in excavated cracks. Frayed nerves jibbed at this manoeuvre – climbing down collapsing rock to an extremely exposed crest of the wall with no prospect of a bivvy ledge. Desperation forced us to scratch out two places to sit with feet hung over the void. At the time, more than any other on the climb, we were extremely close to suffering from severe exposure.

By dawn the wind had not abated and we struggled out of our sacks as the deep red sun rose out of the grey cloud-sea below. With choice of exit barred we tried another way and the secret was soon discovered to be a diagonal descent with aid from the rope in an adjacent couloir on our left. The final two pitches up the steep ice-glazed rocks had to be climbed with numbed hands, often bared to the rocks, with no piton to guide the way or even to secure a fall. Then suddenly the deep soft snow of the summit ridge was reached and instantly the world was changed. On the other side everywhere was brilliantly white with the southern aspect over Italy blinding and dazzling. The wind, that cruel cold wind, could be felt no more. We slumped and made a much needed brew a few feet beneath the summit of Pointe Croz.

The descent is another story in itself. Suffice to say that we survived a high speed fall down a steep snow slope after I had slipped, to be saved by the rope being caught on a small protruding spike of rock. A night in the hut commenced with an unrestrained attack on the plentiful liquor store until my head reeled The descent from the hut to the valley was serious enough with steep snow slopes, avalanche danger, a hidden ladder (which took 2 hours to locate) and soft, soggy snow in the valley floor.

LES GRANDES JORASSES – WALKER SPUR, AUGUST 1980 (EXTRACT)

ROBIN SEDGWICK

"A route to dream of, perhaps the finest in existence" -

– Gaston Rebuffat

"The most beautiful of the extreme alpine routes" -

– Reinhold Messner

"To feel the fascination of the Walker Spur..... is the most wonderful and, at the same time, the most overwhelming experience that a climber can have" –

– Walter Bonatti

245

A last check on the weather forecast at the Guides Bureau reveals "une orage avec tonnere dans la nuit" for the end of tomorrow (Thursday). The prospect of sitting out a few hours of storm doesn't unduly worry us as we've both got gore-tex bivvy bags and the forecast is a return to "Grand Beau Temps" for the Friday. The die is cast and we set off. Two hours stagger up the Mer de Glace and arrange a bivouac on a heap of moraine within half-an-hour of the foot of the face. Awake at four, a quick brew and set off for thebottom of the face where lights are already visible. After our usual route finding cock-ups and numerous detours and retracing of steps we arrive at the bergschrund to find a crowd of competitors for the route – 4 British, 2 Austrians and 3 Japanese – standing around doing very little. So we're out in front. Feeling very smug and efficient with our overtaking.

Two pitches on superb rock, peg pulling strenuosities on the Rebuffat Crack, and then steep icy mixed ground, both moving well, enjoying the climbing. More rock and moves right to the 75 metre diedre. Superb bridging and laybacking in two long pitches. More mixed ground leads to a fixed rope across a belt of slabs. As I'm preparing to follow, there's a sudden loud curse from Paul and a confession that our only copy of the route description is fluttering off to join his axe in the bergschrund. It was obviously going to be "one of those routes". The prospect of 1,000' of difficult rock with no description has little to commend it but the words of Bergführer Scott ringing in our ears spur us on "use your mountaineering sense and experience". We keep going. I arrive at the stance to find Paul belayed to a single, doubtful, in-situ peg that bends under finger pressure, the loose ground precluding any better belay. Sorting gear for the next lead we discover one of our ropes is jammed out of sight below the stance. Pulls and tugs from various angles fail to free it and we realise the only possibility is an abseil and prussic, a possibility too awful to contemplate in that position and with that belay. We keep going on a single 9mm rope. Two more rope lengths on easy loose ground brings us back to a notch in the spur crest at the top of the grey tower. With dusk gathering, two small lie-down ledges, about 4 feet apart, are a welcome sight and we settle in for the night.

I awake some time after four. Light is slowly returning and there's a strange weight on the bivvi-bag. A peer outside and all is revealed. The weight is an inch of fresh snow and the only view is a swirling maelstrom of white. We wait and it gets worse. Bangs and flashes with frightening simultaneity and torrents of ball-bearing like snow that cascades down the rocks. The hours slowly slip by in a daze. We take stock of our situation. We decide to sit tight until the storm stops, but after that the prospects are none too heartening. The idea of 2,500' retreat with a single 45 metre rope and a meagre stock of hardware is uninviting. The storm increases in intensity again as the day slides into afternoon and we pass the time cocooned in our own private worlds and thoughts. It slowly gets dark and the swirling snow continues as we settle down for our second night.

Daylight slowly returns and with it blue skies and a white panorama of snow-plastered rock. The temperature is right down and the snow, piled up around our respective ledges, has a hard frozen crust, so we decide to see if we can thumb a chopper. We spend the morning flashing mirrors and waving vainly at distant aeroplanes to no avail. In the early afternoon it slowly begins to dawn on us that, like buses in England, helicopters are never there when you want one. How long before our friends in the valley raise the alarm? To-morrow? The day after?

"Go for the top?" – "Aye". Paul leads off, smashing ice off the rocks, limbs heavy with inactivity and chill. "Christ it's plastered!". "Keep going". It's good to be going again after our 40 hours of inactivity. Mind and muscles warm to the task in hand and we find we're making reasonable progress. A pitch of tricky mixed and then steep cramponing up the triangular neve to the base of the couloir leading up left of the red tower. A groove on the left of the couloir is capped by an overhang. Paul swings out right on pegs, one pulls and he takes to the air. He bounces to a stop 20' lower but no damage is done. the sun's on us now and it's good to be climbing again, although it's now early evening and the possibility of another bivouac is looming large. A traverse below the tower and on up the couloir on its far side. Dusk is gathering rapidly but we keep moving up, hoping for a bivvi ledge. We're above 4,000 metres, there's a strong bitter wind and we need a ledge. Paul brings me up to the small ledge on the nose of the spur that's exposed to the full force of the wind. It's sheltered across to the right but this is the only available ledge and we decided it will have to do.

246

Dawn eventually arrives but the effort of getting out into the bitter wind and struggling to pack with frozen fingers is such that it's 8 a.m. before we're ready to go. Up to our right the summit of Point Whymper beckons, gleaming white in the morning sun. Our way leads straight up, delicate chimneys and snowed up couloirs for three or four rope lengths until a short snow rib leads to a pull-out onto the sunlit snowy expanse of the summit of Point Walker and it's all over. Italy lies in front of us, to our right Mont Blanc glistens in white splendour while to our left the distant Matterhorn rises majestically above the peaks of the Pennine Alps. Behind and below is the 4,000 feet of the Walker Spur. It feels good to be on top.

Already our thoughts are returning to steak and beer and cream cakes. We plod over to Point Whymper and the long descent to the distant valley below.

A TURN TO THE RIGHT

ROCK HUDSON   *Journal 1981/82*

On leaving the Vignettes Hut, the hard crisp snow indicated a good frost, whilst above, the twinkle of many stars foretold that we should enjoy a perfect alpine day. Chris Bryan set a good pace over the smooth slopes leading down to the Vignettes Glacier. Derek Mountford and I followed; not letting him gain on us, but neither being able to reduce that ten-metre lead.

It was the first route of the 1981 holiday and we were heading for the N.E. Ridge of the L'Eveque which appeared to be a suitable starter, an indication of the conditions on which to base our plans for the following weeks.

We gained on the other parties, passed them, and were quickly nearing the flanks of Mt. Petit Collon, which was now appearing in the pale light of dawn. Glance to the right. Curt comments, 'it looks all right!' followed by a similar detached 'aye, not bad'. We continued following the tracks. Some hidden pretext allowed a change of pace and thus we found ourselves closer together, enabling each of us to notice the others glancing to the right. The north face was now distinct, its icy features producing a beckoning line. We continued, perhaps without a clear sense of purpose, but we each knew. A glance in front showed the track trending to the left – we had turned to the right, but no comment was required from any of the party as we made our way up the steepening slopes below the north face.

The last rucksack was swung onto a back, the axe picked up, and we turned towards the centre of the face at a point to one side of the apex of blocks formed by an avalanche. We reached the steepening ground and moved together on hard nevè, the rhythm only being broken when negotiating the deep runnels. These soon passed into smooth slopes, which swept upwards to a distant skyline, while below the late parties were still following that now narrow ribbon of a path.

With increasing angle, we decided to pitch, and a peg was solidly placed, which allowed the leader to move off and quickly reach the next stance – another good peg. The steep front-pointing continued and, with increasing light, the panorama widened, while the distance to the adjacent right-hand ridge showed that we had gained considerable height.

For some while the snow conditions had deteriorated, the nevè reducing to only a thin skim loosely adhering to the now granular and brittle underlying ice. The pegs would not hold, sending off large splinters of ice, so only a scoop could be made at the contact of nevè and ice; a less than useful loop of rope being wrapped around the head of the axe, which had with great reluctance penetrated a few centimetres into the ice. Looking up the leader made progress more slowly, his crampons hiding all but the edges of his sac, while his axes swung with little effect into the now 'granular sugar'. The last few pitches had reached an angle of 55/60 degree and progress was even slower, but the last of the rock, perched on the adjacent ridge, was below us and we could cut to a snowy shoulder a little distance below the summit.

The sun was warm, the views rewarding, the sardines welcome, the water refreshing, while the 'turn to the right' the best decision of the day.

OLD BRENVA (EXTRACT)

JOHN O'REILLY   *Journal 1981/82*

"For Christ's sake, how much further Chris!?"

"Just keep going – almost there now!"

A none-too-gentle tug at my harness and I realise there are no more loops of rope to quietly lengthen the gap between myself and Rog. I stagger on – the state of stumbling exhaustion has existed for hours or at least it seems that way, as my detached mind wonders at the continued movement of my body.

A mixture of memories and emotions replace thoughts of physical efforts as the struggle continues – "you might as well get fit on a big climb as get fit for one" sounded so simplistic, so logical, in the alcohol-induced comfort of the Bar Nash as to be not worth contesting. The initial sweep of enthusiasm at the thought of the Brenva Face, dampened by doubts at the memory, and stronger image, of a close friend shivering, freezing, storm-bound and not surviving on the same route. The fleeting vision of sunny limestone crags......... dispelled abruptly by another knee-deep blunder, confirming the aching realisation of lack of fitness.

The knowledge begins to form, now too tired to argue or be annoyed about, that I had been conned – "Okay, I agree, we're in no fit state to climb the last 1,500 feet, but we will have to climb over that mound by those rocks before we can traverse" – the mound seemed to go on and on and on.......

.......the knowledge now complete as the mound no longer exists and Chris admits we're on the summit – the summit of Mont Blanc, the highest mountain in Europe, by a classic route – but there is no view, no euphoria, no summit photos, just a gentle throbbing head, aching limbs and the reality of an immediate, wind-buffeted, staggering descent – attempts to concentrate on the insidious tangle of stiffening ropes, views only of three meandering bodies, but visions of shelter, a brew, sleep, sunshine, warmth – strangely, perhaps naively, no doubts that we would get down safely.

Something else to look at and concentrate on now, as the swirling cloud and snow reveal occasional glimpses of the descent path, a few incongruous rock features and then the Hut – clumsy, stumbling crampons on steps slightly too steep, banks of snow outside and in, spreading a thin layer of intrusive spindrift over the creaking floor, a floor covered by the debris of countless grateful climbers – grateful for a windless haven, grateful for an imperfect tin box which would give any health inspector palpitations, grateful in some cases for another chance. The Vallot Hut, still over 14,000 feet on the now stormy flank of Mont Blanc, but a place to relax, to feed, to sleep.

Some thoughts on the Brenva Spur, Mont Blanc, August 1981.

Dave Helliwell, Roger Larkham, John O'Reilly, Chris Wilson.

OREADS IN THE ALPS – 1982

Compiled by Rock Hudson

CHAMPEX AREA

Ecandies Traverse	R. Larkham, P. Wragg, R. Hudson, R. Penlington
Mt. Dolent, E. Ridge	R. Larkham, P. Wragg, R. Hudson, R. Penlington
Traverse, La Portalet	K. Bryan, L. Bryan, J. Muskett, K. Muskett, M. Jaggs, M. Wren

Aiguille du Tour   K. Bryan, J. Muskett, M. Jaggs, J. Welbourn, G. Gadsby

Aiguille Purtscheller   D. Penlington, R. Penlington, R. Hudson
(South Ridge Integral)

Petite Velan   D. Penlington, R. Penlington, R. Hudson

Mont Velan   D. Penlington, C. Barnard, R. Hudson

CHAMONIX AREA

Drus, Traverse (D)   M. Wynne, R. Sedgwick, J. Blackledge & party

Moine, E. Face   J. Blackledge & Party
(Contamine Route)

Petite Jorasses W. Face   M. Wynne, R. Sedgwick
(1st half – more or less)

Aiguille de l'Midi   D. Owen, J. O'Reilly, J. Blackledge & party
(Couzy Route)

Traverse   M. Wynne, R. Sedgewick
(Midi to the Trident Hut)

l'Index, S. Ridge   D. Owen, J. O'Reilly

Aiguille de Peigne   D. Owen, J. O'Reilly
Papillons Ridge

Amone Slab, about 6   M. Wynne, R. Sedgwick
pitches or so
(quote: 'desperate')

Chapelle de la Gliere   M. Wynne, R. Sedgwick
(including new 3 pitch
direct start – 'Cosmic Traffic
Lights' E1 5a)

SWITZERLAND AND OTHER AREAS

Civetta, Solleder VI   P. Holden, H. Lancashire

Civetta, Phillip-Flamm   P. Holden, H. Lancashire
IV plus

Dent Blanche, N. Face   P. Holden, H. Lancashire

Mönch, N. W. Buttress   R. Tresidder & party
(Nollen Route)

Doges Palace, N. Face 1st British Ascent	P. Lancaster, S. Lancaster, P. O'Neill, J. O'Neill
Tour d'Ai, Chimney & the Arete (Leysin)	S. Carter & party
Miroir Slab, Direct	S. Carter & party
Aiguille Argentiere	S. Carter & party
Arete de Belvedere (Verdon)	P. Lancaster, P. O'Neill
Traverse, Bridge of Sighs 1st British ascent	P. Lancaster, S. Lancaster, P. O'Neill, J. O'Neill D. Sedgwick, D. Parnham, L. Freestone, Dot's Mum
Ciarfaron, N. E. Ridge	K. Bryan, L. Bryan
Grand Serra	K. Bryan, L. Bryan
Casnil, E. Ridge (Walter Rische Route)	K. Gregson, M. Pearce
Monte Rosso, Traverse (WNW to S. Ridge)	K. Gregson, M. Pearce
Traverse, (N to S) Gorge d'Ardeche	R. Larkham, P. Wragg
Mt. Argentine (nr. Bex)	D. Penlington, R. Penlington, R. Hudson
Rosenlanistock Engelhörner	S. Carter & party
Ecrins, N. Face, Whymper Route	R. Larkham, P. Wragg
Mont Aiguille, S.W. Pillar, Vercors	R. Larkham, P. Wragg
Via Ferrata de Guiseppo Tofana di Mezzo	D. Wright, A. Ames
Cima Grande, NNE Ridge 1st Half (hard half)	D. Wright, A. Ames

And last but not least, a British attempt on the "Telepherique Route" to the Plan de l'Aiguille – retreated due to bad weather. The retreat involved two stormy bivvies at the Pierre d'Orthaz before a retreat to base camp near Monte Chair Ladder.

D. Helliwell, C. Wilson

THE ALPINE SEASON – 1982 (EXTRACT)

ROCK HUDSON   *Journal 1983*

At the same time, another epic was unfolding on the Schreckhorn. Gordon and Bev. took the E.S.E. Ridge, which was generally steep, loose rock. This and the overall conditions caused them to bivi on the way down. Bev had a pleasant night – Gordon did not. This may have been due to the large amount of extra equipment Bev. was carrying. Gordon was somewhat taken aback by both the contents of Bev's sack and his explanations for same. The items included:–

eye shadow	"not as heavy as goggles"
two spare helmets	"for soup, in case you drop the billy"
spare sleeping bag	"stops first bag being spoiled on ground"
spare piton hammer	"in case normal one too light for large pitons"
2nd spare piton hammer	"in case of loss of tin-opener"
ice axe	"in case snow found hidden beneath scree slope on a rock climb"
Heinz, Crosse & Blackwell, Tesco & Co-op Beans	"you might be climbing with a faddy buggar"
just a small bundle of firewood	"in case primus/bluet dropped and, in any case it gives a homely atmosphere and don't forget, it's Swiss National Day"
dehydrated water	"only inexperienced mountaineers would forget this on a rock route"
35mm, 2.5", half-plate, full-plate cameras & assorted lenses	"I believe it's the only way I shall ever win the photo competition"
Italian, Austrian & Nepalese etc. money	"you might descend by another route"

Bev. Abley and Gordon Wright — *Editor.*

LIVING ON THE FRONT LINE
(EIGERWAND WITH ROB TRESIDDER) (EXTRACT)

ROBIN SEDGWICK   *Journal 1983*

The grey dawn half-light complemented the atmosphere of the third icefield perfectly. Black, glassy ice, embedded with grit and stones, overhung by dark, beetling rock walls. It exuded an atmosphere of sleeping menace. Above and beyond, the Ramp gave four superb pitches on sound rock, the previous evening's trepidations and misgivings dissipated by the smooth flow of movement and progress. The waterfall chimney, a black overhanging nasty, gave a hundred feet of bridging and peg pulling, half blinded by spray, icy water gushing down sleeves and gaiters, a memorable, magnificent pitch. The ice bulge proved to be a wicked little slot between ice and rock, very steep, very Scottish; thrutched by me, wedged much more elegantly by Rob, to an awkward pull out onto the Ramp icefield. A further rope length, curving away right, led to the Brittle Ledges. Following this latter pitch, I heard a crack and looked up to see the sky black with stones. I instinctively flattened against the ice and, seconds later, my very being was engulfed by a total assault on the senses, as rocks whistled, cracked, whirred and thumped off the ice around me, smashing against helmet and rucksack. A sharp crushing blow on the left shoulder, inhaling dust, an acrid smell in my nostril; a timeless period of detachment and waiting, of split seconds transformed into hours; nothing lasts forever, but everything lasts for some time. Slowly, the veil was lifted, the air cleared and silence descended, save for the rattling of small splinters and pebbles still dancing down the ice below me, and Rob's worried shouts from above. Apart from the pain in my shoulder, I appeared to be o.k. – I yelled back and climbed up to join him on the Brittle Ledges.

Two more pitches and we reached the Traverse of the Gods. An excellent lie-down ledge with leaning back wall appeared to offer a protected bivouac and, despite it being early afternooon, we decided to call it a day, as the Traverse and the Spider beyond were undergoing constant barrage.

The White Spider is a magnificent place, an experience to be treasured as a little gem amidst a handful of life's select memories. At the time, a blur of dry mouth, cramping calf-muscles, and radar-sharp senses alert for the by-now commonplace warnings of oncoming stones. A cathedral-like atmosphere, the very epitome of the Eiger, hemmed in by seemingly impossible cliffs with 6,000 feet of clean exposure sucking ones heels towards the meadows of Alpiglen. The Spider is indeed an awesome place. I felt almost as if entering a shrine as I cramponed up to Rob's ice screw belay. As if respecting our benediction, the Spider stayed quiet and we scuttled up a further two rope lengths to relative safety at the foot of the Exit Cracks. A brief halt for a bowel movement, probably brought on by having to hop up the last 30 feet of ice on one crampon and then we were off and away, galloping up the first easy pitches of the Exit Cracks. Rob got the Quartz Crack, possibly the hardest pitch on the route, steep and strenuous, with a thin delicate slab exit at the top, led and seconded, gratefully, without rucksacks. Above, I continued left to the pulpit and a diagonal abseil.

Postscript

KLEINE SCHEIDEGG;

The Eiger was unchanged and yet subtly different. A burning ambition and a sense of purpose had gone forever and irretrievably. I looked down at the fresh scars on my hands, impressions which would soon heal. The impressions in my mind would last longer, though they too would face with time. Fading memories and a set of colour transparencies – is that all you're left with?

Of Air Beds, Harvesters and Gastronomy (*Extract*)

Colin Barnard   *Journal 1984*

Back in the fleshpots, yet more eating and boozing, then off at 7.30 on the Friday morning, to arrive back at Stafford in the wee small hours of Saturday. Oh yes, you ask, what about the air beds and the harvesters? Well a recurring memory of the holiday was of lying in the tent, gazing at the Harvest Spiders in the roof, whilst Rock blew up his leaky air bed. The latter tended to subside nearly completely within a matter of hours. In the same time the Harvesters shifted perhaps one inch. What do they do for a living? I mean, how do they eat? Perhaps they chew holes in antiquated air beds. Something certainly does!

BRENVA, OR ABBO GIVES UP SMOKING (*EXTRACT*)

KEITH GREGSON   *Journal 1985*

Another few minutes and not only is the air blue but the snow round about has taken on the hue of a well matured Stilton. I set off back and eventually see two points of light approaching and we exchange words – short sharp ones! My frustration wins and explodes "How the hell are we going to get up this thing if we have to bugger about standing on the glacier for hours on end?" Rock says, he's lost the spike off the end of his ice axe – I tell him it's nothing to what he's about to lose, and it's about time he bought some bloody kit which had its beginnings in the twentieth century instead of mending his museum pieces with wode and baler twine. Abbo acts as peacemaker and we fix Rock up with a north wall hammer (with spike) which he threatens to test on me. The storm passes, and then begins again as we launch ourselves in the tracks of those who should not be in front.

We passed one or two parties before reaching the bergschrund under the col and another group as we forced our way to the foot of the ridge. The situation at this point was incredible. The moonlight gave an ethereal effect to the surrounding peaks with the Peuterey Ridge and the Eckpfeiler dominating the view to the left and the Brenva Face stretching above us. All the mountain features were in sharp relief with every snowflake intent on being a star. The storm below continued but up here all was quiet, as though in anticipation, but of what? Were we being lured into a trap, was the storm waiting to catch us on the summit?

I must admit that my motivation generally, whilst on a mountaineering route, is geared to an early completion, and I seldom relax until the route and the descent is completed. I suppose that most people share these feelings, though I could be wrong. There were certainly occasions on this route when Abbo would have cheerfully killed for a fag break, and I am sure that on this occasion we all shared the feeling that conditions were remarkable. The higher we climbed, the more we were able to see that the only place in Europe with fine weather was the summit of Mont Blanc! The storm wasn't just confined to the Italian side for we could now see flashes of lightning to the West beyond the Bionnassay.

We eventually reached the final serac barrier which was enormous and we were glad of the tracks left by the previous parties. There were no really difficult sections, except perhaps the odd steep ice of twenty feet or so, but finding the correct route through the seracs was not obvious – it was still dark. Suddenly the slope decreased and we climbed out of a snow filled crevasse onto the summit. We'd done it.

On the descent from Mont Blanc du Tacul we did the British thing and had a brew in a glorious snow bowl. It was the first stop in eight hours and Abbo's first fag. A French party came by, and not realising that we were on the down-line, made with the sarcasm "Zees is no time fur le tay, allez! O les Anglais!" Abbo dropped his fag. They were put in the picture pretty damn quick I can tell you!

An account of the ascent of the Old Brenva Route on August 8th 1979 by Chris Bryan, John Hudson (Rock), Stuart Godfrey (Abbo) and Keith Gregson.

Ice Station Solvay

Rob Tresidder *Journal 1990*

We were all curled up in our bags in the cold pit at the bottom of the hut watching our breath sail into the warm high roof. All day the radio in the corner had crackled with more or less urgent messages – arcane signals of life in another world.

Suddenly........

"Allo, Solvay Hütte, 'Allo Solvay Hütte. Bitte antworten."

I leaped out of my pit and struggled hurriedly to decipher the instructions on the red box which told which buttons to press in what order to transmit.

I heard my own voice, tense with drama, sounding like the chief engineer addressing the skipper on the bridge after a direct hit to the engine room in one of those interminable naval films from the Second World War.

The radio operator wanted to know how many we were and then advised that the forecast for the following day was very bad and we should descend as early as possible. "Over and out".

Did I really say that?

The weather seemed pretty awful now and it would be worse tomorrow. Suddenly we were transformed from a slightly bored, just international quintet, who had been swopping yarns and jokes to wile away the long wait, into a closely knit group of men determined to fight to the bitter end for our survival.

Jan from Czechoslovakia had already had one night in the hut before climbing alone to the summit and back in seven hours. Peter and Brett from Kendal were on the route they had come out to do. Bobby and I, along with numerous others, had found conditions on the North Face unpromising. The ice was very hard and the snow was too fine and dry to stick.

On the North Face too little snow, on the Hörnli ridge far too much, so our climb to the Solvay Hütte the day before had been slow and had felt insecure. We were holed up in the hut because the early morning weather had been so appalling; tomorrow, we were being told, would be even worse

We rose early but not very early, kitted up in the hut and then emerged onto the tiny concrete terrace half banked up with snow. I was strangely glad to climb down off this, the scene of windswept nocturnal terrors on the journey to the bog, overhanging the north face.

Some easy soloing guided by Jan avoided the hard pitches of two days before and then the abseils started.

My hands had been frozen for the first half hour and then all of a sudden, the wind dropped, the sky cleared to give splendid panoramic views: Breithorn, Monte Rosa and then right round to the Dent d'Herens. The sun came out and we were buzzed by two inquisitive helicopters. The whole "epic" suddenly assumed a dream like quality. Had I been a victim of a kind of mass hysteria?

I thought back to other occasions when my judgement might have been interfered with by outsiders. On almost my first Oread meet, at Gardom's, I was warned off soloing a route by a senior Oread, later to be a President, with the advice: "I've seen Pete Holden back off that." I resented the interference but retreated in the belief that I was acting independently.

More recently a friend of long but infrequent experience expressed dismay that he had not been dissuaded by members of his new club from soloing the route he subsequently fell off. He seemed to me to be out of touch with "the ethics and etiquette" of our sport which have caused all of us at one time or another to guard our tongue even when confronted by dangerous bad practice.

In the afternoon and back in the security of the Hörnli hut, the storm returned with increased ferocity.

ERITRICHIUM NANUM

King of the Alps, Lord of the Heights,
Above the Pousett cwm.
Your small blue petals flutter; in the
Wind of the afternoon, the wind
Of an eagle's downward touch,
As he passes you in flight.
Oh, if only you had flight my friend, if only you had flight.
You'd soar above the snowy alps,
The icefall and the sky,
And land in some green meadow
With water running by.
But you would not linger long my friend
For you would surely die, in that
Meadow with the buttercups
And the waters running by.
High, high above is your domain
With the seekers of the heights,
The Chamoix and the Ibex
The Eagles and the Kites.
But when the great north blizzards blow,
They flee the spindrifts fun
And leave this world to you my friend,
You've won, you've won, you've won.
King of the Alps, bluest of blue,
Small flower of a thousand dreams,
This is your kingdom here in the snow
Not down where the buttercups gleam.

Gordon Gadsby

IN MATTERS EDITORIAL

In short, in matters editorial, contentious and deplorable
I am the very model of modern mountain phantasmagorial.....

with apologies to W. S. Gilbert

Newsletters, in much the same style, containing editorial, meets reports, general articles, and club gossip continued up to and including 1975. Radcliffe passed on the editorial chair in 1973 to Paul Bingham, who carried it for two years, until David Appleby took over for a brief period in 1975/76.

This period was also notable for the publication of *Climb if you Will* in 1974. Largely inspired by the death of Geoff Hayes, it told the story of the first twenty five years. Its publication was principally inspired by the late Jean Russell (Editor) and her team: Jack Ashcroft, Paul Gardiner, Gordon and Margaret Gadsby, Mike Berry and Anne Hayes.

At that time I was not very supportive of their aspirations and suspected illusions of grandeur, and an element of pretension, after only 25 years. But I was probably wrong since the book, of very limited circulation, has become much sought after and, on arrival at this half century year, a very valuable source.

For reasons too obscure for current exhumation, the old style newsletter died, but an Annual Journal (editor: Jill Gregson) appeared for 1977 and, from this date, annual Journals came out spasmodically: 1978/79/80 (Ed. R. Sedgwick), 1981/82/83 (Ed. J.O'Reilly), 1984 (Ed. J. Hudson, C. Wilson), 1985/86/87 (Ed. J. Hudson), and 1990/92 (Ed. R. Gilbert).

Editor

EDITORIAL (EXTRACT)

Journal 1981/82

But what of the future – the mainstay of any strong, progressive mountaineering club is its calendar of Meets and the attendances achieved on those Meets. It is to be hoped that a balance can continue to be achieved here which not only caters for all tastes but which tends to unite the various sections within the Club. For this to be effective, a change in outlook is called for in some sections of the Club – too many Members glance through the Meets List and mentally write off half the Meets as not being for them.If everyone was a little more flexible in outlook and was prepared to try Meets, which, in previous years, they have always missed, they might be surprised at the results. The Members who tend towards the walking and mountaineering Meets could well find they fare quite well on what are ostensibly the 'rock athlete's' Meets – conversely, the latter might discover that there are rewards to be gained from a good mountaineering day which they had not thought possible. In the long run, this could only serve to strengthen the Oread as a Club and to avoid a tendency towards, to quote the words of a previous Editor, 'an amorphous association'. We must all remain aware of the need for the expanding Oread to grow together as a club, hence maintaining the spirit which has characterised it in recent years.

John O'Reilly

EDITORIAL (EXTRACT)

Journal 1983

A late night discussion at a recent M.A.M. Meet threw up one of those perennial topics of conversation in established clubs – a topic that I commented on in last year's Editorial – why do younger members not go on the mountain/walking orientated Meets? Ignoring the reverse argument, which is probably just as valid, I looked around the people in the discussion. It occurred to me that the younger members who attend regularly on a Tuesday evening at the Rowing Club, would probably have a fairly fixed view of a lot of these older members – they would be glued to an armchair (emerging only with difficulty to heckle at the A.G.M or Dinner) , hero-worship Mallory or Kirkus, and think that chalk has got something to do with Dover or blackboards (the President, despite attending at the Rowing Club, seems strangely to also hold this latter view).

Given that it is not possible for everyone in the Club to attend the Rowing Club, this communication problem (which is what it boils down to) could be alleviated somewhat if members made more use of both the Journal and, particularly, the Newsletter. Without undermining the Journal and its usefulness in this respect, I feel that the power of the immediacy of the Newsletter is overlooked by many members. Where are the short post-Meet reports and snippets of information that everyone should be contributing to the Newsletter? So, for 1984/85, don't be shy – write a few items for the Newsletter each month and give the Meets Secretary the problem of what to leave out.

John O'Reilly

JOURNALS 1981-1990
"INTERNATIONAL ROCK ATHLETES . . .YOUTH" (*EXTRACT*)

PAUL GARDNER   *Journal 1981/82*

Le Demande is one of the longest routes in the Verdon, making its compelling way up the full height of the Gorge. To reach its foot involves a walk in from the Couloir Samson through the intense darkness and hidden puddles of the tourist tunnel. Pete Holden, our team coach, had woken us before dawn in the frosty cold and driven us to the tunnel end. He left us just as the sun was coming over the horizon melting thefrost and warming the air.

We had met Pete in the bar a few days earlier. He and Howard had been driven off the Eiger – it was too warm. We were all camped on some open ground by the river after being driven off the campsite by the mayor – the campsite wasn't open because it had no hot water, the solar panel being elsewhere. The mayor was very excited about us being there, so much so that we couldn't understand his machine-gun delivery. We heard rumours of his anger and experienced it in the early morning of our second day. Robin attempted to get him to slow down but he just wandered off – something snapped and the teacher in Robin came out – "Hey, come here sunshine, I'm talking to you!" Unlike the lower band fourth years at Bemrose, he was not impressed and went off to throw stones at some Swiss next to us. We loaded everything into the van and moved off down the road.

Pitch followed pitch with complete disregard for Livesey's attempt to define or grade them. Only sections stand out in the mind and even their order is now a jumble. There was one pitch where progress involved scrambling from one twisted sapling to the next, barely touching the rock for twenty or thirty feet, marvelling out loud at the strength of these twigs. Stances came and went, some spacious, others a peg and a horizontal, twisted twiglet. One such stance separated two magnificent groove pitches; leaning out and bridging onto 'goutte d'eau', clipping pegs, deciding which ones to miss to avoid running out of krabs after half a pitch, feeling the sharp-edged holds bite into the pads of our fingers, being aware of the river getting further and further below, but feeling so secure that the space was part of the joy.

Finally this came to an end as the crack, in a remarkable short distance, became a chimney. However, the evil moment when the chimney had to be tackled was put off for a while by a traverse out of the line to avoid a desparate struggle in an off-width, overhanging chimney-crack. A little overhang led to a beautiful airy traverse back in above the monster crack. A stone dislodged by Robin bounded clear to the foot of the route without touching anything. Delightful though it was, the traverse must have been superb before some hammer-swinging vandal had smashed the pockets'sides in to 'improve' the holds, marking the grey rock with yellow scars. After this the chimney was unavoidable.

Pete had briefed us on these chimneys. "Absolutely smooth", he said; "no gear" he said. When he was there, Chris Gibb had failed. We gasped "Chris Gibb!" He had knee-jammed the back crack deep inside, in shorts. "In shorts!" Our eyes were as wide as saucers. "No gear", he said. "Don't bother taking any big stuff", he said. Fortunately, we disregarded this piece of advice. Take a number nine hex.

Actually, the walls of the chimney were not smooth, rather they had the texture of pebble-dash. After this pleasant surprise, the thirty feet to the first runner did not seem too far, particularly as its placement was obvious every time you looked up.

The top came very suddenly. One moment I was pulling onto a ledge with a short wall behind and the next I was on the top. A deeply channelled limestone pavement stretched down to the thorn bushes which masked the road. We had finished the route. Now we could look forward to the bar.

257

Climbing the Napes Needle (*Extract*)

A. A. Milne   *Journal 1983*

Ken and I went to the Lakes together in August 1902, staying at a farmhouse in Seathwaite. We had decided to do a little rock climbing. We knew nothing about it, but we had brought a rope, nailed boots, and the standard book by Owen Glynne Jones. The climbs in this book were graded under such headings as Easy, Medium, Moderately Stiff and Extremely Stiff. We decided to start with a Moderately Stiff one, and chose Napes Needle on Great Gable, whose charm is that on a postcard it looks Extremely Stiff. Detached by the hands of a good photographer from its context, it becomes a towering pinnacle rising a thousand feet above the abyss. Roped together, since it seemed to be the etiquette, Ken and I would scale this mighty pinnacle, and send postcards to the family.

We were a little shy about the rope when we started out, carrying it lightly over the arm at first, as if we had just found it and were looking for its owner.... and then more grimly over the other arm, as one who makes for some well, down which some wanderer has fallen. The important thing was not to be mistaken for what we were: two novices who had been assured that a rope made climbing less dangerous, when, in fact, they were convinced that it would make climbing very much more so. There was also the question of difficulty. To get ourselves to the top of the Needle would be Moderately Stiff; but it was (surely) Extremely Stiff to expect us to drag arope up there too. I felt all this more keenly then Ken, because it had already been decided, anyhow by myself, that I was to 'lead'. Not only had I won the Gymnastics Competition Under -14 in 1892 but, compared with Ken's, my life was now of no value. Ken had just got engaged to be married. If I led, we might both be killed (as seemed likely with this rope) or I might be killed alone, but it was impossible that I would ever be breaking the news to his lady of an accident which I had callously survived. I was glad of this, of course; but I should have liked it better if it had been I who was engaged and Ken who was being glad.

An extract by A. A. Milne from his autobiography 'It's Too Late Now'. published in 1939. Submitted by Gordon Gadsby.

A somewhat offbeat inclusion in an Oread Journal unless you are aware that Gadsby was understudying for Christopher Robin in the Oread Panto. Due to a "confusion of authors" he ended up playing Capt. Hook to P. Janes' Peter Pan — *Editor.*

Further adventues with Poo and Tigger:–

The Belper Crack

30' HVS 4c

In the convent grounds on the E. side of the A6, just to the N. of the bridge over the railway at the N. end of the town.

Takes the obvious overhanging crack on the highest part of the crag. Not well protected.

First recorded ascent: R. Tresidder, R. Larkham, 16.5.84

This is the eyecatching crack on the left as you approach Belper after being rained off at Matlock. Parking at the foot of the climb.

TOM THUMB – PRINCE OF DARKNESS (*EXTRACT*)

BRIAN WEST   *Journal 1983*

I first met the Oread about seventeen years ago. After walking from Wirksworth to an evening Meet at Cratcliffe, I was duly recruited to a rope of half-a-dozen hopefuls who were to attempt Bramley's Traverse.

After much heaving and ho-ing we puffed onto that capacious ledge and there clanked to a halt like a goods train at the buffers. Les Langworthy led the abyss, followed trustingly by Howard Johnson – all blow-wave and tight trousers. Then it was me. Or rather, it wasn't me. One look down that groove and I decided to stay; and, despite all coaxing, stay I did.

With typical Oread solicitude, I was jettisoned and left to my fate. However, I did not go down immediately. I sat for some considerable time on that ledge, fascinated by this Oread chain-gang as it shuffled past, happy in its bondage. In a way I am sitting there still.

"Enough of this ancient history!", I hear you cry. "Who is this Langworthy wally? Who is this Johnson wimp? This is 1983!"

Alright, its 1983; a Wednesday night, and I'm at Cratcliffe again. Unfortunately, so is everyone else. The fair flower of youth blossoms on every conceivable line, and on some that are quite inconceivable. I recognise one wilted bloom levitating mysteriously up an improbable bulge. It is O'Reilly, giving a fine impression of a haul-sack to an unappreciative Martin Roome. Martin hangs tight to his belay; teeth clenched, hernia imminent.

Now all this is bad news, as they say. My repertoire at Cratcliffe is not very extensive. It finishes, quite symbolically I always think, where adjectives fail and numbers begin. Furthermore, I am climbing with Helen (she of the stretch jeans and maidenly blush), and Helen is no mean climber if kept beyond the grasps of her twin gods, Beer and Chips. So here I am, with a personable young lady to impress, and nothing in sight that I can actually climb.

A glance along the crag confirms the worst. I am left with either "Savage Messiah" or some gem quaintly entitled "Reticent Mass Murderer". I can hardly think that either will be suitable for persons of a nervous disposition.

A FAIRY TALE

Anon   *Journal 1984*

Once upon a time in the far flung right hand corner of Drinkbok galaxy on the outer reaches of the known universe was a small pink planet called Dorea upon which the Doreans lived in peace and harmony for around $257\frac{3}{4}$ glinks, (approx. $5,000\frac{1}{4}$ of our years). They were led by a president and his inner cabinet but were greatly influenced by an ancient guru of the Fuzzyfiz sect – Grumpencrapp the miserable. A short portly chap who was followed by several disciples of the same sect.

These Fuzzyfeeze had long ago lost the ability to speak coherently and communicated by a series of knowledgeable grunts. This was for the sole reason that they participated in the disgusting habit of seitt smoking. A seitt was a massive bowl on the end of a stem in which was incinerated huge amounts of weeds, herbs and grom dung from which was emitted great palls of stunkensmoker. These palls had gathered over the glinks to form massive clouds, and because there wasn't any wind on Dorea (due to it having two axes and not knowing which way to turn) the Fuzzyfeeze had lost touch with the other inhabitants and only communicated with the other members of their sect via their peculiar gutteral grunt.

Around about the fifteenth millenium a.p. there came from the neighbouring galaxy a huge comet which had a cataclismic effect on Dorea. For this comet which had been called Dicda-Odd-Dangler, passed so close that the jetstream from its tail set up mighty winds across the surface of Dorea clearing all clouds of stunkensmoker from sight, and for the first time for many many glinks, in fact the very first time for the younger generations, all Doreans could see their little pink planet.

Now the youngsters were beholden at the marvellous sights before them, but not so the Fuzzyfeeze for much had changed since they last cast their eyes about themselves, and as the scientists had calculated that the winds would last for the next 500 glinks they were sore afraid. The youngsters felt free at last, but the fuzzyfiz sect felt naked and exposed and petitioned their government to take some action. The cabinet thought hard and long and finally made a decision. El Presidente Vastmember decreed that a massive windbreak called a musson would be built and behind it the land would be divided into a grid. Each square of the grid would be allotted to a Fuzzyfiz so that he could smoke his seitt in contemplative peace. He would be compelled to record his position on the grid on a document. This great constitutional document was then known as the seitting plan, and until the planet split along the fault line between its two axes, everyone lived happily ever after.

Things Don't Change (Extract)

Rock Hudson   Journal 1984

The same old argument, people wanting change, others that don't. The comments on levels of skill, involvement, good membership or commitment. The pettiness in trying to uphold a minor so-called tradition, when the important point is to still be part of a greater one. Are we to allow members to sit on a fence and look at the view instead of being in that view? Time will only tell, when we find ourselves in that view, with its then welcome fence to sit on.

Tan-y-Coed Llaeth

Brian West   Journal 1984

It is a sodden, sullen night, windy and Welsh-wet. Rain-assailed, tight-nailed casements weep wantonly, lamenting a long lost line to a long lost estuary.

Hush now; it is Tan-y-Wyddfa and the Oreads are sleeping. The hopeless, the hopeful, the damning, the damned; all tomato-saucily sardined in beer-black oxygen-lack torpor.

Come closer; peep into Aran, into Clogwyn, into Hebog; peer at rows of sleep-sacked, cheese-toastie-packed bodies duck-downed in sweet and sour slumber.

So its seems; only you can see their hopes, their fears, their dreams........

Pete Scott is suffering. A cold sweat beads his brow. It is raining on his Gore-Tex.

A similar sweat beads O'Reilly's brow. It is raining on Pete Scott's Gore-Tex.

Martin has a visitor. No it is not Ingrid. It is the Ghost of Craps Past. Martin re-lives actionreplays of those matchless motions of yesteryear, when the world was young, fresh and just waiting to be crapped on.

Sighing contentedly, O'Reilly gently caresses taut swelling curves; curves that belong to the wallet pop-rivetted to his armpit. The wallet bulges with Radder's insurance money. John is on to a good thing. Whose gear shall he set fire to next?

Tip-to-Toe in figure-flattering black, Radders is hanging from a helicopter. Torn by self-doubt, he stares indecisively at the snow beneath. Chris is worried; are his skis quite the right length for the job, and what does he do with the Cadbury's Milk Tray when he gets there?

Martin has a visitor. No, it is not Ingrid. It is the Ghost of Craps Present. Like the Andrex dog, Martin romps in a surrealistic splendour of soft tissues, shimmering pink, white, blue...... Even though he can still outcrap Maurice, and the cool kiss of Twyfords Adamant has lost none of its allure, the reckless days of Izal Medicated are but a fond memory.

Doormouse-deep in her bag, Helen smoulders on. With her metabolism fuelled to magmatic intensity by liquid carbohydrate, she has achieved earth-orbit and now lies dormant, a dying ember. She dreams of more beer......

Dave Wright has had more beer and is orbiting Silverstone. His adoring public roars its approval as he laps Niki Lauda for the second time. Showing masterly control, Dave waves nonchalantly to the cheering crowds. Al Ames, not yet quite so disciplined, lurches reluctantly to an unscheduled pit-stop.

Martin has a visitor. No, it is not Ingrid. It is the Ghost of Craps to Come, looking remarkably like Ray Handley. Martin recoils in haemorrhoidal horror at the Savlon-scented, pebble-dashed portrayal of his anal future.

Pete Scott smiles. The rain has passed, and through the thinning mists a girl bounds bouncily towards him, her long hair flying, her arms outstretched.

"Peter, Peter", she cries, longingly.

Ineffable joy flares in Scott's bony breast. It is Clare!

The smile freezes; that jaw juts. In six-million dollar slow-motion, Clare is about to plunge into a puddle left by the rain. Should he sweep down his Gore-Tex before her? Oh cruel dilemma!

The smile relaxes. Fair wear and tear!

Black dread clutches at O'Reilly's innards. His armpit throbs.

The smile is now confident. There's always the BMC insurance. Down goes the Gore-Tex!

The smile slips. Set to welcome his heart's desire, Pete stares aghast as Clare springs past and on into the mists. There is more than one Peter in the world, it seems; and more than one rip in the Gore-Tex. Scott is having a rought night.

Martin has a visitor. Yes, it is!

Field-Marshal Fisher, Lord of our far-flung battle-line, receives grim news from the Front. The Fuzzy-Wuzzies have taken Smethwick; the Celtic riff-raff are poised to cross the Stour. Corporal Kipling groans in despair.

"Bear up man, bear up!" barks Lord Fisher, stiffening what passes for an upper lip.

Remember, Rudyard, if you can keep your head when all about you are losing theirs ..... "On your way, Gunga!"

A sharp cut from his Malacca speeds a native runner out into a hail of Welsh Nationalist spite; a gunboat is despatched to Stourbridge.

"Grease 'em, baby!" snarls Fisher.......

Ego-driven mercilessly, our hapless players blunder on through the mental maze. Outside the deep, dark, deep-dark night drips on into a wet-slate-gleaming dawn; the rain tempers to a trickle.

Looming out of the sea-fret, Y Garn blows its ballast-tanks and surges skywards, slicing the cloud-wrack in conning-tower majesty.

The Oreads will soon be waking. These mobile, expressive features will slowly congeal, setting into the final familiar masks of everyday. Rebelling, the mutinous neuroses will be thrust deep into spiritual stuff-sacks; horizontal and vertical holds will be adjusted to stabilize the various images for the coming day. Let us be discreet and leave the Oread to its cosmetics.

Already bladders are signalling frantically and Gordon Wright is making an infernal row in the kitchen. Helen is preparing for re-entry, and Radders will soon be down, impossibly hearty, all doubts about the Milk Tray Box completely erased. Fisher will lie long abed, testing his words of the day for euphoney and resonance, before articulating his inanities like some hesitant blackbird essaying the first querulous notes of the dawn chorus.

It is time to go. Remembering not to stub you toe on the chunk of Snowdonia that lies athwart the hall, tip-toe quietly down and ....soft! What's this? Pondering great truths, a noble youth lies austerely before the fireplace; a jug of pure spring-water at his elbow; a crust fogotten, on the floor. A young Greek god, taken unawares?

No, it's only me.

Now we know – that empty box of Milk Tray in the drying room — *Editor.*

THIRTY YEARS BACK *(EXTRACT)*

ROCK HUDSON   *Journal 1985*

For 1955, there are 18 reports on club meets lodged in the Oread Log Book. These show that 40% of them were in Derbyshire, no doubt due to the lack of private transport to go elsewhere. However, despite this, 30% of meets were in Wales and further 10% in the Lakes. Generally meets provided the opportunity for undertaking a spectrum of activities which are appropriate to members of a mountaineering club.

On 55% of meets rock climbing predominated, while walking took place on 60%. Snow and ice climbing was only practised on 5% of meets – again due to the difficulty of reaching the mountains. Or perhaps because it was a poor winter. Interesting to note that for the year only 5% had a social content.

I checked up on the weather reported in these meet reports and found 20% were blessed with very good conditions. 20% had good weather, whilst only fair conditions accounted for 20%. Bad to terrible weather was reported for the rest.

One author complains about the lack of support, a sentiment still heard from someone who has taken the trouble to organise a meet, only to have it very poorly attended.

New members will not unfortunately have the pleasure of staying at the Barnsley M.C. hut on the Snake Pass, for hill creep has made it unsafe and it had to be closed – a great pity. As an innocent youth (some still say so) it was here that I first came into contact with mixed sex sleeping arrangements and that mad rush down to the pub, in this case the Snake Inn, after a day out on the hills.

I'm really just a 'young-un', thus lacking in a vast amount of Oread history and of course associated mountaineerig folk-lore of the past – omissions for which I apologise. I don't know the derivation of the name Chinese Buttress, but I know some older Oread will. With all these accumulated years of being part of our sport, they must surely hold a vast store of knowledge. Perhaps one of them would like to answer the above point on Chinese Buttress, or on any other facet concerned with the Oread's past. The editor looks forward to future contributions.

He didn't have to wait too long. A contribution by Jack Ashcroft in the 1986/87 Journal provided detailed evidence (with illustrations) for the naming of Chinese Wall. I would also argue about Hudson's sense of priorities. The "mad rush down to the pub" generally preceded the "mixed sex sleeping arrangements" — *Editor.*

BULLSTONES '85

BRIAN WEST   *Journal 1985*

Having been importuned quite relentlessly by the Hon. Editor to provide a Meet Write-up, I have had to cobble together something to shut him up. Unfortunately I can raise little enthusiasm for Write-Ups, Journals and the like. To my mind climbers exhibit an amazing conceit, childish almost beyond belief, that their doings are of surpassing significance, their reports awaited eagerly by a world agog. In most circles the subject 'What I did on my holidays' is exhausted usually towards the end of Junior school. It will be less tedious for me, and probably for you if I write not about this Bullstones in particular, but of Bullstones in general.

It occurs to me that there must be a substantial number of what Radcliffe would call 'activists' (a nebulous term referring to the constituents of one's clique) to whom Bullstones connotes nothing at all. Well, the name Bullstones belongs properly to an outcrop on the south flank of Outer Edge, and by association to the cabins once situated nearby. Oread meets were held here until the cabins fell into desuetude and were eventually wrecked. Both the name and the meet live on: a winter weekend traversing the hills, carrying all one's gear and generally roughing it. A form of back-packing, I suppose, if one wishes to use the dreadful neologism.

As a digression, it is interesting to note that these shooting cabins came in pairs, or, if only one, it would be divided internally with separate entrances. The Gentlemen would use one cabin, the others the other. Interior fittings will usually show which one was used by which, but in cases of complete demolition a statistical analysis of the surrounding bottle glass should give the Socio-Archaeologist a ready means of demarcation: a preponderance of clear glass indicating a 'Them' region; of brown glass an 'Us' region.

Now for the heavy going and a pertinent question. The Bullstones and like Meets, have they a place in the Oread of '86 and beyond? I think that their importance is increasing and will explain why.

These meets are needed to maintain the balance of the Oread. They remind us of a simpler and easier time when money was shorter and climbing broader; and they provide links with the origins of the Club, origins rooted in a love of hills for their own sake, of wild places in wild weather, and of the unique camaraderie engendered thereby.

It is by such continuities, insignificant perhaps in themselves, that is preserved the nexus which enable a club to change with time without altering its precepts or its character; an evolution that presently perplexes the Oread.

Climbing Clubs to-day are ten-a-penny; as often as not so are their members. It is not all their fault; one cannot miss what one never knew. The shame is that without some effort they will never know. As in all matters of personal choice, the undiscerning will always take the easy option; they will always follow the crowd; and modern pressures conspire to promote the athletic at the expense of the aesthetic, the shallow at the expense of the profound.

Meets are now anything but. Affluence and personal transport have removed the necessity for making the best of conditions as found and of companions as found. Much is lost thus.

The demand now is for hard rock, dry rock, – quick rock. Indeed, one suspects that for some climbers one of life's dirtier tricks is that rock tends to outcrop in nasty wet windy places, miles from anywhere and usually distinctly uphill. The hill is in fact an embarrassment that could well be done without. Now these conditions, so abhorrent to the rock-athlete, are the very ones which bestow character on our native hills, and which to the mountaineer, give them their perennial appeal.

It should now be clear that we are playing different games: at the limit, mutually exclusive games. It is becoming increasingly difficult to reconcile these two aspects, both at a personal and at a Club level; and it can only get worse. This is the dilemma which confronts the Oread. I will outline one way to avoid the horns; drastic, but logically rather elegant.

Despite what some would have us believe – some indeed, who ought to know better – the Oread is not a climbing club. By its very constitution, the objects of the Club are defined as 'mountaineering in every aspect' Climbing is only a part of that manifesto. Well would it be to remember this. At present, rock-climbing is rapidly becoming an end in itself; it is attracting the attention of the media manipulators; competition climbing is a possibility. Bullstones, Welbourn's Wander, and the like, can maintain the balance of the Oread until extreme rock-climbing reaches the stage, as it almost has, where it abandons any allegiance to mountaineering. At this point, when rock-climbing is de facto a sport in its own right, it can be safely declared beyond the terms of reference of the Oread constitution and consigned to whatever private hell it has wrought for itself. This will leave the Oread free to sneak off quietly whilst the competition climbers and their ilk are belayed by the Sports Council or whoever. I shan't miss them.

Oh yes! This is supposed to be a Meet Write-Up! Bullstones '85 – seventeen people, one dog. I hope that everyone got something out of the weekend: I know that the dog did.

Here is irony or even ambivalence. Embued with "little enthusiasm for write-ups, Journals and the like" the writer exposes himself (again) as a master craftsman........ pamphleteer, and polemicist manqué — *Editor.*

> Mountains! What stuff has been written in praise of them
> what bunkum from dithyrambic pens.

A LONG WALK – LAND'S END TO JOHN O'GROATS

Editor

In 1985, between 25th March and 18th June (79 walking days) Gordon and Pauline Wright walked 1,124 miles from Lands End to Duncansby Head, averaging 14.23 miles a day. This route took in the north coast of Cornwall and Devon, canal routes to the Midlands, the Pennine Way (part), the Forest of Bowland, The Lake District (Kentmere, High Street), the Southern Uplands, a miserable stretch on roads from Edinburgh to Stirling, the old railway from Callender to Crianlarich, the West Highland Way to Fort William, the Caledonian Canal (part) and Lochs Arkaig and Quoich to Glen Shiel, Glen Elchaig to Achnashellach, the Whitbread Wilderness (Shenaval) to Dundonnell, and on via Loch Shin to Strathmore, to Tongue, and along the coast to John O'Groats.

Pauline wrote an account in the 1985 journal, summing up by writing: "It was not our intention to break any records. The aim was simply to get there without walking on roads unless forced to. The further we walked, the more difficult it became to share my thoughts, even with Gordon, and even more difficult to write my diary. Maybe it was the long spells of solitude, and the vastness of the country, with times of complete quiet which impressed me. At times it seemed that everything was there just for the two of us. We had moments when we fell about laughing and others when we didn't. It was quite a way to celebrate our 35th wedding anniversary."

KHARCHA KUND NORTH RIDGE 1987
(PATRON: SIR JACK LONGLAND)

PETER SCOTT

Bobby Gilbert, Robin Beadle, Rob Tresidder and Pete Scott, all members of the Oread M.C. climbed the North Ridge of Kharcha Kund in Alpine style. The mountain is 6,612m in altitude and situated in the Gangotri Glacier area of the Garwhal Himalaya, India. The summit was reached on the morning of 18th September, 1987 after a $5\frac{1}{2}$ day ascent and a 1 day approach from base camp at Sundaban. Descent was by the normal West Ridge route and took $1\frac{1}{2}$ days to base camp. A total of 7 bivouacs was made. The North Ridge comprises a number of rock towers connected by elegant snow/ice arêtes. Difficulties were encountered on rock up to Alpine VI, A1 and ice up to Scottish V. It was the first ascent of the ridge and first British ascent of Kharcha Kund.

The expedition took a year to organise, including defining a suitable objective. We were fortunate after much research to discover and gain permission to attempt an inspiring unclimbed line on an attractive looking mountain suitable for a small team climbing in Alpine style. Two previous teams had made successful ascents of Kharcha Kund via the West Ridge, three teams had previously failed in their attempts to climb the North Ridge, primarily due to poor weather. The weather conditions were exceptionally good in the Gangotri region during the 1987 "post monsoon" season.

The cost of the expedition was £5,000, members contributing £1,000 each. Grants were received from the M.E.F., the B.M.C., Derbyshire County Council, and Oread M.C.

A helpful, detailed expedition report is available.

BOBBY GILBERT (EXTRACT) *Journal 1987*

I arrived in a corner with a very steep exit, placed a large rock runner and pulled up on it to see what I could see. The groove above was blank. So was the one to the left. The runner was wriggling around quite alarmingly, but a couple of blows from my ice hammer had it well jammed in (it was probably Robin's). The thought of comming off with a big sack on, and understandably being pulled backwards didn't bear thinking about.

I decided I would have to aid the next bit, and so I clipped a sling into the runner, stood up, and managed to bang a three-inch blade in about an inch. I tied it off, thinking it would have to do, and stood up on it, praying it wouldn't pull out. The groove above was under two inches of thick lichen and I spent five minutes hacking this away with my hammer before placing another very small bendy blade. This I clipped into and stood on, watching it bend.

From here I could just step into the next groove again on very small holds. I put my right foot on a tiny hold on the vertical wall, smeared my hands on small sloping holds, and leaving the safety of the sling, swung my unwieldy weight across and grabbed a good hold, thankful that my feet hadn't shot off! I was totally exhausted. Hard stuff at 6,000m. The last seventy feet was all steep but on huge holds, so I shot up, belayed and brought Robin up. Whilst he sorted out a bivvy ledge, I 'abbed' down to take the rope across to the others who were waiting at the bottom. I then had to prussic up the pitch again.

Robin had found some small sloping ledges which we tied ourselves onto, and bivvied. We were fairly well sorted out by the time the others arrived. I had my food and brew as quickly as possible and got in my pit. Meanwhile the other two were sorting out their belay in the dark.

The ledge I was sitting on sloped at about 30 degrees and so every time you started to relax, you slipped and were grabbed in the crutch by your harness. This called for careful positioning.

About half an hour after we'd settled down there was a bit of a disturbance from the boys next door. There was a great crash and jongling followed by loud oaths and raised voices. Apparently Rob had put a peg in, belayed to it, hung all his gear, rucksack, crampons, etc. on it and sat underneath it and the whole thing had come crashing down on top of him! I just pretended to be asleep. I didn't want to have anything to do with it.

Next day we got over the next of the GNT, a knife-edged ridge, and then abseiled down two vertical pitches into the unknown to arrive at the North Col. Unfortunately there was another pinnacle in the col, which we were unable to get around, and so had to climb over. This involved hard ice climbing, one pitch led by Rob on rock, hard vertical ice, which we had to traverse. A superb lead, which we took advantage of by all tying on and seconding him. A Scottish Grade V pitch! Then more hard rock climbing up a chimney, and some awkward abseiling and climbing on poor snow, led up to another bivvy site. Our fifth on the mountain. That night the temperature was – 15 degrees Centigrade. Fifty degrees colder than Delhi!

We were within three pitches of the far side of the North Col and so got there in good time after a hard traversing ice pitch (Rob Tresidder speciality) and jamming of one rope, making it necessary to cut fifty feet off it. (Yes it was my bloody rope!) We spent the rest of the day digging a snow hole in the col, ready for an early start for the summit on the following day.

The summit day arrived as our alarms went off at 3.00 a.m. We all had a brew, then promptly all went back to sleep again. Everyone seemed pretty dispirited at this stage. Finally we got up at 6.00 a.m., and after a long plod up the steep snow of summit dome made the summit at 9.00 a.m.

The weather was brilliant. Clouds in the valley with mountains sticking through them, clear blue sky above. We could see for miles in every direction. We spent half an hour on the summit, taking pictures, shaking hands, looking at the view. It suddenly all seemed worthwhile. All the months of preparation, all the hassles of getting to base camp, all the hard work on the climb, but we made it. The first ascent of the North Ridge, and the first British ascent of the mountain.

PETER SCOTT (DIARY EXTRACT)

ALTITUDE

Two deep breaths, one more step
Must rest, twenty gasping breaths.
Now unconsciously holding breath, compose picture, press shutter, utter collapse.
An age to recover.
Now one more step, up steeply, crampons bite, axe holds.
Suddenly ice brittle, picks no longer hooking in, try again, no good, tiring now,
try again, useless, tiring, desperation, steep drop, rope spins down.
Finally pick drives home, collapse, twenty gasping breaths.
Back to normal, one more step.

THE COMMITTED (EXTRACT)

MIKE WYNNE   *Journal 1990*

Taking a last deep breath of the 'fresh' smog filled air outside. M entered the smoky alehouse. After acquiring a pint of 'Brunswick No. 29' (whatever happened to the wonderful names such as 'Bertie's Bottom Blaster'?), he wound his way up the half finished stairs to the little room above.

A quick glance around showed him that he was not the last to arrive. Some of the more strongly committed were there already; some seemed as if they had been there forever. Some looked as if they were not really there at all. Fagin was already there, as usual, peering through his thick lensed spectacles at his book of numbers. He would continue to do this all through the meeting, thought M – as he always did – yet he would still seem to make the right comments at the right time. Did he really listen to all that was said? Or was much said anyhow that was worth listening to?

The note-take was there – early as always. The job of transcribing the meeting's discussion into a brief set of comprehensible notes is an onerous task and obviously not something that we were taught at school. Even with the help of the most up to date word processing machines, the job is not made much easier – yet he sticks religiously at it, year after year. Fortunately, as the note-taker's position is of such importance, the system has provided for a standby in case the note-taker is absent or overworked, a clever little loophole which on occasions can give the notetaker a good opportunity to 'pass the buck'.

Then there is the inner circle of the ultra-committed. This is the team without which the whole organisation may collapse. It revolves around the assets which in theory, are owned and run by all the members, but in practice, are run by the 'cosy little number' who are dedicated enough to put in the time and effort to do it. Various grumblings are often detected within the membership about the situation but they seem to be generally happy with it, being able to enjoy from time to time a few days of palatial luxury in their time-share apartments in the mountains over the border to the west, or even in their more mediocre accommodation which they lease on the local Duke's Estate.

Just as the proceedings are about to start, the latecomers arrive, hot foot from their body building course which always finishes just too late to enable them to arrive at the meeting on time. Brandishing beer and sandwiches, the 'post and publicity' comes in armed with various papers, mumbles the obligatory round of 'eh-ups' to those already present and settles in his place. Next but by no means least comes the Obermeister. In traditional manner the assembled rise, each raising a clenched right hand in salute, symbolising a hand jam in a mean gritstone crack. This is the guy who all the members have chosen by a totally democratic and unbiased election to be their figurehead for two years. His stout stature, rugged features, bulging biceps and chalk under his fingernails, identify him as a real mountain man. He has scaled the steepest cliffs, dangled from the rustiest pegs, survived the most harsh conditions that a Scottish winter can throw at him AND DOES NOT SKI! This is the man who is leading the club into the nineties.

Not one who likes to mess about with trivialities, he uses his new-found power to start by completely rewriting the Agenda for the evening; maybe because he has inadvertently lost or forgotten his copy, or even never received it. There is no arguing with this man – despite the fact that he is veering dangerously away from the 'traditional' way of doing things. Everyone scribbles down the new Agenda:–

1. Potential climbing wall for Redby
2. Publication of magazine/Journal
3. Monthly 'E' point tally
4. Scotlnd's opening hours – an appraisal
5. Annual disco arrangements

and if time allows,

6. Financial Summary
7. Property analysis
8. Correspondence and communications
9. A.O.B.

David Penlington, upper slopes of "A.B.C.", Tien Shan, 1995. *Photo: Rock Hudson*.

Ali Ratna Tibba (5,500m), Kulu Himal. *Photo: D. Williams*.

Kharcha Kund (6,612m), North Ridge 1987. *Photo: Peter Scott*.

Kharcha Kund Expedition 1987. P. Scott, R. Beadle, Sir Jack Longland (Patron), R. Gilbert, R. Tresidder *Photo: Unknown*.

White Edge, Derbyshire 1994: John Shreeve, Auntie Wainwright, Anne Squires, Anne and Bill Kenyon, Peter Janes, Roy Sawyer, Janet Reynolds, Dave Weston, George Reynolds, Colin Hobday.   *Photo: H. Pretty.*

Oreads at Sea: George Reynolds, Roy Sawyer (helm), Dave Weston, Stan Moore (skipper, at rear).
Photo: H. Pretty.

Darryl Kirk, Gordon Gadsby and Mike Hayes,
Froggat 1995.
Photo: Tony Smith.

Eric Beard (Beardie) and Des Hadlum.
Photo: Dennis Gray.

Annual Fell Race, Heathy Lea, Chatsworth: Roy Eyre, Roger Larkham, Richard Hopkinson, Chris Radcliffe.
Photo: Chuck Hooley.

THE NOVICE SUPERVISION SUB-COMMITTEE

RICHARD COGHLAN *Journal 1990*

Friday evening saw the usual rush by the O.M.C. at Portmadoc Station to bag an entire carriage for themselves and their obese rucksacks. Tomorrow's weather forecast was open to some interpretation but was not good. It didn't matter anyway, the details of the previous day's committee meeting in the Brunswick were still fresh in my mind:

"John's still got one to do. You're going to Wales this weekend Richard, can you look after it?"

Damn, I'd copped for it again. I had planned to do some proper climbing with Andrew. After all, that was the whole idea of going to Wales this weekend. He would have to find someone else to climb with. The journey didn't take long because we were being pulled by one of the new Diesels. They saved the Steamers for tourists, and tourists didn't usually want to pay to go on joy rides at this time of night. It still gave time for John to ask all the questions that I would have expected, so I launched into my customary spiel.

"They effectively stopped cars from entering the park in 2002. The rules still say at least four people per car and the toll is now over five hundred ECUs. That's why we're leaving the car in Portmadoc. You don't have to pay if you're on the A5 in transit through Ogwen, but you're not allowed to stop if you haven't paid. I remember when I started climbing, anyone could drive straight in, leave the car anywhere they liked, and walk anywhere they liked".

Streaks of rain began to appear on the windows. At least the hills hadn't changed, nor the weather. I could feel fairly confident that we would be back down the railway to Tremadoc next day. With the current situation that meant Christmas Curry before being able to turn our attention to anything else. John needed to lead another severe on a designated training route before getting his climber's licence.

Christmas Curry hadn't been the same since they put a bolt every 4 metres up the route, but I would still expect John to place gear as if he weren't also using the bolts and, of course, mark the quality of his efforts. I always thought it strange, every time I did this, because I had never been able to do much above V.S. myself. I had been around long enough to gain the status of club instructor. Experience and the ability to climb were all that was needed for this according to the B.M.C.

The train arrived at Rhydd-Ddu station and the carriage emptied into the hut. It was John's first time at Tan-y-Wyddfa, so I had to show him 'round. Who are all these people in the photographs around the room?

"Oh, past presidents. We get a new one every couple of years. Its quite a prestigious position because they say who's in the club and who's out".

What a change from the good old days! The new laws forbade walking away from the road unless one belonged to a B.M.C. recognised club. The club size was limited to 150 in the case of the Oread. The limit on numbers kept down erosion on prime sites such as Snowdonia, and elevated the Oread M.C. and similar clubs to institutions of national repute. John wouldn't get in. Newly qualified climbers needed a few years to 'prove themselves' to stand a chance against the committee and avoid the president's veto.

Working within the confines of European law was not easy at first. All insufficiently active members had to be chucked out. It caused quite a furore when some of the pioneers of the sport had to go, but what else could we do? I kept my place by volunteering to supervise novices. Others made sure that the president was well supplied with beer at the Brunswick.

John was working backwards from the recent, formally posed, suit and tie portraits to the slightly faded photographs of past presidents actually climbing.

"I see some bright red sweaters and some very odd pairs of trousers were in fashion in the early '90's". "Yes, I used to know the individuals concerned. I remember John Hudson leading me up the Triple Buttress on Beinn Eighe."

I didn't admit that I had to glance at the name plate. I couldn't remember names even in my youth. The noise of the front door being shut diverted me from my reminiscences. I remembered that time was pressing, yet everything had to be done by the book because of the legal implications of even a minor accident the next day. No problem. I turned to John and said,

"Coming down the pub? We'll do the briefing session there".

Towards the
Post Modern
1990-1999

The journal for 1990/92 signified the end of a rich period in Oread achievement. The alpine tigers had aspired to the classic greats and had successfully transferred their skills to the higher ranges of the Himalaya and elsewhere.

During the early 90's a number of recent activists disappeared from Oread affairs, and others became attached to other groups. There was a distinct dilution of club spirit. The affairs of the club continued to be administered by a band of long serving members, but there was a shortage of young enthusiasts willing to perpetuate the spirit that had made the Oread a very special club since its earliest days.

It is, I am advised, a universal problem. In this post modern era it is hardly necessary, or even preferable, to belong to a climbing club in order to engage seriously in the great outdoors (or indoors). Climbing, mountaineering in general etc., have always attracted the individual (non team player) and clubs, as the Oread, have only provided a matrix that has created friendship, and some corporate spirit, from the myriad idiosyncrasies of individual members. It is a delicate balance and, over the years, ebbs and flows according to contemporary fashion.

In 1999 it seems likely that most clubs that have prospered from the simple but abiding friendships of the past are heading for a post-modernistic future – one that favours the anarchic and the transitiory. But we shall see.

In many ways any literary traditions that the Oread still aspired to largely evaporated after the Journal 1990/92. Monthly Newsletters resumed but in a miniature desk top publishing format under the editorship and production facilities of Rob Tresidder, who handed the job onto Clive (Rusty) Russell in June 1993. These brief monthly Newsletters are the only written communication circulated throughout the club in the 1990's and, although concentrating on Meets, Hut information, and some post meets reports, often contain esoteric personal interventions by the Editor that might be more appropriate to a Mensa publication, and are little understood by the ordinary member – those below the intellectual salt.

Since they provide mainly factual information, and are not generally rewarding to literary beach combing, they are not rich in source material.

It seems right then that this Journal, up to now a distillation of recent history, should conclude with a number of contributions that reflect the present — *Editor.*

Cradle Mountain, Tasmania (see article by D. C. Cullum).   *Photo: D. C. Cullum.*

50th A.G.M. Meet at Heathy Lea, April 1999. Rear: Harry Pretty, John Shreeve, John Fisher, Brian West. Middle Row: Colin Hobday, Rock Hudson, Anne and Reg Squires, Uschi Hobday, Janet Ashcroft, Stuart Firth, Derrick Burgess, Gill Keeling, Tony Raphael, Mick Keeling, Margaret Russell, Roy Eyre, Derek Pike, Clive Russell. Front Row: Hereward Tresidder, Rob Tresidder, Freda Raphael, Jenny Raphael, Mike Wren, Andy Oakden, Digger Williams, Tim Cairns, David Jones.   *Photo: Jack Ashcroft.*

275

A SHORT DAY IN THE ITALIAN ALPS WITH OREADS OLDISH AND NEWISH

DAVID JONES

Possibly the best thing about the OMC for us "slightly younger" folk is that we can see that neither the patter of tiny feet, nor the advance of years, need stop the enjoyment of crags, hills and mountains. Putting it more simply, growing older gracefully or sedately isn't compulsory. It is also apparent that the OMC upholds some of the best traditions of the British abroad; natty dress, healthy diet, lavish lifestyle, etc.

The Alpine trip of 1997 exemplified all this, combining mountaineering, nappies, grappa, sunbathing and smelly hellies in one heady whirl. And in the midst of it, passing through the meet as part of his season's mission to finish off the Alpine 4,000m peaks, was Dave Penlington: Oread and first ascensionist of old. The Oread trip was to the Gran Paradiso area, based at Pont, and the Gran Paradiso was one of the peaks on the Penlington hit list. So good weather inevitably led to a foray up the thing, specifically Dave P., Tony Raphael, Richard Coghlan and I.

Despite valiant attempts to outflank him, D.P. still outpaced the rest of us to the Vittorio Emmanuel II Hut. Deciding to avoid the crowds as much as possible, we spurned the beds of the hut in favour of a bivvy, but didn't spurn it's beer and food for lunch. Up the tourist track we plodded until we could gain the right moraine of the Gran Paradiso Glacier, and joined the broad west ridge, where good bivvy spots can be found amongst the pancakes of rock.

An early start from the bivvy took us across the glacier and onto the bottom section of the NW face, heading diagonally up to the col between the Gran Paradiso and the Piccolo Paradiso. Our guide book, a 30 year old magazine article, gave the ridge from this col to the summit of the Gran Paradiso a rave write-up.

Unfortunately, water ice was met almost immediately after the bergschrund, and soon we were moving as two pairs, both 'pitching'. After three pitches I must have decided that things were going too easily, as I cunningly managed to drop my ice hammer (after putting in a couple of screws), cords and all, and away it whizzed to the crevasses below, never to be seen again. Three ice tools between two people on hard ice didn't work very well for traversing, so Tony and I devised a cunning plan and decided to go straight up the NW face. After several pitches of front pointing, and one steep ice bulge, we were able to gain a steep rock rib, with the leader sending the hammer down the rope to the second at the end of each pitch. All pretty secure, but slow.....

After two pitches on the rock, and after waving off the unwanted but persistent attentions of a helicopter touting for business, we decided to rejoin the ice, where the afternoon sun was saving us labour by allowing the ice screws to be merely lifted out of their holes. Sadly, the presence of a broken pair of sunglasses on a ledge had removed any faint notion that the rib hadn't been climbed before, and more to the point, we were going even slower than we had on the ice.

A broad couloir brought us up towards the West ridge. A steep and soft snow ridge brought us to the summit ridge just as the sun set, our once-soggy ropes already frozen hard.

We hadn't seen Richard and Dave for many hours, and vaguely assumed that they were already down at the bivvy site or even slurping beer at the VEII hut. But wait! What was that well-spoken voice that rang distantly but clearly through the still dusk air from the North Ridge, below us? What was it saying? It sounded suspiciously like "climb when you're ready, Dave". And there they were. Richard and Dave had had an afternoon exploring the summit of the Piccolo Paradiso in search of alternatives to going along the ridge to Gran Paradiso, but had ended up reverting to 'plan A' and found it easier than they had expected. By the time that all four of us reached the vicinity of the 'tourist summit' it was getting distinctly dark and we were still atop a rock ridge with no obvious descent.

However, flat ledges and clear skies meant that the bivvy option wasn't too daunting, so we took it. Only Richard had a bivvy bag, but everyone else seemed to have a reasonable night (although it was cold enough to freeze in Pont). My pathetic aluminium bag tore apart as soon as I turned over. My cosy little nook turned into a wind-funnel. I couldn't get all of me into my rucksack, no matter how hard I tried. As the sky paled and morning approached, I must have looked a sad state.

A moment changed all that. We noticed a lone figure coming up the glacier on the 'tourist route' towards the rock ridge with the Madonna statue, separated from our bivvy point by only a modest gap. Instantly we perked up and assumed a nonchalant air. What a beautiful spot! What a beautiful sunrise! what a good idea of ours to come and see it. The lone figure across the divide scrambled to the Madonna, keen to have the summit to himself, and then peered nonplussed across at the bivviers (who, he now realised, were higher than the 'tourist summit' on which he stood).

We called to him. "Hello there! Good morning!"

The lone figure replied, "Hello, lovely morning. I thought I'd have the place to myself. How are you?"

We rose with the sun and, after paying our respects to the Madonna, headed swiftly down the glacier and ridge back to the previous nights bivvy site for a late breakfast in warm sunshine (though I discovered my gloves, which had got wet the day before, still frozen hard in my sack). Then back down to the VEII hut for a well earned beer and lunch.

Even I was conscious that amongst the generally lightly laden and smartly turned out folk on the terrace, we stood out in our drab clothes, worn looking kit, and pale faces. I saw a couple of people look at us quizzically One of their colleagues turned to them and said, by way of complete explanation, "Inglese!". Naturally!

ALL AT SEA WITH THE OREAD

Roy Horatio Sawyer

When I was a mere lad or 45 or so and revered such icons as H. Pretty, R. Handley, D. Burgess, P. Scott and C. Radcliffe, imagine how delighted, nay, humble, I felt to be invited to the Golden Oldies October-Fest.

This annual informal gathering of elder statesmen usually took place somewhere on the west coast of Scotland. I thought it would be great to tell the grandchildren that I had actually rubbed shoulders with some of the Oread "Greats".

We were to stay in the bunkhouse in Kinlochewe and I duly arrived on the Friday evening having travelled with Ron Chambers (pre ear-ring era), Graham Foster and the small but not so perfectly formed Weston – "the elder" (or should that be Weston – "the old").

My bright eyed, bushy tailed enthusiasm was soon dampened when a Captain Mainwaring type figure (Pretty) decided to put me in my place: "Now listen Sawyer, you are only here on sufferance because my mate Appleby couldn't make it, so don't get any ideas beyond your station". The thrust of this dressing down was somewhat diluted by his attire. He was wearing a shrunken vest type garment with the faded words "Fleet Air Arm" across what may once have been a proud chest. Red tights did nothing to enhance his authoritarian image.

At this point a rakish, lothario type person slid from the shadows. The epitome of a louche Sergeant Wilson to Pretty's Captain Mainwaring. An ally I thought, but Peter Janes only joined in emphasising my lowly position.

Slightly crestfallen I surveyed my hitherto revered companions. On one side of the table Fred Allen and Jack Ashcroft were wrestling over a half eaten tin of corned beef (we all knew it belonged to Ashcroft as its sell by date went back to some 1950's Norwegian expedition). Derrick Burgess in his inimitable way was half through Ron's semi cooked carrot cake, and Graham was in the corner fiddling with something smelly, old and wrinkled, which in the event turned out to be his usual piece of German sausage.

We had a wonderful week with incidents too numerous to mention. The walk from Dundonnell to the Bothy at Shenavall then onto and over Sgurr Ban and back to Kinlochewe. The climb over Ben Alligin in wild weather, fishing, and pool (snooker) at Badachro with Dave Appleby, (who had joined us later in the week) all set a precedent for the following years of "oldies" fun on the West Coast.

As the others had always organised our trips I felt that perhaps I should do my bit. But where to go – what to do? After seeing an advert in a sailing magazine I suggested chartering a sixty foot skippered ketch, sailing from Armadale on Skye and exploring the small Isles of the Inner Hebrides. The cost was about £150.00 for the week and apart from Burgess declaring that £150.00 shared between eight people was a bit steep, it was all systems go!

Derrick, Graham, Dave Weston and a close friend of mine, one Michael Dunn of drinking fame, embarked on a Saturday morning. A rendezvous with Pretty, Janes and Dave Appleby had been arranged for the following morning in Arisaig Harbour.

The skipper (Charles) an ex-submariner/lay preacher (a bit incongruous we thought) motored us over to the Isle of Eigg and, after dropping anchor in the sheltered bay between Kildonnan and Galmisdale, the four of us traversed the 'Sgurr' in thick mist whilst Charles prepared supper for our return. The evening was spent eating and drinking around a full size log burner onboard before turning in, sometime in the early hours.

The cabins were all of a good size with Burgess bagging what he thought was the best. In his haste, he overlooked the oily steering gear above his bunk and the bilge pump handle at the end. The gear deposited crud over his borrowed sleeping bag each time we changed direction, and he was required to pump the bilge handle each morning – at least that's what he said he was doing.

After gathering the remains of the crew at Arisaig, we sailed away and visited many places not on the normal itinerary, such as – the Treshnish Isles, where young seal pups let us within a few feet: Iona, with fresh fish and the peace of the Abbey: Staffa with a very hairy landing inside Fingals cave. We then sailed to Scavaig and found an anchorage adjacent to the J.M.C.S. Hut where some of the party had spent a very wet and wild week on a previous October outing.

Whilst the skipper collected mussels for our tea, we rowed ashore for a walk around Loch Coruisk before setting sail back to Armadale. Our last evening was spent ashore enjoying a meal and lots of drink in the Hotel at Armadale. Janes eventually forgave us for accidentally locking him into Charles's house and leaving for the pub without him.

The whole trip left us with many happy memories and after a few years the call of the lonely sea and Skye was upon us again.

We left Skye from the same starting off point but with none other than Stan Moore as Skipper. For those of you who have never had the pleasure, Stan Moore is an ex Oread not to be missed.

The boat this time was an Oyster 38 with separate aft cabins complete with en-suite facilities. Of course these quarters were taken by the skipper and his lackey (Pretty) whilst we mere A.Bs. were crammed into the rest of the boat. Dave Weston sleeping on little more than a shelf, and Peter and George shoehorned into the pointy bit. The general consensus was to head north and, avoiding the tide race at Kyleakin, pass under the new bridge and continue north to Torridon. Passing the Crowlin Islands it was a little disconcerting to hear the radio announce that "submarines are operating in your area". But Harry knew all about these things and assured us that all would be well. We had a wonderful sail down Loch Torridon in an ever increasing wind but managed a peaceful night anchored off Shieldaig.

Moving in to Torridon proper, the next day saw us arrive at our anchorage in strong north westerly winds and heavy rain. We dropped the hook about 3 to 4 miles from The Ben Damph bar whence followed a strange walk through rhododendrons which had formed a canopy about shoulder height along the path. A typical Oread rowdy lunch time led to the return journey in torrential rain, bent almost double trying to avoid the overhanging vegetation. A great way to see off the alcohol!

As time to return to home port drew near it proved necessary to set sail in a force 6/7 storm. Around the north of Raasay proved quite exciting with my lunch only being "borrowed" for a short time.

After four to five hours of relentless pounding we finally entered the sound of Raasay and thus into Portree Bay, past *H.M.S. Montrose*, a frigate, which to us seemed concreted to the bottom. Little did we realise that the crew of this vessel were soon to be brought into action.

Pretty had done a sterling job helming the boat all the way from Torridon and only when he steered towards a mooring buoy did we realise that something was wrong. The cable linking the gearbox drive had sheared, leaving us in "forward", thus making it difficult to stop.

The seas in the harbour were still steep and therefore Stan thought it prudent to call for technical assistance. The good old Royal Navy intercepted our call and we soon had an engineer on board to help us moor alongside the jetty.

After repairs, we made our way back to Armadale and experienced one of those rare Scottish days, whether in the hills or at sea. Calm at first, with a watery sun pushing through the mist, the wind picked up to a force 2/3 and, by afternoon, we were anchored opposite Eilean Donan Castle at the foot of Loch Duich. We had a lazy time, wandering ashore, or fishing, followed by a long motor home. The wind had dropped completely, leaving the mountains reflected on a glassy sea.

Perhaps we might have walked the hills a little more, but sailing these waters is definitely a different way to see Scotland. The company was great and my personal thanks go to Stan Moore who helped me achieve a life long ambition. As in all trips there are incidents and experiences, arguments, and many times of mutual enjoyment. Trying to relate a few of these in a short piece is nigh on impossible, but I hope I have given a flavour of another aspect of Oread activities.

It subsequently came to our notice that Princess Anne's husband was at that time, skipper of *H.M.S. Montrose*. It is possible, of course that he assumed that R. G. Pettigrew was aboard our vessel — *Editor.*

ROCKING THE CRADLE

DOUGLAS CHARLES CULLUM

Deloraine, Elizabeth Town, Moltema, in grey pre-dawn light. Try as I might, I couldn't screw more than 130 out of Art's ancient 2.6 litre Datsun station wagon. Kimberley, Railton, Sheffield, and a sudden and splendid sunrise behind us. Some biggish-engined cars are gas guzzlers, but Art's Datsun is an oil guzzler. "Fill her up with 20/50, and check the petrol while your at it." Art, by the way, is a buddy from way back, who had generously given us the free use of his house in Westbury and this old car. Claude Road, Gowrie Park, some spectacular glimpses of an alpine-looking Mount Roland through gaps in the clouds, and at last the National Park Visitor Centre at 8.30 a.m. We had to pay to get in, but you do get a lot for your money. Did I mention that speeds here in Tasmania are in kph?

It was unexpectedly cold, and the clouds were thick and low. The previous day we had had 38 degrees, but up here it was struggling to get into double figures, and we only had shorts and tee shirts. Also the pretty Thai girl in the pub in Launceston the previous evening had told us that Cradle Mountain enjoyed only fifteen fine days a year. We were not ecstatic. However, the visitor centre was impressive, and the ranger said that it might clear up by eleven and added that they only had 10 fine days a year. We drove up to the car park at the north end of Lake Dove and parked facing down the lake towards the mountain. We waited. By 9.30 some of the clouds had golden edges, and by 10 odd scraps of blue were showing through. Good enough. The sack (very small) was packed – tins of fizzy drinks, some chocolate and a very light sweatshirt each. So, up into the singing mountain, but first we signed in, with details of our planned route (obligatory), and made use of the palatial public loos, paid for out of the admission fees.

We headed roughly west along the Wombat Track, where a helpful sign gave a detailed description of wombat turds (they're square and conveniently divided into bite-sized segments). Soon we passed Lake Lilla on our left, very pretty in the strengthening sunshine, and Thrush Forest on our right, and soon afterwards the Wombat Pool. No wombats, but incredibly beautiful, like Disney without the vulgarity. Here the track swung south, and we came to the boardwalk, also paid for out of the admission fees. It's not there to keep your feet dry but to protect the flora and the surface from the effects of tramping boots. We climbed to a grassy ridge where we joined the Overland Track, and could look down to Lake Dove to the east and Crater Lake to the west. It isn't really a crater, but it looks as if it might be, with a cirque of steep crags rising straight out of the water round the southern end. Next there was a short steep bit of scrambling. Nothing to a pair of ageing Oreads, of course, and we soon reached Marion's Lookout at the top, and an easier gradient over Cradle Plateau. The wild flowers were abundant and often spectacular. I wish I could tell you their names. It was starting to get hot, and there was no longer any doubt that this was one of the Ten Fine Days. We plodded on, and suddenly there it was, Cradle Mountain in all its splendour. You may have seen it in calendars – no self respecting pictorial calendar of Tasmania would dream of not having at least one shot of it. It is a dragon's back, running south west to north east, with many jagged spires, and the main summit (1,545 m) is at the extreme right hand (south west) end. The left hand end drops from a great pinnacle called Weindorfer's Tower to a col, then rears up to a lower but very shapely peak called Little Horn, and the whole looks like an old-fashioned cradle. The complete traverse gives an excellent day and is not difficult, but it does need at least two competent climbers with all the gear. Mary hates rock-climbing and we didn't have any gear. Ah, well, another time. We took the first photo's, but had to keep taking more as we drew closer.

At about 12.30 we spotted the Kitchen Hut, which was our intended stop for lunch. It was a very strange wooden building, like a large garden shed, but very tall and with two doors, one directly above the other, i.e. about seven or eight feet above the ground. Well, why do you think? It snows a lot here in the winter, on many of the 355 days that are not fine. Inside there were some primitive bench seats and a table. We had a bite and drank more than was prudent of our drinks and set off up the final wall. Well, it looks like a wall, but it's more of a scramble. No more than 600 feet to the top, and way-marked for the benefit of the stupid and incompetent.

After a short distance the track divided. The way-marked half traversed right and disappeared round a corner. The other half went straight up, clearly the dirittissima. I took the latter. Mary argued (what's new?) and took the way-marked half. "See you on the summit," I said, as she set off, taking the very small sack. With the drinks. And my camera.

The dirittissima got steeper and less well marked. After a while I found myself doing moderate rock climbing, then the track more or less petered out, then the climbing became diff. I was beginning to ponder the wisdom of continuing when suddenly I found myself on a summit. Not *the summit*, a summit. It was Smithies Peak, the second summit, and separated from the main summit by an unbridgeable gulf. Clearly I would have to descend all the way back to where the track had divided, and take the way-marked route. Down then. Ah. Exactly which way is down? Here, in the corner? No, it was more like that slab over there. Or perhaps that little arete to the right? No, don't remember that. I had no idea which way I had come up. Never mind, I'd find the route sooner or later. Or maybe not. It occurred to me that I might be here all night. I was already thirsty and soon I would get hungry. Mary had all the food and drink.

I regarded with greater interest than before the helicopters that were shuttling building materials to some point over the horizon. God, how long shall I have to wait before Mary misses me and raises the alarm? How will they know where to look? How embarrassing, having to be helicoptered off a peak that's no more than a scramble! And how expensive! And how bloody cold in the wee small hours! I wondered if you could freeze to death up here on a summer night, if you were only wearing shorts and a tee shirt. I thought you probably could, and addressed myself more urgently to finding the way down. After a couple of false starts I cracked it, and after that it was all downhill, so to speak.

By the time I reached the fork in the track I was very hot and *really* thirsty. I set off up the way-marked track, which, you will recall, is for the stupid and incompetent, and at last caught up with my spouse. She had followed the proper route without difficulty, but was now slightly gripped by the prospect of the final couple of hundred feet. The top of Cradle Mountain consists of a pile of huge dolerite blocks, scattered in disorder like giant's building blocks. Many are the size of a double-decker bus. The route is a strenuous scramble. She was not to be persuaded to give it a go, so I drank as much as I dare of our remaining liquid and prepared for the final assault. But first, "Where's my camera?" I asked.

"I gave it to a girl."

"You gave it to a girl? What, a hundred and fifty quids' worth of Olympus? Jesus H, what did she do to deserve that? Couldn't I have done it? And do you think she'd do it for me?"

"Well, I thought you'd go straight to the summit, and I'd given up, so I sent it up for you. She hasn't come back yet, and she has to come this way, so she's still waiting. I told her to look for a short fat hairy old Pom called Charlie." "Gee, thanks."

I scrambled up to the summit. It was straightforward and Mary could have done it easily, but she is a decisive woman, and no means no. (What's the old joke? If a lady says no she means maybe, if she says maybe she means yes, and if she says yes she's no lady. My wife is a lady. She has never been known to say yes.) It was very strenuous, and by the time I reached the summit I was sweating like a Pom and dying of thirst again.

There is no water on the top 1,000 feet of Cradle Mountain. On the summit was a very pretty girl with an older woman I took to be her mother. The pretty one had my camera round her neck. "You must be Charlie," she said. Being the only short fat hairy old Pom present, I had to admit it, and camera and owner were reunited. The views in all directions were sensational and I got a few good shots. I spent maybe 15 minutes on the summit and then rejoined my keeper. I was parched, and so was she, for she had been sitting in the blazing sun for an hour or more. We shared the remaining drink but our mouths were too dry to eat anything.

The descent to the end of the boardwalk was uneventful. On the way we met a bloke who commented on how lucky we had been with the weather, because Cradle Mountain only had five fine days a year.

We had chosen to go back via the Face Track, which crosses the northern end of the mountain. On the map the track looks more or less flat, but it zigzags up and down a lot and you have to do several hundred feet of each before you reach the Rangers' Hut at the eastern end. It's very strenuous, the sort of thing you can do without when you're in the early stages of knackeredness and thirstier than you can ever remember. It was still hot and we got thirstier still. It was impossible to speak or even swallow. I tried the old dodge of sucking a pebble, but it just left a taste of pebbles without squeezing out a single drop of moisture. Mercifully when we reached the hut there was a pool that seemed to be flowing a bit, so we deemed it drinkable and had a good guzzle, and then another.

From the Rangers' Hut the track swings north and traverses Hanson's Peak, named after a hunter who died of exposure. There is a steep drop on the left down to the southern end of Lake Dove, which was very beautiful in the late afternoon sunshine. On past some little tarns, the Twisted Lakes, over Bert Hanson's little hill, then lovely views of the same chap's Lake nestling in a deep shady cwm on the right, and finally according to the map, a steady, gentle gradient all the way down to the car park. But what's this? "Track closed because of erosion. Please use alternate route on left." Gulp. Naked rock, if you'll excuse the term, about the height and angle of the east face of Tryfan but without all those comforting ledges. However, someone had thoughtfully banged in some reassuringly hefty iron spikes and attached a beefy chain to them, and the idea was to scramble down hanging on to the chain. It was easy enough, but a fall would have had dire consequences.

The last bit was along a broad track by the waters of Lake Dove. Clouds were forming around the crags and the mountain looked very impressive. The sun was setting as we reached the car park and signed ourselves out. Ours was the only car left, and thank God, there were some spare cans of fizzy drinks in the back. They were luke warm and horrible, but we gulped the lot.

What a wonderful day it had been. When you come to think of it, not very different from many a day in Wales or the Lakes – no more than six or seven miles, maybe 3,000 feet up and a mini-epic almost worthy of Ashcroft himself. No, not very different at all, apart from the temperature, and the appalling thirst.

And the little wallabies that were coming out to graze in the dusk as we started the long drive home.

Cradle Mountain stands near the northern end of the cradle Mountain – Lake St Clair National Park in western Tasmania. There is a strenuous but very popular five-day backpacking trek from Waldheim at the northern end to Derwent Bridge at the southern end. You can, of course, do it from south to north if you wish. There are huts along the way, and plenty of mountains to climb – Mount Ossa at 1,617 m is the highest – and breathtaking scenery. There must be lots of rock climbing, if you can manage the gear. You have to carry everything. I'd like to do it before I am summoned to that great Climbing Hut in the sky. Any takers? Note – the inhabitants of Tasmania are called Tasmaniacs.

THE JOHN MUIR TRAIL

WILLIAM KENYON

The John Muir Trail is arguably the most scenic high level backpacking trail in the world. It traverses 220 miles of the High Sierra in California from Yosemite valley to the summit of Mount Whitney (14,500'). It winds through four wildernesses and passes of 10,000' are common, the highest being Forester Pass at 13,200'. From the rounded, ice smooth granite domes of Yosemite, you travel through 1,000 year old forests, along rushing rivers at 9,000ft and thundering waterfalls in canyons 7,000' deep. one passes through the most diverse scenery imaginable, set with thousands of jewel-coloured lakes. best of all, the climate is sunny and warm – most of the time.

Ann calculated our high calorie food requirements for 19 days trekking, plus two rest days. I wrote and reserved two wilderness permits. at the airports my pack weighed 77lbs and Ann's 38lbs.

We took the bus from San Francisco to Happy Isles camp site in Yosemite where we camped. We had lectures on hanging food (to keep it out of reach of the bears), the bears themselves and boiling water to avoid Gardiasis. Heading for Little Yosemite camp we followed a column of massive wobbly buttocks for half a mile, with both sexes dressed in bermuda shorts.

When we reached camp, the resident ranger warned us about attempting Half Dome as thunder and lightning looked imminent. We hadn't realised that there was a cabled route up the back, a perfect lightning conductor to burn off the unwary in a storm.

That night, more food thieves were on the prowl. A visit from bears resulted in teeth marks on the fuel tin, plus a third of our oil had been drunk. It was remarked that the bear would be able to excrete through the eye of a needle next day.

The morning greeted us with air of such clarity that Half Dome looked only half an hour away. It was a hard pull up through Incense Cedars and Ponderosa pines to the cables where we "hung" our sacks. Then it was up to the summit, over sheets of exfoliated granite, hauling on the cables. The views of the High Sierra were stupendous and worth losing one of our rest days.

Soon, another food thief appeared. As we chatted to two climbers, a little racoon stole our bar of toblerone chocolate. Behind schedule, we camped in failing light at the first spring we came to, in a dense wood. I found a suitable tree and threw the rock weighted bear-line over a branch, only to see the rock carry on minus the line. Ann laughed dementedly at each successive misfire. A counter balance of about 10' 6" was eventually achieved.

Several pairs of green eyes could be seen at various heights in the wood, reflected by our head torches. We retired uneasily, and sure enough – Crash!

Down came the bags and I leapt out like a greyhound – stark naked, brandishing a slick and bellowing, only to see the butt end of a mother and baby bear retreating with one bag plus bearline. The baby had climbed on mum's back and ripped the bottom out of one sack. Disaster!!

We sat up all night on guard by the fire and watched the full moon rise and set. We traced and retrieved the line amongst dried onions, curry mix and coffee next morning. Anything with curry in it had been discarded. We had lost about a third of our high calorie food but Ann decided we could make it if we went on iron rations.

We climbed stiffly over ridges and glacial deposits past Cathedral Peak – solo climbed by John Muir in 1869 – to Tuolumie Meadows where climbers kindly invited us to share their camp before they climbed Half Dome and El Capitain. We fell asleep in front of their fire. Next morning we set off up Lyell Canyon, heading for snow-capped peaks.

On the trail was a very large snake with black and yellow stripes from head to tail. We were apprehensive but it watched us with a curious rather than a menacing manner. We ascertained later that it was a Racer Snake which eats Marmots and Rattlers but is harmless to humans.

Our camp was below Donohue Pass where we met a climber with a badly damaged kneecap and fed him a little rice and olive oil. He was literally fishing for his supper. With splendid views of Mount Lyell, aromatic scents and a hot sun on our backs we headed for Donohue Pass (10,00') on Yosemite's border. We lunched in the snow where a marmot made a daring frontal attack and pinched an empty tin of pate. It jammed on her teeth and made a humorous photo.

Down through meadows of Indian paintbrush flowers we cast a last look at Mts Banner, Ritter and Lyell which we climbed a couple of years later. Suddenly the white cotton wool clouds became dark thunder and my bald patch felt the rain. Arriving at Garnet Lake, the free runner was erected with practised speed. As we cooked a meal inside it bucketed down – just like Wales.

We heard a person shouting about exposure and his lost friend, but he was gone when it stopped raining. What a glorious morning, snow girdled Ritter and Banner silhouetted against the sky and reflected in Garnet Lake.

The terrain was now like a roller coaster past lakes of trout and warm volcanic springs. We saw few people for three days and the opening gambit of every conversation was the storm. We headed for the last trail head at Reds Meadows, along dust pumice trails, past a national monument called the Devil's Post Pile (columns of hexagonally-jointed basalt). On arrival, we purchased meagre supplies of bread and cheese and stashed our bags on top of the toilets. We were awakened by a noise like the Anvil Chorus only to see the "garbage bears" flinging the steel doors of the rubbish skips open and rooting like terriers after moles.

We were now in the "Ring of Fire" – 165 miles left to Lone Pine with no road heads, two or three days walk out and a rumour that the steel bridge was down over Fish Creek. What next? We decided to continue. The next stretch was between two wilderness areas with pools of hot water whose mud bottoms bubbled like witches' cauldrons – no good for bathing.

Here we met a large dog called Clive, carrying two panniers on his back. His owner gave us quantities of home made gorp (???) mixture. We camped at Indian Creek and in the night heard Indian chanting, drums and horses neighing. It must have been the music of falling water or lack of food – or was it?

The aura of mystery remained next day. Anxious to get to the bridge, we were more than relieved to find the rock battered steel span of twisted girders still crossable. it listed at a crazy angle, 500ft above the river, entailing a precarious vertical scramble. I noted with professional interest that none of the friction grip bolts had sheared.

Singing, we trudged up Silver Pass to camp at Squaw Lake. A rampart of rock partly captured the lake from where we had excellent views over Cascade Valley. Ann washed a woollen cardigan (without soap) and found it next morning nibbled full of holes like a paper doily. I laughed until I saw my pullover also looking like a moth-eaten rag.

Over Silver Pass (12,000'), descending via rounded granite domes and waterfalls to Bear Ridge, a daunting sight which has seventy formidable switch backs and no water. Ominously Ann warned that we would have to husband our resources carefully.

To my delight I discovered abundant quantities of Boletus and Edulis but was warned by a passing scoutmaster that they were probably poisonous. I told him we had been eating them for a week and showed him the poisonous Fly Agarics, which contain coatrophine and muscarine which were used to make intoxicating drink during Prohibition, cheaper than bootleg whisky! Impressed he gave us some cereal, almost as good as singing for your supper.

Camping at Sally Keys lake we met a camouflaged group of men carrying bows and arrows (deer hunters). The next morning was sharp and frosty with a smoky mist above the lake. Two timid mule deer, their hind legs hidden in the mist stood outside the tent. Two parties of "Robin Hoods" arrived to shatter the idyll. We sang "Ilkly Moor Baht Hat" to scare the deer away and avoid being shot.

We diverted to Diamond Horse Ranch to visit Adelade Smith regarding her not answering my request for a food drop. She gave us the pick of discarded trail drops, ten tea bags and tin of "wartime dried egg". Ann was presented with an ancient Piute Indian obsidian arrow head for fortitude.

Back to the trail, up a ferociously steep climb, the river thundering over granite terraces surrounded by the jagged peaks of Evolution Valley. We camped by a clear bubbling spring and some wild onions and mushrooms livened our curry that evening. Next morning we forded a particularly treacherous creek with glacier rounded rocks underfoot and a waterfall 60' below. And this was at 10,000'. I tried not to think about it.

At last we could see Mounts Huxley and Darwin, they looked near enough to touch in the frosty air. We had reached the Goddard Divide, what joy. In all their bleak beauty the Jurassic era peaks complemented the stark terrain. We shared lunch with three climbers (theirs) at the hut. The grandfather of one came from Derby. She served us up a veggie meal in his memory.

We traced an indistinct route down a dynamited section of the path to camp with views of Thunderbolt (14,000') and Mount Sill, which we climbed on a later visit. A food check revealed we needed to tighten our belts even further. My beard meanwhile was horrible since my wash bag had been stolen by some creature way back.

Were we going to make it? At first light we retraced 14 miles back up Coute canyon, up the Golden Staircase in a terrific hailstorm which had killed three grouse chicks. We greeted two astounded retreating locals on the Mather Pass, which was now covered in hailstones. Ann found an expensive water bottle but discarded it when she saw the word "piss" written on it.

We spoke to two rangers on horseback leading four burros. They said they had a tough time due to hard snow on the pass. "One falls, they all go," they said. What the heck's in store for us, I thought.

We camped at Palisade Lakes where we met Bob, a ranger, who entertained us with tales of the methods bears use to obtain junk food. Cub on mum's back (our loss), climb tree to gnaw branch, even kamikaze bears who climb above then jump onto the branch to dislodge the food. There was also "Highway Annie" who used to hide behind a rock and chase back packers until they dropped their packs so she could feed. She was shot!

In the night we thought we heard wolves but Bob told us they were coyote. As the passes became higher so did the campsites – colder, and no wood fires, plus the lakes were too cold to swim in. There were still two bears however.

Reaching Woods Creek, the bridge was gone and, fording the fast flowing channel, I lost my footing on a loose rock and soaked myself to the waist. A German youth laughed and took a photo. He had abandoned after five days with blisters – they looked like hinged dustbin lids.

A superb campsite at Dollar Lake with magnificent sunset views of Fin Dome and Dragon Peak gave us a good rest before an exhausting two mile haul up to Glen Pass. The reward was an exquisite panorama of the Kearsage Pinnacles, Rae Lakes, and the distant Forester Pass and Mount Whitney.

We found a good camp with a bear tree and warm granite rock next to the tent. Whilst bathing, Ann remarked how skinny I looked and reminded me of the tale of the woman who gave her donkey a little less to eat each day and had got it going nicely without food when it died.

We waved to two passing vagabonds, the younger one, wearing a Janet Reger garter headband, was carrying the piss bottle and drinking from it!

The next day entailed five miles of exhausting climbing up to Forester Pass (13,200') lagging behind my racehorse wife. I was now hungry enough to eat a horse and it's jockey. We rested and ate our rations and picked out Diamond Mesa and Mountt Tyndal, where Clarence King found an Indian arrowhead on the summit in 1860. Two marmots hastened our departure by rolling rocks at us, in an effort to eat our crumbs.

One of the PC trail lads took our photo and we descended to Tyndal Creek, where we were given burnt spaghetti and cheese by some climbers. In the night we knew Bruno had visited them by the noise of spoons on tin plates which sounded just like Ravel's Bolero. Next day I was lucky to photograph an eagle dropping it's prey as it took fright and swooped away.

The rangers' notice board at Crabtree told tales of woe about bears and their victims. Camping high at Guitar Lake, we were thankful for our winter gear (-5 degrees and frozen water bottles). A donation of peanut butter and honey from some chaps spurred us on to Trail Crest. We left our sacks open, taking food and valuables out first, since we had heard that during a trail repair a marmot's nest was found stuffed full of dollar notes and passports.

Then to the summit of Whitney, with Owens valley 10,000' below. We had made it!! We descended to Lone Pine with $64 left and went for a shower in the barber's shop. I had a shock when I looked in the mirror and saw this bearded skinny ruffian behind me. It was me! No one would take American Express, so a man called Mike gave us a lift to Bishop where Pete and Cheryle gave us dinner, bed and breakfast in their home. Next day I gave Danny some advice about welding and fabrication and he gave us $100 and a lift to Merced.

The food shortage had taken it's toll. I started out a lean 150lbs and ended a skinny 135lbs.

MURRAY KNOWS BEST

BRIAN WEST

On the shoulder of the Ben we went our separate ways. Rob Tresidder and Radders, heavily laden, continued steadily up the Pony Track; great men intent on great things. They planned to set up a bivouac on the summit, then drop down to their chosen route. That left us – myself, Stuart Firth and Helen Griffiths – to fend for ourselves. We turned for the Half-Way Lochan and in unexpected sunshine strolled round to Coire na Ciste.

The right hand icefall of Italian Climb looked to be complete. With three on the rope and a limited amount of gear a route with the crux lower down would be ideal. A descent of the easy half of Tower Ridge offered a quick return to the corrie floor.

Addressing the first icefall it became apparent that Stuart's Ascenbrenner was more or less redundant, a loss resolved by the leader clipping one rope, then when belayed sliding a hammer down the other rope.

In this curious fashion we progressed up pitches various, the main objective danger being the regular approach of a Terror Hammer, coming down your way fast.

Late afternoon saw us sat on Tower Ridge feeling mighty pleased with ourselves. Route done, sun out, and a relatively easy way off. What more could one ask? Well Stuart asked for Tower Ridge; and up not down.

He had a point; here we were, almost halfway, with the whole ridge to ourselves. And was there ever such a ridge? Of course we could do it. Probably finish in the dark, but not to worry. Hadn't Murray himself stated that there is nothing to fear – should one lack moonlight, one has nevertheless a competent party and torches, by means of which one can climb well – nigh anywhere. There was, I half remembered, something by way of a caveat tacked on to this, but what matter to us? Were we not a competent party? Had we not torches? – and a full moon to boot? Onwards and upwards!

The daylight did seem to drain away rather quickly, and where was that moon? Moving out on to the Eastern Traverse we met the advancing shadows, and within minutes the very muscle-tone of the mountain firmed up beneath our axes. The trickles on the rocks have turned to ice.

Lighting up time on the Ben: away across the gulf of Gardyloo twin pricks show high on the last snowy ramparts. Rob and Radders on the finishing pitches of Hadrian's Wall? Down below – a long way below – lights sweep anxiously over those nasty bulging slabs on Observatory Ridge. It is true then, there's always someone worse off than you.

Together under the Great Tower we reach for our head torches. In the mind's eye I see it still: Stuart stretching his brand new Petzl over his helmet; letting go; then staring in disbelief as the bloody thing catapults itself off and into space.

Oh dear. So it's not true then. There isn't always someone worse off than you.

For one mad moment we contemplated resurrecting the Italian Climb system, the leader sliding a torch back down the spare rope. But only for a moment. Anyone who has been the proud possessor of an Achille Little Wonder Lamp will blanch at the prospect of launching same with any expectancy of it arriving in one piece. I always fancied that lamp as a contrivance exported by cunning Frenchmen intent upon confounding perfidious Albion. Anyway, Helen announced that, if pressed, she would prefer to stay tied to her torch rather than to us, thank you very much. So that was that.

Wherever we tried to move up the lamp revealed a similar circle of slippery rock, and beyond the beam nothing that one dared think about. Despite Murray's assurance that we could climb anywhere, it was becoming only too obvious that we could climb nowhere. So much for Murray. At least we wouldn't be needing to worry about Tower Gap.

If it wasn't to be up, then it would have to be across. Could we find a way into Tower Gully? New territory for all of us, but it looked like being a long cold night, and we would keep warm trying.

Working out leftwards, linking up snow patches and ledges that showed well in the darkness, we continued traversing below and then beyond the Gap. Two hours later, the slopes eased and we were in the Gully – Aschenbrenner country.

It would be satisfying to record that here we set to with a will: standing straight in our steps, cutting hard and true from the shoulder; exulting in the fierce joy of battle as the ice-chips flew, etc. etc. Murray would have loved that. But we didn't. We plodded wearily up a winters accumulation of bucket steps, and I was glad of every one.

Above us the gash of the cornice exit stood sharp against the night sky. Toiling upwards, it became something to look forward to, an end. It turned out to be something to look out from, a beginning.

As we broke through to the plateau, the truant moon was there to greet us. After hours in the gloom, the very air itself seemed charged with light. Blinking, we beheld a world wrapped in silver splendour. All the vast sweeps of Lorne and Lochaber lay luminous about us; hill after hill rolling out and away as far as mind could reach. Above, the firmament flashed an infinity of fire. Awful, in the original sense of the word. And not a sound, nor a breath of wind.

Far out on the snow pack a constellation of tiny lights gleamed like earthbound stars: Rob and Radders in their bivouac, brewing up by candlelight. Moths to the flame, we crunched clumsily over to them, our steps out of step with the stillness. Another scraping of snow settled into the pot.

And so, on the midnight of March Full Moon, an Oread party took tea by candlelight on the summit snows of Nevis: and I for one do not expect to do it again – ever.

A week or so later, something was still niggling away at the back of the brain, as these things do. Murray had made his night-climbing assurances conditional, but upon what? I found it at last in "Rocks and Realities", and here I quote: "By means of torches, a strong party can climb by night well-nigh anywhere – provided the line of the route be known." Absolutely correct. Murray knows best. But then he always did.

This was not the first Oread encampment on the summit of the Ben. See Disastrous Chances and the evacuation of Betty Emery's body off Tower Ridge by an Oread party, Easter 1954, and Phillip Falkner's Memories of the Oread in the 50's. From a summit camp Falkner and Cartwright did Tower Ridge and North East Buttress in one day. Subsequently Sutton and Pretty did Observatory Ridge (Zero Gully continuation) and North East Buttress — *Editor.*

MEMORIES

PETER SCOTT

I had only been to the pub in Dufton once before, heading north along the Pennine Way. Ten years later, quite by chance I was in the pub for the second time and casually engaged in conversation with a young German. "I valk your Pennine Way because in Germany I read in our valking magazine about zis Englishman who says, "It was an experience as special as climbing the Eigerwand."!

I could not help but agree since the person he was quoting was myself, a quote from an article written by a German friend from Dusseldorf.

> "... your mother will be proud of you ... you didn't do it to earn memories, but memories you will have in abundance, for the rest of your life ..."

> A. Wainwright

But on the Pennine Way

"....there's nowt ter see but 'ills 'n' trees 'n' watter!"

And the Eigerwand

"....is hollowed like a sick man's chest, often veiled in mist or blotted out by clouds, a heaving vomiting mass of rock and ice!"

Well not quite. There exists an essential difference between one who has been and embraced with all their senses, and one who has not, and relies on a series of conjured sterile images. If the sum total of any single experience in the hills comprised a series of visual images then mountaineering would not exist. The experience is complex, involving all available senses and emotions interacting with the physical environment, other people, and events.

Ten years of reading and looking at images and then the real mountain. The adventure, agony, success or failure. What was to be my lot? Success was likely to be praised, failure to be damned and condemned. Was I experienced enough, how hard was it really, was I strong enough to survive the cold and wet if the weather broke? I almost felt embarrassed at my presumption. The train jerked into motion and whined powerfully up the gradient to Alpiglen. ".....come back safely, my friends."

It began to hail as our fingers clutched the cold rocks of The Wall.

That summer we made a casual last minute decision to walk The Pennine Way and found the promised Arcadia in Teesdale and rested in sylvan sweetness and dreamed. On The Cheviots, we camped on beds of heather and bilberry surrounded by stars and night breezes.

Bernard and Jean-Pierre gave welcoming grins: we were going to have a crowded bivouac on the Swallow's Nest. Suddenly the presence of these two friendly Frenchmen gave a boost to our morale. The 'bedroom' was cramped, but we managed to lash three of us lying down to the ledge while Chris slumped in an ice filled groove.

The lightweight tents in a corner of a field sheltered a slumbering group of Pennine Way friends and walkers from many parts of Britain and Europe. The silence was shattered by a cacophony of bad language from the four occupants of a nearby canvas castle who had recently returned late from the pub. Anger born out of frustration boiled over.

Shortly before dawn we choked down a breakfast of muesli and tea..... and our fear.

The morning was cold, the sky was clear.

We climbed out of the Swallow's Nest up a short vertical wall down which hung a length of fixed rope. Five or so controlled arm-pulls, crampons grating furiously on smooth rock and we pulled onto the First Ice-field. We felt very small and vulnerable.

".....The die was cast, we must win through or die."

At Colden, Lothersdale, and Dufton, farmers provided for our simple needs and around kitchen tables we chatted, drank tea or ate hearty breakfasts as if one of the family. What was the magic ingredient which lifted the heart, brought a smile, a spontaneous thanks and left us with those memories?

In the middle of the Second Ice-field Bernard's axe slipped from his fingers. We watched mesmerised, and reflected, as the axe fled, cart wheeling down the ice to disappear in seconds over the lower edge and down to the meadows thousands of feet below.

What happened to my childhood memories of the farm in Wensleydale? Hot summer days, picnics brought out to the hay makers in the fields, fetching the cows from pastures by the river for milking, the barns, farmyard hens and geese, rides on the tractor, a raft on the river, a myriad childhood sensations. Were they false? There was now no sign of livestock, no meadows or hay making required, and where were the poultry? The barns were sterile units converted to a camp launderette, toilets, shower, and shop. Who was the stranger? Was he born when I was a child?

Death Bivouac!

"….and they went out like a match in the rain. The seasons with their storms passed over, the ropes turned to straw, and one day the rock was bare again as in the beginning"

The ledge was a depressing place that day, banked up with snow, and with water pouring from the bulging rock above. Round the corner danger lurked. One more step ….now?

Great swelling Cheviot fells, rough grass and reeds grazed by sheep, silhouetted against a threatening sky. Stretches of heather, bilberry, cotton-grass and sphagnum relieved the bleakness of the windswept landscape. We remained close together in this lonely spot although the land reached out to meet the sky at every horizon; an illusion of space. Danger. Keep Out. Military Zone. Bombs. Shells. Shooting. Which do you prefer?

'Make tea, not war' some passing wag had remarked wryly.

At that moment a loud detonation high among the summit cliffs froze our gaze to the tiny specks below. Seconds passed as the rocks sighed downwards before raking the ice-field far below. The inevitable happened and one of the tiny figures shot silently downwards.

The Eiger climb was over for the Jugoslavs.

What places of climbing history we trod. It would have been pleasant to linger at the bivouac of Rebuffat and Buhl, the epic Quartz Crack and the Corti Bivouac, but the traditional Eiger storm was brewing. Water showered down, numbing fingers and slowing progress. Just as we exited from the grooves the storm burst. Thunder echoed in the crags and snow whirled in our faces. Waves of snow and rubble from the summit slopes hissed past. Four more rope lengths over 'black tiles' then suddenly it was there, a white summit ice field, now bathed in evening sunlight. We cramponed up the gleaming slopes and along the ridge to the summit. An icy wind was blowing as evening approached.

We passed by farms, windows and doors open to the sun and breeze on a summer's day, and reflected on the free and gentle aspect of the scene. Harsh reality was inconceivable, winter storms and deep snows for months, killing every single living beast at Birkdale, forcing retreat and loss of freedom for a man who was his own master. Life had returned to Birkdale, the door stood open.

The dream had been translated into reality.

OBSERVATIONS FROM PEMBROKE
BOMBS AWAY!

KEITH GREGSON

On one occasion I remember watching D-C (Derrick Carnell) gardening a new route. We (Les, Patti, Eileen and self) were sitting on a promontory looking across at him rolling huge turf's down a slab. It was one of those hot days with hardly a breath of wind and the gardening had been in progress for several hours, as could be seen from the trail of grass sods and heather which meandered out toward the horizon. Nat was supervising the project and belaying a rope on the cliff top. D-C was swinging about below and was gradually peeling a huge carpet of grass and bracken, a veritable axminster, which was maybe 5 yards wide and had been neatly rolled into a yard or more diameter – probably a couple of tons of vegetation, soil and rocks. As he merrily jumped up and down on this potential avalanche there came the unmistakable "put, put, put" of a small inshore fishing boat. We shouted a warning and took cover. I was reminded of a picture on the cover of a Famous Five adventure in which the children were lying in the long grass at the top of a high cliff looking down at a boat in the sea.

The boat came chugging round the point and into the swamp, we couldn't understand how the fisherman could be so oblivious to his grassy surroundings as he checked his lobster pots. If he had chanced to look up his erstwhile tranquil day would have taken a rapid turn for the worse. A hundred feet above him, the carpet was gently rolling and growing, like a huge snowball, while D-C, cowering above it, was doing his best to simulate "zero g". At best the fishing would be a write-off, which was altogether a better alternative to being buried at sea! But he didn't, instead he continued with his work, totally oblivious of the earth and debris which continued to shower about him. We all held our breath for what seemed an age before the boat moved on.

But move on it did, followed shortly by a substantial tidal wave. I often wonder whether the boatman noticed. If so he probably tells an interesting tale of an evening in "The Sloop".

THE NORTH TOWER OF ST. DAVID'S CATHEDRAL

It may come as a surprise to some of you that the Oread can lay claim to a climb on St. David's Cathedral. It's not a long climb so I'll make this a short story. It came about one afternoon following a session in "The Farmers" or was it "The Grove"? We'd been there in order to allow the tide to go out, or maybe it was to come in? Anyway the result was a visit to Cathedral Slabs where we did a couple of routes and were treated to the usual description of latest and possible new routes. D-C mentioned that the arete to the right of Grey Slab hadn't been done and said something about "man for the job". Being gullible, and not of sound mind due to several portions of 'Feeling Foul' ale, I was easy prey. The climbing looked reasonable, the possible fall off the edge appalling and the protection none-existent. Nevertheless D-C assured me that, should I come off, he'd catch me! How gullible can you get? Anyway, once you start laybacking an arete, there are only two things you can do; either continue or fall off. The upshot was a route called "Might'er". However if you want to repeat it you can't because apparently God, during one of His rest periods, let St. David's Cathedral decline a little and so the lesser powers-that-be in that part of the world decided to repair it with our climb! But I'm assured that it still makes a fine line and would be a magnificent and unprotected lead. Maybe one Saturday night late . . .

HOME OF THE PEREGRINE

"I say young man! You can't climb here."

This was clearly inaccurate since I had just ventured over the top of the cliff wearing a rope and all the other stuff which climbers carry.

"I'm sorry?" I questioned. The tweedy lady was clearly confused and it's always a good idea to give a protagonist another chance.

"You can't climb here" she repeated, in that I'm a conservationist voice.

"Oh! and why is that?" I asked.

"Because of the rapture!" she said. (At this point an excitable young man might have risen to the occasion.)

Ah! you mean the peregrine I said. At this she was slightly taken aback.

"You know about them then?"

"Yes, of course we know about them, the peregrines nest in a crack in the cliff which we (climbers) dug out. Before the peregrines could get in, it was used by a kestrel, now the hole is bigger the peregrines can use it. They wouldn't be here if we hadn't cleaned out the crack in the first place."

"Oh! I never thought of that!" she said.

It turned out that she was a member of the nature conservancy and by the time Rock joined me at the top of the crag we were very nearly bosom friends. Ah well! you win some, you lose some.

PURPLE CRACK BY MOONLIGHT OR "CHRIS-TENING THE TENT!"

We'd been to The Rugby Club in St. David's. We always used to go to The Rugby Club on Saturday night, and we always used to get back sometime early on Sunday morning. Chris Bryan and I were about to crawl into our bags when somebody had the idea that we should climb Purple Crack by moonlight. We could see it from the campsite and it did look inviting. So we did. The climbing was excellent and we enjoyed ten minutes at the top watching the moonlight on the waves. Then we crawled into our pits, and Chris threw up! It was the first time I'd used my new tent. Ah well! you lose some, you win some.

TOASTER ABUSE

BRIAN WEST

The curtain rises, disclosing an otherwise empty pub lounge, with large window looking out over car-park to distant hills. It is a fine evening, the sort of evening to be out on those distant hills. For some, however, duty calls....

Four men sit round a table. TITFER and BERKLEY agitated, LUCID calm, FRANKLYN WATTS-DELANEY putting on his glasses....

TIT: Somefinks got to be done about it!

LUCID: About what?

TIT: That toaster. They will keep using it.

BERK: Well if it's a problem it'll have to go. They don't deserve one anyway.

TIT: I've seen 'em doing it! They put muffins in it and spiced buns, and pitta breads... then when it's bunged up they poke about in it wiv their fingers.

BERK: They don't deserve fingers. They've got it all sorted in Chile, y'know. If we were in Chile they'd have had their fingers all cut off by now...

LUCID: I'm sure it's only a littul problem. All we need is a bit of a tightner and...

FWD: We mustn't give them any excuse for misoperation. We'll have to put up a notice where they can't miss it.

TIT: P'raps by the socket marked "toaster"...

FWD: Yes, Titfer. I'll draw up a list of instructions, and next time I'm down I'll...

BERK: But what if someone gets their fingers caught in it? Are we covered?

TIT: I fought they hadn't got any fingers anymore...

BERK: EH!....Oh, I see...It's a joke...This is serious. We must get a grip of the situation. Do we let just anyone use the toaster? We're leaving ourselves wide open y'know...

FWD: We'll have to come up with some sort of bread – gauge then...

BERK: Eh!

FWD: A bread-gauge Berkley. You know, you can only put the bread in the toaster if it's passed the bread – gauge first. Better get Ernie in on this. It'll have to be made of stainless or something that we can sterilise. We don't want E Coli in the club do we?

TIT: Why? Hasn't he been on enough meets? Never been on a working party?

BERK: Eh?

TIT: E Coli. Not been on enough meets. It's a joke. Get it?

BERK: Eh? Oh I see...

TIT: Have you heard the one where Maggie Fatcher goes into...

FWD sighs, crosses to the window and gazes out upon a magical twilight. The last embers of a stunning sunset glow softly upon the far horizon. somewhere out there Burgess is trying to pull in another route. Lost in appreciation, FWD lingers at the window...

LUCID: Magnificent, isn't it?

FWD: Yes Lucid. The Turbo makes all the difference...

TIT: Ev'ryfink OK, FW?

FWD: Yes, Titfer. The cars are still there. (returns to seat.) Now about the toaster...

BERK: We could perhaps say that it's to be used by Full Members only...

LUCID: What about visiting Clubs, and children?

BERK: That's their problem. They didn't ought to have children anyway. Irresponsible, that's what they are... How about then, only if accompanied by a Full Member?

LUCID: I think we can sort this out. It's only a littul problem. Just a simple note in the Newsletter...

TIT: Somefinks got to be done about it!

LUCID: About what?

TIT: That Newsletter...

BERK: Quite right. It's an abuse of power, that's what it is. If he'd been in Chile, he'd have been machine-gunned by now .... What I want is facts and information, not what his dog's done. What use is a brain-teaser to me?

TIT: Just what I was finking...

BERK: Eh?

TIT: What use is a brain-teaser to you...

BERK: Eh?...Oh I see...It's a joke...

TIT: No, that's Not a joke. This is a joke; "Mister President, Mister President, the Martians have landed"...

FWD sighs, crosses to the window, and gazes out. A warm, velvety dusk caresses the casement, those distant hills limned black against a sky of darkest blue. Somewhere out there Burgess has made it to the pub and is scrounging a light for his Castella. Snoddy and Gabbo are still on the crag, but so what?

Anxiously scanning the car park, FWD catches the reassuring glint of chromium...

TIT: Ev'ryfink OK,FW?

FWD: Yes Titfer, the cars are still there. (returns to seat.) Now shall we have a basket of chips or carry on with this toaster business?

We are spared this decision. The curtain falls abruptly, and of it's own accord. It has had enough.

JUST A LITTLE SPANISH
(A TALE OF ANDEAN INSPIRATIONS)

MIKE WYNNE

Titicaca. Machu Picchu. Inca. Nasca.

There can be few people for whom these words do not cause some sort of magical bells to start ringing. Why?

The Corner. The Gates. Dream. Diagonal.

All magical routes at one time in any British climber's life. Routes to inspire which, once achieved, will have left one with an immense feeling of satisfaction and the desire to set new targets for the future.

But what are the connections between these magical, inspiring, routes and the magical names from Peru? In order to find out about the magic of the classic, quality rock climbs one needs time, a partner, the desire and the ability to succeed. To discover the magic of Peru one needs time, money and just a little Spanish . . .

Peru is a high country – very high – or at least the more interesting parts of it are. Trapped between the western and eastern cordilleras, Lake Titicaca stands at an altitude of 3,800m, a respectable altitude by alpine standards. However, when there, due to the immensity of this, the world's highest navigable lake, the brain is tricked into thinking you are at sea level – until you start to climb uphill that is! Here are wild open spaces, great views, and the healthy feeling one gets as one becomes acclimatized to the altitude. At night the skies are crystal clear, silence abounds and there is freedom from pollution. Here the traveller can be rewarded with the same feelings that one experiences on a comfortable, high alpine bivvy when the route is going well. Here life's batteries can be recharged or refreshed, away from the hustle and chaos of our busy lives, congested roads, congested cities and our congested country.

Having been involved in travel (both through work and as an independent traveller) for fifteen years now, I have sometimes been a bit blasé about visiting what should be exciting new parts of the world. In July 1998 my latest venture was to lead a school party on a three week trip to Peru – part trekking, part travelling and sightseeing, which was to leave me with a variety of realisations, new inspirations and a refreshed outlook on life. Peru is responsible for this and for that reason only it deserves some sort of promotion; which is one of the aims of this article.

The second aim is to explore the realisation of acceptance of change from a climber's point of view. When I was younger and freer, a very large percentage of my leisure time was spent rock climbing, mountain walking, or mountaineering. As time has gone by I do not feel that my love for the mountain environment has diminished in any way, but the means of achieving satisfaction from it has changed. Much of the rock climbing has been replaced with fell running, the satisfaction of succeeding on a hard route replaced with the satisfaction of improving one's time over a specific race route or even achieving a respectable finishing position. Much of the mountaineering has been replaced with trekking and travelling, where with opportunities to work as a leader of groups in many mountain regions throughout the world, I have been able to visit and experience areas to which I am certain my own climbing would never have taken me.

Despite all this I still sometimes experience the 'climbers' guilt feeling – I must get out on the rock soon or I will stagnate! One can never forget the immense feeling of satisfaction gained after succeeding on a hard quality route, especially if climbed in good conditions and in pleasant surroundings, and followed with a few good pints of ale. But how often do all these conditions come together? How many despondent hours are spent tolerating grotty weather, feeling that the climbing is not going as well as it should be, wet, greasy rock, before finally experiencing that magical moment when it all comes together at once. Surely, if we have to live in England, there must be easier ways to get through the damp, dark, winters and the damp but not so dark summers, and to still get a lot of satisfaction out of our mountains throughout the year. There are ways – as long as one can dispel the feeling that one 'ought' to climb.

The endemic Peruvians seem to have it sussed. Maybe one reason is due to the fact that their weather is a little more predictable than ours. They get fairly well defined wet seasons and dry seasons; they know when to plant their corn and their potatoes and can be fairly sure that they will grow. The Incas and the pre-Incas have left evidence that amazes and baffles us. Our western technology has recently enabled us to take our rock sport indoors by artificially recreating the natural outside environment under cover (but sadly lacking the ambiance of the outdoors). However, between 500 and 1,000 years ago, the Incas and their predecessors were able to shift whole rock faces in blocks weighing 200 tonnes or more considerable distances and up slopes, and fit these blocks together again with millimetric accuracy. In doing this they were not building climbing walls but temples that seemed to double up as sun observatories to assist them with the correct timing for their cultivation. Simply to see some of this famous stonework in its mountain setting, for whose construction methods modern science has no answers, is certainly inspiring.

Being on the move is definitely satisfying. Who can claim that (with the exception of the occasional rare combination of superb scenery and weather) that they actually enjoy sitting on a belay, being holed up on a bivvy or in a tent, or freezing the gonads off in the howling wind on a ledge in the midst of a Scottish winter? At the end of any epic, pub-talk will diminish the misery we have all felt at times when we are stuck in one place for an unexpected length of time. Travelling, trekking, and fell-running, do overcome this problem to some extent as one can be more in control of oneself and be able to keep on the move if desired.

You may be thinking that I have become a disillusioned climber – which is certainly not the case. I'll still go out when the time allows and the weather looks good, and have a great time. The great discovery though is to find and enjoy the alternatives that suit one when climbing is simply not the best thing to be doing. Being broad rather than narrow minded in one's approach to the outdoors enables one to get far more enjoyment out of it. The Peruvians have *ayni* as a strong part of their culture. This is the mutual agreement to help each other when necessary. The local guides and porters in the Andes could not be nicer people. They work willingly and do not ask for anything beyond the usual rewards for the service that they provide. As a leader I never expect everything to go to plan and am therefore quite happy to accept things that may not be acceptable to a highly structured western way of life.

The Peruvian Cordilleras are very accessible. Being such a narrow range, roads approach close to the peaks. Buses are frequent, cheap and seem to be generally on time. Although my 1998 tour had been prearranged, it was a credit to all the people in Peru involved in its organisation that all the connections from bus – train – plane – boat went like clockwork. During the three weeks that we were there we experienced only one late train! Shops in the main centres provide everything a westerner may desire, while the local markets provided the local flavour. You do not have to eat guinea pig every day; there is plenty of excellent pizza around! The currency is stable and US$ are widely accepted and obtainable from cash machines on credit card. Getting there is not cheap but can be done for around £600. Our summer (July) is the height of their dry season, so why not think about it as an alternative to the Alps one year?

It would help to know just a little Spanish....

BREGAGLIA 1998 – PIZ BADILE
(Cassin Route)

Michael Hayes

Dover Sole on the Ferry, Schnitzel in Germany, Raclette in Switzerland and pizza in every village from St. Moritz to Bellagio. The holiday as usual was going to plan. 10 days of Eastern Alpine sunshine with a few thunderstorms thrown in for good measure, swimming by Lake Como, and eating our way through seven countries. What more could you want?

"Daddy why did you bring your climbing things?" I guess its time for a little exercise!

A warm up was needed! The Leni Route on the Spazzacaldeira, and the Steiger Route on the Punta Da L'albigna, not only provided a suitable introduction to the granite but also managed to wear down the finger ends. A rest was needed (so was more pizza!) The Badile would have to wait.

Three Days of clear weather came at last but was there still time? With everyone heading home the arrival of Paul from Holland gave me one last chance. Sorting gear out was interesting – Spaghetti Bolognaise for the bivvy, Chilli for the Summit, I'll take the gas, you have the stove. It was all going to plan. 7.00 pm in the evening lying in the sunshine on the Bivvy we knew it was going to be a good evening. Soup, spaghetti, cheese and sausage were rounded off by a display of head torches descending the North Ridge. The clear morning sky's meant there would be no turning back. The Cassin was about to take it's revenge.

Pitch after pitch of superb climbing, the occasional peg put to good use and the ever present sun. Time was moving on, quick gulps of water and some melting chocolate passed for dinner, (didn't any one know I needed regular food stops!). Leading VI/A0 on an empty stomach and another sip of water led finally to the exit chimney. Hand jamming with a sack on my back,(I didn't want any skin on my arms any way!) at 8.00 pm we emerged onto the North Ridge. Relief and enjoyment were all too brief. The last of the water consumed – now how do we get down?

An hour of abbing brought us to a small ledge already occupied by 6 Italians. It was here we realised we were to spend the night. It was going to be an interesting evening. Tied to the rock, feet in the rucksack, and sat on a rope shivering, waiting for the sun to rise. Dawn brought its own challenges. First get warm, next team up with 6 Italians and relay 8 abseil ropes down to the col. A huge stone fall passing only 20 meters away on its journey down the north west face had us hugging the rock and glad to be on our way down. The bodies hanging from the helicopter meant not everyone had been so lucky! Finally after 16 hours without water the top snow field offered the first relief. The realisation was beginning to grow. We had done it, were back safe and it was time to get on with the holiday. The family were waiting, the memories would live forever.

After soup and beer in the hut I returned to find Helen busy packing the last few things into the car. Time for one last celebration meal in Vicosoprano before the night drive to Munchen and the luxury of a real bed.

295

ORDEAL ON CRAIG MEAGHAIDH

JULIA STOWELL

I am dozing; too late in Andy's van along with four others. Even Dave Mawer has yet to wake. When he does, the reality of a winter weekend in Scotland will begin.

We discover Graham Weston has been bivvying in the snow outside Kev Allsobrook's car. Soon, everyone is heading expectantly towards the lochan under the crag. The usual banter prevails although it is not long before I am left behind, slithering awkwardly over the bog-avoiding duckboards. A beautiful approach walk, I think, heedless of a moderately heavy sack. In no time at all we are there.

"Well, who's doing what?"

Swift negotiation divides the party into: Kev, Graham, Daryl Kirk and Dave to have a go at Nordwand; me, Trevor Willis, John Salmon, Andy Gale and Robin Van der Heyden to do Staghorn Gully, a suggestion of mine which seems acceptable. Within the second group I am paired with Trevor whom I have never met before. He eyes me suspiciously and enquires politely if I know how to tie on. He relaxes a little when I tell him that although I haven't much winter climbing experience I have been to the Alps, and have been known to lead on rock.

We move together at first and then pitch it on easy ground rapidly catching up with the other three. It is warm; too warm and the slush wets everything and slides off the soft turf below in great dollops. I can hear John ahead questioning the sense of carrying on.

"Just do one more pitch to see if it gets better higher up" is the consensus.

It does, marginally.

After the approach ramp the correct selection of gully is fundamental, as Grade IVs lurk to either side of Staghorn. Robin's team check it out and now we are positioned at the entrance of Staghorn, to one side of the first ice bulge, in pole position. I belay Trevor but cannot see his frustrated endeavor. I can tell though – the lack of demand for rope says everything. Be patient, I tell myself, he must be putting gear in. Indeed, he has an excellent ice screw in lovely turquoise ice but the material above is diabolical and disintegrates at each placement attempt. Eventually we give up. Robin has a go and with determination succeeds to get high enough to latch onto better ice. Now we must climb as a five for this pitch as I am unable to lead it. I patiently wait until last as Robin's team, then Trevor go up. I have little experience of winter gear and find the ice screw placement reassuringly difficult to get out. I am convinced of its security. Still, 'Don't fall off in winter' has been drummed into my head.

I am climbing now, trying to find some purchase for my feet as the bulge disintegrates further. A momentary secure hold is all I need to swing both axes into sounder ice above and I am up into typical gully climbing. Rejoining Trevor and Andy on the belay I discover that we will stay as a five. Probably wise as there are two more ice bulges to deal with and if they are anything like the first we could have problems. In the gloom I can see John belaying Robin. The conditions are better with some frozen turf but the weather is clagging in. And it is late; too late. First Andy, then Trevor leaves the stance and I am left to be patient once more. After an age I surpress the urge to shout and tell myself to wait. At length the all clear to climb drifts down. I have begun to get cold and welcome the chance to warm myself.

The following pitches are a continuous round of climbing; greetings at the belay; disappearing comrades; waiting; cold; waiting; irritation at the delay; waiting; shouting "What's happening?"; waiting and once more climbing.

Now it is dark and I have my head-torch on. It is snowing too and the wind is gusting. The final ice section is steeper than ever and the base has almost completely fallen down. Somehow I manage to struggle up, my awareness confined by the immediate pool of light in front of me. The extra effort involved results in a pain-consumed minute of hot aches in my fingers, worse than I can remember from my years of winter rowing. I arrive at the belay to find everyone together; a mini-triumph as the last ice bulge is behind us. But the elation is short lived because now we must get to the top and navigate off. Will there be a monster cornice? No. Mercifully there are only steady snow slopes to the top but the welcome on the ridge is fearsome. It is very dark but in the torch lights we can see the snow driving horizontally. We can't hear each other over the wind and huddle together to look at the map. I stare and try to make some sense of it but my brain is reluctant to work and I am aware of a desire to lie down. It is perhaps 8.00 pm but feels like 2.00 am. We have been on the go for 12 hours.

John and Robin have decided on a bearing. I feel inadequate but am glad for their competence. Even walking on a bearing, roped up, is difficult in the buffeting wind. We walk straight into it, heads bent to minimise the blinding effect of the driving snow. Andy shouts a warning that we have moved off the level ground of the ridge and we correct ourselves. I catch sight of a marker post, a reassuring landmark that Andy remembered from a summer walk several years ago. Then another one. We are on the right track. Looking slightly away from where I think the Lochan should be I can make out a pale shape but if I look directly at the place it is elusive. I sink down in soft snow and hope the slope we are descending now is not avalanche prone. Relief floods through us as we reach the Lochan and the walk out seems academic. We stop for a bite to eat.

I am asking Andy once again for a rest. He is encouraging and patient as I slump down, convinced I cannot go on but knowing I must. The track is interminable before we reach the duckboards but worse still after – they seemed to come so soon after starting this morning. Now it goes on forever, our Creag Meaghaidh ordeal, until we find the sanctuary of the van.

The Nordwand team have abandoned us and gone home, anxious to avoid the possibility of having to send out a search party. But I don't mind, I just want to sleep.

THE OREAD FAMILY

Uschi Hobday

I was first introduced to the Oread in 1962 who, at that time, met regularly at the Bell in Sadler Gate, Derby. The club was full of young and single chaps, all on the lookout for a partner and ready to pounce if a suitable fair maiden appeared on the scene. Well can you blame them. It was never easy to find a partner who also enjoyed extreme sports like climbing, mountaineering and skiing, and prepared to rough it on cold and windy campsites in tiny Vanguard tents. As it happened Geoff Hayes and Colin did succeed in luring Anne and myself into marriage even though we played hard to get.

When I returned from Germany in 1965, having just married Colin, things seemed to have changed. Various people had got married in the meantime and there were lots of young couples about. In the first few years, the Oread became my replacement family and helped enormously to settle into my new life far away from the "real" mountains and my old climbing friends. We went away most weekends and generally had a good time. Various couples already had children but I was too busy to take much notice. There were the Ashcrofts, Allens, Janes, Prettys, Penlingtons, and of course the Welbourns and the Westons.

However, things soon changed. The moment our first offspring Steff arrived in 1967, we suddenly had become a family and had to re-orientate ourselves, as things were not so easy anymore and every weekend away needed a lot of planning and organising.

We were in the throngs of the baby boom years of the sixties, not just nationally but also within the Oread. I believe this generation of kids were the first truly mobile ones. It was now possible to take babies out in slings and carriers from a very early age, which made life much easier for the young

297

Oread families. (This meant that we Oread mums did not have to spend every weekend at home minding the children) Some of our equipment came from Ruth Welbourn who had bought it in Norway and both Lisa and Helga were introduced to the hills from a very early age.

We now tended to get together with other Oread families in a likewise predicament. In those days children were not allowed in any pub so consequently, on a day out walking or climbing, the route was not chosen according to where the pub with the best beer and food was, but where the best shelters were for eating sandwiches and feeding stations for babies. So we were normally huddled behind a wall for shelter.

As is typical of the Oread, something funny usually happens. I particularly remember the year the Ashcrofts travelled with their boys Ian, David and Peter to the Alps, loaded to the top with a borrowed luggage rack. Somewhere along the Autobahn, the whole load took off and discharged itself onto the motorway. There were pushchair babywalkers, coloured wooden bricks, camping equipment etc. scattered at a distance of 100m. Jack stopped on the hard shoulder, rushed out to retrieve the bits, but luckily the motorway was not too busy, so it was relatively safe. Just as everything was tied down safely, the Police arrived, issuing a warning to Jack saying in a stern voice "You cannot stop here, move on". Jack was only too happy to oblige and grateful for his lucky escape from a heavy fine.

We had good weekends at Tan-y-Wyddfa, especially when the children were small, as even then it was fairly comfortable and reasonably dry and warm which is worth gold after a wet weekend camping with small children. There were of course always those, who did not like young families taking up bed space and disturbing the peace of the Hut, saying this is a "Climbing Club". Just to mention John Fisher, who called them "Hammelkeule" which translates into "leg of lamb". It was one of the words which John picked up in Germany and one which he liked the sound of, so consequently he used it frequently. He also gave them ear rubs. This resulted in them usually trying to avoid him whenever they could. Nowadays, of course, things are very different, since he has become father to Peter and Robert, even though he is financially "RUINED" since becoming a family man.

Our best times were the Alpine Meets, where we all got together as one big family. There used to be a great exodus from Nottingham and Derby, with about 40 to 50 people arriving in dribs and drabs at the chosen campsite. Frequently it was chaos, but so what. I always remember the Ashcroft boys as being very lively and active, especially David who impressed everyone with his gymnastics and backflips. He later became Junior Gymnastic champion of Sheffield. Some years later we were joined by new members Roy and Chris Eyre with their three girls, who were on their first Alpine Meet. It was in the Aosta valley, a very popular meet, to be repeated several times. That particular year, little Heather was not very well, so they called in Nurse Sue Wren for a consultation. Nurse Wren soon diagnosed "Mumps" and immediately mum and the girls were put under quarantine, leaving Roy free to carry on with the climbing. It was really hilarious. We made a big sign, "Danger – Keep out – infectious disease".. No doubt it was not amusing for Chris. However, we kept them well supplied with food and gossip. Ever since then Heather has been left with the name "Mumpy".

Mike and Sue Wren had a sure method of keeping their children under control. Whilst climbing on Birchen, they simply tied Lucy to a tree, gave her a banana to keep her happy and got on with the climbing.

Eric and Merle Wallis went even one step further, they tucked their children into a backcarrier and climbed with them on their backs. At that time Eric was working as a climbing instructor in Wales.

Reg and Anne Squires, however, took their boys into deepest Africa for 2 years, perhaps to teach them to speak like the Zulus or to learn how to track wild animals.

Whilst there were so many youngsters within the Oread, Rusty got rather fidgety and restless. All his friends were slowed down by children and the mileage for the day's walking was not at all to his liking. So in turn he carried them all on his broad shoulders. It was one way for him to work off surplus energy. Believe it or not, even now, 25 years later, he still needs slowing down, and he still carries Oread children on his back.

In 1978 a large group of Oreads and their families went to Trafoi – Italy, to climb in the Ortler Region. The campsite was very small, no facilities, no shop, no restaurant, in the middle of nowhere. Even now in 1998 Oreads still talk about the fantastic campsite, its atmosphere and its situation. It was the washhouse, which became the focus over the next two weeks. As the campsite had no electricity, the camp warden arrived every morning very early to light a wood fire in the boiler house. Soon after we had hot water to wash and shower. At that time the Church of Rome was in the throngs of electing a new pope. As is the custom after each round of voting if black smoke rises from the chimney of the Vatican, no one has been elected, however, if the smoke is white, then we have a new Pope. So our first look in the morning was the boiler of the chimney house to look for the colour of the smoke. Soon after, Pope John Paul III was elected. When we were all in basecamp we tended to frequent the local pub where they made us very welcome. On the last evening we all went there for dinner and we presented the landlord with a carved wooden plaque with a mounted Oread badge. I have it from a reliable source, that it still graces the shelf behind the bar. The only real problem with the campsite was the walk back in the dark. No streetlight to guide you, just the stars. We had to walk through the fields and through the churchyard. Austrians tend to have the eternal candle burning on the graves. The flickering lights made it really spooky, and it became a real test of courage for the children.

When I think of the Hut in Wales it reminds me of the wonderful Christmases and New Years. The community spirit of the Oread was brilliant in those days. Everyone brought goodies for the communal dinner and everyone helped to cook under far more primitive conditions than now,. Everybody exchanged presents, the children thought it was wonderful, specially fetching your own Christmas tree straight from the forest. There was no need to go out to the pub, entertainment was in the hut. I can just visualise it when I close my eyes, the lounge, a big fire roaring, Ernie Phillips sitting comfortably in the big red velvet chair near the fire fast asleep. On the table a barrage of bottles, the children playing games, and everyone happy. New Year used to be just as much fun, with a great buffet in the dining room contributed by all, and the old traditions being kept alive with silly games like the submarine, and the statue of Nelson, and bringing in a piece of coal as well as bread and salt straight after midnight. Frequently the chaps took their sons and walked up Snowdon to welcome the New Year with a sunrise.

More frequently however, it was dull, grey and wet, and no sunrise to be seen. Sadly those days are gone, when it was a fight to get into the hut. There were always the Gadsbys, the Welbourns, the Squires, the Hobdays, and Ernie and Ronnie Phillips, and others. Now sadly, year after year, the hut is empty at Christmas. Do we like too much our home comforts or has the community spirit gone?

Not many of the Oread children carried on with the mountaineering tradition in their adult life or kept their ties with the club.

There is of course Michael Hayes, who plays an active role, as a climber, mountaineer, and also as an active committee member. We have Lisa Welbourn, a good climber and skier, now heavily into Trail Quest competitions on mountain bikes. She became Great Britain Ladies Champion in 1997. She too played a role as a committee member. There is also Graham Weston who leads meets for the younger generation, attends Alpine Meets, climbs and skis. There is also Chris Bryan who climbed very hard routes in the Alps when quite young, specifically with his dad Ken Bryan. Of the younger ones there is Matt Chambers, a prospective member, and Jenny Raphael, now married to Dave Jones.

Those that are still active but live away are Roger Penlington, Steff Hobday, who has climbed in America and in the Alps in summer and winter, frequently with Graham Weston. There is Simon Wren who became a very hard climber who often takes his father Mike on desperate routes on the climbing walls. Annette Hobday who has been living in Germany since 1992 has the Alps at her doorstep and attends an Alpine Meet if it is in Austria. She skis seriously, snowboards, and does mountain biking. Peter Hayes also lives in Munich and attends most Alpine Oread family meets.

To finish off I give you an amazing statistic. This is only rough, and I may be out by a few on my count, but the Oread in the Sixties and Seventies either produced or adopted more than 70 children. Well done you Oreads. It just goes to show how active the Oread was in more than one way. However out of these only 8 have become actual members in their own right.

In the Eighties there was a big lull in new children and only now in the last 7 years or so, is there a new batch of small children and a new group of Oread parents who go together on meets, who socialise with each other, and actually organise their own family meets in the Hut in Wales. So the cycle repeats itself. May the Oread continue to prosper and continue to be a family orientated club. Lots of people grumble that the Oread does not have many hard climbers, but to me a Mountaineering Club means everything from walking to mountaineering to skiing, etc. To me, the Oread has given me 33 wonderful years of companionship, wonderful weekends in the hills and on Alpine Meets and, for that, I am grateful.

Sponsored by Mothercare and Aldi — *Editor.*

WHAT'S ALL THIS ABOUT MUNROS?
EASTER 1994

JACK ASHCROFT

I returned from the Highlands on the 9th April 1994 after what must have been the worst Easter weather that I can remember. It snowed on the mountains every day with considerable accumulations in the corries, and the formation of large unstable cornices on the tops. The beginning of the week had the added bonus of gale force winds. These calmed by the end of the week. Temperatures increased a little and it was rain in the valley. That was a general report of Easter 1994 in the Glen Affric and Strathfarrar Hills. Not that it made too great an impact on a determination to get on the hill. A brightening of the sky and Nick Evans enthused "The sun will be out soon". "And so will the thaw" was the rejoinder. Caution was high with some of the team, particularly bearing in mind that from the word go on the Saturday John Linney, followed by Colin Barnard, had the misfortune to walk through a cornice in white out conditions and gale force winds. They had found themselves alive several hundred feet down the east slopes of Tom A'Choinich, Colin having leapfrogged over John. On stopping in the murky conditions, John shouted uphill "I'm OK" to Colin who had arrived stationary on the slope below him.

They gathered themselves together and descended the mountain on a route which had been rudely determined for them by the involuntary fall. The major injury was a bruised leg and sprained hand for John. Colin had lost his axe and compass. That was bad news.

The good news was a day when Rock Hudson, Nick and I traversed Mam Sodhail and Carn Eighe via the Sgurr Na Lapaich Ridge. The day started in bright sunlight with an inch of fresh snow on the road up Glen Affric. From Affric Lodge the whole setting was idyllic. Glen Affric was living up to it's reputation of being the most beautiful glen in the Highlands.

This was only short lived, and at the 700m contour in came a storm. Crampons on, we walked over Sgurr Na Lapaich cairn in the face of a further deterioration in the weather. At this time the Elder of the party began to whimper "Not going on in this", reversing the bearing on his compass. "Stop Moaning" was the retort through the blizzard. The Elder had traversed the main summits many years ago in fine weather. What the hell was he doing traversing them again in poor weather. Ah well "Don't split the party". The young men wanted their Munros – "Don't mess the day up", so on we went.

Half an hour later there was a clearing of the sky and a ray of sunlight – just before a rise in the ridge blended with one of the most spectacular mushroom cornices I've seen for many a year. Camera out, waiting for Nick to walk onto the top, photograph taken, but a minute too late. The ray of sunlight and the cornice silhouetted against the unlit summit ridge behind had been a perfect picture. The image remains a memorable moment.

A few minutes later storm again, the camera went back into the rucsac and remained there for the rest of the day. The last few hundred feet of the Sgurr Na Lapaich Ridge to Mam Sodhail looked a spectacular icy edge but proved easy. Snow arêtes often appear more spectacular than they are.

Our arrival at the large circular cairn, which was a principal point on the primary triangulation of Scotland by the Ordanance Survey in the 1840s, coincided with the arrival of two others who had walked to the summit via Coire Leachavie. They said their route at the head of the corrie had proved difficult – too much fresh snow. The five of us sat at the summit munching our lunch relatively sheltered in the lee of the cairn. In 1840 the cairn had measured 60 feet in circumference and 23 feet high. It had shrunk since those heady days when the Industrial Revolution was gaining momentum across the world. But the now modest size, worn away by the ravages of nature over the previous 150 years, was appreciated as a shelter for our lunch on one of the two highest mountains west of the Caledonian Canal.

There was a strong wind as we set course for Carn Eighe, but the visibility was good in reasonable sunlight. Soon over the summit we embarked on the long east ridge of Carn Eighe, onto the narrow rocky ridge with a snowed up crest, and fine views in all directions. The Elder must have been engrossed with the temporary magnificence of the situation since he got his rucsac jammed in a little 'V' notch near the summit, with crampons flashing in space. The tail man, Rock, gave a 'heave-ho' to the sac and a sense of terra firma was re-established. The beallach between the Pinnacles and Sron Garbh, the weather having come in again, decided us on a direct descent south into Glen Nam Fiadh, and so it was a steady 500m descent at speed as, simultaneously, the snow storm gathered pace.

Some two and a half hours after a laborious plod through soft snow we descended to Glen Affric Lodge and the car park. The sun came out again to end the day. The late afternoon sun gave Sgurr Na Lapaich an ethereal presence. Glen Strathfarrar was visited, and Sgurr Na Muncie, but we'd had enough of snow blizzards and soft snow by Friday.

Only Nick who was intent on Tom A'Choinich (hill of the moss) ventured far. A straight forward stalkers path in summer, but in stormy winter conditions and poor visibility, he experienced a similar day to the one with which John and Colin started the week. When overcorrecting his compass bearing to avoid their error, he in turn plopped through a cornice. No harm done.

Jack Ashcroft had completed the Munros by 1994 — *Editor.*

A COMMENT – OUR CLIMBING HERITAGE

JACK ASHCROFT

When Ronald Clark and Edward Pyatt wrote, in the final chapter of their excellent book, *Mountaineering in Britain* (1957), of "the cheer leader philosophy of mountaineering", I am sure they hardly saw the great growth in climbing wall development and its coming to majority in the 1990's.

Their thesis in 1957 was that climbing as a spectator sport, much the same as tennis and cricket, would rob mountaineering of much of its original appeal – wildness and solitude of hills.

No problem. I would advance the proposition, that we have weathered the storm and the competitive and technically competent have moved into the gymnasium where points can be awarded by judges for standard of difficulty, stylishness and speed on artificial slab, crack, chimney, groove or overhang. If you wish to translate onto the crag O.K:– Green Death – Millstone; Quietus – Stanage, Kilnsey roof – Limestone. More reasonably, Allen's Slab – Froggat; Grooved Wall – Gardoms; Trafalgar Wall – Birchen.

My objective in these few comments is to quickly recap on how one unapologetic club mountaineer sees the development of our recreation for the better: one who has often glanced through contemporary British climbing guides and found nothing accomplished above 5a – and it won't be again! (?sic — *Editor*).

The unique value of our recreation is that whatever innate ability you may possess, what ever skill you may demonstrate on the hill, whatever your age, you can take part with unabashed enjoyment. Of course no one denies a level of general fitness is desirable. But that comes with regular exercise, fresh air, the company of friends, or by ones self. You can derive from the mountain environment, speed, suppleness, and stamina, and develop the mental and physical balance to truly gain satisfaction in mountain and moorland activity. Agreed, things slow up a bit with age. But you can still get out there without getting too uptight about the big 'C' of competition and the wages to go with it.

You can enjoy recreation in the hills of Britain, the Alps, the Himalaya, or where-ever, and take on board the recent words of Ken Wilson (AJ 1998 "....quite easy climbs can contrive to offer high challenge to the person of matching experience or fitness. In this manner far from being elitist, a sport that takes care to preserve the full character of its environmental challenges, remains demanding at all levels and thus quintessentially egalitarian. A sport rigged up for safety and performance will probably soon become highly elitist and at the same time be performance obsessed and conformist"..... Ken Wilson on Traditional Values and protection on climbs.

The next time you visit or cycle along the High Peak Trail, look up at Black Rocks (Putrell, Harding, Moulam); or Mickleden, Rossett Ghyll, or the Stake Pass (Dolphin, Bower); Sty Head (Haskett Smith, H.M. Kelly); the Miners Track, Ogwen (Kirkus, Edwards, O.G. Jones). The list associated with tradition on nearby crags is endless and I haven't mentioned Snowdon, Glen Coe, Nevis, Skye or indeed Birchen, Gardoms, Curbar, Froggatt and Stanage. An ageless tradition. And finally, on the Pennine Way, Widdop and Laddow. Full circle – walking and climbing.

FAR KINGDOMS

'Tis distance lends enchantment to the view
And robes the mountains in its azure hue.

Pleasures of Hope – Thomas Campbell, 1777-1844

JOHN (ROCK) HUDSON WRITES....

High altitude forests with a weird flora of giant groundsels and lobelia, the flash of the malachite sunbird, the hum of countless insects, adjacent to the ruined Kitandra Hut, at 4,027m, deep in the Ruwenzori Mountains.

The only thing out of place is Dave Penlington peeling potatoes. No dried pom for him, for he remembers that fish and chips were staple food back in the early days of Oread meets in Derbyshire. So why change in the heart of Africa. We had obtained not a single view from the summits of Vittorio

Emanuelle, Stanley, or even Baker. But the mists cleared and the rock and snow peaks of Mounts Philip and Elizabeth appeared. Dave noted that these mountains were only recognised and named a couple of years before the founding of the Oread. Who would have thought in those days that members would be able to climb amongst them within a holiday of three weeks?

Editorial Note:

Hudson is writing about his venture, with Penlington, to Uganda and Kenya in 1994. Penlington's travels in the distant ranges are only rivalled by those of Rock Hudson, although other Oreads have followed in their footsteps and yet others have struck out on their own to many far flung corners. In this context it is worth recording Penlington's long term achievements, unique in the Oread, at home and abroad.

Both Penlington and Ashcroft completed the Munros at different but unspecified dates but D.P. notes that the Ben was his first in 1947. Penlington has also completed the Alpine 4,000m peaks. He writes: "The first 4,000m came in 1951, with Ken Griffiths, during a failed attempt on Mont Blanc. We had been snowed in at the Gouter Hut for two days. The Custodian had taken everybody down shortly after K.G. and I arrived. We refused to go. The storm started two hours later and continued for twenty four hours".

"Two feet of new snow and cold forced us to give up our attempt about thirty minutes from the summit. If I had known we were so close, we would have made it. Anyway we had been over the Dome de Gouter but I did not realise it was in excess of 4,000m until years later. My last 4,000m peak was the Piz Bernina, solo in 1997, third time lucky, but not by the route I would have wished; the Biancograt. Thus the Munros and the 4,000m tops occupied forty six years".

"My best day in the Alps (not 4,000m peaks) was the Wildefrau, Morgenhorn, Weissefrau, Blumisalphorn traverse with John Fisher, a 6½ hours round trip, about half the guide book time. I had done it the previous day with Peter Biven, John and Mary Fowler, and was so impressed that I had to get Fisher onto it on one of his "official off days".

Since retirement Penlington's activities have spread widely beyond Europe as the following list shows.

1991	Himalaya; Rowaling peaks with Rock Hudson
1992	New Zealand/Australia
1994	Africa; Ruwenzori and Mount Kenya
1994	Tien Shan (Kazakhstan) with Richard Coghlan
1996	Tien Shan (Kirghistan) with Rock Hudson (Kaingdy Expedition)
1996	New Zealand/Tasmania
1997	Tien Shan
1998	Peru/Bolivia with John Green

In addition to the above Rock Hudson has been displaying his bachelor characteristics on a regular basis;

Cordillera de Blanca, Peru including Aconcagua

Himalaya: Karakorum trek

Nepal: Mount Api, Mount Chamar, and Island Peak (Winter), and in 1998 he managed to pull in Greenland (East Coast), Tibet, and Cho Oyu.

A quick survey of other Oreads displaying in distant places shows that Myke Wynne has circled the world in his quest for mountains. Jack Ashcroft has travelled widely in Ladakh, Kulu, and Eastern Nepal, and Richard Coghlan, when not accompanying D.P. to the Tien Shan, has (with Julia Stowell and other Oreads) ventured to Aconcagua and Mount Mera, Nepal.

1998 has seen Oreads scattered around the globe: The Eyres in the Karakorum, Daryl Kirk on Mount Kenya, Helen Griffiths in the Canadian Rockies, Ron Chambers and Ruth Allen in Nepal and, in June, a few Golden Oldies, The Reynolds and the Gadsbys, met up with the Prettys in Alaska.

Also in 1998 the Great White Sahib, R.G. Pettigrew, did a moderate tour of Kulu with Ernie Phillips and Digger Williams – to the D.H.E. '61 base camp with six porters and six ponies.

Since Kharcha Kund in 1987 Peter Scott and his partner Judy have not been idle and post cards, recording arduous travel through Hunza and Chitral to the meadows below Nanga Parbat, and across the Bolivian Andes, have been a regular feature.

The above listings do not include the Hopkinsons and the Males who climb regularly in North America, or Gregson, who commutes to Oregon to disperse his particular brand of Yorkshire humour (at an academic level of course). Nor does it take account of Bill and Anne Kenyon trekking widely in the Himalaya and an Oread first, completing the legendary John Muir Trail. Nearer home, in the late eighties, Pretty, Janes, Williams and Appleby wandered the badlands of Corsica and H.P. subsequently produced a new guide to the G.R. 20 and other long distance routes. During the same period Pretty completed an obscure long distance walk from Mt.Grammos (Zagoria) to the Agrapha Mountains through the North and South Pindos (Greece), taking in many of the big peaks en route.

But one could not complete this discursive overview without mention of the man in black, Christopher Radcliffe, depositing his boxes of milk tray around the globe. From the Drakensberg to the Bugaboos his privately chartered helicopters are even now searching for new peaks and passes. If it has been climbed, or has potential, Radders has been there, or is about to go. There is a whole secret world here of mystery and intrigue that we shall never know unless it explodes in quadraphonic sound; the only true accompaniment to the master who may fade in, or fade out, but always in exemplary style.

Harry Pretty

Rites of
Passage

RITES OF PASSAGE

The Oread year is marked by certain events in addition to A.G.M.s and Annual Dinners. These are the rituals whereby the Oread marks the passage of time .... each appropriate to the season.

John (Rock) Hudson throws some light.

Club Meets (Wednesday Evenings)

Rock Hudson

For the rock climbing section of the club, changing from G.M.T. to B.S.T. is something longed for, because they can now be out knocking off the routes midweek. For over two decades now, with near universal car ownership, increasing numbers of members form part of the Wednesday evenings climbing scene. From midday in office, factory or while teaching, they have one eye on the weather, hoping it will keep fine, or if raining stop before six o'clock, so that two or three hours sport and freedom can be spent on limestone or gritstone cliff – from Cromford to Dovedale, Roaches or Stanage.

The Dolomite limestones of the Brassington area are the traditional venue for the first evening, being easy of access, short in length and not too serious. The evening, also short in length, so there's pressure to solo though, on Trident Buttress, Colin Hobday and Clive (Rusty) Russell are roped on Trident Arête, while Tony Raphael and Tony Smedley tackle Trident Face, using a selection of modern protection. Back in the early sixties, Ray Handley made the first ascent with only hawser laid rope and perhaps a single rope sling.

Back at the Gate Inn in Brassington village the group meet up with those who have been on Rainster Rocks. Had a good evening? Great, and nobody was stung to death by nettles on the way in. Another succession of routes soloed, though Nick Evans and Roy Eyre were impressed by Penlington's Progress and Two Step, first climbed by Dave Penlington way back in 1950, no doubt with only a length of hemp and not a bit of protection.

Must be at least twenty out on a dull but dry midweek evening on Gardoms Edge. Parties of twos and threes gravitate to the Apple Butress Area, crags having a close association with the Oread, particularly in the early years, when some members were part of that select band of 'hard men', able to put up new routes, which were considerable achievements for the period.

Mike Hayes and Mike Wren are soon on Finale Groove, while Rock Hudson, Keith Gregson, and Beryl Strike go for the exposed Apple Arete, both routes first climbed by' Penno' in 1951 and 1952. Several ropes are tackling the routes of Capillary Crack and Babylon's Groove, while Kevin Allsebrook and Daryl Kirk are coming to terms with a typical route put by a young Oread Tiger, Ernest Marshall in 1953, Orchard, and still graded at HVS.

There is drizzle in the air, so down to the Robin Hood for the second phase of the evening. A beer, and we talk of the climbing skills of those Oreads, with the most basic equipment nearly fifty years ago.

The evenings have lengthened by July, so the venues are further afield. Willersley is on the calendar, but typical of the Oread's fickleness we hear later, at the Queen Victoria, that many have been elsewhere.

Derrick Burgess went to Willersley and climbed Babylon (HVS), noting that Derek Carnell's route was no 'walk over'. On Wildcat, Tony Howard, Steve Bennet and Gill Heyes, considered Cougar Cleft a death trap, not easy for severe. On ticking it off in the guide it was noticed, that it was the first route climbed and that back in 1948 by Nat Allen.

Another party arrives, darkness having fallen ages ago. All confirmed it was a beautiful evening, and the last route climbed was 'topped out' as the last rays of the sun lit up the sky. What a great classic is Nat Allen's Slab to finish off the evening, though the earlier attempt on another of his routes, Neb Crack, was found to be beyond their abilities, even with friends. They were still wondering after the second pint of beer, how it could be climbed without any protection. It's closing time, so a quick drive to the nearest fish and chip shop: By the time they roll into bed, there's only a few hours of sleep before those eight hours of work reappear.

The Quiet Woman at Earl Sterndale is packed with climbers after attending the last of the evening meets, for it's mid September, and the days are drawing in. There's a typical atmosphere, with Brian West bemoaning the fact that another summer is over, and it's going to be a long cycle home unless some kind person will find room for him and his bike in the back of the car. Gordon Wright is moaning about the beer, but he's already tucking into the fourth pint. Burgess is telling the story of the first ascent (1965) of Cummerbund on Ossam's Crag and how clean it now is compared with then.

Ron Sant is given a pint by a prospective member for taking him up his first VS, Simeon, on Tissington Spires while, out of the spotlight, young Chris Bryan, is now making steady progress, chatting up a pretty female with no transport. Chris is asked about plans for ski-ing this winter, only to turn round and see that Pete O'Neill, twice his age, has smartly stepped in. Can't mix climbing and pleasure, some observant member says.

A closely packed set of bodies are asked "what they've done on Beeston Tor"? or "what happened on the Alpine Meet?", while others show off a bit of new gear, and Ron Chambers passes a comment that "Storm" on Thor's Cave is never 5a, which brings Pete Scott into the conversation, recalling that it's another good route put up in the past by Dez Hadlum and Eric Wallis. Wendy Lawrence, probably the youngest in the bar, is congratulated by Burgess, having seconded her hardest route – The Webb, complaining that his joints would not allow a repeat of his first ascent.

Final order please! A few go for a last pint (jug). Others make late arrangements for a coming meet, while information is asked for and passed on about crags, routes and campsites, or somebody remembers the holiday photographs of America or Asia, which only brings forth more questions and answers.

"Good evening, Great! Lot of climbing done – It was a beautiful walk down the dale, see you in Wales this weekend, yes?", "or, on the climbing wall next Wednesday?"

WINTER TALKS

ROCK HUDSON

Where can you go for the price of less than a pint of beer on the first Tuesday evening between October and March and see a series of talks on the widest range of topics, be it travel, exploration, mountaineering or rock climbing? It's the Oread!

For many years members have been welcome at the Royal Oak in Ockbrook. In rain, snow, frost or fog, between 20-100 have been able to spend a few hours sharing the experiences, knowledge, problems of both members and guest speakers, on the widest range of mountaineering topics. However, to provide even more interest, you can take part in a quiz. Though questions such as; the size of Reg Squires' boots, the maiden name of Sherpa Tensing's mother, or highest mountain in Madagascar, were only known to a few. We all like a true bargain, so the Oread provides an auction. Bidding is slow, very slow and members ignore any level of inflation. Nearly new boots can go for five pounds, a pair of ski for little more, while a set of rusty old nuts are withdrawn at twenty pounds for not reaching their reserve price.

A new season with Chris Radcliffe's extravaganza of quadraphonic music, synchronised projectors with fade in and outs, produced from hours of dedicated planning, only to be let down by an intermittent power supply. John Hudson takes days drafting introductory maps, diagrams and archival illustrations only to run out of time during the narrative. Tim Cairns turns up with a few tatty slides, a completely discounted commentary, but provides the greatest of laughs for the whole session. We see the wonders of caves with K. Waltham, the pleasures of ski-ing in New Zealand with R. Hoare, and the desperation of portage over the watersheds of Canada with Hank Harrison. Crossing the White Spider with Robin Sedgwick, or achieving the first ascent of the Croz Spur in winter by P. Holden and C. Radcliffe, to the reminiscence of Ray Colledge on the first British ascents of Nesthorn and Grosshorn.

Over many visits Denis Gray has given his life story but, up to now, only reaching his early thirties! We all know the Tatras by following Colin Hobday, and vast areas of the Great Himalayan Range from Jack Ashcroft and others. Those present, wish they too could join expeditions to Alaska with Roy Ruddle, the wastes of Greenland with Phil Nixon, and the Whittaker Couloir on Mount Everest with Ken Rawlinson.

What's the rock like on Jersey? Ian Smith told us. 'How easy are the routes in Wadi Rum? Tony Howard told us. Travelogues from Bleaklow to the Bregaglia by Gordon Gadsby, and around the world from Mike Wynne.

All Oreads know it's better value than looking at 'soaps on the box' or seeing all that bare flesh at the cinema.

Rock Hudson, a confirmed bachelor, has a strange notion of what most red blooded Oread men would prefer — *Editor.*

HUT WORKING PARTY

ROCK HUDSON

On the meets calendar, it's a working party at the weekend. The name implies two days of unremitting toil, damaged fingers, fear of not being able to knock in a nail straight and, for the prospective member, the trauma of being black balled by the hut sub committee for failing to achieve levels of competence.

The Welbourns are up at the crack of dawn and by 7.30 we are handed tea in bed by Ruth, for work must start at a respectable hour. After a healthy breakfast of bacon, egg, beans, sausages, black pudding and fried bread, we, skilled workers, assistants, support staff and 'bodies', are "lined up" by the bosses in the form of John Shreeve and Chuck Hooley. For months they have been planning; drawings, materials, tools needed, manpower required to fulfil the endless list of jobs to be done.

They scrutinise us all, for the difficulty of the task must match the real or perceived D-I-Y skills – not easy, and mistakes over the years have led to disaster. Typically, Ron Chambers, the plumber, is given the painting job, Kim Davidson, the policewoman is to sort out the electrical supply but, being young and pretty, will later become John Shreeve's personal assistant. Volunteers are asked to dig out and remove trees from the garden, but nobody steps forward so three are conscripted, and the rest start cutting the grass, painting the hall, while curtains are hung by two females.

Minutes pass and the most important person on the work party Margaret Hooley says: "Tea is ready!".

Michael Hayes is painting the back of the lounge magnolia, but Tony Raphael, following orders, is painting it white, while Nick Evans is repairing the back door, and Richard Coghlan is putting hinges to a new one. Stuart Haywood is putting up a panel with six inch nails, when all the power tools fail due to an electrical short.

Tea and sandwiches are taken outside, and conversation as ever ranges from Chuck recalling jobs done in the early years, to Rock telling about his last trip, and Daryl moaning that he's losing a good weekend on the crags. Down from Snowdon come a bunch of walkers and ask what the cost is for food and drink. Keith Gregson tries the old dodge, about needing to get a saw from the village before it closes at 2.30 p.m.

By now three small jobs have been done, one of which required Chuck to put up another notice; "a guide to understanding the hut notice board". On the negative side a tin of paint has been spilt over the new carpet and the new doors fitted in the kitchen prevent each other from being opened. In the hall, painting is stopping the laying of new tiles, the stair carpet is too short and, now that the old ceiling is removed, somebody recalls that he's left the new plaster board at home. The final straw: the total work force has to go outside to prevent the bonfire spreading onto tinder dry grass on the slopes up to Snowdon.

The hut sub committee calls all the experts for a meeting on how many sticks should be cut for winter and how many toilet rolls should be kept in stock.

Outside a team is painting the walls, while in the bedrooms Lisa, Shirley and Uschi have replaced all the mattress covers in minutes. It's mid afternoon, tea and home made cakes, then back to finishing off a new bit of wiring, cleaning the chimney, realigning the shelves from the previous working party.

It's good sitting in the lounge, chatting about the climbing, ski-ing, and what's proposed for the autumn work party only to be interrupted by Steve Bennett, who informs us that it's pouring with rain and the paint is washed off the outside walls, the gutters are blocked, and, he believes there is a patch of damp rot by the back door.

Oread Meet
Wednesday Before the Wednesday Before Christmas

Rock Hudson

What sort of mountaineering club would include on its calendar of events, an evening's climbing in mid December and then call it 'The Wednesday before the Wednesday before Christmas'; it's the Oread.

Another car pulls into the car park below Black Rocks, followed by another. Indistinct figures are pulling on tatty, very tatty anoraks. Another calls out that we must all be a load of silly buggers while someone else drapes a rope over his shoulders, its looks indicating its age. But then traditional club members never heed the call of the modern retailer and their intense sales campaigns. A prospective member asks, "Shall I take a couple of racks", only to be informed a couple of slings will do and those PA's, which only shows up his age, are bloody useless on a night like this. Yet another body calls out: "Anybody got a spare head torch?"

While wandering up to the crag we hear yet another tale, regarding what happened on this evening the previous year. Two panda cars sped into the car park, out tumbled, what appeared to be a number of under employed constables: "What are all those lights doing scanning the sky?" asks one. What answer could a sharp Oread give, apart from:– "Searching for enemy aircraft!" A flood of questions followed; "Who are you all? What are you doing? Have you permission?". "It's a climbing meet", explained Keith Gregson. Blank faces indicated that this was more than strange. The interrogation continued:– "Are you all experienced? Have you got your equipment? Don't you think the weather is too bad?" Without answers we are informed that the police do not want any more details. Finally we are told not to expect any help if there is an accident, the police have better things to do than rescue people like us!

Below the crag shadowy figures answered to their names on enquiries as to who they were, while others shone the torches upwards, picking out a section of rope, before it was lost beyond the rim of light. Higher, but at an unknown distance, there appeared a series of dancing fairy lights, at times in twos, then in threes, now rotating, followed by swinging left and right.

It started to sleet and gusts of cold wind, followed by "climb when ready" brings you back from day dreaming. Only a 'diff, but tonight the rock has a veneer of shiny green slime in the light beam. Vibrams slip and find no purchase, hands are cold and wet groping for a hold that is merely an illusion. On Queens Parlour Slab somebody is gripped, another unsure of the line; while nearby grunts and groans, a rapid scraping boots, indicates a little epic. Someone states it's impossible to judge distances to holds with head torches and comes onto a tight rope to prove it. Out left, a voice tells us that the pockets are full of frozen slush, while above, another with no name, gives a sigh of relief, for he's on top. A leader is 'farting' about on Queens Parlour Chimney, so several teams are passing the time at the belay, asking each other what they are doing for Christmas. A couple are off to Spain to climb in the sun, another off to France ski-ing, while another is down at Tany-y-Wyddfa to enjoy the company of Oreads and the hope of a few days out on the hills.

In the depths of Original Route, flashes of light indicate a little progress. Then it's pitch-blackness, followed by swearing and cursing from the man at the sharp end, who announces that he's knocked his head torch off. This only brings comments: "I'm cold", or "hungry", "prat", or "it's time we got off to the pub", from those waiting below. With bruised shins, skinned hands and banged head the leader emerges to sliver clouds scudding across the moon's face, while the lights from Cromford to Matlock cast an orange glow up to the sky.

Walking back to the car one feels content as are those, met on the way, who have had a walk along part of the High Peak Trail. All agree it's been another fitting end to the year's activities. Down at the car park some late comer has arrived, having cycled up from Derby. In the gloom, those present are informed that the meet leader has booked pie and peas at the pub and also Keith and Mike have their musical instruments so, after the shouting match, we can have a good sing-song.

Before Their
Time

Brian Cooke 1923-1981

Oliver Jones 1906-1983

J. Norman Millward 1928-1990

Nat Allen 1928-1995

"....... for enriching my life, giving, not just for me, but for many others, a different perspective on life itself, an enthusiasm for it, and an even greater satisfaction from it. I am proud and happy to have known you."

Derek Carnell

BRIAN JOSEPH COOKE
1923-1981

Brian Cooke's sudden death robbed the Oread of one of its most loyal and long serving members. Brian, with his wife Marion, first came into contact with the Oread one evening in late 1952 in the Llanberis Pass. Some six months or so later a change of job brought them to Derby – thus began a long, devoted membership of the Oread. Very shortly after election to membership, Brian became a committee member, which was quickly followed by a long term as General Secretary. On the 3rd March 1962 he was elected President.

Brian became interested in the hills at a very early age. Evacuated to Penrith at the outbreak of the war, he was soon rock-climbing in the Lakes. War service took him to India and the Himalayas. His coolies on an expedition into the hills considered him to act in a most dangerous manner when he climbed bare rock rather than, as they did, the vegetation.

After the war, he returned to his native Newcastle and made a major contribution to the production of the Northumbria Climbing Guides. During this period he came to know the Cheviots in detail and produced a number of fine rock climbs. Many members have experienced Brian's patient encouragement, whether they were a novice receiving advice and instruction or a tiger putting out a new route.

Brian, a Civil Engineer, also left his mark on many fine road works and bridges. The older Nottingham members appreciated the original improvements to the A52. A major bridge over the Mersey cut the time of travelling to the lakes by hours. One of Brian's later achievements was the Keswick By-pass.

Brian was a man who was dedicated to helping others, of a high standard and integrity in all that he did, winning the respect and affection of all those who came to know him.

David Penlington

The world will be a sadder place without Brian Cooke. He was quietly dedicated to his work and recreation. His family have requested donations to the Coniston Mountain Rescue Team. He was first on the scene after the accident on Dow Crag in 1971 when Geoff Hayes, with whom he had climbed a lot, died. He was forever appreciative of the prompt help the team gave on that sad day.

Jack Ashcroft

CRAG LOUGH

A cold depressed cliff,
A precipice to the lake below,
Diminishing in size; reeds devouring all;
Silver boughs sway, bare of leaves:
Autumn is near.

As predictable as the next blade of grass
For the sheep on the hills,
The unchanging posture of climbers on the rocks.
Wind tearing at their clothes,
As they proceed strategically across the face.

A clicking of hammers against metal,
An occasional word catches one's ear on the wind –
Climbing jargon, relevant only to climbers.
Ropes strung across, uniting
The elements of achievement.

Margaret Cooke, 1974

OLIVER JONES
1906-1983 (HON. MEMBER)

Oliver died on the 19th April after a short illness. A loyal Scot, he was born in Glasgow in 1906. He was elected to club membership in 1949, the year of its foundation. He remained an active member throughout his life. After having two artificial hip joints fitted a couple of years ago, he climbed in South Africa and was on Ben Nevis the following Easter. His climbing itinerary was simple – Ben Nevis at Easter, Glen Brittle for two weeks in August, with Wales and, to a lesser extent, Derbyshire and the Lakes in between. There were also trips to the States, Canada, Arctic Norway, Switzerland, South Africa, etc....

At sixteen he left home for America and, in the next five years, he had 50 or so jobs ranging from cleaning sewers, to building aircraft, to being a lumberjack, etc.... In his later years, up to retirement, he ran his own engineering works in Birmingham with a product range from cake trays for Lyons to the famous 'cuillin' climbing nail – he also made 'B.P.' nails for his competitors.

Oliver was not only a mountaineer, he played rugby (until well after retirement) for the Old Edwardians in Birmingham. His support of international rugby took him on regular visits to Cardiff, Twickenham, Paris, and so on. The Americans loved him and a number of features on the O.A.P. player appeared in various 'States' and South African newspapers.

After rugby came Scottish Dancing, swimming and cycling, the latter activity leading to his arrest on the M6 motorway extension into Birmingham. This, in the end, turned out to be very embarrassing for the two policemen involved – how could they do such a thing to a poor O.A.P.!

Oliver's background made him an ideal member of the Oread. After a hard day, out would come the guitar for an equally long session of singing and drinking. In Glen Brittle the Macraes invited him to play with the other pipers at the annual Summer Ceilidh, indeed a unique honour. Most members will remember Oliver as the bachelor who presented the tankards to the newly-weds at the Dinner. This tradition, which commenced with Nan Smith and Keith Axon in 1950, was only broken in the one year when Oliver was in dock being re-fitted with his new hip joints. A tradition which will no doubt have died with Oliver.

A great man in so many ways. He will be remembered by countless members who have enjoyed sharing his life, whether actively or just watching from the sidelines.

David Penlington

313

J. NORMAN (NOBBY) MILLWARD
1928-1990

"Nobby was a very private person" to quote Ernie Phillips, who, of course, was a fellow member of the Stonnis M.C. in 1946 when Norman started climbing at Black Rocks. But there was a lot more to Nobby Millward than that, and I am grateful to Tony Moulam for a few snippets from their early climbing days on Gritstone and in North Wales.

A.J.J.M. remembers meeting him for the first time at a Black Rocks Stonnis Meet in September 1946 in the company of Peter Harding, Ronnie Lee (later Phillips), S. Ball, K. Brindley and R. Bickerstaff. Moulam also recalls Nobby belaying when Harding and A.J.J.M. were trying the then unled Prom Traverse, and subsequently joining them on the same route in October 1947 ("all in rubbers). There is an early marker for Oread "Wednesday before Wednesday" antics when, after a Stonnis November A.G.M., they climbed at Black Rocks in the dark, in a state of inebriation, after a surfeit of fish and chips. This was followed by Nobby participating in the traditional Christmas Day ascent of the Grimmet – and a first ascent of Chalkren Stairs on Gallt yr Ogof, "after many fraught attempts".

Nobby appeared in Oread circles before the demise of Bryn-y-Wern, following the migration of those other R.R. characters (ex Valkyrie, Stonnis) Janes and Handley. Although originally a railway engineer he translated smoothly to nuclear engineering and achieved distinction, if not legendary status, by solving lesser men's complex problems on the back of his fag packet. An amazingly modest man it was a long time before one realised that he could tailor a suit, or an overcoat, with the same expertise that he built an extension to his home, turned out a superbly finished tool on his lathe, or led a hard severe on sight, and all with the same matter of fact economy of effort that left ordinary mortals gasping.

In the early '60s', before the later mass invasion, small Oread family parties spent Bank Holidays encamped on the north coast of Pembroke, and on the headlands of the Lleyn Peninsula, where night time fishing inevitably meant descending, traversing, and escape climbing unknown cliffs. Occasionally these jaunts became small epics and, although we never recorded a single climb, it was generally Norman who cracked it to ensure that Janes and I (and occasionally Paul Gardiner) returned safely to camp – generally after sunset.

Not physically strong in terms of carrying heavy loads, he was never a participant in the rough excesses of Pennine or Welsh long walks but with Norman and Judy, Molly and I spent some of our happiest days exploring odd corners of Derbyshire with a 25,000 map for he was, as in all his activities, a consummate map reader, a man with style, a complete original, and ten years later I miss him dreadfully.

Harry Pretty, 1999

JOHN REGINALD (NAT) ALLEN
1928-1995 (HON. MEMBER)

When, on the next Bank Holiday, I travel down to Pembroke, it will be in the knowledge that a major strand in my life is broken and that an era is ended. With the death of Nat Allen in June, the interwoven pattern of our lives was ended, and the spirals of our rope forever severed. Now, whilst I grieve his loss, the many, notable memories of the 46 years I spent climbing and socialising with Nat, remain at least to cheer me. I remember my first climb with him – Black Slab on Stanage – then many more on Gritstone, Limestone and Granite peaks: in Wales, the Lakes, Scotland and Ireland too. The Alpine holidays, rock climbing and mountaineering routes among the great and lesser ranges. In good or bad weather, scorching heat, frozen, wet or baked – we tried them all, but always his enthusiasm, skill, and indomitable spirit, coupled with an innate stubbornness to achieve his goals, made Nat a cherished partner.

From the 1960s until his death, we found a common purpose on the Pembrokeshire sea-cliffs, regularly climbing together, doing new routes (some 200 plus), and with others, exploring the possibilities. Nat's enthusiasm was boundless. He always had ideas on where to go, what to do, and was a source of inspiration, if not competitiveness amongst our little group. 'Secret Crags' abound, and we hugged ourselves, each time we forged another route.

My final memory of Nat is of climbing together in Pembroke on the last day of May this year; neither of us in the best of health – me with a knee op, he with the debilitating effect of his illness. We both crept (in every sense of the word!) away from our friends doing their hard routes, to climb a couple of slabby V Diffs in a secluded bay. Summer's End was to be the last climb Nat did in Pembroke. We sat, watching the setting sun pointing a rosy finger along the sea in Ramsey Sound and I saw a serenity in his face and felt with him his pleasure at having done the routes despite his illness. Ruth had joined us and we laughed and talked easily in the euphoria of just sitting there, in the grass, above the crag, above the sea, reliving the earlier times and making plans to visit Ireland again before too long. Just over 3 weeks later Nat was dead.

With his death the climbing world loses a most active, erudite and friendly man; one who had managed to mix easily with people of all levels, ages and experiences while still remaining true to his own principles. On the personal side, I lost the truest, closest friend that I have ever had. Thank you Nat for your steadfast and reliable companionship in the hills, for enriching my life; giving, not just for me, but many others, a different perspective on Life itself, an enthusiasm for it, and, an even greater satisfaction from it. I am proud and happy to have known you. You live forever in our hearts.

Derek Carnell

315

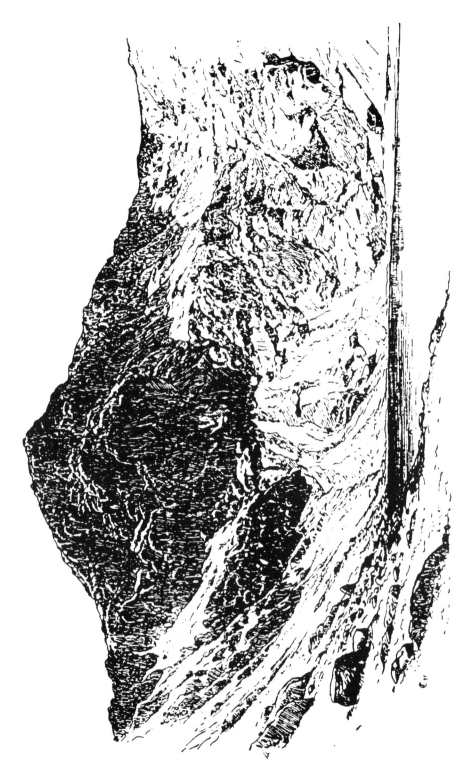

SNOWDON FROM GLASLYN

End Game

"They think it's all over", at least I did before the post brought three contributions that I would not want to leave out. Peter Holden adapts, with tongue in cheek, Brian West is at his magisterial best, a lesson to us all, and finally young Michael Gregson (aged 11), with impressive simplicity, is wise beyond his years — *Editor*.

Oreads

High above – teams ascending
Where crags are bare and steep,
You may see the Oreads clinging
Where awesome voids are deep.

The glistening summits they beckon,
With 'friends' and wired 'rocks',
They climb so steadfastly,
Clipping pitons and their 'chocks',

Feet swathed in 'Fire' slippers,
Stealing up the finest routes,
No fear or wilting bodies,
Keeping rock-fast with their boots.

Wraiths of the 'Rock and Ice',
Even up the frozen waterfall,
Mate with us – do be 'nice',
'Case we fall, – we fall.

Peter Holden

Adapted from August Oreads, The Faery Calendar by Bernard Sleigh and Ivy A. Ellis.

Tan-y-Wyddfa

In echelon facing Snowdon: this is how our cars should sit.
I tried at times to find a space but never seemed to fit.
Too late, perhaps, when I arrived, and always there the doubt
That should I ever once get in, I never would get out.
And so I park beyond the pale; beyond the security light;
Where it helps to have a little torch, and familiarity with the night.

In echelon facing Snowdon: in procession past the hut,
They all go to their mountain. That gate does not stay shut.
A recommended track upon a map they did not help to make,
Content, it seems, all towed along in someone else's wake.
Performance by prescription; not hard to understand,
Life taken from the guide book can at best be second-hand.
What exists in this to set the mind alight,
To fire imagination, to clarify the sight?
In echelon facing Snowdon: alignment is implied.
But with whom, with what, we each of us decide.

Sometimes in the still of a sea-trout night, where Llyfni meets the sea,
And shooting stars clash with the lighthouse flash from far – off Anglesey,
I catch the siren – song of those hut-bound souls who own to a different custodian,
But am not moved.
For I fear they lie sleeping there, in echelon facing Snowdon.

Brian West

UNTITLED

My dad and I go to the mountains,
To look at the hills and the sky,
We walk over the hills in the sun, rain and snow
And marvel at all things, wherever we go.

My dad and I go to the mountains,
To climb on rocks, never mind why,
We've looked down on buzzards and eagles
As they soared down below in the sky.

My dad and I've been to the mountains,
Been lost in the fog up on high,
And seen the white hare and wild ponies
On the slopes of the wild Carneddau.

My dad and I've been to the mountains,
Had a swim in the lake and the stream,
And sometimes, when we can't get back there
We just lie on our backs and we dream.

Michael Gregson, aged 11

APPENDIX

Presidents

C. B. Machin	1949-1951
E. Byne	1951-1953
G. A. Sutton	1953-1955
H. Pretty	1955-1957
P. R. Falkner	1957-1959
R. G. Pettigrew	1959-1961
B. Cooke	1961-1963
J. Ashcroft	1963-1965
P. Janes	1965-1967
R. Handley	1967-1969
D. Burgess	1969-1971
P. Gardiner	1971-1973
N. Allen	1973-1975
G. Gadsby	1975-1977
C. Hobday	1977-1979
C. Radcliffe	1979-1981
P. Scott	1981-1983
K. Gregson	1983-1985
R. Sedgwick	1985-1987
J. Linney	1987-1989
J. Hudson	1989-1991
R. Gilbert	1991-1993
R. Chambers	1993-1995
B. West	1995-1997
C. Russell	1997-1999
H. Pretty	1999-2000

Honorary Secretaries

G. Sutton	1949-1950
E. Say	1950-1951
H. Pretty	1951-1952
G. Gibson	1952-1954
C. Webb*	1954-1955
B. Cooke	1955-1957
L. Hatchett	1957-1959
R. Handley	1959-1961
P. Janes	1961-1963
C. Hobday	1963-1964
R. Turner	1964-1965
Mrs. V. Langworthy	1965-1968
L. Langworthy	1968-1971
P. Scott	1971-1975
C. Hobday	1975-1977
D. Williams	1977-1980
R. Sant	1980-1987
C. Barnard	1987-1988
Miss L. Welbourn	1988-1990
S. Bashforth	1990-1997
Mrs. S. Wainwright	1997-

* C. Webb's period of office was interrupted by his joining the British South Georgia Expedition.

Newsletter Editors

D. C. Cullum	1953-1958
H. Pretty	1958-1959
T. Frost	1959-1961
R. Turner	1961-1963
G. Hayes	1963-1970
C. Radcliffe/P. Scott	1970-1971
C. Radcliffe	1971-1973
P. Bingham	1973-1975
K. Gregson	1975-1977
Miss B. Strike	1977-1978
R. Sant	1978-1980
C. Wilson	1980-1981
R. Freestone	1981-1984
J. O'Reilly	1984-1986
R. Larkham	1986-1987
J. Hudson	1987-1988
Miss H. Griffiths	1988-1990
R. Tressider	1990-1993
C. Russell	1993-

Journal Editors

P. Bingham	1974-1975
D. Appleby	1975-1976
Mrs. J. Gregson	1976-1978
R. Sedgwick	1978-1981
J. O'Reilly	1981-1984
C. Wilson and J. Hudson (Joint)	1984-1985
J. Hudson	1985-1988
R. Gilbert	1990-1993

Honorary Members

C. B. Machin	1951
E. Byne	1953
A. Bridge	1956
Jack Longland	1956
G. A. Sutton	1959
H. Pretty	1960
N. Allen	1963
L. Burns	1971
C. D. Milner	1973
M. & C. Hooley	1984
J. Welbourn	1984
E. Phillips	1989
K. Griffiths	1989
D. Penlington	1989
D. Burgess	1993
C. Hobday	1993
D. Gray	1993
J. Shreeve	1995
P. Janes	1998

CRIB GOCH